D1800132

Grit Alter

Inter- and Transcultural Learning
in the Context
of Canadian Young Adult Fiction

Fremdsprachendidaktik in globaler Perspektive

herausgegeben von

Prof. Dr. Christiane Lütge
(Ludwig-Maximilians-Universität München)

Band 5

LIT

Grit Alter

Inter- and Transcultural Learning in the Context of Canadian Young Adult Fiction

LIT

Cover image: Susanne Liljeroos & Gary L. Musselman

D 6

This book is printed on acid-free paper.

Bibliografische Information der Deutschen Nationalbibliothek
Die Deutsche Nationalbibliothek verzeichnet diese Publikation in der
Deutschen Nationalbibliografie; detaillierte bibliografische Daten sind
im Internet über http://dnb.d-nb.de abrufbar.

ISBN 978-3-643-90675-5
Zugl.: Münster (Westf.), Univ., Diss., 2014

© LIT VERLAG GmbH & Co. KG Wien,
Zweigniederlassung Zürich 2015
Klosbachstr. 107
CH-8032 Zürich
Tel. +41 (0) 44-251 75 05   Fax +41 (0) 44-251 75 06
E-Mail: zuerich@lit-verlag.ch   http://www.lit-verlag.ch

Auslieferung:
Deutschland: LIT Verlag Fresnostr. 2, D-48159 Münster
Tel. +49 (0) 2 51-620 32 22, Fax +49 (0) 2 51-922 60 99, E-Mail: vertrieb@lit-verlag.de
Österreich: Medienlogistik Pichler-ÖBZ, E-Mail: mlo@medien-logistik.at
E-Books sind erhältlich unter www.litwebshop.de

To my grandmother,
Omma Inge Klara Alter.

Susanne Liljeroos – du vet vem du är

Table of Contents

Acknowledgements

When I first started studying at Greifswald University in 2001, I had no idea where Prof. Dr. Hartmut Lutz's lecture on Canadian literature, Dr. Margitta Kuty's seminar on teaching English as a foreign language, and various eye-opening discussions would lead me. What lay in store for me, you now hold in your hands. This book, which was originally accepted as a PhD thesis at the University of Münster, Germany, in 2013, is the result of a long journey that began with a spark of fascination for literature and teaching, and which has allowed me to discover different routes; some taken, some not. On this journey, I have met many interesting and wise people who have asked questions, engaged in discussions, given advice, challenged my ideas, and thus contributed in their own special ways to this project.

I would like to acknowledge the essential contributions of my mentor and supervisor Prof. Dr. Christiane Lütge who has constantly provided open doors and mailboxes, offered her opinions and supported my academic advancement. She has always encouraged me to think further and explore new territories. I am also genuinely grateful to Prof. Dr. Laurenz Volkmann for his time, patience and valuable advice; I highly appreciate his support.

I am especially indebted to The International Council for Canada Studies (ICCS) for granting me the Graduate Student Scholarship in 2011. This allowed me to conduct research at different libraries and institutions in Canada and to meet people who have been so helpful for the development of my ideas. At the Centre for Research of Young People's Texts and Cultures (CRYPT) at the University of Winnipeg I had the honour of working with Prof. Dr. Perry Nodelman, Prof. Dr. Mavis Reimer, Dr. Naomi Hamer, charlie peters and Dr. Heather Snell. At The Canadian Children's Book Centre in Toronto, Meghan Howe opened their huge collection of Canadian books for young readers for me and provided me with a comfortable desk and atmosphere to discover more resources. Prof. Dr. Ingrid Johnston at the University of Alberta has helped me refine my perspectives and broadened my horizons. Nik Burton at Coteau Books in Regina, and the authors Barbara Sapergia and Hiromi Goto (whom I had already met in 2005 and who first introduced me to the "In the Same Boat" series) welcomed me to their offices and homes with open arms and patiently answered questions, many of which led to new ones. I would like to thank Sharon and Colin Jeffares for providing me with a home away from home. Dawn Maracle has been highly influential for my approach to literature and cultural studies – Niawenko:wa.

Academia attracts many talented people and I was lucky to be working with some who now have become close friends. Tanja Aho, you deserve special appreciation and thanks. Your sharp mind already impressed me when we were academic kids in G'wood and it still guides my current adventures, not least through your intensive reading of and commenting on the first manuscript and your helpful recommendations. Special thanks go to Johanna Marks, Thorsten Merse and Dr. Stephan Gabel who discussed my ideas, challenged my approaches and critically read drafts. You endured my moods, the good and the bad ones, and knew exactly when I needed a fresh cup of coffee or an open ear. I would like to extend collective thanks to my friends who have believed in me and this project and always knew when I needed a break, more coffee or just a short chat in between. No matter what time of day or how far away, Lexi, Ralf, Flo, Birgit, Tina and Verena – you were always there for me and provided valuable support. Toni, Gianmaria, Luca y Elizabetta, muchas gracias por su apoyo. Las visitas de la feria cada miércoles juntos muchas veces fueron lo mejor de la semana. Grazie mille per tango, bollita e un poco di giogia di videre mediterranea in Münster.

Marcus and Christiane Möhring, and their children Abelina, Lennard, Malte and Linea have been and remain a save haven, your home offered a space for recreation, for recharging my batteries and gaining trust in myself. Thank you.

Finally, I need to express my deepest gratitude to my family, especially my parents, Doris and Bernd, without whom this project would never have been possible. I could always rely on your encouragment and I am sincerely thankful for your understanding when I had to hide behind books instead of visiting. Thank you both so much for everything.

Introduction

Within the last decades, scholars, researchers and practitioners have established a strong link between teaching English, literature and cultural learning. They have suggested various texts for English language teaching (ELT), outlined their benefits and designed lesson plans and possible classroom procedures that are meant to achieve the objective of developing students'[1] inter- and transcultural competences. From Surkamp and Nünning's (2008, 2009) or Hesse's (2009) suggestions, one can generalize that these texts often represent a multicultural scope and increasingly belong to the genre of young adult fiction. Yet, in a changing society the connection of literature, culture and ELT offers new perspectives which demand extended conceptualizations of cultural learning.

That the endeavor of increasing cultural competences with multicultural young adult fiction also entails challenges and limitations can be illustrated by the anecdotal experience of a colleague of mine. She reported that after she and her students had finished discussing a 'multicultural book', which described the hardships of a protagonist of color and his struggle against disapproval, discrimination and racism in a 'mainstream' society, one of her students had left the classroom commenting "I'm glad that wasn't about me!" Although the protagonist's fight was successful in the end, his pain and despair were overwhelming, causing this student to feel pity, shame and conscious non-identification with the ethnic other. These responses run counter to common objectives of inter- and transcultural learning as both are actually supposed to develop students' ability and willingness to identify with others, to be open toward them and engage in respectful negotiations of meaning and communication (cf. Norton 2011, 73). Such communication is characterized by mutual tolerance and respect, honest openness and empathy, and a willingness to understand the other from within their specific cultural frames.

There can be various reasons why in this incident these objectives had not been achieved. Some could be traced, for instance, to the choice of texts on which cultural learning was based, the methods used in approaching the text, or the student's previous learning and real-life experiences. Additionally, a possible reason could be found in the objectives of the teaching unit, in the sense that these might have been too ambitious and remote from what is feasible in a classroom context. In this particular case cultural learning was restricted to experiences mediated through literature. This is a dilemma that teachers often face when trying to promote cultural learning through literature, a dilemma which this study tries to resolve. I will argue that if certain practices in cultural teaching are altered, such reactions cannot only be prevented, but could even give way to reactions like "Hey, that was about me!" By critically investigating conceptualizations of inter- and transcultural learning based on young adult fiction,

---

[1]   The terms 'student(s)', 'learner(s)' and 'reader(s)' are used as synonyms as this study is situated in an educational context. These terms include all gender identifications of the members of classrooms, audiences and readerships.

I will argue that the current understanding of transcultural learning does not suffice to enable students to benefitially engage with otherness in a local and global context.

Since the publication of Michael Byram's seminal text *Teaching and Assessing Intercultural Communicative Competence* (1997) new conceptualizations of cultural learning in the English as a foreign language (EFL) classroom have gained increasing attention. This tendency manifests itself not only in theoretical approaches, such as Lothar Bredella's extended notion of the other in ELT (2010) and Werner Delanoy's effort to implement a new didactic approach in literary and cultural studies (2005, 2006, 2008, 2011), but also, and more concretely, in the empirical research by Christiane Fäcke (2006) and Britta Freitag-Hild (2010). They focused on the emergence of transcultural competences and provided tools for the closer investigation and classroom evaluation of such competences. Recently, Eberhardt (2013) put forward an empirically founded model of cultural competence development.

Although intercultural communicative competence (ICC) remains the central foundation of ELT, a closer look at current trends in cultural learning and teaching reveals that the theoretical foundations of inter- and transcultural learning are facing constant shifts, for example changing assumptions about the meaning of 'culture.' Therefore, inter- and transcultural learning remains an attractive field of interest for further investigations. Another critical area is the evaluation of students' cultural competences. Few empirical studies on cultural learning have been conducted. In these studies students' competences and performances[2] are not always sufficiently differentiated, but scholars seem to assume that students' answers in the classroom reflect their unfiltered inter- and transcultural competences detached from teachers' or society's expectations.

The following chapters discuss these reservations in more detail. Within the critical context of inter- and transcultural learning one of the focal points lies on the perception of the other beyond national or ethnic otherness. I suggest that such an extended perception agrees more with societies' diversity and plurality at the beginning of the 21st century. One interesting question to ask in this context is who should actually be regarded as the other in societies which are characterized by multiculturalism and hybridity. Closely connected to this aspect is the observation that ethnic and national others are usually represented within issue- and problem-laden paradigms, which reduce them to certain prob-

---

[2] Interestingly, Byram refers to such a differentiation: "Since the five *savoirs* include attitudes (*savoir être*) [,] dispositions or orientations to act (*savoir s'engager*), knowledge (*savoirs*) and skills (*savoir comprendre, apprendre, faire*), it is evident that the distinction of competence and performance introduced by Chomsky and developed by Hymes is not adequate. It is here that the advantage of using the term '*savoir*' holistically becomes clear, since it includes the whole range of skills, attitudes and knowledge, and simultaneously allows us to distinguish among them by adding a second infinitive" (1996, 89, emphasis in original). A so-called "'performance assessement', in which knowledge and abilities are evaluated as they are used and evident in activities which might be an application of what has been learnt" sounds rather vague. Therefore, I would still like to critically investigate this distinction in more detail.

lem-identities. Yet, as Laurenz Volkmann analyses in his comparison of inter-cultural learning and postcolonial studies, the "unlearning of binaries and Other-ing" (2012, 177) is a necessary tool for cultural learning. He notes a "marked development to move beyond simplistic and reductive polarities such as the dis-tinctions between […] oppressor and oppressed […], black and white, rich and poor, male and female, good and bad" (ibid., cf. Antor 2010, Delanoy 2006, Schulze-Engler 2009, Welsch 2000). Transcultural learning, which – due to the original etymological meaning of the prefix 'trans' – refers to learning 'across' or 'beyond' culture(s), carries the potential to investigate not only these spaces in-between, but also connections to other others. Additionally, 'trans' allows to explore spaces of representation between and beyond good and evil or oppres-sor and the oppressed. It is this depiction of otherness that I regard as making a valuable contribution to differentiating between the concepts of inter- and trans-cultural learning.

Such deconstructions have been explored by Delanoy (2005, 2006, 2008, 2011, 2012) and Volkmann (2011, 2012), for example, but it remains questionable in how far they have found entry to ELT, both conceptually and regarding the choice of literature. Therefore, the unlearning of simplistic di-chotomies, which is essential for cultural learning in the face of multicultural societies and globalization, will be discussed in much detail. As I will argue, the analysis and discussion of narratives on which cultural learning is currently founded tends to reinforce stereotypes[3] rather than to deconstruct them. Moreo-ver, the Teaching English as a Foreign Language (TEFL) discourse of cultural

---

[3]   The term 'stereotype' was introduced to political and socio-psychological studies by Walter Lippmann in *Public Opinion* first published in 1922. He assumes that human thought is orga-nized by "pictures in our heads" (1997, 3-22). These pictures help to understand the com-plexity of people's surroundings and to categorize and process information. As stereotypes function to generalize, abstract, simplify and systematize information, they are an important mental tool. However, stereotypes are only partly based on experience, personal or mediated. "For the most part we do not first see and then define, we define and then see. In the great blooming, buzzing confusion of the outer world we pick out what our culture has already de-fined for us, and we tend to perceive that which we have picked out in the form stereotyped for us by our culture" (ibid., 54-55). And further "[t]he subtlest and most pervasive of all in-fluences are those which create and maintain the repertory of stereotypes. We are told about the world before we see it. We imagine most things before we experience them. And those preconceptions, unless education has made us acutely aware, govern deeply the whole process of perception" (ibid., 59). Interestingly, Lippman here refers to the potential of education to unlearn stereotypes. Yet, as I argue, it remains to be seen in how far this unlearning is suc-cessful in connection to a certain choice of literature (for further scholarship, also language education specific see Bredella/Delanoy 1999, Burwitz-Melzer 2003, Eisenmann 2004, Lö-schmann 1998, Löschmann/Stroinska 1998, Maijala 2006, Nünning 1994, O'Sullivan/Rösler 312-321). Stereotypes are assumptions or images directed at a certain group; they can be posi-tive or negative. Usually, stereotypes generalize certain behaviors or traits of character which are ascribed to a collective group or individuals. Stereotypes can be differentiated in hetero-stereotypes which are assumptions or images members of a group have about another group, and auto-stereotypes which are images members of a group have about their own group. Both are said to support identity formation in terms of membership and differentiation of self and otherness, but also pave the way for discrimination and oppression.

learning seems to limit 'culture' to ethnicity and nationality – it does hardly provide a perception of multicultural protagonists beyond ethnic and national identity.

Generally speaking, texts and literatures from English-speaking countries are seen as valuable and beneficial material to support processes of understanding otherness within a theoretical framework of increasing inter- and transcultural competences (cf. Bredella/Burwitz-Melzer 2004, Burwitz-Melzer 2003, Carolli 2008, Hall 2005, Lazar 2009, Surkamp/Nünning 2008, 2009, Thaler 2008). However, realistic fiction about multicultural characters, which is used most commonly to achieve this objective, may support readers and learners in upholding their dichotomous perceptions of cultural otherness. Compared to texts which invite learners to openly engage with balanced otherness, these texts rather create ties that blind. Despite the fact that the intercultural approach apparently needs cultural otherness and problematizations of cultural identity, the question in how far transcultural learning needs to be based on a similar paradigm is still awaiting an answer – a question that is addressed and conceptually further developed in this contribution to the study of inter- and transcultural learning in ELT.

The reduction of otherness to cultural otherness has been criticized by few academics in TEFL research, for instance by Laurenz Volkmann and Helene Decke-Cornill, who edited a collection of essays on *Gender Studies and Foreign Language Teaching* (2007). In this publication, Volkmann demands that in the age of globalization cultural learning and teaching necessarily need to pay tribute to a new, continuously and rapidly changing cultural diversity (cf. 2007, 145). In my reading, this not only refers to culture in a narrow sense, but also includes aspects of sexual orientation, gender identity, religion, aspects of psychological and physical abilities and/or age and milieu or class.

With increasing academic attention being paid to postcolonial studies, cultures and literatures of previously ignored and marginalized ethnicities and 'minorities'[4] are moving toward the center and receiving consideration in philology as well as in new methodological approaches to teaching English (cf. Hallet 2010a, 154). The increasing diversification and plurality brought about

---

[4]   The terms 'minority' and 'visible minority' reflect attitudes and hierarchies imposed by a dominant group that assumes power over others and could therefore be contested. In *Making a Difference* (2007), Kamboureli raises critical awareness for using the term 'minority.' For her anthology she selected literature as a "counterreading of what we have come to call mainstream and minority literatures in Canada. Multicultural literature is not minority writing, for it does not raise issues that are of minor interest to Canadians. Nor is it, by any standard, of lesser quality than the established literary tradition. Its thematic concerns are of such a diverse range that they show the binary structure of 'centre' and 'margins', which has for long informed discussions of Canadian literature, to be a paradigm of the history of political and cultural affairs in Canada" (Kamboureli 2007, xx). When this terminology is still used in current discourses (e.g. Merkl 2013) such race and ethnicity-based power structures are re-implemented and indicate that the hierarchical perceptions of people are not yet overcome. Therefore, I avoid using this term, or put it in single inverted comma to distance my approach from this connotation.

by the postcolonial and global age has given rise to manifold options for forming social and cultural identities. Those need to be integrated in educational contexts if young people are to be prepared for participating critically, reflectively and more productively in the social, economic and political life of the 21st century. As many of these developments stem from English-speaking countries or from contexts in which English is the lingua franca of the global village, and have global impact, negotiations of cultural meaning must have their place in ELT. Foreign language education can and should take up the social discourses of everyday life and the corresponding experiences; if these are implemented in lessons, they can in turn affect discourses outside the classroom (cf. Hallet 2010a, 155).

Apart from contributing to inter- and transcultural learning, I also wish to engage in the challenging discussion of assessing and evaluating cultural competences. Whereas the development of cultural competences is based on solid ground, their evaluation and assessment remain a challenging endeavor for teachers and researchers. Cultural competences address students' personalities and are located on a cognitive, affective and pragmatic level. While these can certainly be influenced by education, it is difficult to evaluate and assess instances of a successful implementation of affective and pragmatic cultural competence. Fäcke's (2006) and Freitag-Hild's (2010) empirical studies on inter- and transcultural learning have indeed provided first insights into suitable methods of assessment. Nevertheless, certain difficulties can still be unveiled when taking into account that students could be aware of the democratic and institutionalized environment in which their reflections of cultural issues take place – namely in the classroom – and of a certain underlying social desirability. In this respect, this study suggests alternative methods and critically discusses evaluation tools between Standards of Education and complex and dynamic discourses of culture and identity.

The concluding remarks in Freitag-Hild's investigation of British fictions of migration and transcultural learning offer further justifications for the approach in this work. She states that the canon of texts read in ELT needs to be extended (cf. 2010, 355). Following this claim, I argue that in addition to multicultural literature currently used in ELT, narratives need to be read that do not limit multicultural protagonists to mere problem-identities but which depict multicultural protagonists who experience fantastic adventures for their own sake. This is especially important in view of transcultural learning.

Moreover, Freitag-Hild stresses the importance of implementing transcultural learning in Grades 5 to 10 (cf. ibid., 357). The texts that are discussed in chapter 5 meet this call as they are suitable for students aged 12 to 18 and for a language level of B1 onward (cf. Council of Europe 2001). I generally support the researcher's further demand to represent diverse cultures in ELT (cf. Freitag-Hild 2010, 357), but would like to expand it to diverse options for identification, because reducing otherness to ethnicity and nationality can be misleading, one-sided and too narrow in a frame of transcultural learning.

Hence, while Volkmann sees blind spots of cultural learning and teaching in view of an in- or rather exclusion of a "postcolonial element" (2012, 169-180), I additionally see blind spots of transcultural learning in view of the representation of different degrees of othernesses. Volkmann points out that in the postmodern turn also feminist literature, literature of 'ethnic minorities', and literature of the popular and the marginal were included in critical reflections and have been, and still are to be, increasingly applied to English classrooms as well (cf. 2007, 145). Besides this broad understanding and inclusion of social and cultural diversity, I believe that the question *how* the protagonist is represented is essential for increasing transcultural competences. Therefore, using 'cultural identity', I explicitly refer to a broad understanding of culture, including various identity markers such as gender, age, social milieu, religion etc. and their different realizations.

My account of cultural learning elaborates on and further develops the concept of transcultural learning in the EFL classroom. In the course of argumentation, I consult psychological and literary-didactic concepts to support my perspectives. One central claim will be a call for a different kind of literature that is necessary if the 'trans', i.e. the cross-cultural component is to be emphasized. Moreover, I argue that inter- and transcultural learning based on literature could make use of different classroom procedures, which can lead to more serious and honest reflections of cultural and identity issues. Therefore, my research aims at scrutinizing the concepts of transcultural learning and transcultural competences, re-evaluating the perception of otherness and, based on this, suggesting young adult fiction in English, exemplarily from Canada, which is suited for promoting transcultural learning in ELT.[5] This discussion will help to distinguish transcultural from inter- or multicultural literature. Finally, as a more practical outlook, means of evaluating cultural competences will be examined, build on which underlying principles of methods prevailing in contemporary ELT are altered to be more fitting for transcultural approaches.

Using examples of Canadian children's and young adult literature as a foundation for a critical discussion of transcultural learning and teaching is neither an arbitrary decision nor should it be seen as a mere search for a perfect text for cultural learning. New texts can always be suggested, found and taught. Eisenmann, Grimm and Volkmann's (2010) publication on the potential of New English Literatures for ELT supports this view. Instead of a hyper-optimization of texts for classroom reflections, I attempt to develop an understanding of transcultural texts in differentiation to intercultural texts, which holds promises

---

[5] As I focus on teaching English as a foreign language, I will not include Canadian literature for young readers in French. A diverse and resourceful body of French Canadian literature for young readers exists that could be used for a similar approach. The interested reader may refer to Lemieux's *Pleins feux sur la littérature de jeunesse au Canada français* (1972) or to Madore's *La littérature pour la jeunesse au Québec* (1994) for general information on French Canadian literature for young readers. Additionally, I am aware that French Canada plays a different role in teaching French as a foreign language than English Canada does in teaching English as a foreign language (cf. chapter 3).

for transcultural learning objectives specifically. It remains to be seen, though, in how far clear lines between both types can be drawn, in how far a dynamic continuum can be defined or whether a text can be read inter- as well as transculturally.

My exploration of Canadian literature for young readers[6] relates to Volkmann's demand that teachers are increasingly obliged to expand the content of ELT beyond the U.S. and Great Britain. They need to see it as their task to gradually become acquainted with further Anglophone cultures, not only in contrast to those but also for their own sake (cf. 2007, 143). A selection of literature for ELT which is based on habit and is oriented at the availability of teachers' notes and ready-made interpretations cannot be exclusively used in ELT that is understood as a global village (cf. ibid.).

What is more, the extension to Canadian texts helps to fill the gap of representing Canada in ELT. I will reveal that textbooks hardly touch upon Canadian content, not even regarding topics in which Canada provides beneficial points of reference and food for thought such as multiculturalism, diversity, or environmental issues. Although suggestions of texts and supportive arguments have been put forward, Canada is widely ignored in ELT. A study on Canadian 'minority' literature in the frame of identity and understanding otherness within a university context has only been published recently (Merkl 2013).

Although he uses a wide range of novels and short stories by diverse writers, I see Merkl's usage of the term 'minority' in the title and throughout the study as problematic. I believe that this re-establishes a hierarchy of a Euro-Canadian non-visible 'standard' literature and additional texts by 'other' writers who supplement these to offer incentives for developing understanding otherness and identity formation. Such an approach seems to reflect Eurocentric modes of power. The term also questions in how far Euro-Canadian literature can trigger inter- or transcultural learning processes that focus on identity formation and understanding otherness. In my study, therefore, I refrain from seeing 'other' literature as 'minority' literature, because in multicultural societies, and especially in Canada where multiculturalism has been official policy since 1988, such approaches are not applicable, even when official multiculturalism did not always hold what it promised to be and achieve (cf. chapter 4). Furthermore, a focus on 'minority' literature which disregards texts by 'white' authors does not agree to a transcultural scope as will be seen in the definition of transcultural literature.

---

[6] In my work, the term 'young readers' refers to readers who are younger than 18 years of age. Because of their complexity I chose to label the books included in this study 'young adult fiction' (cf. chapter 5). I estimate that the implied readership of the different books I analyse is between 11 and 18 years of age. I am aware that the lower limits of this age group are often labeled 'child readers' of 'children's literature.' However, 'children's literature' often connotes shorter stories that are told in text and illustrations, whereas the books I analyse are complex narrations in length and plot with hardly any illustrations, and multifaceted protagonists between the ages of 11 and 22. As the topics of the novels are intricate and demanding, using the term children's literature would not suffice.

While Merkl's study focuses on tertiary learners at university and analyses how texts create cultural identity (not their effects on the students' identity), I focus on Canadian young adult fiction and on how this frame can trigger developing awareness of alterity and identity formation in younger learners. Despite the benefits of Canadian literature, this national frame functions as a model and should not be understood as contradicting a transcultural scope.

The novels I include in this work have been selected for their inter- and transcultural merit; they offer points of references for negotiating alterity and understanding otherness. The texts represent different forms of otherness, and therefore do not limit otherness to ethnic markers, but reflect society's diversity, including Japanese Canadian, First Nations[7] and 'white' Canadian perspectives.[8] It may come as a surprise that a white male author is included besides a Japanese Canadian and First Nation author, which could be seen as de-marginalizing formerly excluded voices. Yet, as my argumentation shows (cf. chapter 6.1, 7.1), 'whiteness' cannot be excluded from a multi- and transcultural approach as this would imply a Eurocentric perspective which is not compatible with current changes toward multicultural societies. The texts provide an extended view on Canada and support a non-stereotypical encounter while at the same time they offer a first glimpse on Canadian society. A balance of both approaches is important as it can be assumed that learners between 12 and 18 years of age may not have come across Canada in their career as English learners.

I focus on contemporary authors of different backgrounds and their more recent publications post 2000. While the texts cannot be seen as representatives of whole ethnic groups, they are, however, exemplary for the experiences and developments they narrate. As I will argue, Ruby Slipperjack's *Little Voice* (2002), Eric Walters' *Run* (2003) and Hiromi Goto's *The Water of Possibility* (2001) are representative as they offer inter- and transcultural readings and illustrate a continuum from inter- to transcultural learning.[9] More importantly,

---

[7] In the following, First Nations and First Nations people should be understood as including Métis and Inuit peoples. I am highly aware of their high diversity, but would like to use this shortened form for matters of readability.

[8] Although I offer the background of the writers I discuss, I do not perceive of them as representatives or speakers for their background. I am well aware of the diversity of Japanese Canadians and First Nations peoples and admit that one can wonder what a 'white perspective' actually represents. In close proximity to Kamboureli, I also consider these writers "Canadian writers, and not as representatives of cultural groups. The tendency to read multicultural literature through the racial or ethnic labels affixed to its authors more often than not reinforces stereotypical images of the authors themselves and of their cultural community. Labels are vexing and sneaky things because they are intended to express a stable and universal representation of both communities and individuals. By implying that there is a specific essence, say, to the writing of First Nations authors, labels prematurely foreclose our understanding not only of the complexity inherent in individual communities but also of the various ways in which authors position themselves within their cultural groups and the Canadian society at large" (Kamboureli 2007, xxi).

[9] The selection of these titles is the result of a two-month research stay in Canada in 2011 dur-

especially *Run* and *The Water of Possibility* integrate other others, which is considered to be essential in the approach to cultural learning and teaching given here. Slipperjack's and Goto's text are published in Coteau Books' series "In the Same Boat," which was created from the desire to close the gap of a lack of enjoyable reading material for multicultural children: "'Why aren't there any stories about us?' has been a heartfelt cry of Canadian children" (preface *The Water of Possibility* by Janet Lunn) of immigration or multicultural background. Children of diverse descents wanted to read books in which children like them engage in adventures, in their own environments, sharing their experiences. Thus, those books offer options for identification, and allow various children to recognize themselves for their human qualities and give readers insights to Canada's diverse cultures (cf. interview G.A. with Nik Burton, August 2011). The third book under investigation, Eric Walters' *Run,* is a fictional account of Terry Fox's "Marathon of Hope" (April to September 1980). After the amputation of his leg, the young man attempted to run across Canada, a marathon a day, to collect donations for cancer research.

The Canadian texts I select for my account provide options for creating ties that bind instead of ties that blind. This is a reference to Rudine Sims (1982, 70, cf. chapter 7.1.1) who suggested using children's books in order to establish ties that bind inter-generational relationships of African-Americans. Yet, one needs to be careful with such readings as a certain representation of cultural identities could easily establish a very limited and stereotypical perception. I believe that compared to the young adult fiction I discuss, texts that are currently used for cultural learning in ELT re-establish and re-construct stereotypical assumptions of otherness instead of de-constructing those and offering balanced representations of alterity. In this sense, readers are blinded with respect to the complexity of alterity rather than enabled to establish beneficial links between members of diverse communities and societies, including themselves.

The depiction of other others in the three selected titles transfers a modernization of traditional canons in literary and cultural studies to the classroom and allows students to encounter diverse forms of identity formation beyond national and ethnic markers. In the texts, determination, will-power, strength and trust define the protagonists, not their search for ethnic identity. This attention to othernesses is in accordance with Jürgen Einhoff's statement that multicultural texts in the classroom – I would add 'need to' – give insights to basic phenomena and situations which are common in various cultures (2003, 8). In the academic debate of cultural conceptualizations and their didactic implications, this assumption is reflected in the furtherance of intercultural to transcultural learning and teaching.[10] Volkmann's references to topics such as childhood,

---

ing which I studied at several universities, visited scholars specializing in Canadian literature for young readers and explored various bookstores across Canada. I additionally had the chance to interview writers and children's book editors as well as publishers in Saskatoon and Regina. Those interviews are included in chapters 4.1, 4.2, and 5.3.

[10] It needs to be noted that both should not be perceived as one being better than the other. Ra-

coming-of-age, family structures, age, education, relationships between genders, friendship and love (cf. 2007, 150) mirror a direction of cultural teaching that Bredella calls 'transcultural' (cf. 2010b, 122-123). This approach is also foundational in my investigation. While it is important that students identify "the many contextual differences between various cultural and political situations" (Antor 2000, 258), they should also be enabled to see commonalities without running danger of universalizing diverse shapes.

Within my approach to inter- and transcultural learning, literature for young readers serves as the main focus; if not indicated otherwise, the term 'literature' as used here implies young adult fiction. As this field has gained significance for ELT in the past decade, which is for example visible in publications like *Teenage Fiction the English Classroom* (Hesse 2009) or *Children's Literature in Second Language Education* (Lütge/Bland 2012), the following part reflects in more detail on the readership of literature for young readers.[11]

Who are young readers? How experienced does one need to be in order to be a young reader? It is hardly possible to find universal answers to these questions due to a multitude of approaches and needs for justifications.[12] As the term suggests, on first sight it seems as if young adult fiction is defined by its target readership. However, this readership is in turn understood under the influence of adults' assumptions of who young adults are, what they like and how and what they read (cf. Nodelman/Reimer 2003, 79). It does not seem to be difficult to define literature for young readers, yet recent publications reveal that a differentiation of children's and adult literature is everything but easy.

Beyond a readership, the age of the protagonist is considered to be decisive: children's literature revolves around a child protagonist; young adult fiction revolves around young adults. However, novels such as Zusak's *The Book Thief* (2005) or Boyne's *The Boy in the Striped Pyjamas* (2006) show that this is not necessarily the case. Both novels present child protagonists – Liesel Meminger and Bruno, both nine years old – yet, the complex books are set during World War II and describe the horrors of the Nazi regime from the innocent perspective of children. Therefore, these novels can be considered as part of a "crossover genre" which dissolves the frontiers of adult and juvenile fiction (cf. Hesse 2009, 18, Hunt 2007, n.p.). Rowling's *Harry Potter* or Mayer's *Twilight* series are popular with young and adult readers alike. These examples denote one crucial debate about children's and young adult fiction: the implied readership (cf. Iser 1972).

This refers to the "gulf between [...] writers and their intended readers" (Nodelman/Reimer 2003, 14). As Nodelman and Reimer explain, literature for

---

ther, both gain validity based on the objectives pursued (cf. chapter 1).

[11] Chapters 2.1 and 7.2 will refer back to this issue.

[12] Cf. Hillman (2003), Lynch-Brown/Tomlinson/Short (2011), Nodelman/Reimer (2003) for children's and young adult literature and Latrobe/Drury (2009) for a specific perspective on young adults and young adult literature.

young readers is written by adults for people who are younger than they are themselves and who are convinced that those young people are certainly different to themselves, so that they need their own kind of literature. The authors observe that adult readers of children's literature not only have to pay attention to their own enjoyment of or interest in those texts but also "remain conscious of ways in which [these] might differ from other texts" (ibid., 16). This leads to the concept of the "implied reader" that was introduced by Wolfgang Iser (1974). It entails that each text, through its style of writing and the topic it addresses, has a certain reader in mind for whom the text is comprehensible. More specifically, these implications regard "the reader's tastes and interests," the reader's "knowledge of literature and life" as well as the reader's ability to engage with a text, respond to it in order to make it "meaningful [and] comprehensible as a use of language" (Nodelman/Reimer 2003, 17). Those aspects of a reader becoming the implied reader indicate that age is not necessarily a marker that ascribes a text to a certain audience. Tastes and interests can certainly be shared by members of different age groups, not every adult is by definition an experienced reader who has a lot of knowledge of literature; responses to texts can take on manifold realizations. Thus, a definition of children's and young adult literature based on the implied reader proves to be problematic. Yet, the difference between the implied reader of a nursery rhyme and a sonnet by Shakespeare seem obvious. Whereas adults may find access to both, Shakespeare would be a challenge for young readers. What, then, distinguishes literature for adults from literature for young adults from literature for children?

Cadden's interesting line of arguments sees literature for young readers as a nexus, a "core of connections and links" (2011, 303) which contribute to the difficulty of defining it. Using the example of *Harry Potter*, he concludes that "mode is the most important consideration of all – not genre" as the *Harry Potter* books include many genres by crossing "portal fantasy to school story to family novel." What readers "ultimately care about is how the thing will end" (ibid., 307). Whalen-Levitt offers a similar individual approach to how literature could be categorized "in terms of what a given text calls upon a reader to know and to do: to know, in terms of experience of both life and literature; to do, in terms of producing a meaning for this particular text, in time, from start to finish" (1983, 159). This distinction extends the theory of the implied reader in so far as it adds a qualitative and a quantitative level to the responses readers give to a piece of writing. Taking up the example above, it becomes apparent that a nursery rhyme and a Shakespearean sonnet evoke different responses in children compared to responses in adults. This allows to see both texts suitable for both and partly negates a strict differentiation.

Additionally, as this discussion is in the present context applied to reading in English as a foreign language, certainly language needs to be added to both categories of knowledge and response. In ELT, the reader is supposed to understand the text and to respond to it in the foreign language. This aspect is of special importance as language level and content are often decisive for the motivation and success of reading a text in a foreign language. An English text that is originally written for 9-to 12-year-old children can most often not be read by foreign language learners of the same age group, because the text's English level can be expected to be too high. Older students who would have the appropriate language level could find the content too childish.

Another twist to grasping the readership of literature for young readers is added when taking into consideration that most publishers and buyers of what is assumed to be literature for young readers are actually adults, especially in the case of children's literature. It is therefore questionable whether the authors of literature for young readers really have the young reader in mind when writing books or whether they rather think of the potential publishers and adults who select and purchase books. This aspect became known as the "dual audience," as May recognizes that children's books are indeed regarded and read by adults and children alike. Children's writers certainly write for one audience, the children, but at the same time they need to appeal to an additional level, namely the norms, values and attitudes of the adults who potentially buy the books (1995, 37, 55).

Nodelman's discussion of conventional assumptions about childhood sheds a new light on understanding children's literature as texts that are defined by adults' expectations and their need of what children want to and are allowed to read. In "The Other: Orientalism, Colonialism, and Children's Literature" (1992) he draws parallels between Said's "investigations of European attitudes towards Arabs and Asians" and "assumptions about childhood and children's literature" (ibid., 29). Nodelman elaborates on the similarities of Said's observation that "what we call 'the Orient' has little to do with actual conditions in the East – that is more significantly a European invention that has a powerful influence of how Europeans have not only thought about but also acted upon the East," and the way in which adults and educators perceive the child and thus create children's literature accordingly. What he calls "self-confirming description" entails that children behave and act in ways adults and educators expect them to:

> If we assume that children have short attention spans and therefore never let them try to read long books, they do not in fact read long books. They will seem to us to be incapable of reading long books – and we will see those that do manage to transcend our influence and read long books as atypical, paradoxically freaks in being more like us than like our other. It may well be for that reason that [...] children do seem to like the kinds of books that adult experts claim to be the kind of books children like. (ibid., 32)

Nodelman parallels this with the manipulation of a mindset that makes the 'Oriental' *Oriental*, its description and agreement to Europeans' imaginations as a kind of self-fulfilling prophecy. In a similar sense, also adults' prevailing assumptions of what a child is capable of doing confines children to certain images and roles.

For the content at hand, especially Nodelman's power-dimension is an interesting case in point as it seems to correspond to certain convictions that educators have about the cultural competences children are equipped with or could manage: offering them intercultural books with a certain cultural context, adults and educators see those to be appropriate for children's cultural competences. Moreover, they see the message entailed in these to be appropriate for the social, educational and political context in which the respective book is read and child is brought up and socialized. This thought is fruitful when investigating the kind of realistic fiction that is read in ELT and the modes of representation of otherness that are visible in those (cf. chapters 3.1, 7.1 and 7.2).

This study approaches transcultural learning from a perspective that is grounded in the assumption that literature which is suggested and reflected in current discussions of developing transcultural competences needs to be extended by alternative texts. I believe that this literature re-establishes stereotypical perceptions of cultural otherness which are meant to be deconstructed in transcultural learning. In order to argue for this assumption, transcultural literature and competences are discussed and outlined within a theoretical frame that draws from TEFL theory but also neighboring academic fields such as post-colonial studies, philosophy, psychology and literary theory. It is assumed that changes of local societies, perceptions of culture and global dynamics find reflections in alternative approaches to cultural learning and teaching and bring forward ideas like intercultural learning, intercultural communicative competence, didactics of understanding otherness and transcultural learning. Those concepts find a common ground in their objectives to enable students to be respectful toward others and try to understand them from within their cultural frames. In sum, this investigation combines the aforementioned fields of research and aims at

- discussing and further developing the critical discussion of transcultural learning with transcultural literature,
- making Canadian young adult literature accessible for the EFL classroom by focusing on its inter- and transcultural potential, and
- re-evaluating concepts of teaching literature and culture in ELT contexts with a special view on transcultural competences, including suggestions of alternative methods and critically viewing procedures of evaluation and assessment.

The main thesis can be summarized as follows: in order to increase transcultural competences in students, material, for example literature, is needed which prevents a perception of the other within a problem-laden paradigm and which goes beyond a mere representation of the other as an object of social and cultural issues and discrimination, as a victim of the way in which mainstream society

treats him or her. Instead, the other needs to be presented as an active partici-
pant in social life who has power over his or her own decisions and whose individual development revolves around human characteristics and not only around
overcoming ethnic identity struggles which were caused by a malevolent society. I argue that if a differentiation of inter- and transcultural learning and competences exist, both also need to be differentiated in their practical application
to ELT, either with different texts, different methods, or both. I assume that a
distinction of both concepts could add decisively to the discourse of cultural
learning.

Breaking this main context down, this study assumes that inter- and transcultural competences form a continuum in which one does not take a hierarchical position over the other. Further assumptions of this discussion include:

- In order to meet the demands of and agree to the theoretical foundation of transcultural learning and the development of transcultural
  competences certain key features and commonly accepted aspects of
  implementing literature to ELT need to be extended.
- Children's and young adult literature from Canada can serve as a beneficial resource for transcultural literature.
- Curricular guidelines (exemplified with the curricula of North Rhine-
  Westphalia) do not provide the necessary content to support transcultural learning.
- Transcultural learning needs an adapted set of methods and activities,
  as well as underlying principles.
- Cultural and linguistic competences need to be seen as different
  spheres, as someone can be culturally very competent but lack the
  tools to express this in the foreign language.

To argue for those aspects, the text is divided into three main parts, each
containing three chapters. Part A offers an overview of the development of concepts of cultural learning to give insights into the state of current research.
Chapter 1 critically discusses different conceptualizations of cultural learning as
they have evolved within the past few decades. This is followed by reflections
upon key features of using literature in the EFL classroom, of which literature's
potential for increasing intercultural competences is most essential (chapter 2).
In a last chapter in Part A, curricula and literatures on which the development of
ICC has been grounded are investigated and analysed. This sheds light on gaps
within the practical application of ICC and point to a lack of transcultural approaches. Chapter 3 also suggests Canadian literature as one possible option to
fill the gaps that are identified.
Based on these elaborations, the potential of Canadian literature for
young readers is presented in detail in Part B. First, Canadian literature for

young readers is encountered from a historical perspective (chapter 4) which helps to frame the three example texts discussed and analysed in chapter 5. As the focus of this investigation lies with bringing forward the scholarship of transcultural learning and teaching, chapter 6 summarizes the potential of the selected texts for developing cultural competences. The observations made in this part serve as a basis for a more general approach to transcultural learning and transcultural literature.

Part C draws conclusion from the first two parts in that it re-investigates selected key features of using literature in ELT in view of chapters 1, 2 and 5. It defines transcultural literature as a conclusion of chapter 3 and Part B and introduces a continuum from inter- to transcultural literature. The critical discussion of the challenges and limitations of inter- and transcultural learning as outlined in chapter 1 and 3 and the potential of Canadian texts as analysed in chapters 5 and 6 culminate in alternative suggestions and alterations to existing approaches and methods in transcultural teaching and learning (chapters 7 and 8). Resulting from this discussion, chapter 9 suggests identity competence and awareness of alterity as important sub-competences and extensions to the current concept of transcultural learning. Finally, future perspectives and a critical outlook shed light on further challenges and the need for further research into the topic and its larger frame. The conclusion serves as a summary of the interrelation of Part A, Part B and Part C.

As this discussion is based on the analysis and interpretation of texts, the methodological approach will follow hermeneutics in the tradition of Heidegger and Gadamer. I analyse the literary texts in view of selected topics from inter- and transcultural perspectives. Within the texts, I reflect upon central questions of identity and depictions of otherness and add a didactic perspective which reveals the potential for understanding and negotiating otherness. An overview of the current discourse of inter- and transcultural learning and understanding otherness with respect to the underlying concepts of cultural and postcolonial studies serves as a background for the literary investigations. Within my research I refrain from empirical applications because I see certain challenges of empirically investigating cultural competences that I believe need to be solved first. This aspect is reflected in detail in chapters 2.3 and 8.

This study contributes to the ongoing discourse of transcultural learning in ELT by suggesting an extended view on otherness beyond national and ethnic markers and by adding titles of Canadian literature for young readers to ELT on which the development of transcultural competences can be based. I also suggest a definition of transcultural literature and offer alternative methods and classroom approaches which provide a more thoughtful and in-depth approach to transcultural teaching and learning.

Part A: Didactic Foundations of Cultural Learning and Teaching

Within the German laws of education,[13] the main objective of education is based on principles of gender equality and tolerance; it is defined as the development of versatilely interested personalities who are willing and able to take responsibility for living together in a society with other people and nations, and for future generations (cf. e.g. Ministerium für Schule und Weiterbildung (MSW) 2005, §2; Ministerium für Bildung, Wissenschaft und Kultur, 2010, §2, §3).[14] It is school's duty to develop the knowledge, skills and competences as well as attitudes which enable students to participate in social, economic, cultural and political discourses actively, creatively, critically and responsibly. This should support students in unfolding their personalities and making independent decisions. Each subject of the curriculum needs to contribute to the implementation of these general objectives of education in their syllabi according to their subject-specific and interdisciplinary potential.

The aforementioned responsibility for living together in societies characterized by mutual respect and openness gains additional validity as processes of economic, social and political interaction on a global level have increased the cultural and social diversity of everyday experiences. As a consequence, TEFL theory and curricula guidelines for ELT attempt to translate different conceptualizations of cultural learning into formats applicable to language teaching. Key terms such as intercultural communicative competence, intercultural discourse competence or competence to engage in intercultural encounters ("interkulturelle Handlungsfähigkeit") are frequently used to discuss and theorize these applications.

With respect to foreign language learning and teaching, the competence to negotiate meaning is intrinsically present (cf. Byram 1997, 28 in reference to National Standards for Foreign Language Learning 1996), as it includes more or less intercultural and content-related dimensions directed at a respective culture (cf. Klippel/Schmid-Schönbein 2001, 111). Foreign language teaching aims at enabling students to adequately communicate with people who do not share their mother tongue or to function as mediators between people who do not share a common language. Furthermore, it aims at students becoming aware of cultural differences and similarities. European policies of language education

---

[13] In Germany, federal countries are responsible for setting rules and regulations of the public and private school system. Therefore, each federal country has separate laws that regulate objectives and guidelines for schooling. The main objective as mentioned here is usually set within the first five paragraphs of each law of education.

[14] For my research I use resources in German as well, as my argumentation refers to the current TEFL discourse in German-speaking countries. Whenever the bibliography at the end of this work reveals that the original text quoted or referred to is in German, I provide the translation myself. I only quote the German original in specific cases in footnotes as to support readability.

have acknowledged this central importance of raising critical cultural awareness by implementing ICC in the *Common European Framework of Reference for Languages: Learning, Teaching, Assessment* (CEF, Council of Europe 2001) which serves as the foundational guideline for language education in Europe. This implementation is the result of complex developments in the field of cultural learning and teaching. The following chapters present a detailed introduction to conceptualizations of cultural learning and to realizations of this central object of language education. As these conceptualizations are grounded in discourses of TEFL theory and research in both literary and cultural studies, the explications regard both field s and discuss their mutual integration. Additionally, in Part A I refer to some of the key features and justifications of using young adult literature in ELT (chapter 2) and explore and analyse in how far young adult literature is implemented in curricula and teaching material currently used in ELT. In order to argue in favour of reading Canadian young adult fiction, this analysis focuses on Canadian content specifically (chapter 3).

1. Conceptualizing and Promoting Cultural Learning in ELT

The term intercultural competence took a central role in TEFL discourses in the 1970s and 1980s when the development of multicultural societies in the U.S. and Canada increasingly gained political attention. Within those societies, tolerance and respect between people from different cultural backgrounds was seen as an essential educational objective of social integration (cf. Volkmann 2010, 21). Intercultural competence's high value for educational purposes has been granted when it was incorporated as an "existential competence" (Council of Europe 2001, 11-12) in the CEF, be it as an element of "plurilingualism" (ibid., 4-6) or as part of para- and sociolinguistics (ibid., 13-14, 89-90). The CEF was created in order to find a common base on which languages are taught, to make stages of education and language improvement comparable among the member states of the EU and to set standards for language education for these states. This document frames the development of skills and competences in an "intercultural approach" to teaching languages. Within this intercultural approach "it is a central objective of language education to promote the favourable growth of the learner's whole personality and sense of identity in response to the enriching experience of otherness in language and culture" (ibid., 1). In its further explanations, the CEF describes a complex interaction of numerous competences that support the development of intercultural communication. These competences revolve around various aspects, for example the "[k]nowledge of the shared values and beliefs held by social groups in other countries and regions, such as religious beliefs, taboos, assumed common history" (ibid., 11). Increasing such competences provides for the development of intercultural awareness which is understood as acquiring knowledge, awareness and understanding of the relation (similarities and distinctive differences) between the 'world of origin' and the 'world of the target community.' Intercultural awareness also covers a critical awareness of "how each community appears from the perspective of the other, often in the form of national stereotypes" (ibid., 103).

The CEF furthermore suggests intercultural skills and know-how as a support of learners' identity formation. These include

- the ability to bring the culture of origin and the foreign culture into relation with each other,
- cultural sensitivity and the ability to identify and use a variety of strategies for contact with those from other cultures,
- the capacity to fulfill the role of cultural intermediary between one's own culture and the foreign culture and to deal effectively with intercultural misunderstanding and conflict situations, and
- the ability to overcome stereotyped relationships. (ibid., 104-105)

The importance of connecting personal and cultural competences is likewise underlined when explanations of "'existential' competence" (ibid., 105) define

> openness towards, and interest in, new experiences, other persons, ideas, peoples, societies and cultures; [the] willingness to relativize one's own cultural viewpoint and cultural value-system, [and the] willingness and ability to distance oneself from conventional attitudes to cultural difference (ibid.)

as essential contributions to students' personal identity. These aspects also mirror intercultural awareness.

In order to compare the levels of language proficiency, the framework provides complex and detailed descriptions of six developmental stages for the skills of reading and listening comprehension, as well as speaking and writing, unfolded into respective sub-skills and variations.[15] Although intercultural competence takes center stage and is regarded as the essential objective of education, the framework does not include descriptions and stages for this foundational competence. This unveils that two very different discourses clash, namely that of cultural learning, which is said to be subjective and individual, and standardization, which aims at providing objective descriptors for language use (cf. Hu 2008, 290-291/2010, 63, cf. chapter 2.2.1).

Within the culture discourse, one central question focuses on the possibility to understand cultures in order to learn about and from them. This question demands two main reflections: the aspect of understanding other cultures which is anchored in TEFL theory, especially through the scholarship of the Gießen Graduate School of "Didaktik des Fremdverstehens" (Didactics of Understanding Otherness, cf. chapter 1.1) and an elaboration of the term 'culture' borrowed from cultural studies discourses. As the latter has influences on concepts of inter- and transcultural learning, I reflect on it before the TEFL specific discussion is entered in the following sections.

'Culture' is a highly multidimensional, complex, flexible and dynamic term. As culture is located within discourses of individuals and society, structure, cognition and communication, action and interaction as well as continued and disrupted processes of development, it is difficult to define culture detached from certain contextualizations. Most of the approaches and definitions of culture agree that on a formal level, it is understood as an organized and self-organizing structure which is complex and relatively autonomous, which is con-

---

[15] The sub-skills and variations to those main skills are very complex and diverse. Reading, for example is divided into reading for general orientation, reading for information, reading and following instructions, reading for pleasure, reading for gist, for specific information, for detailed understanding, for implications. The CEF provides scales for overall reading comprehension, reading correspondence, reading for orientation, reading for information and argument, reading instructions. For each of those forms can-do-statements for the levels A1 to C2 are provided (cf. Council of Europe 2001, 68-71).

stituted of various elements in which language takes a central position. On a content level, culture is defined as a concept which mediates between people and their environment; it offers cognitive connections of information and communication and provides options for interpreting the world. In this sense, culture pre-structures contexts of thought and generates a reality in order to guide members of a community with rules, schemata and patterns for understanding behavior and interaction – both on an individual and collective base. As such, culture is ever present, is re-established through human concretizations and presents a frame of categories of human behavior which is shared by its members, though to different degrees (cf. Witte 2006b, 31). Through socialization and observations, young members recognize this frame, imitate and take over roles and tasks which contribute to the manifestation of the culture; the cultural frame is implicitly transferred to younger generations.

However, such reflections on culture often run the risk of establishing essentializing positions. Yet, an anti-essentialist position toward culture has become prominent in academic discourse not least since Edward Said's critique of inaccurate representations and understandings of cultures based on which European and Western forces justified their imperial and colonial attitudes toward the East, an argument that he discusses in *Orientalism* (1978). This postcolonial perspective was further established in Homi Bhabha's scholarship on "hybridization," which reflects upon worldwide migration and the consequential development of new cultural identities, multicultural societies and new options for *Location[s] of Culture* (1994) (cf. chapter 1.3.2). As culture is an open construct, individuals while being socialized into a certain society, continuously reshape and contribute to culture and keep it dynamic and flexible.

Within the last few decades, concepts that underline cultures' hybrid, dynamic, fluid and flexible character have been further developed and suggested by scholars like Benedict Anderson (*Imagined Communities*, 1991), Gloria Anzaldua (*La Frontera/Borderlands*, 1999) and Zygmunt Bauman (*Liquid Modernity*, 2000), who take recent phenomena such as globalization into account as well. These topical emergences have caused some scholars to reject the concept of culture altogether, for example Welsch as expressed in his idea of transculturality (1999, 2000, cf. chapter 1.3.2). There, culture is based on a "colonizing agenda," as the term cannot do without binary oppositions of 'we here' and 'they there' or 'civilized' and 'primitive,' which are ascriptions that always stigmatize the other as the other (e.g. Derrida 1972 in Witte 2007, 8). However, as a consequence of those critical voices, the culture term should not be reduced to mere individual differences and experiences as this ignores meta-individual aspects of cultures and societies (cf. ibid.).

An open and dynamic culture term which pays tribute to historically developed, negotiated and mutually shared meanings and schemata of a society offers a solution for this issue. As such, culture is not fixed and static, but rather provides its members with cultural patterns of interpretation (cf. Altmayer 2004, 154 in ibid.). This understanding also pays tribute to members' active and creative contributions to culture. As the discussions in the chapters on intercultural and transcultural learning show, this terminology has gained further attention regarding its conceptualization in modern societies.

The term culture as it is applied in this thesis places special emphasis on its multilayered and dynamic character. This will become visible in a very broad understanding of cultural identity which can be located in close proximity to alterity and various forms of otherness (cf. chapter 7), but also in the difficulties of assessing cultural competence (cf. chapters 2.3.3 and 8). I believe that when emphasizing transcultural perspectives and identity formation, a culture term needs to go beyond an understanding that implies ethnicity only and needs to include various options for identification. This argument will result in suggesting a competence that places identity and alterity center stage, rather than culture (cf. chapter 8).

Since the 1990s, TEFL theory and ELT see a stronger link between language and culture (cf. chapter 1.2.1). This is based on the assumption that language serves as a main tool of communication and understanding, be it verbal or non-verbal. Thus, language is one of the main means through which one gains access to culture and is enabled to understand the other. Yet, in the discourse of cultural learning, differing positions regarding the options and possibilities of understanding a cultural other and the role of language have gained ground: it is either viewed rather critically or claimed to be achievable. Understanding the other with an awareness of a certain part that cannot be understood forms a consensus between both. The following chapters reflect upon this discourse which is essential for cultural learning.

1.1 Understanding Otherness as an Intercultural Objective

When models of intercultural competence include the self in their conceptualizations, this reveals a strong tendency to regard the learner in processes of language acquisition and also in processes of negotiating cultural meaning. Thus, discovering and understanding the other, which is the central process in cultural learning, is extended to discovering and understanding one's own cultural embeddedness and cultural self. The Gießen Graduate School of Understanding Otherness elaborated upon and extensively researched this hermeneutic dialogue. Within its years of existence (1991-2000), the Gießen School published a large number of texts on the theory of understanding otherness and its application to ELT which had an immense influence on the development of models of cultural learning in TEFL discourses.[16]

---

[16] For example Antor (2007), Bredella (1995, 2002), Bredella/Christ (1993, 1995, 1996), Bredella/Christ/Legutke (1997, 2000), Bredella/Delanoy (1999), Bredella/Meißner/Nünning /Rösler (2000), Christ (1992), Christ/Legutke (1996).

One of the main assumptions that underlie understanding otherness in ELT is that people learn a different language to be able to enter a dialogue with others who do not share a similar language. In order for this dialogue to be successful, learners need to try to understand others from their specific frame of cultural references; this entails taking the others' perspective and simultaneously establishing a distance to one's own perspective (cf. Bredella/Meißner/Nünning/Rösler 2000, xiii). The debate of understanding otherness heavily draws on the philosophical position of Gadamer's *Truth and Method* (first published in 1960) in which he tries to uncover the nature of human understanding. Influenced by Heidegger's teachings, Gadamer assumes that people cannot be perceived as independent actors, but that they are unconsciously embedded in their particular culture that shapes and forms them. Partners of cultural encounters carry with them particular worldviews which are influenced by a certain cultural setting that affects these frames. Within successful processes of encountering otherness, both partners negotiate meaning; both change their mindsets and alter their perspective in order to understand the other.

In Gadamer's terms, this can be described as a "fusion of horizons." Horizon is "the range of vision that includes everything that can be seen from a particular vantage point" (1997, 302). If people are not aware of this horizon, they do "not see far enough and hence over-value[s] what is nearest to [them]" (ibid.). Having a horizon, on the other hand, means that someone is "not being limited to what is nearby, but being able to see beyond it" (ibid.). Enlarging one's horizon through negotiating otherness can also be transferred to literature: when texts are read, readers approach these from their specific perspectives and try to make sense of them. Interpreting and understanding texts involves a kind of "fusion of horizons" during which readers negotiate the meaning of the text by using their own backgrounds as points of references. Here, Gadamer's hermeneutics and understanding of horizon and TEFL theory of ICC and understanding otherness find a common foundation.

This foundation becomes even more profound when acknowledging that Gadamer's hermeneutic assumes that understanding is only achievable when the self and the other engage in some kind of interaction. As undestanding between both can be realized through dialogue, communication is also the major cornerstone of developing intercultural competences and understanding the other. Through the dialogic negotiation of meaning, 'self' and 'other' engage in a discourse which aims at finding a mutual agreement (cf. Gadamer 1972, 363). Both have to regard the position of the other and apply it to their own mindset. It is this dialogic negotiation of meaning which entails changing perspectives and altering one's standpoint that Bredella includes in the concept of understanding otherness (Bredella et al., 1997). For him, being able to see an issue in a different light serves as an indicator for a successful dialogue (cf. ibid., 17).

How is understanding otherness in language education characterized? According to Bredella and Christ (1995), learners of a foreign language encounter otherness in three different dimensions: first, the other language as such;

second, the other language as a part and as a concept of the culture in which it is spoken; and third, the representatives of this culture. People who learn a specific language and who are confronted with otherness have to allow themselves to change their personal perspective and regard the perspective of the other in order to openly meet and be able to understand them. Thereby, the subjects experience new perspectives and insights to otherness as beneficial and contributing to their own personality and identity (Bredella/Christ 1995). In this change of perspectives, this widening of horizons, it is essential that the learners perceive the other from the other's own and specific cultural context, namely from the other's inside perspective, and be comfortable to leave their own frame of cultural references. Then, a kind of understanding is introduced which also changes the view of one's own culture (cf. Burwitz-Melzer 2003, 45). Understanding involves processes of mutual negotiation of meaning between self and other, and within the self, too. Hence, the change of perspective is not only essential but necessary.

The application of this universal approach to understanding otherness is challengeable, as understanding the other, becoming at home in the other (cf. 1990, 19-20), could lead to an appropriation of the other. This concept finds further criticism in relativistic approaches which are reflected in the following chapter.

1.1.1 Conceptual Limitations of Understanding Otherness

The concept of understanding otherness reflects a normative reaction toward curricula alterations of including cultural competences as major objectives of ELT. Yet, this concept, and especially the term 'understanding' are highly disputed, a discourse that is informed by epistemological objectives as well as by cultural, postcolonial but also didactic perspectives.

Whereas understanding the other and the self forms the central element of understanding otherness, this dialectic should not be mistaken as a static or ontological binary (cf. Bredella/Christ/Legutke 1997b, 11-16, Hu 1997). Rather, self and other are relational, dynamic and subjective entities, which are open to change and influence. Especially in times in which trade, migration and communication have gained global expansion, this perception is essential. In a multicultural and transnational society it is almost impossible to speak of absolute otherness; something or someone is not 'other' as such, but in reference to the self or in reference to something and someone else (cf. Bredella/Christ/Legutke 1997b, 11). Still, I would like to underline that otherness should not be simplified. As I argue later, one way of acknowledging the dynamics and complexity of otherness is to refer to it in the plural as othernesses.

One positions which sees understanding otherness critical puts language as the medium of negotiating meaning center stage. This shows traces of Humboldt's idea that language always limits human beings to a certain space and that people are not able to have unrestricted points of view beyond this space (cf. Humboldt 1973). Language not only represents reality but this reality is also constructed by mental and linguistic representations; thus, language is always culturally bound (cf. Witte 2007, 11). Language and cultural categories are based on conventions, which in turn are based on mutual experiences, traditions and shared convictions. Language usage in everyday situations is culturally determined. Hence, understanding within one cultural frame is relatively easy as interlocutors usually share similar rules in which language is used. This assumption could, however, be questioned as intracultural differences of social class, sexuality or religion could increasingly complicate even intracultural negotiations of meaning (cf. also Hu 1996). Understanding others from a different frame of reference is highly challenging, too, as the rules and points of references of language may not be familiar to both interlocutors. A lack of shared experiences and knowledge can ultimately lead to misunderstanding. Therefore, a relativistic perspective on understanding otherness takes empathy and distancing oneself from one's own cultural setting stronger into account (cf. ibid.).

Further criticism of the concept of understanding otherness finds it roots in postcolonial theory, a perspective from which understanding the other entails imperialist and appropriating notions. One essential opponent of assuming to understand the other is Said, who in his seminal text *Orientalism* (1978) criticizes that Western academia has not understood the cultures of the Orient but rather presents a "Western style for dominating, restructuring, and having authority over the Orient" (1978, 3). In this sense, understanding the other reflects exercising power over the other. In Foucault's terms, the will to knowledge as understanding the other is nothing but a veiled will to power (in Bredella 1995, 5). Geertz draws attention to the fact that not being able to completely understand others by emphatically engaging with them allows people to recognize otherness in the first place (in ibid., 8). From these two perspectives, although they were developed in different times and under different circumstances, one can derive that understanding the other is always situated within certain power structures, that knowledge is already a product of power dynamics and that power could also flow in both directions. As power structures can change, understanding otherness is limited and bound by time and place, culturally inflected and highly unstable.

I would not go as far as saying that this results in assuming that understanding the other is neither possible nor desirable. Negating understanding the other per se does not provide a valid direction for establishing a theory of understanding otherness and for translating cultural learning into practical applications. Rather, the aspects mentioned above indicate the high level of complexity of understanding otherness and increase the difficulty to grasp what 'understanding' really entails. It is debatable how one can understand certain aspects if not through one's own experiences and from one's own cultural setting. If the discussion of Geertz and Foucault as presented in Bredella (1995) is strictly followed, one not only negates understanding otherness but the central aim of modern foreign language education as well.

Yet, it is this underlying power relation which foreign language teaching tries to overcome by creating open and respectful encounters of otherness. It could be assumed that, therefore, cultural learning puts much emphasis on the ability to change perspectives, to distance oneself from one's own culture and to regard the other from their cultural frame. However, beyond these processes, also the interlocutors need to be focused. In order to pay tribute to multicultural societies, the rather monolithic notion of "one's own culture" should be critically reflected: What if the student's culture is not the majority culture? What if students have more than one culture? Are these seen as separate? From which culture do they distance themselves? Which perspective would they have to change? This awareness and recognition furthermore increases the complexity and challenge of understanding otherness.

A further critical notion to this perspective on understanding otherness is added in Banerjee's "Fremdverstehen meets Indo chic" (2011), in which she uses references to Grewal's "Travelling Barbie's" and the two novels *Life Isn't All Ha He* by Meera Syal (2001) and *Brick Lane* by Monica Ali (2003) to assert that "turning a moving target into an understandable one may itself be an act of epistemic violence" (Banerjee 2011, 40). In fact, the assumption of understanding a cultural other could reduce the multidimensional other in its complexity and interfere with the perception of the other.

This aspect – the risk of incorporating the other into one's own mindset and of reducing the other to a selected subjectivity which is simplified, stereotyped and does not meet the complexity which constitutes the other in their cultural frame of reference – is one cornerstone of the model's criticism. In this context, Bredella, Christ and Legutke (1997) see a fruitful contribution in differentiating contrastive and complementary hermeneutics. The former focuses on differences toward the other as it aims at determining the self in contrast to the other (cf. ibid., 12). Whereas this hermeneutic approach prevents the self from incorporating the other, it may also exclude the other and lose sight of commonalities. Contrastive hermeneutics not only ignores intracultural differences, but leaves similarities which are the foundation for seeing differences unnoticed (cf. ibid.). Understanding otherness from a complementary position offers the potential of emphasizing similarities (cf. ibid., 14-16).

These references show that the development of a concept of understanding otherness and its critical reflection is not reserved for cultural studies but is strongly anchored and discussed within TEFL research itself. The question whether understanding the other is actually possible and desirable has caused intense debates among scholars of foreign language teaching and learning (e.g. covered in Burwitz-Melzer 2003, Eberhardt 2013, Fäcke 2006, Freitag-Hild 2010, Nieweler 1995), among which one of the most common debates is the exchange between Bredella (cf. 1993, 1995, passim) and Hunfeld (cf. 1991, 1992, 1994, passim).

Hunfeld, in response to Bredella's positive interpretation and approach toward understanding otherness, states that keeping a distance between the self and the other in principle is not only necessary but cannot be avoided. He contradicts the proponents of a theory of understanding otherness and its implications for language teaching because the foreign language classroom aims at overcoming as well as preserving the other. His perspective of skeptical hermeneutics (cf. Hunfeld 1991, 50) calls for a recognition of the mysteriousness and normalcy of the other (cf. Hunfeld 1994, 97) which entails a certain part that cannot be understood. With this reflected distancing, he warns of incorporating the other, which can only be prevented when a certain distance toward the other is kept. Thus, boundaries and limitations need to be recognized, the other needs to remain a mystery. This incomprehensible rest would be especially visible in literature that provides a hermeneutic challenge for learners as it is based on a certain degree of otherness and distance to the reader's experiences (cf. Hunfeld 1990, 62, also in Fäcke 2006, 14).

Additionally, Hunfeld states that the approach to others is always influenced by a limitation of one's own knowledge and by stereotypical preconceptions. The learning process cannot do without simplifications of the foreign language and the other world; yet, without multiple meanings and diverse perspectives of the other, a necessary distance, which the learning process tries to overcome, cannot be kept (cf. 1992, 5). For Hunfeld only the recognition of differences between the self and the other can prevent subsuming the other under the self (cf. Burwitz-Melzer 2003, 43). For conceptualizations of cultural learning, his perspective offers a more open and fruitful approach, because the other is left with more space to unfold (cf. Fäcke 2006, 14).

Although he is one of the leading proponents of understanding otherness, Bredella is aware of the challenges of understanding otherness. Understanding would often already be difficult within one's native language and culture – how is a learner then supposed to achieve understanding across cultural boundaries? (cf. Bredella 1995, 2) Yet, one learns a foreign language to understand and communicate with the other in the first place and certain methods and media can support such processes.

Antor grounds understanding otherness in the context of intercultural learning on Gadamer's hermeneutics. However, Antor (2007) explains that the separate entities between which understanding is negotiated do not exist; rather cultures always overlap even if only to a limited extent. He further argues that without such basic similarities intercultural contact and discourse would not be possible. Regarding Gadamer's objective of the process of understanding, Antor sees the need to relativize such processes as complete understanding is rather unlikely in intercultural encounters: negotiating otherness always leaves a certain part that will remain 'other' and that will not be understood (cf. Antor 2007, 119). Therefore, he argues, it is rather possible that both positions move closer together. Antor advises a certain degree of hermeneutic modesty in order to prevent self-abandonment or colonizing the other (cf. ibid.). In Hunfeld's and Antor's perspective, intercultural competence entails the ability to accept alterity even after extended and intensive contact without trying to obliterate it.

Compared to understanding otherness, it would be more important to benefit from alterity and use it for changing into the perspective of the other and reconsidering one's own position from this perspective (cf. ibid.).

Within his criticism of understanding otherness, Altmayer points at a tautology that a certain terminology entails. He refers to the neglect of critically reflecting the terminology that has increased since the beginning of the Gießen School's research. Terms such as "Fremdverstehen" (understanding otherness), "Fremdkultur" (other culture) and "eigene Kultur" (own culture) would no longer be challenged or discussed controversially. According to Bredella, Meißner, Nünning and Rösler (2000), "Fremdverstehen" means to understand something not within one's own, but in a different context (cf. Bredella et al. 2001, xii). Altmayer states that this explanation is only sufficient to solve the problematic notion of the tautology 'understanding otherness' if there was an understanding that would be possible from one's own perspective exclusively. 'Understanding' intrinsically entails understanding something other than the self, every process of understanding attempts to comprehend an 'other' context, understanding always regards understanding otherness. According to Altmayer it would not be reasonable to reflect upon otherness if it did not regard the 'other,' 'somebody different' or something 'not me' (cf. 2001, 6).

Most interesting in Altmayer's elaboration are the concluding remarks in which he raises the question whether the category 'understanding otherness' truly makes sense. Is the dialectic approach of self and other (national) cultures useful when it assumes that 'self' and 'other' can be strictly separated and, moreover, when it implies that 'cultures' are homogeneous structures between which a clear distinction can be made? This questions leads to my assumption that the understanding of cultures as dynamic and fluid needs to be integrated in TEFL discourses more clearly, as phenomena like mass migration, globalization and mass media have proven that separate cultures, if ever, no longer exist (cf. the discussion of the term transculturality in chapter 1.3.2). Therefore, Altmayer asks whether the usage of the term 'understanding otherness' leads toward re-establishing traditional images of national identity and mentality which have become obsolete in post-nationalism. He assumes that concentrating on the 'other cultures' and 'otherness' contributes to constructing otherness in the first place and, thus, solidifies existing stereotypes and prejudices. Talking about the cultural other and the cultural self would be based on the same models which assume a strict separation of cultures and nations. Rather, he suggests questioning this mindset of 'collectives' in general, putting individuals into the center of attention and perceiving of these as individuals rather than as representatives of larger general groups. This line of argument shows traces of a transcultural approach to negotiating otherness on which I focus in chapter 1.3. Furthermore, this offers a linkage to my suggestion of identity competence and awareness of alterity (cf. chapter 9).

An additional aspect I see critically in understanding otherness are the conditions of cultural learning. Nowadays, young people, some for a long time, some rather recently, have grown up in multicultural societies. It is not unlikely that students regularly encounter cultural incidences which are only made visible as 'other' in ELT. It could be the case that otherness only becomes apparent through classroom reflections. In these encounters, negotiation of content does not necessarily aim at finding a common truth, but rather needs to be content with reconstructing worldviews and the self-conception of the other (cf. Bredella et al. 1997, 18).

One major issue within the concept of understanding otherness is reflected in its remaining within a traditional approach to cultures as homogeneous and separable. The respective scholars only marginally refer to the problem of using an essentializing culture term and an apolitical perspective, and publications only seldom question this understanding of culture from a deconstructive perspective or include anti-racist points of view in their argumentations (cf. Fäcke 2006, 13). Those are indeed necessary in order to make transparent a cultural teaching and learning which agrees to lifestyles and modes of societies in the 21st century. However, more recent publications have paid tribute to this aspect (cf. Delanoy 2011, 2012, Volkmann 2011, 2012).

This critical reflection shows that the topic 'understanding otherness' is highly complex and challenging. I believe that its central position in ELT could also be seen in the potential that is entailed in a failure of understanding otherness: a resulting misunderstanding could be regarded as a confusion that serves as a foundation for further negotiations of meaning and intense dialogue rather than as a final disruption of the intercultural encounter. Yet, another reaction to the dilemma of understanding otherness could be to investigate a consensus of the impossibility and possibility of understanding otherness (cf. Witte 2006b, 33). A constructivist approach that mediates between a universal and relativist approach to understanding otherness can balance both poles and still pay tribute to its normative setting.

1.1.2 Reconsideration of Understanding Otherness

Whereas chapter 1.1 stated that negotiations of otherness lead to understanding otherness and summarized the contributions of changing perspectives and enlarging horizons for understanding the other, the previous chapter revealed that the process of understanding otherness entails notions of power, of appropriating and incorporating, even negating the other when the process is successful. Additionally, linguistic features can limit mutual understanding. Nonetheless, social, political and cultural changes on a global and local level make understanding otherness a necessity in increasingly multicultural societies. It is, therefore, established as a normative aim of ELT; in curricular guidelines it is the central objective of teaching English. Thus, understanding otherness indeed needs a theoretical and conceptual base on which teaching programs can be built.

Despite the challenges that are entailed in the concept, the foreign language classroom serves as a beneficial space for understanding otherness. Learning the other language is a first step toward further processes of learning about and from the other culture. The ELT classroom is a relatively save space in which students can experience otherness via various media and be cognitively and affectively prepared for actual encounters. Although the Gießen School's concept remains within a dichotomy of self and other, both cannot be negated because cultural discourses need participants and interlocutors who engage in negotiations of meaning. If these were not different, their exchange would be reduced in its meaningfulness. Negotiations of meaning between and beyond the cultural and linguistic borders of self and other allow students to express an individual standpoint (cf. Fäcke 2006, 17) which can indeed remain dynamic and open for new influences.

As was mentioned, Bredella's contributions to finding didactic answers to the cultural turn of language teaching were decisive in developing cultural learning. When curricular norms demanded the inclusion of cultural perspectives, TEFL academia faced the challenge of translating these into conceptualizations which are applicable to classroom practices. Didactics saw beneficial starting points in certain philosophical concepts, which it attended to and further developed for its own needs. Seeing Gadamer's approach to texts as most beneficial for this challenging endeavour, the Gießen School of Understanding Otherness certainly contributed largely to the TEFL landscape. Basing elaborations of understanding otherness on this approach is still essential, even if the concept has been altered and extended in the past few years and even if critical statements, e.g. regarding evaluation and assessment have been brought forward (cf. Casper-Hehne 2008, Dervin 2010, Eberhardt 2008, 2009, Hu 2008, Schulz 2007, 2008).

In view of these alterations and extensions, conceptualizations and critical reflections of understanding otherness need to enter a productive discourse in order to make cultural learning applicable for the 21st century. As to support processes of understanding otherness, Bredella and Christ (1995) demand that foreign language education provides the prerequisites for successful communication. One attempt to do so is the adaptation of transculturality to conceptualize transcultural competences (cf. chapter 1.3) and the investigation of modified versions of understanding otherness (cf. chapter 9 as a conclusion of the critical discussion).

For reconsidering understanding otherness, details of this complex process can be emphasized which carve out certain notions that add to the applicability of understanding otherness to cultural learning. Such a productive approach not only needs to ask how the cultural other can be identified within the self, but also how the individual is able to discover and understand the other within itself (cf. Witte 2007, 12). Just as culture, the individual self is no homogeneous and static entity, but is flexible in occupying certain spaces and evolves from continuing processes of performance and adaptation (cf. chapter 9.1.1).

From the various options a cultural frame offers, the individual foregrounds those options that contribute to its identity formation. The different choices continuously add to changes and incidents in which otherness is implemented in the self.

Negotiations of understanding otherness are mainly characterized and influenced by language as the individual cannot move beyond the limitations of this linguistic sphere. In order to communicate with other members of a cultural group, however this group is constituted, and to develop one's identity and make choices, the individual needs to make use of semiotic symbols that are available and shared in the community and that have been formed by certain social and cultural patterns. At the same time, speakers are not fully determined by their surroundings, as available categories need to be filled or new categories need to be created. Individuals constantly need to negotiate meaning, communicate with others and make themselves understandable. This space between the individual and the other represents negotiations of understanding (cf. Witte 2007). In this space it becomes apparent that individuals are no closed systems, but are influenced by social and cultural entities and positioned in certain historical contexts; they are open to change and able to change their environment.

If this negotiation of meaning is successful, the other does not necessarily have to remain the other. This does not mean that the other is incorporated into the self, but rather that both entities discover shared categories which are filled by differing or similar details. If the foundation of the concept includes strong dynamic, fluid and open notions, it can be acknowledged that understanding is possible, even when a certain rest is not understood, and even though it is highly complex, constructed, multidimensional, and needs to be based on detailed and respectful reflections.

For critically discussing texts currently used in intercultural learning and suggesting alternatives, the reflections on understanding otherness are important with regard to the following questions:

- What does 'otherness' mean and to whom can this term be applied? 'Other' is generally understood as representing another culture, but when looking at the texts and discourses on which understanding otherness is based, it seems as if the 'other' is limited to an ethnic or national 'other.' Does that apply to multicultural societies?
- In how far does intracultural otherness play a role in understanding otherness? Does a multicultural society demand intracultural competence? Or can a general cultural competence be covered by transcultural competences?
- Is it actually possible for young learners to really understand otherness, or should foreign language education rather lower this teaching objective and assume that experiencing otherness is sufficient because it is more realistic? (cf. chapter 7)

–   How are learners to reveal that they have understood the other? Which
    methods and activities can be applied that transcend a superficial in-
    corporation of the other? (cf. chapter 8)

This critical discussion and the open questions indicate that understanding otherness indeed remains a multifaceted concept. Reconsidering different perspectives on understanding otherness, I claim that this process is challenging for
students in view of necessary prerequisites and consequences. At this point of
my argumentation, I would like to leave this open and not further engage in the
debate. The elaborations in later sections point out that the difficulty of understanding otherness can be taken a few steps further when considering empathy
and identification (cf. chapter 2 and 7.2.2) as well as the results of the discussion of example texts in chapter 5. I will refer to understanding otherness again
in chapter 9.1.2 and suggest an applicable concept for ELT, which could help to
relativize the opposing positions of understanding otherness.

   As mentioned, in TEFL research understanding otherness is set as a normative objective of ELT, similar to the development of ICC. The critical reflection on understanding otherness therefore leads to a more detailed view on intercultural communicative competence.

1.2 Competences and Literacies in the Context of Intercultural Learning

From Volkmann's depiction of aspects and dimensions of intercultural competence (cf. 2002, 11-47) one can conclude that students increase cultural competences in three different areas: pupils learn about a) the nature of cultures themselves, b) about other cultures, and c) about their own cultures, and similarities
and distinctions of their own and other cultures.[17] Based on the plurality of cultural identities in literature and the manifold lines along which cultural identity
can be realized, special emphasis needs to be put on the plural in which these
levels are to be understood which accounts for the target cultures as well as for
the cultures of the learners.

   In order to show how nuanced the development of cultural competences
can be, the following overview introduces further aspects that need to be taken
into consideration when reflecting upon ICC:

–   While it is true that in descriptions of ICC phrases such as 'willing-
    ness to engage with the foreign culture' are essential and often used, it
    is important to be aware that in their later lives learners meet individu-

---

[17] Byram uses a similar differentiation to illustrate how the categories of *savoirs* are interrelated
(1996, 96).

als, not cultures. Although this reference is entailed in the conceptualization, cultural learning needs to put more emphasis on people.

- When stating that "on a daily basis, we all have to interact with different people from our very own environments" (Dervin 2010, 162), Dervin explains that the absence of an interlocutor in most definitions of intercultural competence makes it quite monological and individualistic. "Most definitions only mention the 'user' of the competence and ignore the influence of the interlocutor and the context of interaction on acts of interaction" (ibid., 163).
- In the EFL classroom the self is present in the form of students who negotiate meaning with a target culture. Their interaction with otherness is not based on face-to-face encounters, but is substituted through various texts (fiction, non-fiction, pictures, video or sound material etc.). As each text only entails a limited insight to a culture, it only offers a single representation to which counter-representations can often be found. An awareness of this particular context is essential as stereotypes or one-sided representations are to be avoided.
- The multitude of selves in the classrooms needs to be taken into consideration, as students may have different perspectives on the issues encountered. Not only Anglophone target cultures are characterized by multiculturalism, but also German ELT classrooms. Consequently, it is necessary to speak of own and other cultures between which meaning is negotiated in the plural.

This overview indicates that ICC and its development face certain critical issues. Before this discussion is continued and cultural literacy is considered as an extension of the concept, ICC needs to be reflected in order to frame those aspects.

1.2.1 Intercultural Communicative Competence

Intercultural competence has been widely discussed within the TEFL discourse.[18] The concept of ICC that is implemented in the CEF has its conceptual roots in Michael Byram's seminal publication *Teaching and Assessing Intercultural Communicative Competence* (1997a). In this, Byram differentiates between intercultural competence and intercultural communicative competence. Whereas the first is also important in discourses in the mother tongue, when reading translations of foreign literature or in intracultural encounters, the latter entails the ability to interact with people from another country and culture in a

---

[18]   For example Antor (2007), Bausch/Christ/Krumm (1994), Bredella (2002a, 2002b), Bredella/Delanoy (1999), Buttjes/Byram (1990), Byram (1997, 1999), Byram/Fleming (1998), Eckert/Wendt (2003), Kiesling/Paulston (2005), Knapp/Knapp-Potthoff (1992), Levine/Adelman (1993), Schuhmann (2005), Seelye (1988) and Volkmann/Stierstorfer/Gehring (2002).

foreign language, or to act as mediators between people of different cultural origins. People with ICC are able to negotiate a mode of communication and interaction which is satisfactory to themselves and the other. Their knowledge of another culture is linked to their language competence through their ability to use language appropriately, and their awareness of the specific meanings, values and connotations of the language they use. Based on the experience of learning a foreign language and negotiating meaning in that language, they have also acquired a basis for cultural understandings (cf. Byram 1997a, 71).

These aspects point out that ICC is a very complex construct that includes a certain number of sub-skills. They derive from a social-psychological tradition of covering knowledge, skills and attitudes as well as an ability to interpret and understand texts and cultural events, a cluster which reflects a hermeneutical perspective (cf. above, cf. Risager 2012, 147). Additionally, a pragmatic dimension is reflected in the demand to discover and interact with people in actual intercultural encounters. In more detail, Byram labels those sub-skills the five *savoirs* which refer to different levels on which ICC can be developed. The first of these *savoirs* is called "*savoir être*" and refers to the emotional level of ICC. Learners need "attitudes of curiosity and openness, of readiness to suspend disbelief and judgement with respect to others' meanings, beliefs and behaviors" (1997a, 34). They also need the "willingness to suspend belief in one's own meanings and behaviors […] an ability to 'decentre'" (ibid.). In order to do so successfully, learners have to abandon their ethnocentric attitudes in view of the other and relativize the self; they have to value the other.[19]

As a second stance, Byram suggests "*savoirs*," a cognitive level which includes "knowledge about social groups and their cultures in one's own country, and similar knowledge of the interlocutor's country […]; knowledge of the processes of interaction at individual and societal levels" (ibid., 35). This strongly reminds of former area studies in which learners had to memorize facts, figures and knowledge about social interaction within the target culture. As knowledge forms an essential base for interaction, this second level would be "fundamental for successful interaction" (ibid.).

Furthermore, Byram distinguishes "*savoir comprendre*," the skills of interpreting and relating documents from another country (cf. ibid., 37) and "*savoir apprendre/faire*" which refers to actual cultural discovery and interaction in real-life encounters (ibid., 37-38). In order to interpret documents, learners need "specific knowledge and general frames of knowledge which will allow them to discover the allusions and connotations present in the document" (ibid., 37). Compared to "*savoir apprendre/faire*," this skill does not necessarily involve interaction as it is "confined to work on documents" (ibid.). "*Savoir apprendre/faire*" as a skill of "discovery is the ability to recognise significant phenomena in a foreign environment and to elicit their meanings and connotations,

---

[19] Although Byram's model refers to the self, chapter 1.2.2 points out that for some scholars the self was only implicitly included in his model, a fact that became one of the main points of criticism.

and their relationship to other phenomena" (ibid., 38). Moreover, "the skill of interaction is […] the ability to manage […] constrains in particular circumstances with specific interlocutors" (ibid.); the learner needs to be able to deal with "dysfunctions".

"*Savoir s'engager*" can be seen as the culmination of the four other sub-skills as it refers to the critical evaluation of the other's and one's own culture. Byram defines this as "[a]n ability to evaluate critically and on the basis of explicit criteria perspectives, practices and products in one's own and other cultures and countries" (ibid., 53). For this central aim of developing critical cultural awareness, learners need to be able to change perspectives, for example by critically comparing cultures and regarding the other and their own cultural frame of reference. This adds the notion of "clarifying one's own ideological perspective and engaging with others consciously on the basis of that perspective" which could result in a conflict of these perspectives (ibid., 101, also in Byram/Gribkova/Starkey 2002). With those five levels, Byram establishes an understanding of ICC which entails cognitive, affective and pragmatic specifics: interculturally competent people are able to integrate their cognitive knowledge of other cultures in their open and respectful approach to others in intercultural encounters in which meaning is negotiated through communication in the foreign language.

A closer look at the historic development of language teaching shows how language teaching has always had a cultural dimension and how culture has always been significant for ELT. Already in the early 18th century, scholars regarded the ability to speak and understand a modern foreign language as a key to participating in a foreign culture (cf. Klippel 1994, 272).

In the 18th century, the English language was learnt as to be able to read English texts (cf. Klippel 1994, 47, 271, Klippel 2001, 63). A certain selection of texts was supposed to reveal insights to cultural aspects of the foreign language. Such selections were provided in literary textbooks like Herrig's "British Classical Authors" (1849) (cf. Klippel 2000, 53). When teaching cultural aspects was included before the 1880s, it had a strong national orientation, which stemmed from the formation of nations within Europe (cf. Risager 2012, 145). English language teaching focused on England, the English people and its language, attempting to convey a uniform picture of the country and its culture.

Whereas the inclusion of cultural elements in language teaching in terms of critical cultural reflections only gained importance within the last few decades, concepts such as

> Realienkunde: the knowledge of realia or facts about the country, Landeskunde: knowledge of and insights into the country's geography, history and society […], Kulturkunde: knowledge of national culture (literature, arts, etc.), and Wesenskunde: knowledge of national mentality or psychology (Risager 2012, 145, also in Klippel 1994, 2013)

had been known and applied from the 1880s to the 1970s. Especially the term 'Landeskunde' was very common in German discourses and foreign language teaching as, for example, Abendroth-Timmer (1998), Baumgratz-Gangl (1990), Buttjes (1990) and Melde (1987) have elaborated in detail.[20]

Apart from Lado, who included a chapter on "How to compare two cultures" already in his 1957 publication and was thus one of the first to include the self in the perception of the other culture, these tendencies show a rather one-directional view within culture teaching. The learner discovers facts and gains knowledge of the other culture as a by-product of learning the other language. In the beginning of ELT, successful communication was defined by the correct usage of lexis and grammar, which was trained by pattern drills and practicing dialogues. In the audio-lingual method cultural aspects of language learning were regarded as supplementing language acquisition and only had a supportive function. This becomes visible when recognizing the unsystematic inclusion of cultural information in older textbooks (cf. Witte 2007, 7). Nowadays, this national perspective has moved into the background, and research and teaching display a tendency toward transnational approaches to teaching and learning languages (cf. Risager 2012, 145) and on raising awareness for intracultural diversity.

In the 1970s, language teaching gradually included different text genres in order to increase the visibility of different cultures in classrooms. This comprised fictional and non-fictional texts like newspapers and magazines, and likewise texts that are part of everyday life, like timetables, menus and street signs (cf. Risager 2012, 146). Such a selection reflected a greater need for knowledge of the outside world than purely literary knowledge. The increasing emphasis on the pragmatic level of culture teaching was thus, for example, visible in Erdmenger and Istel's "call for a needs analysis of pupils before starting cultural teaching" and Seelye's practical teaching techniques which included acting out minidrama in order to "illustrat[e] a typical cultural misunderstanding to be reflected upon" (in ibid.). In both minidrama and the extension of text types, roots of an intercultural perspective can be identified which in fact refers to the other and the self.

---

[20] Klippel provides a comprehensive overview of the general development of foreign language teaching and teaching methodology (1994, 2000, 2013). Her publications go beyond a cultural perspective of ELT and offer a very complex approach to the advancement of foreign language teaching in general. For example, she refers to teaching English in primary schools, bilingual teaching, new media and self-assessment and the usage of portfolios (cf. Klippel 2005a, 19), and also elaborates on the role of literature in ELT in the 19th century (2005b). A detailed overview of the development of TEFL theory is offered by Doff (2008). The publication on TEFL research in the 20th century (Doff/Wegner 2006) offers interesting insights to the development of this academic field and includes chapters on teaching methodology in the former GDR (Siebold in ibid., 177-192), on the early phase of teaching methodology in West-Germany (Doff in ibid., 193-207) and future perspectives of TEFL research (Klippel in ibid., 273-287).

This approach to culture teaching changed significantly when humanities witnessed a general cultural turn in the 1980s. Geertz promoted an anthropologist perspective on culture and "advocated an interpretive or hermeneutical approach to the analysis of culture, especially as it is produced in cultural events like the football match or the marriage ritual" (ibid.). This influenced the perspective on culture in language teaching as it addressed multiple layers of culture which transcend pure language teaching.

One of the first documents that asked for a transnational communicative competence was the *Stuttgarter Thesen zur Rolle der Landeskunde* (cf. Robert-Bosch-Stiftung/Payer 1982). This publication not only saw the development of cultural competences as a main objective of teaching foreign languages but called for an inclusion of adequate, historic- and content-based knowledge about the learner's own and the other culture as well as a critical approach to analyzing social structures (cf. in Burwitz-Melzer 2003, 39). Foreign language education only reaches its objectives when it is able to put the experiences of the learner and the realities of the people of the other country in explicit relations with each other (cf. Robert-Bosch-Stiftung 1982, 11). Within the development of the academic field of TEFL, Byram was one of the essential scholars who established a theoretical foundation for this approach (cf. above).

New developments in technology provided innovative and more detailed representations of cultures in the classroom, when it became possible to record movies and films and apply these to increase cultural knowledge and experiences. Working with visual images made reflections on nature, clothing, interior designs and non-verbal communication possible in a more realistic and authentic[21] manner (cf. Risager 2012, 147). Nowadays, the reflected use of online media can offer manifold options for inviting other cultures, when Web 1.0 overcomes mere textual representations by covering local distances digitally and Web 2.0 enables students to digitally interact with people in other countries.[22]

However, it was not until the 1990s that cultural contents in language teaching were strongly emphasized in ELT and successful communication entailed adequate usage of language regarding existing norms and values. Adequate in this context meant that foreign speakers became aware of culturally different settings, which could hinder but also support communication. Claire Kramsch, who researched the connection of language and culture in a postmodern perspective, and aforementioned Byram, for example, advocated the close connection between language and culture (cf. Kramsch 1993, 2009a).

---

[21] In ELT contexts, authenticity is a highly disputed term and is extensively researched and reflected. For an introduction and overview see e.g. Breen (1985), Dantas-Whitney/Rilling (2010), and Gilmore (2007). In this work, the term and a critical discussion will be refered to in the context of representating otherness in literature in ELT (cf. chapters 2 and 7).

[22] Certainly, Web 2.0 applications should not be understood as a tool for language acquisition which is automatically motivational and successful, but needs to be seen critically as well (cf. Grimm 2012, Viebrock 2012, Volkmann 2005).

In line with the main objective of ICC to develop intercultural critical awareness, Byram (1999, Byram/Zarate 1997) and Kramsch (1998) suggest the goal of educating an "intercultural speaker" who "is able to establish a relationship between their own and the other cultures, to mediate and explain difference – and ultimately to accept that difference and see the common humanity beneath it" (Byram/Fleming 1998, 8). The respective learners are "aware of their own identities and cultures and of how they are perceived by others; and also [have] an understanding of the identities and cultures of those with whom they are interacting" (Byram/Zarate 1994 in ibid.). As modern foreign language teaching aims at enabling learners to successfully communicate in intercultural encounters (cf. Volkmann 2007, 130-131), learners need intercultural pragmatic competence rather than native speaker competence which was the previous aim of second language acquisition (cf. Byram 1997, 48, also Byram 1996, 240-241, Byram 1997b, Byram 2001, 5). This concept strongly anchors cultural aspects in language teaching.

Byram's model has recently been altered by various scholars who include current social and global shifts and observations in their conceptualizations of cultural learning. Antor, for example, defines intercultural competence as a profile of skills and abilities which enable a subject to act appropriately in contact situations with different cultures. The contact with the other is characterized by peaceful, communication-oriented, constructive and productive intercultural exchanges (cf. Antor 2007, 112). Antor emphasizes that this competence can only be thought of in the plural, as it is constituted of different sub-competences. Witte differentiates these sub-competences into declarative knowledge, facts and information, procedural knowledge, the development of empathy, strategies and competences of dealing with other cultures (cf. 2007, 8). Volkmann states that, likewise, techniques and strategies to engage in communicative interaction are essential in the model of ICC when it focuses on communicative negotiations of contents (cf. 2010, 17).

Kramsch and Whiteside (2008) extend communicative competence by "symbolic competence" which includes a "systematic reflexive component that encompasses subjective and aesthetic as well as historical and ideological dimensions that communicative language teaching (CLT) has largely left unexploited" (Kramsch 2011, 355). Symbolic competence has three dimensions:

- symbolic representation (denotation and connotation of a stable reality through lexical and grammatical structures, focus of discourse on "what words say and what they reveal about the mind"),
- symbolic action (focus of discourse on "what words do and what they reveal about human intentions" in terms of speech acts, speech genres, symbolic interaction rituals etc.), and
- symbolic power (focus of discourse on "what words index and what they reveal about social identities, individual and collective memories, emotions and aspirations"). (ibid., 357)

According to Kramsch, this alternative and extending perspective on communicative competence has become necessary as participants in intercultural encounters and discourses need the ability to read semiotic symbols beyond language and "need much more subtle semiotic practices that draw on a multiplicity of perceptual clues to make and convey meaning" (2006, 250). Compared to vocabulary or communication strategies, the symbolic also entails "embodied experiences, emotional resonances, and moral imaginings" (ibid., 210).

As such, symbolic competence is conceptualized in close proximity to intercultural learning, as

> [t]he interculturally competent speaker, then, when reflecting upon discursive practices between people who speak different languages and occupy different and sometimes unequal subject positions, asks the following questions:
> - Not which words, but whose words are those? Whose discourse? Whose interests are being served by this text?
> - What made these words possible, and others impossible?
> - How does the speaker position him/herself?
> - How does he/she frame the events talked about?
> - What prior discourses does he/she draw on? (cf. Kramsch 2011, 360)

Kramsch further elaborates that asking these questions "shows an awareness of the cultural or cross-cultural context in which language unfolds" (ibid.). Interestingly, literature offers special potential for symbolic competence, as it increases the complexity of language and discourse, and as readers can "find through the symbolic use of language in a foreign literature alternative scenarios of possibility for life in the real world, other ways of desiring and belonging" (Kramsch 2006, 251).

The model of ICC, including its variations and extensions, has long been the foundation of developing cultural competences in ELT. For many it is still seen as the standard according to which cultural teaching is defined, not least based on its inclusion in the CEF and other national guidelines. Nevertheless, the concept of ICC had to face criticism and modifications, which is explored in the following chapters.

1.2.2 Objections to Intercultural Communicative Competence

One of the scholars who read Byram's ICC critically is Adelheid Hu (2008), who states that the concept is independent of any context, it is too abstract in the face of political, social and cultural conditions in which school education and foreign language teaching and learning are always integrated. Moreover, she criticizes that Byram does not describe which level of ICC can be reached at which developmental stage or age. While Byram poses the question of the relation of a general development and ICC himself, he would not provide an adequate answer (cf. Hu 2008, 297). Byram describes his model and the sub-skills entailed, but leaves open important aspects of practical procedures.

Apart from these objections, the underlying concept of interculturality was seen critically as well. As will be elaborated in detail in chapter 1.3, in Welsch's view interculturality does not agree with the changes and shifts which cultures have gone through during the past few decades. Interculturality and multiculturality are based on Herder's concept of cultures as homogeneous and separate islands (cf. Welsch 1999, 194-197), yet this is "not only descriptively unserviceable, but also normatively dangerous and untenable" (ibid., 194). As this perception is "factually incorrect and normatively deceptive" (ibid., 198), neither the one nor the other can be used to describe current cultures (ibid., 196-197). Instead, cultures need to be thought of "beyond the contraposition of ownness and foreignness" (ibid., 196). Flechsig (2000) concurs with the argument that interculturality focuses too much on the differences between cultures and puts the effort of understanding the other center stage (cf. chapter 1.3.2).

Antor's argues in a similar way: in "Inter-, multi- und transkulturelle Kompetenz: Bildungsfaktor im Zeitalter der Globalisierung" (2007), he explains that intercultural competence is incomplete when its definition does not entail a strong notion of understanding the self and a confident establishment of a personal opinion. He elaborates that this personal opinion needs to be based on a position which enables people to meet the other as a subject that has a clear identity while simultaneously being open toward the alterity of the other. Thus, the subject ought to take the risk of being influenced through the encounter with the other (cf. ibid., 118). Furthermore, Antor correctly points out that unreflected mimicry and the attempt to uncritically copy the other culture are as fatal as xenophobic attitudes. For intercultural learning it is essential to know and accept one's own difference toward otherness as this supports negotiating the self. Rather than assimilating the other culture or rejecting it in principal, one essential aspect of inter- and transcultural learning lies in understanding otherness by contextualizing both one's own and the other's culture, relating both to each other and interact with both in discourse (cf. ibid.).[23]

Antor's and Welsch's approaches focus on the essential question whether the underlying understanding of culture and intercultural competence is still adequate today. They argue that the concepts are based on an essentializing culture term and an apolitical perspective. Yet, such assumptions need to be deconstructed in order to make transparent a cultural teaching and learning which agrees to lifestyles and modes of living together in societies in the 21st century. These are increasingly complex, diverse and heterogeneous – students need to be prepared to come to terms with such changing social and cultural structures.

---

[23] Although inter- and transcultural learning seem to be interchangeable in this reference, both differ in their emphasis of the self, for example. Whereas a critical reflection of the self was indeed included in intercultural learning, this aspect takes a more prominent and central position in transcultural learning (cf. below).

This discussion reflects the complexity of the academic field of cultural learning and its application to ELT, when concepts like understanding otherness, ICC and intercultural awareness seem to be overlapping and a clear differentiation may not always be possible or convincing. On top of those, academia has extended the view of the aforementioned competences to inclusive literacies in order to add a more pragmatic notion and include a skill level which specifically refers to students' ability to be part of cultural discourses on a meta-level (cf. e.g. Burwitz-Melzer 2013a, Hallet 2007b, 2008, 2009c, 2010b).

To be literate in a field refers to the ability to take part in "the discourses in a particular discipline, i.e. to be able to use the language and terminology that a discipline has developed to describe and conceptualize the phenomena that it investigates and seeks to explain or describe" (Hallet 2009c). At the same time, learners need to be enabled to communicate this knowledge in

> everyday cultural contexts and social situations. Learners must be able to use their content knowledge to participate in cultural and public discourses, engage and interact in problem-solving processes and negotiate controversial issues. (ibid., n.p.)

The application of 'literacy' to education contexts carries the potential of translating knowledge to everyday life, a central aspect that is sometimes pushed to the background. By focusing on this application, school content gains a higher level of relevance and sustainability.

For the context at hand, consequently, I suggest that cultural literacy could be understood as the ability to gain knowledge of political, social and cultural conditions of everyday life, to recognize cultural discourses in texts, media and daily experiences and to be able and encouraged to critically take part in the discourses that evolve. Based on this recognition, a culturally literate person critically negotiates differences and similarities by regarding their own and the other's perspective and alters their point of view accordingly, yet not without critically stepping back from what is perceived. Taking a critical distance to texts and media, cultural literacy assumes the confident development of personal opinions and reflective participation in cultural discourses. The critical stance on texts and media also entails the ability to discover mechanisms of othering and approaching others. Reading, understanding and interpreting texts critically leads to the ability to discover and debate (mis)representations of culture and alterity.

Despite its wider scope and inclusion of agency, such a concept of cultural literacy as outlined above does not help to solve the critical perception of cultural learning in terms of ICC, as it is based on a similar perspective on culture. In order to balance this criticism, Wolfgang Hallet and Ansgar Nünning further discuss concepts of cultural learning and integrate various paradigm shifts in terminology and understandings of culture, literature, text and subject in *Neue Ansätze und Konzepte der Literatur- und Kulturdidaktik* (2007) and unveil their interconnectedness. The contributors to this publication not only elaborate on insights based on a connection of literature and culture didactics, but also suggest new approaches and material to make literature and culture more comprehensible for the individual learner. Werner Delanoy elaborates on the connection of literary and cultural learning, too, and sheds more light on alternative concepts that consider the aforementioned criticism of intercultural learning (cf. chapter 2). Yet, as already implied above, one possible answer to the criticism of ICC can also be found in transcultural approaches which have recently become more popular in contexts of teaching literature in ELT (e.g. Fäcke 2006, Freitag-Hild 2010).

1.3 Broadening the View to Transcultural Approaches

As the last chapter indicated, a central criticism of the concept of intercultural learning regards the question whether the underlying understanding of culture is still adequate in the 21st century. This argument was developed in light of social, cultural and economic phenomena closely connected to the widely spread term globalization, which Larsson describes as

> the process of world shrinkage, of distances getting shorter, things moving closer. It pertains to the increasing ease with which somebody on one side of the world can interact, to mutual benefit, with somebody on the other side of the world. (2001, 9)

This interaction can be understood as communication for pleasure, but regards trade, tourism, politics, peace-keeping and journalism, too. Based on these interactions beyond national borders, not only the relations between, but also within these nations and cultures have changed. Both the changes within and between these groups of people have been described differently in cultural studies discourses, emphasizing certain features and seeing others more critically. One of the central concepts concerned with a cultural reflection of global changes is that of "hybridity," which was most influentially discussed by Bhabha (1994) and Hall (1990, 2000). Another line of arguments that is closer to describing the circumstances under which people live together in culturally diverse societies and that alters the view of the intercultural is Welsch's transculturality.

Welsch (1999) questions the appropriacy of interculturality as a concept to describe relationships between nations as it is based upon a traditional understanding of cultures that exist separately and are rather homogeneous. As such an understanding negates complex and diverse perspectives on cultures, he suggests the concept of transculturality which has been adapted as a basis for altering intercultural toward transcultural learning and competences (e.g. Fäcke 2006, Freitag-Hild 2010, Risager 1998).

1.3.1 Transcultural Competences

The aforementioned changes and shifts are translated into TEFL theory by the conceptualization of transcultural competences. Compared to the intercultural approach, transcultural competences entail a strong global reference, for instance in that the English language is perceived as a lingua franca. More importantly, transcultural competences focus on human experiences beyond national and cultural borders, for example regarding concepts such as birth, love, friendship, relationship of younger and older generations as well as between different genders and sexes (cf. Bredella 2010b, 122-123). On a third level, while intercultural teaching implies a negotiation of cultural meaning between separate cultures (cf. Fäcke 2006, 17, Welsch 1999, 2000), the transcultural scope pays tribute to postmodern diffusion, connections and interweavement of groups, and also takes the individual more into account. This last level of transculturality is based upon an understanding of cultures that does not entail a single allocation of individuals and culture, but rather one that focuses on ambiguity and diversity regarding identity (Bhabha 1997a), culture (Bhabha 1997b) and nation (Bhabha 1997c). As will be encountered, an understanding and definition of transcultural competence is still in the making and the field faces various challenges. These challenges are the foundation for critically discussing transcultural learning and offering alterations in chapter 7.

One of the early scholars who integrated a transcultural approach in teaching cultures was Gisela Baumgratz-Gangl in her publication *Persönlichkeitsentwicklung und Fremdsprachenerwerb. Transnationale und transkulturelle Kommunikationsfähigkeit im Französischunterricht* (1990). Although she focuses on teaching and learning French, this can still be applied to ELT as mechanisms and contexts of foreign language acquisition are similar. The confrontation with the other reality that contains commonalities and differences should be seen as a mirror in which the self can see itself more clearly (cf. ibid., 26). Consequently, for her the objective of foreign language teaching which strives for transcultural communicative competence lies with engaging in human relationships that involve a necessary negotiation of an intercultural consensus based on affective dispositions. Essential for the notion of transcultural learning is the inclusion of the self and the other in cultural encounters which go beyond a mere comparison of both by reflecting the self in view of the other. A transfer is not complete unless learners also negotiate what the other means for the perception of the self.[24] Extending values and dispositions of behavior that

---

[24] Ashcroft sees high value in the metaphor of a "mirror" for transculturality, as it "reflects the continual possibilities of negotiation, transformation and change. The mirror metaphor does

the self acquires in the cultural context are central objectives of this complex process (cf. Nieweler 1995, 293). Burwitz-Melzer (2003), Freitag-Hild (2010), Nieweler (1995) and others, who are involved in the ongoing discussion of transcultural competences, agree that one central medium with which such competences can be achieved is literature, especially young adult literature, as this usually reflects the interests of young learners (cf. chapter 2).

Trompenaars and Hampden-Turner understand transcultural competence as the ability to reconcile cultural dilemmas and differences (1997, 195-211). In the context of business and economics, cultural dilemma are seen as people's different cultural orientations which need to be solved for business transactions to be successful.[25] To do so, Trompenaars suggests a process from recognizing and increasing cultural awareness, to appreciating and reconciling cultural differences, to implementing reconciling actions (cf. ibid.). When people of – what they call – different cultural orientations meet, they apply certain strategies in order to reach the suggested reconciliation. Those can also function as a foundation of a didactic of transcultural learning (cf. Flechsig 2000). These reconciliation strategies (cf. Trompenaars/Hampden-Turner 1997, 200), for example include recognizing that oppositions should not be perceived as contradictions in principle but rather as sequences that can be altered, or recognizing that a certain behavior stems from a certain cultural frame and should not be judged negatively without further investigation. Flechsig adds an additional strategy when he considers it important to acknowledge and teach that attitudes toward other groups always express a certain relation ("Beziehungsaussagen", Flechsig 2000, n.p.).

These strategies relate to transcultural learning as they entail a strong notion of raising awareness of one's own attitudes toward otherness. They move beyond showing empathy and respect for the interlocutor and ask students to critically reflect upon themselves, too. If transcultural competence is to be increased in the EFL classroom, students need to be equipped with skills and competences which prepare them to use those strategies. Although this is also said to be part of ICC, in transcultural learning the self and the students' culture are stronger put into focus (cf. below). This aspect needs to be taken into account when applying certain methods to the development of transcultural competences (cf. chapter 8).

Risager sees cultural learning in language education more broadly, too. For example, she adds the concepts of a multicultural and a transcultural approach to the existing discussion of intercultural learning (in Burwitz-Melzer 2003, 51). Whereas intercultural learning was based on the relation between two

---

not construct the other as the same, but rather subordinates identity to difference, reversing the othering process" (2011, 17).

[25] Interestingly, cultural dilemmas are also used for intercultural learning in ELT, when students have to discuss, evaluate and find solutions for critical incidents. Based on their reflection of these critical incidents which follow a similar concept as cultural dilemmas, teachers assess their students' cultural competence (cf. the discussion of Göbel's study in chapter 2.3).

cultures of different countries (home country vs. target country), in the multicultural approach this monolithic culture term is abandoned in favour of a culture term that pays tribute to the complexity and diversity of cultures within national boundaries or within a society (cf. ibid.). This understanding of culture implies the recognition of cultural and ethnic diversity within countries and tries to reject discrimination and stereotyping of 'minorities' (cf. in ibid.). For foreign language education, this entails that learners undergo a similar process of recognizing diversity as the language they learn is the official language of a country, but at the same time it is the second or third language to many people of the same country or culture respectively. Although this multicultural teaching aims at supporting learners in seeing that diversity is also part of their own society, Risager emphasizes that it still assumes homogeneous cultures between which meaning is negotiated (cf. in ibid., 52). Therefore, it does not agree with a reality of cultures that are characterized by mutual penetration and transcended borders. Byram, too, extended his concept of ICC to a multicultural perspective stating that foreign language teaching "should not introduce learners to a 'national culture' at all. They should not be introduced to the dominant culture, precisely because it is dominant and represents the interest of a powerful (middle class) minority" (Byram 2000, 14 in Volkmann 2007, 153).

Volkmann uses the term multicultural competence in differentiation to transcultural competence, as he warns of the danger of unifying cultural identities in a transcultural approach that generalises cultural differences toward 'McDonalization' (cf. Volkmann 2007, 153-154). For him, multicultural competence, not transcultural competence, is able to go beyond an intercultural understanding. Although multicultural competence does include transcultural communicative competences, these would focus on specific English-speaking countries (Great Britain and the United States) and pay tribute to certain cultural specifics, and not, as transcultural competence, ignore and negate cultural differences. Linguistic, verbal communicative competence is supplemented with non-verbal and para-verbal communication as well as differing perceptions of time, space, power, individuality, gender and nature (cf. ibid., 154). Thus, Volkmann concludes, a multicultural teaching of foreign languages can exemplarily draw on authentic texts to show how differently Anglophone cultures form perceptions of human beings in their social surroundings which each underlie specific culture-bound imaginations (cf. ibid.).

In a later publication, Volkmann states that while it is difficult to distinguish intracultural, intercultural and multicultural competences, a transcultural personality is marked by recognizing the task to responsibly deal with one's own hybridity, to deal with circumstances in which "various cultural experiences are superimposed upon each other" (in Volkmann 2010, 24). Referring to Beck (2008, 40) and West-Pavlov (2005, 221), he believes that one essential moment of transcultural competence is the ability and willingness to reconsider one's own perspective and position by engaging in intercommunication with the other (cf. Volkmann 2010, 22). For transcultural learning, understanding otherness is as important as understanding the self since only then is it likely to discover similarities as possible connections to the participants of a discourse (cf. Flechsig 2000, n.p.) – in this stronger emphasis of the self, transcultural learning can be differentiated from intercultural learning. A discourse gains transcultural elements when the participants reflect their own position according to the input of the other. Through this mutual incorporation of cultural patterns (cf. Welsch 1992, 20), one establishes a newly defined cultural position.

One important result of transcultural learning and an indicator for transcultural competence is the recognition of shifts regarding the perception of 'self' and 'other.' One sees parts of the cultural self reflected in the other; something that was perceived as specifically 'other,' now appears as an element of the cultural self (cf. Flechsig 2000, n.p.). In transcultural learning processes a bipolarity of the learners' and the target culture cannot be assumed. Rather, cultures lose clear national boundaries, which increases their heterogeneity, while their intertwining with global media, global food and fashion industry etc. simultaneously increases homogeneity. Furthermore, transculturality entails a broader perspective that refers to other Anglophone cultures such as Australia, India and South Africa, too. As the English language is perceived as a lingua franca, cultures that do not share English as an official or widely spoken language (cf. Volkmann 2010, 22) are included in the transcultural frame, too.

These reflections indicate that it is necessary to offer a more profound discussion of transculturality as a concept for understanding modern cultures. As the following chapter reveals, this is also closely connected to 'third space' which has become highly relevant in elaborations on cultural learning in ELT. Both are introduced before engaging in a critical discussion.

1.3.2 Transculturality and the Relevance of "Third Space"

In 1991[26], Janice Kulyk Keefer published an essay with the intriguing title "From Mosaic to Kaleidoscope: Out of the Multicultural Past Comes a Vision of a Transcultural Future," which not only introduced a new metaphor for describing multicultural societies but also included a new concept of understanding cultures.[27] Kulyk Keefer's starting point is a critical reflection of Canada's

---

[26] As Tunkel analysis in her account of history and globalization in contemporary Canadian literature, origins of transculture can already be identified in the Québécois cultural scene in the early 1980s with the publication of *Vice Versa* (Tunkel 2012, 107). Keefer's concept shows similarities to this Francophone version. For more details see Tunkel (2012).

[27] The mosaic is a popular metaphor for describing the ideal of Canadian multiculturalism. It consists of individual parts which are different from each other, but which still contribute to a coherent pattern. However, each single piece, which resembles a cultural group within Canada, is also ascribed a certain position from which no movement is possible without changing the pattern. Once a certain position is taken by or given to a piece, its position is fixed. Keefer's suggestion of a kaleidoscope rather than a mosaic critisices this static nature and prefers a more dynamic and changing pattern which is still coherent and unified, but which acknolwedges diversity and is open to change. This, e.g. allows groups that enter Canada at

much-praised multiculturalism stating that "[w]hen multiculturalism seeks to preserve and succeeds in paralyzing cultures, transculturality [...] brings out the dynamic potential of cultural diversity, the possibility of exchange and change among and within different ethnocultural groups" (1991, 16). This refers to a transcultural experience

> which challenges the fixed and fragmented separation of the multi-
> cultural mosaic and urges the crossing of all borders and bounda-
> ries, not only between self and other or between past and present,
> but also between the different selves that co-exist with a person's
> variegated and constantly changing identity. (De Luca 2009, 67)

Transculturality gained more attention with Wolfgang Welsch's account in 1999. His approach was initiated by dissatisfaction with the concept of inter-culturality which for him resembles an understanding of cultures as homogene-ous and separate islands (cf. chapter 1.2.2). In comparison, transculturality per-ceives of cultures as entities that "pass[...] through classical cultural boundaries" (Welsch 1999, 197). This acknowledges the process that cultures have moved closer together and are mutually intertwined; the 'trans' is under-stood as beyond, through, transcend or across (cf. Iljassova-Morger 2009, 38). Cultures can no longer be described as socially homogeneous, interculturally separated and ethnically consolidated entities (cf. ibid., 39, Welsch 1999). As cultures spread beyond national borders (cf. Flechsig 2000, n.p.), it is necessary to view them beyond a binary of 'self' and 'other.' Volkmann points out that transculturality is a reaction toward a global upheaval, which includes the de-velopment of multicultural societies, a plurality of lifestyles and living condi-tions, and the tendency toward a post-national world citizenship and cosmopoli-tanism (cf. 2010, 23-24).

Welsch's concept of culture and transculturality reacts to processes of globalization and offers links to concepts such as hybridity and third space, which describe postcolonial cultural changes from a cultural studies perspective. One of the most influential scholars who worked on conceptualizations of cul-tures in a global age is Homi Bhabha, who in his seminal text *The Location of Culture* (1994) draws on the ideas of Said, for example, to describe cultures within processes of hybridization. He links this hybridization to "global cosmo-politanism [...] that configures the planet as a concentric world of national soci-eties extending to global villages" (Bhabha 1994, xiv). This is seen as a positive development "so long as the demography of diversity consists largely of edu-cated economic migrants" because Bhabha also refers to "the problems of di-versity and redistribution at the local level, and the rights and representations of 'minorities' in the regional domain" (ibid., xv). Although nations would be rela-tively open toward newcomers, there is "however, [...] a structural injustice,

---

the margins to reach the center.

shown towards African Americans or First Nation Peoples whose ethical and political demands for equality and fairness are based on issues of reparations and land-rights" (ibid., xv). As soon as demands and claims of certain groups within a nation begin to question the "sovereignty of national traditions and territories" (ibid., xv), political and social infrastructures find limitations. Nevertheless, globalizing nations need to acknowledge and recognize their inner diversity.

Furthermore, Bhabha questions the perception of culture as a "homogenizing, unifying force, authenticated by the ordinary Past, kept alive in the national tradition of the People" (ibid., 37). Rather, cultures are in a continuous process of negotiation and hybridization within in-between spaces. Bhabha understands this 'third space' (1994) and hybridity as reactions to unifying and essentializing concepts of inter- and multiculturalism, an understanding that is also visible in Welsch's concept of transculturality. 'Third space' emphasizes the margins, the spaces of negotiation of meaning and resulting cultural hybridizations which are based on cultural encounters and developed by the mediation of differences and diversity (also in Freitag-Hild 2010, 38). This 'third space' can be localized in spaces of cultural encounters in which values, norms, interests and meanings are negotiated and modified (cf. Bhabha 1994, 37) and which often leads to a creative development of new hybrid meanings. As Bhabha explains "hybridity [...] is the 'third space' which enables other positions to emerge. [...] The process of cultural hybridity gives rise to something different, something new and unrecognizable, a new area of negotiation of meaning and representation" (in Rutherford 1990, 5). Thus, 'third space' can also be seen as a tense space of cultural confrontations (cf. Bachmann-Medick 2004, 285) in which former identities are transcended and explicit differentiations of race, gender, religion and milieu are no longer possible (cf. also Freitag-Hild 2010, 38). As a consequence, cultural identities and cultural differences are no ontological entities, but necessarily need to be negotiated and interpreted, and are thus dynamic and fluid.

Hybridity and 'third space' refer to individuals who are part of a larger social network and who are not only affected by their immediate local surroundings but are influenced by and contribute to the shaping of their cultural frames in a wider scope. From the various choices their surroundings provide, individuals can ideally select those which contribute to their identity formation. In this process, they can differentiate themselves from and attach themselves to others. This includes the relation of the individual to the community and to the mindsets in which negotiations of meaning take place. Within this complex network, culture is increasingly understood as a hybrid and dynamic product of cultural agents (cf. Altmayer 2002, 7-8, Freitag-Hild 2010, 34-35, Hansen 2003). Likewise, the concept of transculturality structures a complex and partly confusing modern world and answers the question about what it is that holds lifestyles together which are drifting further apart, which simultaneously are horizontally and vertically connected, diverse and also contradictory: transculturality can be applied to both the global and a local sphere, and includes both unifying and particularizing tendencies (cf. Iljassova-Morger 2009, 39-40).

These changes of cultures are acknowledged in Welsch's concept in that it distinguishes between a macro- and a micro-level of transculturality and justifies why the separatist view of cultures is no longer valid. On the macro-level, transculturality is a consequence of an "inner differentiation and complexity of modern cultures" (1999, 197), an interesting aspect when a later criticism of understanding otherness explores the question what actually defines otherness in an area characterized by transculturality (cf. chapter 7.1.3). Additionally, cultures engage in various external networks: migration, mass markets and international communication have led to the development of lifestyles that are not bound to certain political territories. Various worldwide discussions, for example human rights debates, feminist movements and ecological awareness (cf. Welsch 1999, 198), decrease the assumption that cultures may be fundamentally different.

The micro-level of transculturality refers to individuals rather than to complex cultures. The underlying notion is that, as individuals, humans are no longer shaped by a certain culture only but face manifold influences from all kinds of spheres. Individuals are facing a multitude of cultural references systems (cf. Flechsig 2000, n.p.). On the one hand, there is the tendency to understand oneself as an individual within a complex construct of far reaching social influences. On the other hand, people try to pin down cultural backgrounds in their local environment. This shift of national and cultural identity calls for extended processes of identity formation which in turn lead to increasing negotiations of 'self' and 'other' (cf. Welsch 1999, 198-199).[28]

In the EFL classroom, similar negotiations of cultural meaning are at work. This has led Kramsch (1995, 2009a) to transfer the concept of 'third space' to ELT: within intercultural learning contact between cultures also leads to the creation of 'third spaces.' Delanoy even assumes that based on the recognition of cultural differences, the development of a distance to one's self and regarding the other, the foreign language classroom itself can be perceived as a 'third space' (cf. 1999, 125). In this 'third space,' different positions and perspectives meet as participants negotiate cultural meaning based on their personal and socio-cultural standpoints, and as cultural experiences are often mediated through texts. Accordingly,

> this third place should be 'popular', 'critical', and 'ecological' in orientation, i.e. it is conceived of as a contact zone where as many people as possible (popular) are invited to (self)-critically participate (critical), and where extra care is taken to give the less power-

---

[28] I believe that although this aspect is essential in conceptualizing transcultural learning, it has received minor attention in the current scholarship of the field. Chapter 9.1.1 therefore suggests a respective extension of transcultural learning.

ful a platform to bring in and further develop their interests (eco-logical). (Delanoy 2012, 160)

The potential of the metaphor of 'third space' for ELT is also discussed by Hallet (2002) and Müller-Hartmann (1999), among others. Hallet and Müller-Hartmann agree that foreign language teaching is regarded as a space of cultural operations, and that within this space negotiations of cultural meaning take center stage. Foreign language teaching becomes a classroom of intercultural encounters in which several cultures participate, but which is located between those and presents and creates something new which is different to the participating cultures (cf. Hallet 2002, 37).

While the concept of the 'third space' has been transferred to the intercultural discourse of language teaching and understanding otherness, it cannot be limited to intercultural learning. Delanoy (1999) and Müller-Hartmann (1999) use 'third space' to argue in favour of transcending a dichotomy of self and other and of critically reflecting the cultural self or culturally shaped perspectives. This can be achieved by a change of perspectives and dialogic processes of negotiating cultural meaning (cf. Freitag-Hild 2010, 42) – elements which are entailed in the transcultural concept, too. In the foreign language classroom 'third space' is usually formed by the learners who experience the other culture based on texts: the voices of the others are integrated through reading literature, watching films or discovering further cultural products (cf. also Hallet 2002, 54). The foreign language classroom is, thus, not only a hybrid space of cultural encounters but at the same time a hybrid space of discourses (cf. ibid., 39), in which meaning is created through a "Spiel der Texte" (Hallet 2002).

Participants of this "Game of Texts" are the learners themselves, who can be characterized as cultural agents (cf. ibid., 34), and also the texts they encounter. According to the transcultural paradigm, awareness needs to be raised that both are no ontological entities but dynamic and diverse participants who are open to change and interpretation respectively. Thus, I would emphasize that 'third space' is not strictly understood as an encounter and hybridization of cultures and is located at their margins, but includes and is extended toward spaces in between individuals, the learners and the interlocutors they encounter in texts. This would emphasize the transcultural perspective on these concepts without negating their intercultural relevance.

1.3.3 Critical Reflection of Transculturality and Transcultural Learning

Despite the extended and promising perspective on understanding modern cultures, the transcultural concept as suggested by Welsch can also be seen in a critical light. For one, transculturality cannot do without a specific culture terminology. Through the usage of culture as the key-part of the term, it does refer to a concept that the 'trans' actually tries to overcome (cf. also Iljassova-Morger

2009, 41). Welsch himself acknowledges this problem and explains a solution for this issue with a double significance: single cultures still exist and serve as a kind of reservoir for the development of new networks (cf. Welsch 2000, 341); accordingly, cultures change and are seen as points of references in correspondence to transcultural realities. As Iljassova-Morger concludes, this adds to the perception of transculturality as a process of transculturalization, of a development of new dynamic structures (cf. 2009, 41).

Sommer (2001) and Schulze-Engler (2006) point to transculturality's ignorance of power structures and questions of cultural participation; both scholars suspect an elitist program. Especially for so-called 'minority groups' which have been the target of discrimination and racism, cultural identity has gained enormous importance in postcolonial discourses: for oppressed groups a fading identity bears the danger of becoming invisible within a social power network and of losing their postcolonial voice for which they often had to fight (cf. Sommer 2001a, 54). A 'trans' understanding of cultures would deprive them of the self-determination they struggled for, because voicing cultural identity is an important step on the path to cultural and social participation (cf. Appiah 1996, Hall 1991, Taylor 1993). Beyond this, it can be asked under which circumstances the individual is actually able to access globally connected common resources (cf. Delanoy 2006, Schulze-Engler 2006, 46, a similar discussion can be found in Freitag-Hild 2010, 35). Cultural hierarchies do not disappear (cf. Iljassova-Morger2009, 43), they rather shift to other levels and spheres. Asymmetries between cultures that are placed in the center or at the margins of a society and the power structures which are entailed in this allocation need to be critically included in the mindset of transculturality.

Another question which is interesting for my approach is in how far the concept of transculturality is generally valid and collectively applicable to various lifestyles. This aspect partly goes in a similar direction as the power argument above. It focuses, though, on the fact that many people still see themselves strongly rooted within a certain nation or culture and have established a strong connection to a collective 'we-identity.' At the same time, an increasing number of people cannot define themselves as being part of one particular national, cultural or geographic group (cf. Iljassova-Morger 2009, 41). Schulze-Engler has labeled this a simultaneousness of inter- and transcultural paradigms which will characterize societies in the future (cf. 2006, 47, cf. chapter 9) and which seems to offer a solution for the discrepancies of inter- and transcultural learning.

The question whether inter- or transculturality are applicable gains further challenges as it can be assumed that often people living in urban centers, younger people and generations which have been socialized within the last few decades are more affected by transculturality than older generations and people living in rural areas. This is thought-provoking for the didactic argumentation of developing transcultural competences, as learners are part of the younger generation socialized within a transcultural mindset and may actually be more transculturally competent than their educators. I continue this essential discussion in the context of the effectiveness of cultural learning in chapter 2.3 and draw conclusions in chapter 9.

The overarching aim of cultural learning is defined as enabling students to respectfully approach and deal with people who are members of other cultures. In TEFL research and publications about cultural learning, 'culture' often seems to be limited to a national or ethnic frame. Yet, in my view otherness also unfolds according to markers of identity such as gender, sexual orientation, age, religion or questions of ethics (cf. above). Hence, the concepts of inter- and transcultural competence should be explored according to their full potential and not limited to a certain dimension. If 'transcultural' is applied, it is essential to extend its connotation to include various shades of diversity. If this is acknowledged, the choice of literature on which cultural learning is based needs to be altered, too; a critical discussion of this aspect follows in chapter 7.

As this elaboration on transculturality for didactic purposes shows, it can be adjusted, applied and implemented in various ways. It offers potential for supporting or rejecting understanding otherness, for describing multi- and transcultural competences in opposing terms or for perceiving of 'inter' and 'trans' as a continuum (cf. chapter 7 and 9). It is this partly confusing and contradictory discourse to which my work adds an important contribution. In fact, transculturality has recently been used by some scholars as a new paradigm of cultural teaching in foreign language education. Empirical studies on transcultural competences and foreign language literature (Fäcke 2006) and on the theory, task typology and practical application of inter- and transcultural teaching and literature in ELT in view of Sommer's (2001) analysis of British fictions of migration (Freitag-Hild 2010) try to merge a theoretical account and a practical development of transcultural competences. Nevertheless, as will be seen from the following sections, I believe that this can be challenged with regard to the methods and literatures that are applied.

Additionally, a critical discussion could reveal that a transcultural mindset actually does not provide any benefits for increasing cultural competences, that these prefixes should play a minor role, and that education should rather be seen in broader perspectives, for instance as developing cultural competence in terms of humanities (cf. chapter 9).[29] Besides, one may argue that developing cultural competences in classroom settings remains a general challenge, and that further issues like assessment and methodology need to be solved (cf. chapter 2.3). When later chapters suggest the term 'transcultural literature' as a furthering of intercultural literature, the present discussion will be extended to yet another dimension. However, this may also shed light on options to differentiate the concepts of cultural learning.

---

[29] One may, however, ask why other concepts such as transdifference are not used in order to elaborate on new approaches to cultural learning. As I will mention in the conclusion and further research desiderata, I believe that the potential of concepts in use should be fully investigated before inviting further concepts from neighboring fields into the didactic discussion of teaching English (cf. chapter 9.3).

In the elaborations above, a connection of cultural learning and using literature in ELT has repeatedly been mentioned. In order to emphasize this interesting link, the following chapter looks at key facets of this connection. This also serves as a basis for a critical view on teaching culture and the development of cultural competences. Overall, this prepares a critical reflection of the representation of otherness in young adult fiction in educational context.

2. Key Facets of Young Adult Literature in the EFL-Classroom

In the context of teaching languages the negotiation of understanding otherness and increasing ICC are mostly prompted through a variety of texts, fiction or non-fiction, poetry and drama, or texts included in a broader sense, like pictures, films or audio material. Having established a theoretical background that locates cultural learning in different academic discourses, the following sections focus on justifications for using young adult literature in ELT. The beneficial contributions of literature to the development of cultural competences in ELT have found widespread support in TEFL theory.[30] Scholars such as Bredella (e.g. 2008, passim), Burwitz-Melzer and Bredella (2004), Carolli (2008), Hall (2005), Lazar (2009), Nünning (2000), Surkamp and Nünning (2008, 2009) and Thaler (2008) have published extensively about the potential of literature for language and cultural learning. Hesse has narrowed this perspective by focusing on *Teenage Fiction in the Active English Classroom* (2009) specifically. The options for (re)negotiating self and other are seen as general justifications for using young adult literature as a foundation for developing ICC. Yet, the quality of these (re)negotiations is a direct consequence of the methods and tasks applied and the literature that has been offered in the first place.[31]

Despite the many benefits of using young adult fiction to extend literary and cultural competences, its application to ELT also poses questions regarding the representation and hybridity of cultures, the de facto development of cultural competences, as well as the assessment and evaluation of these competences. The following chapter sheds light on these questions and discusses the usability of young adult fiction in more detail. In order to do so, I apply a rather general perspective and look at key features of literature in the EFL classroom as they are commonly referred to in the respective scholarship. As the aspects of understanding otherness and identity formation are more complex, these are focused separately. However, I consider some of the justifications of using literature in ELT to be debatable. Therefore, the general reflection in chapter 2 serves as an outlook to reinvestigating and re-evaluating selected key features in chapters 7, 8 and 9 based on the results of Part B.

In my account, reflections upon literature in ELT are perceived in the light of reader-response criticism.[32] One central representative of this approach

---

[30] However, literature is relevant to various subjects, not only languages. Thaler, for example, points at literature's potential for language development, intercultural learning, personal enrichment, motivational value, interpretational openness and social prestige (cf. 2008, 23) which cannot be limited to foreign language education but account for education in general.

[31] The underlying assumption of using literature for developing social competences is neither new nor original but can be traced to Plato's *The Republic* (circa 375 BCE) in which stories are said to be essential for educating young people.

[32] This approach is also followed by other scholars who apply literature to the development of ICC, e.g. Surkamp/Nünning (2008, 17) or Hesse (2009, 18-20). Reading literature is seen as an interactive process, as in this approach the text only gains meaning when it is perceived.

is Wolfgang Iser, who sees the perception of a text as a dynamic process between two poles: the text itself and the perspective of the reader (cf. 1974, 7). Within this reader-response criticism lies great potential for the development of ICC as readers actively engage with texts. By discovering gaps, for example, readers can interpret the text using their world-knowledge, while the text also alters their understanding of the world. Iser's conviction that the "production of the meaning of literary texts [...] entails the possibility that we may formulate ourselves and so discover what has previously seemed to elude our consciousness" (1980, 68) is the essential basis for processes of identity formation and understanding otherness. The readers' individual reading of a text can, thus, contribute to their cultural competences.

In the field of using literature in ELT, the publication *Rezeptionsästhetische Literaturdidaktik* (Bredella/Burwitz-Melzer 2004) was especially influential. Building on Iser's approach, this concept focuses on the readers' intensive interaction with and their discussion of texts (cf. ibid., xiii). Readers are actively involved in the process of reconstructing a text's meaning based on its content and their world knowledge and are able to develop competences through this interaction (cf. ibid., xiii-xiv). This strong focus on the learners' involvement and engagement with texts also indicates the importance of selecting appropriate titles for cultural learning in ELT.

2.1 Literature in Cultural Learning

Following the cultural turn of teaching and learning English in the 1980s (cf. Risager 2012, 146-154), literature was perceived from a new perspective – it is not only beneficial for increasing linguistic competences but cultural competences as well.[33] The discourse of developing ICC with texts has especially been supported by scholars such as Byram and Fleming (1998), who focus on the potential of drama, Burwitz-Melzer (2003), who transfers the concept to intermediate learners, and Zaharka (2002), who specifically focuses on multi-ethnic texts from the U.S. Recently, some scholars have seen literature through a

---

[33] Further functions of literature in ELT have extensively been described and analysed and should therefore not be further investigated here, for example in Bredella (2010b/c, 2002), Brown/Stephens (1998), Burwitz-Melzer (2003), Bushman/Haas (2006), Fäcke (2006), Freitag-Hild (2010), Grenz (1999), Müller-Hartmann/Richter (2002), Richter (2000), Sommer (2000), Surkamp/Nünning (2008, 2009), Volkmann (2010) and Zaharka (2002). This justification of using literature in order to enhance cultural learning could also be seen critically. The function-based perception of literature could run counter to the general approach of language learning beyond functionalizations (e.g. of grammar and vocabulary). However, even if in contexts of extensive reading or seeing literature as a piece of art and cultural artefact, this entails a certain function. Therefore, it is rather difficult to see literature in ELT beyond functional contexts.

transcultural lens (cf. Fäcke 2006, Freitag 2007, Freitag-Hild 2010).[34] Bredella is one of the scholars who brought forward the connection of intercultural competence, teaching literature and understanding otherness (e.g. 2002b, esp. 306-330). He sees literature's potential for increasing intercultural competences in its narrative structure of experiences and plot. Literature does not require specific knowledge but rather speaks to world knowledge and the readers' individual experiences and their understanding of norms and values (cf. ibid., 307). Literature often offers insights to new and possible life scripts which may challenge the readers' pre-knowledge and expectations; it therefore entails specific potential for understanding otherness. When readers encounter protagonists, their feelings and thoughts in a narrative structure, they are likely to see the world through their eyes, they change perspectives and are thus led toward an understanding of the other from the other's point of view. They are involved in the story – a process of identification that is supplemented by developing empathy for the other.

Literary texts confront the reader with other and new perspectives and demand active comprehension processes (cf. Hesse 2009, 78, cf. Nieweler 1995, 293). Although texts are included in course books, these seldom have the necessary depth for a mediation of (cultural) otherness because they still foreground grammatical and linguistic progression. This, Nieweler argues, reduces cultural complexity to a stereotypical representation of otherness. If foreign language teaching is to prepare learners for understanding the other, it not only needs to facilitate an integrated text-language approach (cf. Zydatiß 1992), but also a methodological approach that aims at developing inter- and transcultural competences (cf. Nieweler 1995, 294).

One of the challenges studying the potential of literature for young readers faces regards the definition and understanding of such literature. "The lack of a clear demarcation of the field" and unanswered questions like "Where does children's literature end and adolescent literature begin?" and "What makes a crucial distinction?" (Coats 2011, 322), are still critical issues (cf. ibid., cf. introduction).

The beginning of young adult literature is "usually dated [...] to the publication of S.E. Hinton's *The Outsiders* (1967)" (Trupe 2006, vii). Hinton wrote this book when she was 17 years old, because it was the book she wanted to read, "with characters who were both tough and vulnerable, who faced real social and emotional problems, who had economic worries and life choices to make, in a well-plotted, exciting narrative" (ibid.). For Latrobe and Drury young adult literature is "what YAs [young adults] are reading," which cannot be fixed to a certain genre but entails an "overlapping set of works from picture books to graphic novels to adult fiction and non-fiction" (2009, 3). Characteristics of young adult literature include writing "from the viewpoint of young people," a focus on a "young character [who] solves the problem," "make[s] worthy

---

[34] This aspect will be focused and critically reflected in chapters 3 and 7.3.

accomplishments," and it "deal[s] with emotions that are important to young adults" (Nilsen/Donelson 2009, 20-35). It is literature that "is fast paced," is "basically optimistic," and "includes a variety of genres and subjects, many different ethnic and cultural groups" (ibid.). Scholars more or less agree on the age group to which young adult literature is aimed, ranging between 12 and 20 (cf. ibid., Alsup 2010, Trupe 2006), an age at which they usually attend Grades 7 to 12 or have just finished secondary education. Young people at this age are also referred to as teenagers or adolescents so that the literature they read could be referred to as teenage or adolescence fiction. In my perspective, however, the term young adult literature resonates a more grounded and serious attitude which mirrors the significance of many of the topics around which young adult fiction revolves.

Beyond a "universal appeal of stories," "make-believe" (Hesse 2009, 17), and processes of distancing oneself from real life, young adult fiction is popular with young readers because they can find themselves in these books. Hence, one special feature that makes this genre appealing to young readers is connected to the characterization of the main protagonists. These are usually of a similar age and have to deal with challenges and issues that are considered to be typical for that age. Such issues include, but are not limited to,[35] first love, family issues, rebellion against authorities, temptations of crossing the law, peer pressure, friendship, school and parents (cf. Müller-Hartmann 2001, Richter 2000). In such situations the young protagonists have to make certain choices by considering different options which could be similar to the readers' experiences. Based on a similar age and trials and tribulations, it is possible that the readers identify with the protagonist and find models for their own quests (cf. Hesse 2009). This specific design of protagonists and plot developments are likely to trigger the young readers' interest in the text and to facilitate processes of identification, empathy and understanding.

Because such narrative structures offer manifold points of references for classroom reflections, young adult fiction is a valuable medium for ELT. Literature from English-speaking countries holds a central position, since it immanently depicts foreign and other cultures and can support students in understanding these. It is often assumed that compared to didactized texts that were especially written or edited for learners of English, texts originally written for native speakers are more authentic and, therefore have the potential to increase learners' motivation to engage with them (e.g. Collie/Slater 2007, 3-4, Goshn 2002, 172, Lazar 2009, 15, 17, 25, Lütge 2013b, 98).[36] Nodelman and Reimer also address the issue of authenticity in that they state that "writers who share the race or ethnicity of their characters are likely to be able to describe them more convincingly than those who are not" (2003, 173). Accordingly, it would be rather unlikely that a book can teach about tolerance toward others when it

---

[35] Cf. Nodelman (1992) in the introduction.
[36] However, this view is also debatable, as for example Hermes (2007) sees benefits in using graded readers as well.

does not tell the truth about others (cf. ibid., 174). However, it can be asked what this truth actually is.

As indicated in chapter 1.2.1, authenticity is debatable. While it is often assumed that something is authentic when it is in accordance with the experiences of who is represented, it can be asked whose experiences this actually refers to. There is, for example, hardly any authentic way of representing First Nation cultures as these are highly complex and diverse. Experiences depend on a number of aspects such as age, gender, sexuality, religion, as well as geographic surroundings and rural or urban environments. As an alternative to authenticity, Bradford suggests using focalization and positioning of the characters (cf. 2011, 136). For Breen (1985), who reflected upon authenticity from an ELT perspective, authenticity is a relative term as a text can be authenticated by a teacher through the teaching process or by a learner through reading the text in a specific light.[37]

Authenticity is also a leading concept in the CEF when it calls for authentic texts (e.g. Council of Europe 2001, 49, 145-146, 152) or authentic language (e.g. ibid., 143). The CEF implies the potential of literature to increase ICC as "[n]ational and regional literatures make a major contribution to the European cultural heritage, which the Council of Europe sees as 'a valuable common resource to be protected and developed'" (ibid., 56). This points at a general appreciation of literature as presenting a cultural good to be valued. However, the CEF remains at such a general level and does not go into further detail. Apart from this common agreement for using literature in language education on a European level, federal governmental guidelines for teaching English include similar, yet more detailed references to the value of literature (cf. chapter 3.1). There, a closer connection of reading, cultural learning and language development is visible when texts should explicitly provide for language acquisition (cf. e.g. MSW 2007, 37) and readers shall use literature as an aesthetic medium of communication and as a language model (cf. MSW 1999, 14).

Federal curricula offer more details by referring to certain cultural topics in relation to specific texts. For example, in advanced classes the presentation of Anglophone realities in literature is one central aspect (cf. ibid., 6, cf. below). The focus of literary and cultural learning lies with negotiating constructions of reality in the past and present, applying challenges and problems that are described in literary texts to one's own experiences, changing perspectives, discovering aesthetic characteristics of texts, and, finally, suggesting personal and creative interpretations of texts (cf. ibid., 30-34). A change of perspective and understanding of the target culture shall be achieved by means of diachronic or synchronic approaches (cf. ibid., 27), for which active and creative tasks should be applied (cf. ibid., 9).

---

[37] Fox and Short's *Stories Matter: The Complexity of Cultural Authenticity in Children's Literature* (2003) discusses authenticity with a special focus on multicultural children's literature.

However, the proposed presentation of Anglophone realities in literature in the curricula guidelines can be seen critically, as chapter 1 referred to the dynamic character of cultures and the perspectivity with which texts depict culture. This phrase seems to imply a static set of characteristics which according to selected texts is likely to be transferred to a complex group of diverse people subsumed under the collective item 'Anglophone.' When taking the aim of ELT into account, which also includes raising awareness for the diversity of English-speaking countries and cultures, such contexts need to be deconstructed by teachers and lesson planners.

This line of thought calls for a more detailed account of the relationship of fiction and reality. In Aristotle's *Poetics* (circa 330 BC) 'mimesis' is a central term, which entails the notion that a work of fiction is a representation or imitation of the world. When Halliwell (2002) explains that 'mimesis' rather needs to be understood as 'world-making' or simulation, he assumes that fiction and reality mutually create and re-create themselves.[38] Similarly, Volkmann does not regard literature as purely mimetic because it not only reflects reality but can intervene in reality, change perceptions and can determine political power structures (cf. 2010, 251). He illustrates this with reference to *Uncle Tom's Cabin* (1853) by Harriet Beecher Stowe and the abolitionist movement in the U.S. American North.Volkmann points out that fictional texts also combine elements of reality to create new models of reality only existing in the literary sphere (cf. ibid.).[39] For him, the process of constructing meaning while reading can therefore be understood as an act of negotiating one's own needs, schemata, understandings and expectations of the printed text. This would always be an act of co-authorship and co-creation in which imagination plays an important role. Based on such alternative and simultaneously virtual "world concepts" and manifold incentives for identification, literature offers various opportunities for changing and adapting perspectives (cf. ibid.).

Nevertheless, when focusing on the multitude of voices involved in creating texts, the question 'Whose reality is reflected in the texts and in which socio-historic context is this reality seen?' is central to my line of arguments. For this critical approach it needs to be emphasized that literary texts refer to selected topics and present these from a specific perspective. Texts re-interpret and thus re-create culturally specific experiences based on which they entail a productive character; in this sense they guide the readers' cultural orientation and negotiation of meaning (cf. Surkamp/Nünning 2008, 36). Yet, the depiction of the different protagonists, especially in the context of inter- and transcultural learning, influences processes of identification, options of identity formation

---

[38] This important argument will be extended when discussing the influence of young adult texts on young people's identity formation (cf. chapter 7.2).

[39] Bredella sees mimesis in a similar sense elaborating that it has the power to generate and open up the world ("Mimesis [...] besitzt sowohl eine welterzeugende als auch eine welterschließende Kraft") (2007, 77).

and the development of cultural awareness (cf. chapter 7). This description sets the frame in which readers can fill gaps and actively construct meaning.

Initially, readers participate in the narration from an outside perspective, they have a distanced point of view which enables them to take a critical stance, for which cognitive and emotional competences are necessary (cf. Alsup 2010, 10, Bredella/Burwitz-Melzer 2004, xv, Surkamp/Nünning 2008, 15). While dealing with texts, learners have to engage in changes of perspective and identify with protagonists for which they need to overcome this distanced perception of the text and interact with the otherness that is presented. Hence, it is essential to carefully select appropriate texts that purposefully support understanding the other culture (cf. Surkamp/Nünning 2008, 46, 49) and that invite students to actively and respectfully participate in intercultural encounters (cf. ibid., 27-38). Here, an idealized picture of otherness needs to be equally avoided as its total depreciation. Being able to productively fill gaps and attempt to understand otherness, and to apply a critical view to the depiction of otherness present a high level of cultural and literary competences.

As multicultural literature provides readers with the option of intensively encountering otherness, it has been established as one of the most useful tools to develop critical cultural awareness. Through presenting alternative worldviews, social and cultural norms can be reconsidered (cf. Surkamp/Nünning 2008, Volkmann 2010). Therefore, literature offers readers the chance to reassess their self in view of the other depicted in texts. Such engagements with texts can be extended to intertextual discourses and can serve as foundations for actual face-to-face encounters and, thus, also have the potential of forming students' identity.

Additionally, Fäcke (2006), Nünning (2000),Volkmann (2000, 2012) and Zaharka (2002) point out that processes of negotiating identity based on narratives are especially recognizable in literatures of 'minority' groups, fictions of migrations and texts from the past. In Müller-Hartmann and Richter's line of arguments, "the formulation, or re-formulation of personal identity" (in Müller-Hartmann/Richter 2002, 5) serves as the main task of young readers. Literature depicts different realizations of identity which could be role models for readers, for instance in view of coping with difficulties. Substituted by the protagonists, students can experience different cultural encounters and derive features that they consider to be relevant for themselves and their own identity. In this sense, engaging with questions of identity serves as a bridge to understanding the self, which is seen as a foundation for being able to understand the other; both have been established as closely linked in chapter 1.

2.1.1 Young Adult Literature and Understanding Otherness

One argument why literature as a medium that supports developing ICC should be included in ELT lies with the assumption that students can understand otherness beyond their everyday surroundings. Literature is perceived as balancing a lack of experiences in the students (cf. Volkmann 2010, 250). It not only conveys background knowledge but also offers participation and being involved in a text:

> [t]he students [value] literature as a means of enlarging their knowledge of the world, because through literature they acquire not so much additional information as additional experience. New understanding is conveyed to them dynamically and personally. Literature provides a living-through, not simply knowledge about. (Rosenblatt 1970, 38)

Experiencing otherness rather than just learning about otherness contributes to the high value of literature in ELT. For this, the insights to feelings, thoughts and wishes of protagonists that are presented through literature carry the main potential. Through reading about others, students are not only involved in the other culture but they see themselves in relation to that new input. Hence, readers can reflect their own culture in the mirror of the "other" (cf. Grenz 1999, 195) and broaden their horizons.

The possibility for experiencing otherness is facilitated as literature offers narratives which present a (fictional) reality that is, to a certain extent, different from the readers'. For young readers this is especially appealing and effective when dealing with young adult fiction, with literature that entails protagonists and quests which are similar to the readers themselves (cf. chapter 2.1). When the readers are affected by the narration, it is more likely that they are actively involved in constructing meaning from the text and actually engage in processes of identification and changing perspectives.

In order to reach a high level of ICC, it is important to see the development of ICC as a process which may begin with identifying otherness, showing openness toward otherness, comparing self and other as to negotiate meaning and understanding of self and other. This negotiation of self and other entails opportunities for the students to change perspectives and challenge egocentric perceptions (cf. Surkamp/Nünning 2008, 14-15). Such processes are mainly achieved when otherness offers alternatives, virtual constructions of worldviews and a multitude of possibilities for identification. As Delanoy states "participation in [...] secondary worlds may help readers develop empathy with and solidarity for the characters portrayed. Thus, such an aesthetic approach also has a strong ethical dimension" (2005, 57). Identification and empathy are vital key terms in the current debate of increasing ICC and shall therefore be devoted separate subchapters (cf. chapter 7.1 and 9.1).

Nünning's distinction of different levels of understanding otherness (cf. Nünning 2000, also in Surkamp/Nünning 2008, 29-31) reveals the complexity of this process. On the one hand, one needs to be aware of understanding otherness within the literary text as such; on the other hand this awareness needs to be expanded to include the readers' interaction with the text. The first aims at processes of understanding otherness as represented through the protagonists, the second at how the reader perceives the plot that deals with intercultural aspects. The narrative transmission which could be difficult to understand in reference to a multitude of perspectives, or an unreliable narration that presents a plot, could contribute to the otherness in the text. An additional level is included in transforming understanding otherness in literary encounters to intercultural encounters in real life situations (cf. Surkamp/Nünning, 2008, 29-30). On all four levels, the reader needs to be aware that each representation only gives a partial insight to the other.

Apart from that, I would include an additional level. This refers to the students' attitude with which they approach a text and which influences how they perceive and understand otherness: What is the learners' general knowledge of the context of the narration? Have they had encounters with the other prior to reading a text? Are they close to this culture or perhaps members of the particular group themselves? These questions could determine the access students have to a text. Jordan, Purves, Cruz, Meléndez and Ostrowski's (1997) study about students' responses to culturally diverse texts offers answers to the questions raised above. These and reflections on the importance of choosing texts that are read in class will be shared in chapter 7 which critically reflects upon general assumptions of the benefits of using literature in ELT.

Through the literary contact with different kinds of othernesses, readers are invited and encouraged to negotiate assumptions about the other. As the following chapter discusses, this could indeed affect the readers' personality and their self-perception, because certain assumptions may be challenged, altered or even contradicted.

2.1.2 The Influence of Fiction on Readers' Personality

How is it possible that teaching literature increases cultural competences? Which underlying processes take place and how do these relate to ELT? As mentioned, young adult fiction follows a certain narrative structure; the plot is often action-driven and problem-oriented, solutions to issues can be found when protagonists overcome obstacles and personal challenges (cf. e.g. Bredella/Meißner/Nünning/Rösler 2000, Ewers 2000, O'Sullivan/Rösler 2002). This can be appealing to readers of all ages, but specifically to young readers. The narrative structure personally engages readers with the story and leads them to identify with the protagonists and to change their perspectives; this in turn causes empathic feelings and contributes to understanding the protagonists. As especially multicultural literature presents young protagonists who face cultural challenges, these processes are often directed at a cultural other who is to be understood, which then is supposed to contribute to understanding the cultural other. In secondary literature this process is often said to culminate in identity formation (cf. chapter 9.1.1, e.g. Blell 2013, Burwitz-Melzer 2013b).

My research of the scholarship in this field has revealed that the complexity behind such assumptions tends to be underestimated and is only partly seen critically. In this context, I would like to focus on the representation of cultural otherness (cf. chapter 7) and the quick conclusion that are drawn about identity formation (cf. below and chapter 9). In order to offer insights into the current TEFL scholarship of the development of aforementioned expectations, I first reflect upon the research results in this field.

In the scholarship of cultural learning and teaching literature in ELT one of central objectives is the formation of learners' identity, for instance through enhancing the self by taking the others' perspective and trying to understand the other (cf. e.g. Bredella 2002b/2010b/2010c, Bredella/Christ 2007, Bredella/Delanoy 1999, Bredella/Meißner/Nünning/Rösler 2000, Byram 1997). Here, the students' cultural background needs to be taken into account, which Lazar complements by referring to students' "social and political expectations [...] [which could] help or hinder their understanding of a text" (1993, 53).

Fiction's influences on the development of personality traits have been empirically researched by a group of scholars at the University of Toronto and York University (Djikic et al. 2009, Mar/Djikic/Oately 2008, Oatley 2011). By applying personality and reading tests and drawing on their subjects' experiences, the scholars investigated whether reading fiction, understood as a kind of simulation of experiences in a social world, contributes to developing better social skills and changes the personality. One of the experiments applied is the 'Mind-in-the-eye' test "which measures empathy and understanding of others' minds" and shows that "people who read mainly fiction had substantially greater empathy than those who read mainly non-fiction" (Oatley 2011, n.p.). The results of a test in which participants either read the short story "The Lady with the Dog" by Chekhov or a documentary form of the same text presented as the proceedings of a divorce court (cf. ibid., Mar/Djikic/Oatley 2008, Djikic et al. 2009), indicate that those who read the short story "underwent larger changes in personality than those who read the control text, with the type of changes varying from person to person" (Oatley 2011, n.p.).[40] The authors conclude that "reading of narrative fiction probably plays a role in developing social expertise" and that "practice at understanding the fictional social worlds represented by narrative appears to improve our empathic abilities" (Mar/Djikic/Oatley 2008). The authors estimate that the effect of reading narrative fiction involves a softening of usually rather rigid boundaries of self-schemata (cf. ibid.) and explain that "by projecting ourselves into fictional stories and the minds of fictional characters, we open ourselves up to greater possibilities for who we may become" (ibid., 127-137).[41]

---

[40] The authors provide very interesting insights into their Social-Improvement Hypothesis and their Self-Improvement Hypothesis, of which a detailed account is unfortunately beyond the limits of this work. For more details refer to Mar/Djikic/Oatley (2008).

[41] It is significant that within the study the participants did not show the same changes, which indicates that they were not persuaded by any moral embedded in a story. The authors also

Although reading fiction can indeed improve social skills such as empathy, Mar et al.'s research could not identify the extent to which this is possible. Still, the observation that reading literature increases empathy because it simulates social experiences has beneficial consequences for ELT as it helps to justify the inclusion of literature in ELT in order to meet the objective of increasing ICC. Students reading young adult fiction in ELT may experience the fictional encounter with otherness as a broadening of their own identity and could reflect possibilities of who they may want to become. However, this research design has not been conducted at school, and certainly not in German ELT contexts. Therefore, its applicability to foreign language teaching and increase of cultural competences may be limited (cf. chapter 7).

Despite this objection, such research shows that fiction indeed influences certain personality traits. Yet, in order to reach such teaching objectives, teachers and educators need to be aware of the responsibility they have for choosing and offering books. It depends on texts and approaches to reading in how far readers can "change through various experience; they can grow, develop, ask new questions, think new thoughts, and even feel new emotions" and in how far a complete "engagement in a narrative world is powerful and can create internal, personal narratives of self that, some argue, might guide a reader's behaviour in future" (Alsup 2010, 5). Above all, students need to develop a positive attitude toward reading in the first place. If students are "lost in a book" (Nell 1988), empathic responses may be more likely and, thus, also understanding otherness and identity formation may be more thorough.

Beyond the responsibility for providing students with good reads, questions of ethics need to be taken into consideration, too: What if a teacher decides to develop students' identity by teaching literature that a surrounding community may consider to be harmful, for example when it demonizes or praises homosexual relationships, neutrally presents teenage pregnancy, fosters revolutionary political ideas or other values that some see as immoral or unethical? Alsup asks a number of similar questions, which go one step further:

> To what extent is the job of the literature teacher to effect personal change among students? Are English teachers qualified to elicit purposefully the identity change or growth of their students? Is it ethical to teach a book because a teacher believes it will make her students 'better,' 'more moral,' or 'more empathetic' people? (2010, 5)

As these questions provoke a more detailed account, the selection of texts for ELT will be referred to separately (cf. chapters 3 and 7).

Nevertheless, and beyond aforementioned effects, one can still ask what there actually is to teach if fiction functions as a limited mirror of reality. Chap-

---

address the critical aspect of the temporary effect of the changes in self or social abilities.

ter 1 indicated the difficulties that surround descriptions and understandings of cultures which are hybrid, fluent and multilayered entities that offer a frame of references for various individuals. As the following chapters outline, another challenge is posed by classroom procedures which not only include discussions and reflections upon the other culture, but also assessment and evaluation of students' competences and performances.

2.2 Teaching Cultural Contents

When approaching cultures in foreign language teaching, a "broad and inclusive access [...] must basically be possible" (Witte 2006a, 213). This also entails a long, carefully planned and maintained learning process that demands a critical reflection of the cultural concepts, norms, values, patterns and assumptions of this foreign culture (cf. ibid.). In order for students to successfully discuss foreign cultural issues, it is the responsibility of the teacher to carefully suggest, preselect and didactically prepare the materials on which the learning process is based, and to enable students to reflect upon cultures in correspondence to their own specific needs and interests.

Based on their dynamic diversity it is difficult, and according to Witte it cannot even be the aim, to raise a claim for an all-embracing teaching of cultural elements. Rather, teaching culture should raise awareness for diversity and provide learners "with means of arriving at their own conclusions concerning the cultural context of the foreign language and the source language" (ibid., 215). In reference to Witte's demand to expose learners to relevant aspects of the other culture, one can reply that deciding upon this relevance can easily lead to a superficial selection and thus facilitate a stereotypical view of the other culture. Which aspects of the other culture are relevant – for students and for a general understanding? In how far does that support including aspects beyond the core of a culture? For teachers and learners it could be difficult to know which facts comprise a general understanding. As Bernhardt and Berman estimate with reference to teaching German:

> Despite the 'cultural presentations' in modern textbooks, beginning learners perceive cultural presentations in a vacuum. No matter how analytic, cultural presentations are little more than a few paragraphs of 'facts'. There is simply no way to get at the why this 'cultural fact' may or may not be an important issue in contemporary Germany because there is not enough language in the learners to understand it *auf deutsch*, there certainly is not enough time, and they are not equipped with the prior knowledge base to make the point anything more than trivial. (Bernhardt/Berman 1999, 24 in Schulz 2007, 10)

Although this seems like a rather pessimistic view and needs to be relativized for older students and current inclusions of literary works, the conclusion entails important notions of cultural learning: What is actually included and how deep a negotiation of meaning does a certain selection permit? In how far are students able to really comprehend cultural issues?

Different layers of culture complicate the issue of selecting material for cultural teaching. These layers include a

- national level according to one's country (or countries for people who migrated during their lifetime),
- regional and/or ethnic and/or religious and/or linguistic affiliation level, as most nations are composed of culturally different regions and/or ethnic and/or religious and/or language groups,
- gender level, according to whether a person was born as a girl or as a boy,[42]
- generation level, which separates grandparents from parents from children,
- a social class level, associated with educational opportunities and with a person's occupation or profession, and
- for those who are employed, an organizational or corporate level according to the way employees have been socialized by their work organization. (Hofstede 1991, 10-11)

Additionally, one needs to be aware that members of a certain culture can identify with multiple layers and categories simultaneously. As Hofstede emphasizes, the different layers can sometimes be conflicting, and additions to these layers can easily be made. For example, they can be extended to unemployment and productivity, but also to sexuality and politics. Furthermore, it should not be forgotten that these layers have developed fluid and hybrid forms; they do not represent cultural determinations as collective truths. For ELT, this adds to the complexity of teaching cultures, as one can ask which of those layers are to be included in classroom reflections and how such a selection can offer balanced insights to cultures without appearing relativistic and partial. In this context, the translation of such layers into metaphors, the iceberg- and the onion-model,[43]

---

[42] This is a rather traditional distinction. Certainly, gender is a socially ascribed and constructed role depending on whether someone was labeled male or female at birth based on the primary sexual organs. Scholarship has also identified variations, e.g. that people can be intersex.

[43] Further descriptions of cultures are offered for example by Tomalin and Stempleski's model of three different elements of culture (1993, 7), which consists of 1) products like literature, folklore, art, architecture, music and artifacts, 2) behaviors such as customs, habits, dress, food, leisure, and 3) ideas which refer to beliefs, values, institutions, rules and patterns of thought. Hall differentiates three levels of culture: "an underlying, hidden level of culture that is highly patterned – a set of unspoken, implicit rules of behavior and thought that controls everything we do [...] it defines the way in which people view the world, determines their

can be helpful to reveal which layers can become accessible depending on the students' age and progression in ELT.

2.2.1 Multilayered Cultures

In order to go beyond one's own culture and learn about and from the other's, it is necessary that humans "must first recognize and accept the multiple hidden dimensions of unconscious culture, because every culture has its own hidden, unique form of unconscious culture" (Hall 1976, 2). This assumption can be related to the image of an iceberg, which has become a common metaphor in the scholarship of cultural learning (cf. e.g. Aigner 2002, 99-100, Volkmann 2010, 51-53). The model compares the culture of a society to an iceberg of which only the top part is visible and a larger part is hidden below the surface of the water. The surface of the water differentiates between the visible and invisible, the conscious and unconscious, the aware and unaware. This means that a culture's food, music, arts and literature, festivities, national symbols and dress are part of the visible iceberg and relatively easy to access as members of a culture are primarily aware of these features. Notions of self, religious beliefs, conventions of body language, friendship, politeness, attitudes toward nature, time and gender, understandings of beauty, modesty etc. which are part of beliefs, values and thought patterns are below the surface and only accessible through deep engagement as those features are usually beyond awareness (cf. AFS Orientation Handbook 1984, 14).

Hofstede states that "cultural differences manifest themselves in several ways [for example in] symbols, heroes, rituals, and values" (cf. 1991, 7). As he suggests, those can be represented as the skins of an onion (ibid., 7-10). Symbols are placed on the outer skin as they are most evident; values are at the core of the onion as they are the deepest manifestation of culture; heroes and rituals are in between. Under the category of symbols, Hofstede subsumes words, gestures, pictures or objects but also dress and hairstyles. Interestingly, he points at the fluency of this level as new symbols are easily developed and old ones may disappear, which supports a dynamic terminology of culture. The category heroes includes "persons, alive or dead, real or imaginary, who possess characteristics that are highly prized in a culture, and who thus serve as models for behavior"; these could even be fantasy figures such as Batman or Snoopy in the USA or Asterix in France (cf. ibid., 8). Rituals are "ways of greeting and paying respect to others" or "social and religious ceremonies" (ibid.). These are "collective activities, technically superfluous in reaching desired ends, but which, within a culture, are considered as socially essential: they are therefore carried

values, and establishes a basic tempo and rhythms of life" (1989, 6), b) secondary level culture "is normally hidden from outsiders [...]" (ibid., 260), cultural knowledge shared by insiders of a culture, but not by outsiders, c) "tertiary or explicit, manifest culture is what we all see and share in each other, it is the façade presented to the world at large" (ibid.). This level is easily manipulated and open to change.

out for their own sake." Finally, values at the inner core of cultures are "broad tendencies to prefer certain states of affairs over others. Values are feelings with an arrow to it: they have a plus and a minus side" and include understandings of "evil vs. good, dirty vs. clean [...] ugly vs. beautiful, [...] abnormal vs. normal [...] irrational vs. rational" (ibid.).

A comparison of the iceberg and onion model with an analysis of the curriculum (MSW 2008) for primary English in North Rhine-Westphalia shows that younger learners only approach English-speaking cultures on the surface level, the top layer of cultures, which matches their assumed cognitive skills and level of psychological development. Intercultural learning in primary schools focuses on getting to know and comparing life worlds and being able to act in intercultural encounters on a very basic level (cf. MSW 2008, 10). This is mirrored in the "fields of experience" the curriculum suggests for classroom reflections, for instance the seasons, food and drinks, special days, children of the world or our environment (cf. ibid., 13). Students are supposed to put together scrapbooks (including photographs, texts and advertisements) that represent the other culture, they should know daily routines of children in other cultures and be able to perform common speech acts of introducing, greeting, congratulating and being polite toward people of other cultures. This should contribute to their general openness.

The curricula for higher grades and more advanced learners include a deeper approach to cultures, which should not come as a surprise because learners are more mature and have a higher level of English. They are expected to deduce and critically reflect values and attitudes based on single observations and recognitions, and to be aware of culture-specific conventions in intercultural encounters with native and non-native speakers who use English as a lingua franca (cf. MSW 2007, 38). The objectives of teaching culture are distinguished into

- knowledge of orientation: e.g. relationships between genders during adolescence, the value and system of education in the target culture, the political system and attitudes toward human rights and democracy,
- values and attitudes: e.g. the ability to understand and compare culturally determined differences and similarities of living conditions and life styles of members of the other culture; it refers to the ability to explain non-fictional texts according to their cultural features and to understand literary texts from different cultural perspectives, and
- intercultural encounters: e.g. the ability to recognize cultural conventions in various discourses and respond emphatically to cultural misunderstandings. (cf. ibid., 39)

Comparing these descriptions of cultural competence at the end of Grade 4 (primary school) and at the end of Grade 9 reveals that with an advancement of foreign language education, learners' reflections touch upon more hidden features of culture and move toward the lower part of the iceberg and the inner core of the onion, toward underlying concepts which demand more profound considerations. This also indicates that for the competence level of more advanced learners, the pragmatic and affective parts of ICC gain more importance which is connected to their psychological development and their higher linguistic competences.[44]

Identifying the content of cultural teaching and learning only meets one of the central challenges of increasing ICC, as ICC also includes aspects such as language competence in grammatical, socio-linguistic, pragmatic, and paralinguistic spheres as well as knowledge, experience, and empathy. Thus, the development of ICC appears as complex and multilayered as the discussion of cultural contents. Which of these different layers determine(s) students' intercultural competence?

It is often stated that intercultural competence goes beyond a mere knowledge of facts and a cognitive understanding of cultures, while this simultaneously establishes the foundation for understanding further aspects of cultural issues. Yet, the cognitive aspects of cultural competence reflect an approachable subject of assessment compared to the affective and pragmatic aspects. Still, those cognitive aspects run the risk of being static and outdated (cf. Eberhardt 2013 in chapter 8.1). In this context Paige et al.'s definition of cultural learning as "the process of acquiring the culture-specific and culture-general knowledge, skills, and attitudes required for effective communication and interaction with individuals from other cultures" could be helpful. The understanding that "[i]t is a dynamic, developmental, and ongoing process which engages the learner cognitively, behaviorally, and affectively" (Paige et al. 2003, 177) includes the different elements that were outlined above and need to be taken into consideration.

2.2.2 From Hybridity to Standards?

The dynamic and open character of constructed cultures can furthermore be contrasted with the recent debate of competence development and standard orientation. Within the discourse of cultural learning, key terminology like identity, cultural complexity, hybridity, intertextuality, negotiation of meaning, and diversity are prevalent. On the side of the CEF and the intrinsic orientation of increasing complex competences terms such as quality, standardization, strategy, competition, monitoring, ranking, efficiency, and management of knowledge are mentioned (cf. Hu 2008, 290-291). From this juxtaposition, Hu concludes that in cultural learning those two discourses, which appear to be exclusive of each other, attempt to find a common base. I agree with Hu in seeing essential differences in both discourses. These differences regard the perception

---

[44] One further aspect that contribtues to the challenges of teaching culture is the competence of the teachers themselves. This will be reflected in more detail in chapter 8.

of learners and of processes of learning, the perception of language and culture, and the objectives of foreign language education in general. Hu warns of an economization of education (cf. ibid., 290) and asks which consequences this entails for the future of intercultural foreign language teaching and learning. This contrastive approach to both fields of expertise could lead to the conclusion that the discourse of ICC in foreign language education reacts more differentiated, theory-bound and contemporary to current social changes and conditions (cf. ibid., 285-286). At the same time Hu points to the fact that the discourse of ICC often lacks the attempt to clearly describe, if not define, an appropriate model of developing intercultural attitudes and awareness of desirable objectives in respect to the age and ability of the learners (cf. ibid., 286) (cf. chapter 2.3).

Within the development of ICC it is essential to be aware that intercultural foreign language education is understood as a much-diversified space in which understanding otherness is increased based on negotiating meaning between participants of multilayered discourses. Through this negotiation of meaning, the participants de-construct, re-construct and co-construct their understanding of cultures, the other and their own. Due to the fact that the discourse is not only multilayered, but also multilingual and the participants are heterogeneous on various levels (age, ethnicity, gender, religion, and life experiences etc.) it is challenging to frame cultural competences in competence descriptions.

Through processes of distancing oneself from one's own culture and taking the foreign culture into account, advanced learners find themselves in a 'third space' which has been described in detail above. However, it can neither be the aim to establish in students attitudes of relativizing cultural identity toward indifference, nor for them to completely adopt the foreign. While it is the learner who develops intercultural competence through intercultural encounters, it is the teacher who serves as a guide in order to prevent students from being lost in this multifaceted, multilayered and dynamic continuum.

Despite the challenges pointed at above, ICC is a central feature of foreign language education. Thus, it can be asked in how far ICC can be included in and made available for an education that aims at reaching and fulfilling standards and agreeing with the competence-oriented reform of foreign language education. How far can learners' progress be made comparable and assessable? In fact, if ICC is to be supported in ELT, educators should also be able to identify certain levels of cultural competence. Such models have been suggested by various scholars, most recently by Eberhardt (2013) who developed a model of describing cultural competences in the context of German Standards of Education. This aspect of standardizing, empirically researching and assessing cultural competences lays the foundation for the reflections in the following chapter.

2.3 Developing Cultural Competences

The educational turn toward outcome orientation and the description of teaching objectives as competences led to a standardization of teaching and learning. The Standing Conference of the Ministers of Education and Cultural Affairs (KMK) set those standards which for intermediate grades are defined for functional, intercultural and methodological competences (KMK-Standards 2003, 7-10). For advanced grades those are extended to additionally include text- and media competence, language awareness and language learning competence (KMK-Standards 2012, 10-12, cf. chapter 3.1).[45] Functional communicative competences refer to skills (reading and listening understanding, viewing skills, writing, speaking and mediation) as well as lexicon, grammar, pronunciation/intonation and spelling. Methodological competences include the ability to read and produce texts, to use learning strategies, to present and use media, etc., and intercultural competences include socio-cultural knowledge, negotiation of meaning in intercultural encounters and the respectful approach to cultural differences (KMK-Standards 2006, 8). The competences for advanced grades are defined similarly but more complex (cf. KMK-Standards 2012, 10-12).

However, and although ICC is stated as the main objective of learning languages, compared to the other competences, neither the CEF nor the Standards offer detailed descriptors or can do-statements which would support an assessment of cultural learning processes. Within the discourse of competence orientation, this main objective, hence, also poses the main challenge: operationalizing developmental stages of cultural learning and assessing affective and pragmatic competences is difficult. Various scholars from different fields of expertise have contributed to the important question of modeling and evaluating ICC, for example from the perspective of business communication (Bolten 2007), comparative cultural psychology (Bennett 1986), psychological exchange research (Thomas/Simon 2007), or pedagogical psychology (Hesse/Göbel 2007) as well as foreign language education research (Byram 1997, 2008, De Florio-Hansen 2010, Eberhardt 2013, Volkmann 2002). This list already shows how complex this topic is and how many different perspectives and suggestions have been made. Different arguments can be brought forward to challenge the respective approaches and findings. Therefore, this chapter offers a rather detailed insight into this field. The standardization of ICC is of pressing interest because certain scholars see ICC vanishing from curricula if its evaluation is not brought to a reliable level (cf. 2.3.3).

---

[45] The Standards of Education are defined in the "Educational Standards for the First Foreign Language in Secondary Schools" (KMK Standards 2006/"Bildungsstandards für die erste Fremdsprache (Englisch/Französisch) für den Mittleren Schulabschluss") and "Educational Standards for the Continued Foreign Language in the A-Levels" (KMK-Standards 2012/"Bildungsstandards für die fortgeführte Fremdsprache (Englisch/Französisch) für die Allgemeine Hochschulreife").

2.3.1 Models of Staged Development

In the Intercultural Development Inventory (IDI), which is based on the Developmental Model of Intercultural Sensitivity (DMIS), Bennett suggested six stages which reflect the advancement of intercultural competence (1993, 1986a, 1986b, cf. Casper-Hehne 2008, Eberhardt 2013, Hu 2008, Larkey 2008). These are multi-dimensional measurements referring to an individual's cognitive, affective and pragmatic reactions to cultural differences (cf. Casper-Hehne 2008, 317). According to Bennett, the six stages are divided into ethnocentric and ethno-relative phases of development.[46] It is noteworthy to mention that Bennett's model runs the risk of ignoring the diversity and hybridity of cultures as well as commonalities when an item in stage four, for example, reads "I generally enjoy the difference that exist between myself and people from other cultures" (cf. also ibid., 320). Eberhardt agrees to this criticism and adds that this model neither differentiates intercultural sensitivity on a horizontal level nor does it take the interdependence of linguistic and cultural competences into consideration (cf. Eberhardt 2013, 132-137, 447).

Further models are the Cross-Cultural Adaptation Inventory (CCAI), developed by Kelley and Meyers (1993) which is "rooted in psychological personality assessment values of extraversion, openness to experience, neuroticism, agreeableness, conscientiousness" (Larkey 2008, 262), and the Intercultural Adjustment Potential Scale (ICAPS)[47] created by Matsumoto et al. (2001). These

---

[46] To the ethnocentric phase, Bennett counts the stages of "denial" (ignorance toward intercultural difference, inhuman denial of recognition), "defense" (recognizing differences but direct rejection) and "minimization" (de-emphasizing the value of differences, tendency to universalize values of one's own culture). The ethno-relative phase is characterized by the stages "acceptance" (cultural differences are seen as normal and are generally respected, recognition that cultures are dynamic and constructed), "adaptation" (ability to adjust action and mindset according to culturally different settings) and "integration" (ability to regard differences and relativity of cultural meaning from an inside perspective) (cf. Casper-Hehne 2008, 317-318, Hu 2008, 295-296). The IDI consist of 50 statements which aim at measuring how culturally sensitive people are and how they construct cultural difference. Subjects are asked to comment on statements such as "It is appropriate that people do not care what happens outside their country," "I can change my behavior to adapt to other cultures," "people from our culture are less polite compared with people from other cultures," or "people in our culture work harder than people in other cultures" (in Larkey 2008, 263). According to the subjects' reactions to these statements, the conductors are said to be able to identify a person's intercultural sensitivity and propose "training needs, guiding interventions for individual and group development of intercultural competence, contributing to personal selection" (Hammer/Bennett/ Wiseman 2003, 441). Similarly, the DMIS seeks to develop intercultural sensitivity by "attaining the ability to construe (and thus experience) cultural difference in more complex ways" (ibid., 423). Interestingly, this procedure attempts to diagnose cultural competences before training, an aspect that will be relevant in chapter 2.3.3.

[47] The scale of the ICAPS tries "to reliably and validly predict the degree to which a person will be able to adjust to living, working, and playing effectively in a new and different cultural environment" (cf. Larkey 2008, 270). Similarly to the CCAI it is divided into categories such as emotional regulation, openness, flexibility and critical thinking. In this scale, too, the learner has to agree or disagree with certain statements from which cultural competences are derived,

scales differ to the IDI in that they are mostly concerned with particular inter-culturally salient values. The CCAI, for example, is meant to "help people focus on specific aspects of their personality, behavior, skills and/or knowledge to become more conscious of their strengths and weaknesses in these areas" (Kelley/Meyers 1993, 1).[48]

Those models are not grounded in foreign language education specifically, but are included in this overview as they show how scholars attempt to set stages for the advancement of cultural competences. Bennett's model refers to the evaluation of suitable sojourners for work experiences abroad, yet, it was still used as a basis for the DESI study.[49] A closer look at those models of a staged development of cultural competences reveals that the scales are indeed not easily applicable to foreign language teaching and learning. In reference to Bennett's model, this critical recognition regards

- – the model's normative setting as it describes a continuous development from bad to good behavior whereas also counter developments are possible (cf. Hu 2010, 68-69),
- – an understanding of homogeneous cultures which are characterized by their intercultural differences (cf. Hu 2010, 68-69, Larkey 2008, 263),
- – the model's neglect of language learning as only one option of gaining intercultural competence (cf. Hu 2010, 68-69),

---

including "I rarely feel anxious or fearful," "I get angry easily," "I don't get much pleasure from talking to people," etc. (cf. Matsumoto 2001, 504 in Larkey 2008, 270). What is striking about these items is that the ICAPS was developed to adjust and assess a person's strengths and weaknesses prior to departure to an intercultural experience (Larkey 2008, 207). Matsumoto reports that some of his students were able to raise their scores by 80% when the questionnaire was repeated after the learners took part in the intercultural training class. He admits that others were not that successful and suggests that those discrepancies can be traced to different teaching methods. Similar to the CCAI, the ICAPS can only be applied to ELT to some extend, as ELT not necessarily aims at preparing students for exchange programs but focuses on developing ICC in general. However, for the content at hand both scales are interesting as they show attempts of translating such complex competence descriptions into learning processes and progressions.

[48] In intercultural encounters, this inventory focuses on the self-understanding of individuals and how they are able to cope with their cross-cultural adaptability, and on their readiness to interact with people from a different culture (cf. Larkey 2008, 268). The categories that are included refer to emotional resilience, flexibility and openness, perceptual acuity and personal autonomy etc. When implementing the CCAI in teaching English, a teacher can use this inventory to detect fields and categories to focus on and identify how these could be encountered in real life; certain methods and activities could help students with their anxieties and uncertainties. Yet, since language teaching is closely connected to contents, the implementation of the CCAI as such is not advisable.

[49] The DESI-study was conducted in 2001 to investigate German students' language competences in German and English (Klieme/Beck 2007, DESI-Konsortium 2008).

- the addressees, as only young people with a migration background have the preconditions for achieving the last two stages of his model (cf. Casper-Hehne 2008, 319),[50] and

- the different connotations of items addressing the affective level in different contexts; anxiety and openness can appear in changing graduations and refer to different objects – a differentiation that the scales do not provide. (cf. also Larkey 2008, 273)

Based on this criticism, for the content at hand I rather focus on Byram's *savoir*-model, which distinguishes different spheres in which ICC can be recognized (cf. chapter 1.2) and on LOLIPOP, which describes can-do-statements of cultural learning (cf. De Florio-Hansen et al., no year). LOLIPOP was specifically designed for ELT and is the first attempt to describe a staged development of cultural competences from A1 to C2 according to the CEF. Additionally, I refer to Eberhardt's suggestion of an empirically based model of cultural competences for the German Standards of Education, and empirical approaches (cf. Fäcke 2006, Freitag-Hild 2010, Eberhardt 2008, 2009). The latter are used to translate the theoretical assumptions and models into practice and show how learners are affected by intercultural learning activities, methods and materials.

LOLIPOP (Language Online Portfolio Project) is a multilingual, interactive online-version of the European language portfolio with a specific focus on the intercultural dimension (cf. Neuhoff 2008). It establishes a scale for intercultural competence ranging from A1 to C2 in correspondence to the CEF. Each competence level is described on a general level which is distinguished into further sub-competences. For example, the overall description for the lowest intercultural competence of A1 reads 'I am able to recognize basic differences between my own and another culture and would like to know more about the other culture and its people' (cf. LOLIPOP n.y., n.p.).[51] The general description of the highest level of intercultural competence (C2) reads 'Based on my previous intercultural encounters and various theories of culture with which I am so far familiar, I am able to assess and correctly interpret the cultural behavior of people. I identify myself as an intercultural mediator' (cf. LOLIPOP, n.y., n.p.).[52] Similar descriptions of competences, sub-competences and examples

---

[50] As a reaction to this critical view on Bennett's model, Paige et al. (1999) suggest a three-factor model, which in turn has been criticized by Casper-Hehne (2008) and Hesse/Göbel (2007) because of its proceduralization and differentiation of cultural learning.

[51] Sub-competences include 'I can say something about the other country (capital city, geographic details, climate, political structure, main festivities),' 'I am increasingly able to understand everyday situations of the other culture (eating habits, politeness, address and greetings),' 'I acknowledge that cultural encounters serve as personal enrichment although I have not had that many personal experiences' etc. (cf. LOLIPOP, n.y., n.p.).

[52] The sub-competences of this stage include 'Based on my previous multicultural experiences, I am able to act according to different and new sets of values and worldviews. This enables me to take various perspectives which are not shaped by my personality or another culture,' 'I am

can be found for the respective levels in between these two. While the first stages remain within abilities of describing and recognizing, higher stages demand correct interpretation, mediation of and participation in intercultural encounters. This indicates a progression from a cognitive level of intercultural competence toward an affective level and includes references to a pragmatic application of intercultural competence – a progression that reminds of the progress of cultural learning in national curricula that was paralleled to the iceberg and onion model of culture (cf. chapter 2.2). However, it is questionable, and LOLIPOP does not discuss, how teachers can assess whether students have reached these stages.[53]

Göbel and Hesse used a combination of Bennett's scales and critical interaction situations as a foundation for the investigation of ICC within the DESI study (Göbel/Hesse 2004, Göbel/Hesse 2007, Hesse/Göbel/Jude 2008, 180, cf. chapter 2.3.2). As pointed out above, I believe that while these scales are the basis for drawing general conclusions about an individual's main attitude to members of other cultures and their willingness to engage with them, I would challenge their application to classroom practices and foreign language teaching (cf. below).

Witte (2006a, 205) offers a more ELT-specific approach to a staged development of ICC suggesting seven stages of cultural progression in foreign language learning. These are based on Hall's differentiation of three levels of culture (1989, cf. chapter 2.2) and Tomalin and Stempleski's model of three different elements of culture (1993, 7, cf. chapter 2.2). Although he does suggest such a general account, Witte emphasizes that the stages are a highly individualistic construction: learners act and react toward cultural aspects and encounters to which they individually ascribe meaning (cf. 2006b, 42).

Witte's first stage tolerates learners to reduce foreign elements to "native culture-centric categories", which in the process of getting to know the other, "will be increasingly expanded" (ibid., 218). This aims at "generat[ing] an awareness and understanding on the part of the learner that people act the way they do because they are using the options provided for them by their culture to satisfy basic needs." (ibid.). Stage 7 is the highest stage and is

> concerned with an integration of the many elements of the foreign and the native cultures so that the learner can move between linguistic and cultural patterns of the cultures involved and transfer his or her skills and knowledge to other aspects of intercultural encounters, in the sense of applying her or his acquired openness to his or her thinking and behavior. (Witte 2006a, 226)

---

able to view my own and other cultures from an inside as well as an outside perspective. This allows me to mediate between cultures and to take an objective position' etc. (cf. LOLIPOP, n.y., n.p.).

[53] I will only signpost some of the criticism of a staged development of cultural competences in the following section and expand this in a separate chapter (cf. chapter 2.3.2).

Learners are expected to "handle cross-cultural differences in constructive manner" and to "negotiate ambiguity of meaning and roles arising from ongoing attempts to empathize with the foreign constructs" (ibid., 217-226).

Traditionally, progression is referred to in grammatical contexts, but learning a language refers to much more than the correct combination of grammatical rules and semantics: "understanding the immediate situational and the broader socio-cultural context of a human language in general and speech acts in particular is a prerequisite for meaningful and competent usage of any human language" (Witte 2006a, 205). This is especially recognizable when speakers use idioms and metaphors, or are sensitive to culturally specific connotations of certain words and phrases, both of which often reflect rich cultural resources. As communication has strong social, cultural and pragmatic connotations, I agree with Witte in that progression also needs to be accountable to cultural competences. Language reflects cultural values, therefore, the furtherance of pragmatic and socio-cultural knowledge is essential to the learning process of a foreign language if the speaker is to become a competent and confident user of that language.

These stages reveal that cultural learning and cultural progression are no linear processes. The individual learner is involved in complex and dynamic negotiations of meaning which continuously challenge and shift self and other, their own and the foreign culture into different directions. The learner has to withstand ambiguities and uncertainties which can sometimes not be solved for a longer period of time, if at all. Therefore, I believe that it is extremely difficult, it not almost impossible, to assess the progression of cultural competences.

A further reason for challenging staged developments and scales for cultural learning lies with the relevance of some of the items for ELT, as some seem to be somewhat "detached from both FL [foreign language] classroom context as well as from specific intercultural encounters," as also Larkey estimates (2008, 271). Using these would demand an adjustment to classroom procedures and objectives. Another problem is the wording and phrasing of some items and their concreteness: Teachers would need to relativize items such as "new experiences, emotions, and thoughts" (ibid.), as the actual referent remains opaque, especially when testing young people who are multicultural themselves or grew up and are educated in multicultural environments. A "new situation," for example, can be constituted of moving to a different neighborhood, recognizing new levels of poverty or a trip overseas to an unfamiliar country. This criticism applies to several of the items and categories that are included in the scales (further examples in ibid., 273-276).

To this criticism I would add that the development of certain stages of intercultural competence depends on certain topics or issues, too, and that, thus, a generalization of a level a learner has achieved is hardly possible. While one may have a high intercultural competence regarding a general openness toward others, learners may be lacking a similar competence level regarding this openness when it comes to aspects that interfere with their profound norms, values and convictions. For example, someone could be open to the diversity of U.S.-American cultures in general, but be reserved toward their dealing with Native American policy or questions of same-sex marriage. It could be the case that the categories openness, flexibility, perceptual acuity and personal autonomy interfere with each other. Which of those is then important and decisive for being interculturally sensitive and competent? It is also debatable on which cultural encounters the answers and reactions to the statements in the different scales are based, and whether a disagreement with certain cultural practices can actually be seen as positive as these may negate human rights or other values that are considered more important.

Additional factors which make a staged development of cultural competence in ELT problematic are the different spheres of language and culture competence. Just as it cannot be assumed that young learners necessarily enter formal ELT on an A1 level, it cannot be assumed that young learners automatically have a low level of cultural competence or cultural sensitivity, and approach other cultures with ethno-relative attitudes when they start learning English. Hu (2010, 68) estimates that this correlation is based on elusive reasons, as intercultural competences do not solely depend on language competences (cf. a detailed discussion in chapter 2.3.3). Moreover, Eberhardt points at a lack of sub-competences which describe cultural competence on a horizontal level (cf. Eberhardt 2008, 279 and 2009, 208).

A similar conclusion as in earlier criticism of implementing ICC in foreign language education needs to be applied here: Despite the challenges of a staged development of intercultural competences and the difficulties the mere teaching perspective of cultural content pose, the development of ICC is deeply anchored in the CEF, the national guidelines and curricula of foreign language learning and teaching. If these are to be part of the curriculum, they have to be made available for measuring tools. The dilemma of assessing and measuring cultural competences is grounded in positions which severely criticize such endeavours. Simultaneously, the respective scholars warn of the danger that competences which are not assessable lose their relevance for learners and that foreign language teaching's ability to increase intercultural understanding loses its credibility (cf. Schulz 2008, 247). The counter-position implies that if a competence exists in some amount, it can also be measured (cf. Zydatiß 2006, 261, cf. below and chapter 8.2). When arguing in favour of one of those positions, the consequences that are drawn are crucial: What happens to central aspects of ELT if they are excluded from outcome orientation and standardization? Does the objective become insignificant because it cannot be tested? Is it excluded from classroom practices? Does it have to remain an ideal that cannot be achieved? Or is it indeed made assessable under certain parameters? Empirical studies, for example by Fäcke, Freitag-Hild and Eberhardt (cf. below) take up these pressing questions and try to establish a foundation for teaching and assessing cultural competences. However, as my descriptions show, these are not free of limitations and challenges.

2.3.2 The Empirical Investigation of Cultural Learning

As intercultural competence is part of the curriculum and official guidelines for teaching English, this competence was part of the studies that were conducted to compare and define educational standards within Germany. One of the first of such surveys was the DESI-study which tested students' competences in German and English. Göbel (2007) conducted a study of the general quality of English lessons in which teachers were explicitly asked to dedicate one of the two videographed lessons to an intercultural topic (Göbel/Hesse 2008, 401).[54] The intercultural content was evaluated based on teachers' and learners' references to culture or country-specific aspects of the target culture (such as norms, values, attitudes, behavior, etc.). While the general attempt to measure the quality of cultural learning needs to be valued, due to this specific procedure Göbel's research can also be seen critically in different respects.

On the one hand, a focused dedication of lessons to cultural issues suggests a separation of culture and language. On the other hand, when (mere) references to the other culture are seen as indicators of ICC and the quality of English lessons, the role of the self in intercultural encounters is not included in the reflection process, neither is the relevance of negotiations of cultural meaning. These aspects contradict what has been established as cultural learning and ICC in earlier chapters. However, students' competences were rated according to these teaching and learning processes. Furthermore, I believe that conclusions about the intercultural competence students can perform in such an environment can only be drawn within strict limitations.

In the DESI study, learner's intercultural competences were operationalized on the base of Bennett's staged model and on learners' reactions to critical incidents (cf. Göbel/Hesse 2007, 256-272). The usage of critical incidents assumes that specific intercultural awareness reveals itself best when dealing with actual and imagined intercultural conflicts. Learners are presented with an intercultural situation in which something (seemingly) unexpected happens or in which someone is faced with a cultural challenge. For the empirical research it is then interesting to see how the students understand this incident and how they interpret the situation – their approach to the critical incident is used to draw conclusions about the students' ICC (cf. ibid., 264).

This implementation of critical incidents in analyzing students' ICC followed a certain structure. The students first read the critical incident, are then asked questions about it which refer to cognitive, affective, pragmatic and transferal aspects and are finally given pre-formulated answers from which they can choose, all of which are related to a stage in Bennett's model (cf. ibid., 265). Within this strict and pre-structured procedure it is disputable in how far the given answers reflect the students' opinion or whether they would have ideas beyond the ones provided. As the students need to base their answer on prox-

---

[54] For a detailed account cf. Göbel/Hesse (2004), Göbel/Hesse (2007, 2008), Göbel/Hesse/Jude (2008).

imity to the given answers, this procedure may not demonstrate an in-depth evaluation of their ICC. Besides, it is possible to react to such dilemma situations by applying common sense or by reflecting upon what kind of reaction is socially desired.[55]

Moreover, in order to use critical incidents in such a study, it would be necessary to establish common quality markers of critical incidents which so far have not been defined. Which standards do critical incidents need to fulfill in order to be applicable to cultural learning? Which cultural situations are especially beneficial for cultural learning? Although it should not be disputed that critical incidents may be useful for triggering communication and debates about cultural situations, these questions have not been answered, and yet, critical incidents are regularly used to practice, measure and assess cultural competence.[56] Additionally, the usability of Bennett's model for the development of ICC in the EFL classroom is questionable as was elaborated in chapter 2.3.1. It would be interesting to actually gain insights to the questionnaires and critical incidents that were handed out (cf. Küppers/Trautmann 2008), but these are not included in the respective publication. Besides, it can be noted that although Göbel points at a changing terminology and understanding of culture (cf. Göbel/Hesse 2007, 257-259), the critical incidents focused on particularities of British culture and ignored the high level of heterogeneity of the population, especially within London (cf. Hu 2010, 66). Eberhardt furthermore questions whether it is in general possible to evaluate a complex competence like intercultural sensitivity, competence and awareness based on two critical incidents and a multiple-choice test only (cf. Eberhardt 2008, 279).

For her empirical research design on mental processes of primarily mono- or bi-culturally socialized young adults, Christiane Fäcke widens the scope of cultural research to include transcultural approaches. She describes different stages of cultural learning which are labeled understanding, transcultural understanding, and transcultural opening (cf. 2006, 53-55). These stages differ, for example, in their construction, coding and interpretation of texts and cultural contexts, different levels of comparisons of culturally specific text passages, the individual's experiences, and the level of assessment, balancing and discussion of one's own hypothesis according to a text and other contexts. The stages of transcultural opening, for example, are defined as

- taking the other's perspectives,
- tolerance of ambiguity,
- constructing similarities and differences,

---

[55] De Florio-Hansen criticizes that solutions to critical incidents are often based on memory, that the texts would not be authentic but manipulated, that there is a lack of involvement of the learners in the situation and, finally, that critical incidents are based on a static and obsolete term of culture (2010, 76).

[56] Göbel (2003) only offers an introduction to critical incidents and their contribution to education.

- relativizing one's own constructions,
- consciously deconstructing separating categories,
- deconstructing through contextualization,
- reinterpreting discomfort, mutual penetration of hybrid *Lebenswelten* (life worlds), and
- reflections of currently performed processes of understanding on a meta-level. (cf. ibid., 54-55)

These stages would support a continuing process of developing transcultural competences; various sub-competences are implicitly included. In how far these stages differ from intercultural understanding, however, needs further explanation.

In order to investigate mental processes in cultural learning, Fäcke used research tools such as thinking aloud, diary studies, and guideline interviews. Thinking aloud activities are based on a short reading section which the learners reflect orally right after they have finished reading. From these immediate introspections Fäcke hopes to draw conclusions about the learners' mental processes of negotiating meaning (cf. 2006, 69-71). Due to a certain time interval between reading and reflection, diary studies provide a more retrospective account. As diary studies entail a low level of structured schemes, they aim at having learners freely reflect upon their thoughts, impressions, feelings and the challenges they see in the given text.[57] Although both methods have been criticized regarding a transfer of results, Fäcke justifies their usage as her study aims at uncovering individual constructions of meaning and the individual's mental processes. Her interviews include open-guided questions which allow the researcher to investigate learners' more detailed and in-depth attitudes toward the content of the texts and to compare these to the spontaneous reactions of the thinking aloud reflections. Beyond those aspects, interview questions offer the researcher the opportunity to point to issues which the learners themselves may not have recognized (cf. ibid., 74-77).

In her detailed analysis, Fäcke relates the learners' answers and reactions toward the texts to the stages and differentiated phases of understanding, transcultural understanding and transcultural openness (cf. 2006[58]). In one example, Fäcke refers to a learner who explains that by reading a text about a Moroccan family, she was able to reduce her stereotypes and preconceptions of Moroccan culture and that she would now be way more tolerant if she met a Moroccan family than before reading the text. Based on the reading experience, she would know in what they believe and would try to understand them as she

---

[57] In order to prevent learners from not being able to phrase their impressions and to prevent limited reflections, Fäcke allowed them to write their diaries in German and only provided them with open and guiding questions (2006, 72-74).

[58] On pages 105-106, 117, 127-128, 137-138, 149, 161-162, 172-173, 185-186, 197-198, and 210 Fäcke comments in detail upon the single students who were part of the study.

reflected upon the meaning of their behavior (cf. ibid., 101-102). Although these statements seem to indicate that the learner has changed her attitude toward the Moroccan family, she also applies the characteristics of a single family to a collective cultural group; based on this one example she may now be open toward any Moroccan family. In Fäcke's categorization, these statements reflect the levels of 'transcultural understanding and transcultural opening.' However, one could ask in how far such learning processes reflect transcultural rather than intercultural learning, and it remains open in how far such an opinion reflects awareness for cultural diversity.

Similarly, I would like to point out that the learners' statements and their opinions were recorded in an institutionalized and artificial classroom environment in a democratic society. I believe that when evaluating the students' answers in the interviews and diary entries, the influence of social desirability needs to be considered. According to my point of view, social desirability has a huge impact on the learners' in-class opinions, reflections and performances (cf. below and chapter 8 for a detailed critical discussion and suggestion of alternatives).

In the evaluation of the transcultural approach, Fäcke reveals that many of the students demand a stronger link between the topics and contents of lessons and their personal and affective responses as well as a more conscious reflection, self-reflection and critical negotiation of contents (cf. 2006, 280). This demand and approach to foreign language learning from the learners' perspective strongly agrees with the transcultural approach to teaching and learning foreign languages, which offers the learners and their holistic identities a more central role in the learning process. On a more pragmatic level, this also implies that students and their opinions are taken more seriously. Although Fäcke is only able to derive this notion of transcultural relevance from the ten students she included in her study, it could be assumed that more young adults feel that way as they are personally affected by increasingly diverse societies and see the need to reflect upon their skills and competences to successfully live in them.[59]

Britta Freitag-Hild (2010) sets out to explore a theory, task-typology and practical application of inter- and transcultural learning in ELT which enables learners to become aware of increasingly diverse and complex cultures and identities that surround them. As a foundation of her study, she defines certain principles, which need to agree to the following demands:

- textual representations need to support learners in recognizing individual and cultural multiplicities of perspectives;

---

[59] However, it can additionally be asked in how far it is necessary to develop such competences when it can be assumed that young people may already have such competences. As was pointed out earlier, nowadays many students grow up in multicultural societies and learn in multicultural classrooms so that it cannot be assumed that they are culturally incompetent. Therefore, a diagnosis of students' ICC would be necessary (cf. chapter 2.3.3).

– activities and methods need to be oriented to the learners so that they are motivated to negotiate this multiplicity and are open-minded toward other perspectives in order to be encouraged and invited to broaden their own points of view through dialogues. (cf. ibid., 61)

For the task-design the principles of multi-perspectivity,[60] interactivity[61] and reflexivity[62] are essential (cf. ibid., 61-62).

Regarding approaches to inter- and/or transcultural teaching of literature, Freitag-Hild refers to Schuhmann's suggested "empathic reading" (cf. Schuhmann 2008, 89-99 in ibid., 62) and Hallet's "intertextual" and "cultural reading" (cf. Hallet 2007a, 43 in ibid., 62). Empathic reading aims at enabling learners to take the protagonist's perspective, to develop empathy and to reconstruct their worldviews, conflicts and challenges from their inner perspective. This should support the learners in understanding the others' socio-cultural situations, their processes of identity formation and individual advancement. In order to be successful in this, learners need to activate their pre-knowledge, engage in critical self-reflections, distance themselves from their own views and coordinate inner and outer perspectives (cf. ibid.). Cultural reading is understood as seeing the literary text as a part of the cultural discourse and identifying references to other cultural discourses and contexts. Recognizing and understanding intertextuality and references between cultural texts of the same topic is supposed to facilitate learners' expansion of cultural knowledge (cf. ibid., 62-63).

Freitag-Hild's research design aims at reflecting and finding out about learners' perception of cultural others, their negotiation of meaning and in how far their change of perspective contributes to their approach to otherness and their understanding of the self (cf. ibid., 140). From the lessons she attended, interviews she conducted and from learners' products she analysed, Freitag-Hild

---

[60] This entails a selection of texts which introduce multiple and diverse perspectives and intertextual text arrangements. These texts are said to add variety and a multitude of voices and perspectives to the classroom which learners need to be enabled to understand, deconstruct and interpret.

[61] This principle places dialogues and active negotiations of meaning in the foreground. Dialogues are to initiate intercultural negotiations of understanding, a transcultural process of exchange and processes of identity formation on the side of the learners. Recognizing and experiencing differences can be challenging, but also broaden the learners' perspectives and intercultural competences. Tasks thus need to ask learners to reflect upon their individual perception of and their personal responses to the texts in order to initiate dialogic interactions among learners and between leaners and teachers.

[62] This entails the notion of inter- and transcultural learning as a decentralized and critical reflection of content which moves beyond Eurocentric perspectives, essentializing images of culture and identity and a transcendence of fixed schemata. Learners are to become aware that the texts they encounter only represent one of many possible perspectives and experiences which are fictional and not necessarily similar to the other cultures' reality. Still, those texts could give insights to other cultures and thus be useful to negotiate meaning (Freitag-Hild 2010, 61-62).

draws the conclusion that British fictions of migration are indeed useful for offering young readers models of identification and are thus considered to be relevant for them. Students made use of manifold changes of perspective and eagerly negotiated cultural meaning regarding (inter)cultural conflicts, the search for identity, belonging and mechanisms of exclusion in multicultural societies. Students' ability to change perspectives beyond cultural borders, negotiate meaning dialogically, or soften fixed structures of perception depends, as Freitag-Hild estimates, on their willingness to decenter, on their cultural knowledge, the task design and the role of the instructor (cf. ibid., 351).

Although Freitag-Hild's study gives important insights into the design and effects of inter- and transcultural learning processes, I believe that the application of transcultural awareness as an awareness of heterogeneity, diversity and hybridity of cultures and identities (cf. ibid., 194, 331) is still limited. The scholar refers to otherness and identity, but focuses on processes of cultural changes and suggests further "fictions of migration" and diaspora and exile literature (ibid., 355-357). Yet, such texts remain within a limited scope of national and ethnic identity. As I go on to argue in the discussion of the sample texts and their relevance in chapters 5 and 6 and as my definition of transcultural literature in chapter 7.2 reveals, important aspects that reflect a transcultural reading only find minor consideration in Freitag-Hild's and other current publications.

Furthermore, Freitag-Hild estimates that learners' negative responses to certain characters in a narration would be signs of a lacking ability to change perspectives. Here, a self-critical reflection of an individual reading response could lead to changing a learner's negative evaluation of and emotion toward a protagonist and to supporting the willingness to change perspectives (cf. ibid., 337). Yet, these aspects are seen critically in my thesis (cf. also Alsup's objections in chapter 2.1.2). Although the suggestions for alternative activities which facilitate a change of perspective, for example on behalf of the parents in *Ae Fond Kiss* (Freitag-Hild 2010, 341-346) are meaningful, learners should have the option to reject certain positions because this can indeed be a result of their individual reading and cognitive and mental processing which Freitag-Hild rightly emphasizes in her conclusion (cf. ibid., 358-359). If this is not done and a relativity of opinions and perspectives is overemphasized, cultural competence may result in universalist thinking which does not provide orientation for a negotiation of cultural meaning.

Eberhardt (2008) tried to overcome the challenges of empirical research of ICC by conducting a qualitative study of the development of intercultural competence in 10th graders. He seeks to explore whether the objectives for intercultural learning as defined in the educational standards in Germany pose a realistic learning objective for learners at the end of their 10th year in school. In order to do so, he designed open questionnaires in which learners were asked to comment on and evaluate "culturally laden" photographs and intercultural dilemmas. They also had to report on their own experiences with members of a different culture and language (Eberhardt 2008, 282, cf. Eberhardt 2013). Moreover, he conducted dilemma interviews in which learners discussed intercultural encounters based on film clips. As to emphasize the learners' personal and individual points of view, Eberhardt designed the tasks and questions as non-suggestively as possible. For example, from a selection of eight pictures, learners were asked to choose those which would invite them to stay in France for a longer period of time or which cause them to rule out staying there (cf. 2008, 286). This part of Eberhardt's research design focuses on the learners' individual experiences and their personal links to examples of French cultures. Compared to tasks in which students are asked to change perspectives and see a certain situation from the point of view of someone who is discriminated against or who is suffering from social inequality, tasks like these avoid running the risk of activating students' answers and opinions based on social desirability.

Interestingly, neither Fäcke nor Freitag-Hild refer to the staged development of inter- and transcultural learning. While they empirically try to show that learners increase inter- and transcultural competence, are able to change perspectives and generally recognize and acknowledge hybridity and diversity, they leave an evaluation of the quality of those reflections for further investigations. Yet, Eberhardt uses his results to suggest his own staged development of cultural competences according to a further sub-categorization of Byram's *savoirs* (cf. chapter 8.1).

However, in order to describe in how far the learners increased their cultural competences, I believe it would be useful to diagnose their cultural competences prior to the studies. Taking the elaborations about ICC, transcultural competence and the design and results of the empirical studies together, further challenges of measuring, evaluating and assessing cultural competences are to be unveiled in the following chapter.

2.3.3 Challenges of Assessing Cultural Competences

The problematic issue of assessing cultural competence has caused an intense debate among scholars of foreign language teaching.[63] The discrepancy of standardization and operationalization of cultural competences on the one hand and personal involvement, identity formation, developing empathy and respect on the other hand mark the main challenge of assessing ICC. Output- and competence orientation and the development of affective attitudes toward otherness seem to be difficult to combine. Hu sees a similar concern in ICC as a key competence of ELT and defining operators and standards of assessment for this complex competence (cf. 2008, 284, cf. 2.2.1). As a consequence, she assumes that psychometric aspects of language learning that are difficult to assess will be

---

[63] E.g. Byram (1997, 2009), Byram/Gribkova/Starkey (2002), Byram/Zarate (1997), Casper-Hehne (2008), Eberhardt (2009), Hu (2008), Lafayette/Schulz (1997), Larkey (2008), Schulz (2007, 2008) and Witte (2006a, 2006b).

marginalized; I would even say that this contributes to a functional teaching and learning of languages. Hu predicts two different future scenarios:

1. Competences which are easier to assess (such as listening and reading understanding, speaking) leave enough space for intercultural, reflexive, ethical and aesthetic aspects of language learning, although they may not be easily subsumed under standardization and output orientation;
2. Competences which are difficult to operationalize are described according to standards, norms and levels anyhow in order make them assessable. (cf. Hu 2008, 285/2010, 61-62)

For Zydatiß (2005b) the second option is a strict necessity, as literary and cultural competences are threatened to be eliminated from curricula and from the contents of foreign language teaching if their conception and validation based on tasks and descriptors of competence levels is not clearly formulated and included in seminal documents. In a similar vein, Volkmann (2009) discusses the compatibility of output orientation and foreign language teaching that focuses on literary and aesthetic aspects of language teaching and on developing learners' personality and identity. How can output orientation and teaching culture find agreements?

As has become apparent in the discussion above, the development of ICC in the EFL classroom poses challenges in a number of aspects. The following section attempts to reflect upon these challenges in more detail. Based on the discussion of transcultural literature and alternative suggestions for classroom procedures, solutions for some of the challenges are suggested in chapter 8.

In her essay "The Challenge of Assessing Cultural Understanding in the Context of Foreign Language Instruction," Schulz (2007) discusses the difficulty of assessing such competences and refers to portfolio assessment[64] to evaluate students' emerging awareness. Although they are suggested in manifold publications as a suitable tool to document progress in cultural learning, Byram, for example, sees portfolios critically. A portfolio would be an "autobiography of intercultural experiences [...] which is problem-focused, it only deals with experiences which reflect difference and there may be a tendency to focus on difficulties rather than pleasurable experiences" (Byram 2005, 14). However, as

---

[64] According to Schulz, portfolios are "structured collections of a student's work over time, based on specific objectives that can [...] be related to individual student interest" (2007, 18). They are tools in which students can record and reflect on their language learning and intercultural experiences (Council of Europe, European Language Portfolio (ELP)). Within the last years, portfolios have increasingly gained importance as learning and recording tools, esp. in autonomous learning environments. Bräuer/Keller/Winter (2012) and Flächer (2009) as well as the homepage of the Council of Europe offer detailed perspectives on using portfolios in school. Documents such as the EPOSTL were designed to support teacher students in diagnosing and developing their competences and identity as teachers (Newby/Fenner/Jones 2011).

he correctly notices, "'key experiences' are not necessarily difficult or problematic." A portfolio "requires a high degree of literacy and analytical skill" (ibid.), which many learners would not necessarily be able to master because autonomous learning and acquiring competences of analysis require training (cf. Dervin 2010, 165). Although portfolios are considered to be useful for the intercultural training programs mentioned above, Casper-Hehne estimates that they are difficult to use in other contexts such as teaching in school (cf. Casper-Hehne 2008, 321), because they rely on the self-perception of the subject. Especially for younger learners a critical distance to their perception of cultural others is challenging. Casper-Hehne thus summarizes that the assessment of ICC still remains an unresolved problem (cf. ibid., 322). Moreover, portfolios are tool of students' self-assessment and using them for external assessment was originally not intended.

In order to make cultural competences assessable, Schulz suggests a summative assessment of culture-specific knowledge and abilities only (cf. Dervin 2010, 166). This could also be seen critically, because culture-specific knowledge is highly diverse and dynamic as the discussion about intracultural hybridity and diversity indicated (chapter 1). Currently, there are no instruments available that allow researchers or teachers to draw conclusions about the extent and the development of intercultural competence in intercultural foreign language teaching or about the effectiveness of methods and tasks that are said to develop intercultural competence (cf. Casper-Hehne 2008, 32).

The reflections upon ICC revealed that this competence is composed of a cognitive, affective and pragmatic level, each of which can be further divided into a number of sub-competences (cf. chapter 1.2.1). Additionally, ICC is not only complex, but revolves around dynamic, fluid and heterogeneous concepts of culture and self. Therefore, it can be asked what kind of knowledge actually serves as a foundation for intercultural competence (cf. also Schulz 2008, 244, chapter 2.2). This points at the assumption that, on a cognitive level, facts are a mere selection of what is possible to know about a culture, and that the cognitive level of cultural competence can only refer to samplings that are regarded important in a certain context; in a different context, this selection could be very different. Yet, just as cultures are characterized as dynamic and heterogeneous, so is cultural knowledge changeable. Teachers and learners need to be aware that their knowledge is only selective, as would be important for Fäcke's student who generalizes her knowledge of one Moroccan family to other Moroccan families. In some publications (e.g. Byram 1997, 96, Schulz 2008, 244) the amount of factual knowledge of a culture is described as basic knowledge – but what does this entail? In how far can cultural knowledge be reduced but still pay tribute to complexity and diversity? As Witte states, "culture is not a body of rule-governed factual knowledge like grammar that can be learned with precision and accuracy. And inherent to any attempt to teach about the foreign culture is the danger of essentializing cultural elements and thereby misrepresenting them" (2006a, 210). What kind of cognitive knowledge, regarding quality and quantity is sufficient to fulfill a certain level of intercultural competence?[65]

A similar approach holds true for the affective level of ICC. The concept aims at developing openness and a respectful and friendly approach to other cultures. It is not only a challenge to teach and develop such attitudes, but also to assess in how far students are actually successful in increasing these. When students express empathy and respect toward others in classroom discussions and essays this does not necessarily mean that they truly feel that way and react similarly in intercultural encounters outside the classroom. Dervin follows a similar line of arguments stating that "the scholar [Byram 2008, 222] rightly claims that openness to others, critical self-awareness and self-analysis are basic values in education, yet there is no way we can prove or test (or trust) if somebody *genuinely* believes in them." He concludes that "[t]herefore assessing these *savoir être* summatively is [...] impossible" (Dervin 2010, 163, emphasis in original). In an earlier publication, Byram grounds assessment criteria for *savoir être* on the definition of an intercultural speaker as someone who is interested in the "daily experience of a range of social groups within a society" (1997a, 91) and establishes that an evidence for this would be "an expression of preference" (ibid.) for such experiences. Yet, it is challenging to conclude from having students "choose between two representations of an aspect of a foreign culture in order to use the representation [...] as a basis for explaining the other culture to an interlocutor from their own culture" (ibid., 91-92) to the students' *savoir être*.[66]

Dervin's and my argumentation show traces of social desirability: learners adopt those opinions that are acceptable in democratic societies and school environments. They know which kind of responses are appreciated by teachers, they are well aware of appropriate attitudes and the teachers' expectations[67] and it is not unlikely that they remain in a mindset that agrees to what is socially desirable in testing situations. Although democracy and tolerance have been established as foundations of German laws of education, these concepts could, at times, also prevent students' honest and serious discussion of cultural issues. Dervin's analysis reveals a similar idea as he points at the misconception

---

[65] Cf. references to the value of facts and knowledge in relation to assessment and evaluation in chapter 8.1

[66] Byram mentions a further thought-provoking point in reference to this category and in view of a "readiness to engage with the conventions" of a culture stating that intercultural speakers "may not wish to adopt conventions which engage their whole personality and cultural identity [...] They may be able to accept intellectually that a particular gesture is a norm of greeting, but resist doing it themselves because it is very different from their own non-verbal behavior" (1996, 94). This example is a concrete distinction of competence and performance, of cognitive and pragmatic cultural competence. I consider Byram's estimation that students develop a "*modus vivendi*," that evidence for this category "is likely appear over time" and can be included in a portfolio, to be rather vague for the content at hand.

[67] Interestingly, an older study by Trager and Radke Yarrow (1952) revealed that already third-graders know "how to be polite about race relations even though they really thought otherwise" (in Derman-Sparks/Ramsey 2006, 41) (cf. chapter 7).

that researchers are caught in a naïve belief in their subjects' honesty – "defini-tions of intercultural competence […] are based on what people have to say about what they feel about Others, what they have learnt about others… and not on how they say it" (ibid.). This indicates parallels to portfolios, diaries and per-sonal reading logs which Dervin also considers to be problematic. In reference to Ruben (1989, 235) he states that

> if teachers ask students to keep diaries and logs, there is a subcon-scious belief that learners are honest and blunt about their experi-ences, while intercultural learning usually takes place through 'vagabond learning' which the learner may not always like to share […]. [The] analysis of the portfolios and diaries which is carried out by the teacher not only leads to big ethical problems, but also to problems of validity, interpretation and objectivity. (in Dervin 2010, 165)

Considering Havighurst's and Kohlberg's scholarship offers similar in-sights from a psychological perspective. Both have extensively researched hu-man and moral development and analysed the influence of peer groups and au-thorities on decision making. Kohlberg's moral development describes the process of learning what is wrong and right in reference to three levels, each consisting of three stages. On the first level, children generally react according to awards they receive for good and punishment they receive for bad behavior. The children perform and act within a pre-conventional phase. In the conven-tional phase, "children see certain groups (parents, teachers, policemen) in soci-ety as those who have power to determine what is right and what is wrong. At stage three, children value conformity and loyalty and often identify with those involved in maintaining the order of things." The motive of their behavior is to please others. In stage four children try to maintain and support "fixed rules and […] show […] respect for authority" (Kohlberg 1975, 49). From his research Kohlberg concluded that most people reach stage four and remain there. Hav-ighurst identifies the developmental task of young adults between the ages of 12 and 18 as "acquiring a set of values and an ethical system as a guide to behav-ior", as "developing an ideology" (1972, 69-75) and as "desiring and achieving socially responsible behavior" (ibid., 75-82) which all contribute to achieving identity.

Despite the criticism that was applied to both theorists and their work,[68] both theories help to justify a careful interpretation of students' performances of cultural learning in institutionalized environments. Children and young adults could mainly orientate their answers toward what is expected from them and not

---

[68] Kohlberg was criticized, for example, for excluding females from his investigation. Hav-ighurst's differentiation of sex and gender roles as well as his strict perspective on class can be criticized as these are socially and culturally constructed and his theory, accordingly, sup-ports limited possibilities for individuals.

independent of social norms. In these theories, the parents, peer groups, teachers and other authorities play an important role in forming opinions and displaying behavior. This is especially the case when Havighurst implies that students "should be made to feel that [their] moral convictions are important to the teacher" (ibid., 73).

Here, Butler's concept of "performativity" which describes constructions of identity as a result of performing actions within social norms and laws, adds a further relevant facet. "Performativity" entails the notion that performances are always realized within certain social contexts in which existing structures have established norms and laws. These are not static but open to change, and so is performativity. Butler understands performativity "not as a singular or deliberate 'act,' but, rather, as the reiterative and citational practice by which discourse produces the effects that it names" (1993, 2). Further it is a "reiterative power of discourse to produce the phenomena that it regulates and constrains" (ibid.) which can be applied to further markers of identity beyond gender on which Butler focuses. For the discussion at hand, this aspect is important as also the EFL classroom sets a certain socio-political and educational frame dominated by certain rules of discourse and norms. I assume that students are highly aware of this frame and are likely to participate in cultural discourses accordingly (cf. chapter 8.3).

In a similar sense, Block estimates that identities are "bodily and linguistic enactments of discourse at particular times and in particular places" (2007, 17). Thus, if school and ELT classrooms are understood to represent a micro-society, students' performances in this particular time and place of ELT are likely to be in accordance with the underlying norms of ELT, of which tolerance and respect for the other are main features. Students' performances when reflecting upon cultural issues in ELT could be in accordance with expected and constructed ideas, and not necessarily represent performance and competence outside the classroom.

Furthermore, it can also be asked in how far teachers actually have the right to interfere with learners' identity formation and influence the development of their personality (cf. 9.1.1). Besides, observations of learners are often influenced by various subjective feelings of the observer, be it fatigue, certain emotions and other exterior factors; they tend to be subjective and co-constructed, lacking validity and reliability (cf. in Dervin 2010, 165). Beyond these issues, it is debatable whether assessment of cultural competences can actually be achieved in a normative classroom. Schulz considers the assessment and grading of cross-cultural attitudes to be most problematic, too, as it runs the risk of indoctrination (cf. 2008, 246). Both teachers and students are simply expected to develop positive attitudes toward people from their own and other cultures and toward beliefs that are implemented in their culture's social and political system.

Finally, the pragmatic level of ICC can be seen critically in terms of assessment and evaluation as well. On the one hand, it is possible that certain competences only manifest themselves in retrospective, which is especially true for *savoir s'engager* and *savoir faire* (Byram 1996, 103). On the other hand, as certain in-class reflections do not mean that a similar attitude is visible in the daily life of the students, a (huge) gap can exist between classroom performance and internalized competences: Knowing that members of certain cultures are offended when someone looks them directly in the eye does not mean that a learner does not do this anyhow; knowing that some cultures tend to offer open invitations to their houses does not mean that one is not disappointed when the dinner party never happens. In a similar sense, expressing empathy toward a character in a text does not reflect a respectful approach to other people in real life. As Dervin describes, "there is lack of reliability between acts and discourse/discourse and acts: an individual may behave in an 'appropriate' manner in a certain situation, though he/she may be disgusted by his/her behavior" (in Dervin 2010, 163, de Florio-Hansen uses a similar differentiation, cf. 2010, 64). Thus, teachers need to be aware that a desired opinion in the classroom does not necessarily mean that the learner applies this opinion outside of the classroom. Students can be able to write great essays using perfect language and vividly engage in discussions about respect toward otherness, but this has no immediate consequence for how they experience otherness in real life and how they actually engage in intercultural encounters. Even if students engage in intercultural encounters and repeatedly have contact with citizens of a particular country, this would not mean perfect mastery of intercultural competences (cf. Zarate 2003, 113), if one accepts that this is what education should strive for.

From Anderson's concept of understanding nations as "imagined communities" one can deduce that the cognitive knowledge and affective and pragmatic codes of behavior that are included in cultural teaching and thus assigned and applied to a culture are social and socio-cultural constructions ascribed to that culture. Volkmann, too, points at the constructedness of imagined communities which is even supported when students mediate cultural understanding by changing perspectives and perceive the other culture from an inside and outside perspective (cf. 2010, 102). Putting McLaughlin's estimation in a classroom perspective, this negotiation creates a "mythical 'other'" which becomes "quite easy to understand" (2007, 33) as it is based on the constructions of the self. In a similar line of arguments, Bauman's understanding of society as a "liquid modernity" rejects notions of cultural knowledge, as cultures and societies cannot "keep to any shape for long and are constantly ready (and prone) to change" (2000, 2). As Delanoy states, for language education this means that "habitualised knowledge is no longer sufficient to cope with changing demands" (2012, 163).

Taking the cognitive, affective and pragmatic level of ICC together, it can moreover be asked whether all three are of equal importance, and which combination of them is sufficient in order to be culturally competent (cf. also Hu 2010, 66, Schulz 2008, 245-246). Could a lack of cognitive competence be balanced by respectfully engaging with members of a different culture? In how far is a pragmatic application of intercultural competence more important than being able to reflect upon critical incidents in pen-and-paper tests? Should assessment take into consideration that "a person who is 'normally' competent in certain contexts may be very incompetent in other situations" (in Dervin 2010, 164)? The correlation between different levels needs to be taken into account as a high level of cognitive knowledge about a culture does not mean that this knowledge is also used in intercultural encounters; its pragmatic application is no logical consequence.

Furthermore, the assumption that intercultural competence develops in similar stages as language competences needs to be seen critically, as implied above. Even though students may be beginners of learning English, they do not necessarily have a similar level of ICC. It cannot be assumed that an A1 learner of English has an ethnocentric worldview, as benevolent attitudes toward others are not only developed by foreign language education but depend on personal experiences such as socialization, migration or growing up in a multicultural neighborhood, too. A speaker can be way more experienced on a cultural than on a linguistic level. Students may have already learnt another language through which they have gained ICC. At the same time, it can be the case that a learner's level of English is close to native speaker competence, but that he or she is culturally unaware, insensitive and disrespectful. Thus, when a student does not elaborately reflect upon intercultural issues presented in a text, unjustified assumptions about his or her intercultural competence could be derived, as cultural and language competence can develop very differently.[69]

Additionally, the fact that learners who take part in foreign language learning are within the process of socialization in a certain cultural mindset needs to be considered when reflecting on the assessment of ICC. This mindset includes previous knowledge, assumptions and opinions about other cultures transferred through media and information technology. Which role does this pre-knowledge – or these preconceptions and stereotypes play (cf. Hu 1995, Kaikkonen 1995, Volkmann 2010)? Would it not be necessary to diagnose learners' intercultural competence before engaging them in intercultural learning activities in order to draw conclusions about their development and the effect of the learning process as such? If learners are exposed to activities and methods that advance intercultural competences, how can they demonstrate that they have gained this cultural competence or are making improvements and extending their competences to a more advanced level? A competence increase can only be seen if learners had not possed certain competences before they took part in the actual learning process. Thus, a diagnosis would be necessary in which learners may show that they are culturally incompetent or lack certain aspects of cultural competences. However, it is questionable whether the learners

---

[69] This is also one reason why Fäcke allowed her students to rely on German in their cultural reflections (cf. chapter 2.3.2).

would allow teachers to diagnose this because they are aware of the importance of such competences.

In this context the question arises in how far classroom reflections actually influence the cultural competence of learners. On the one hand, many young people nowadays grow up in multicultural societies and are, for the most part, surrounded by cultural otherness and diversity on a daily basis (cf. above). Maybe they are already culturally competent and classroom reflections point to certain problems of intercultural encounters in the first place. Could raising awareness of stereotypes in ELT not unlearn respect and reflective understanding of the other which learners had already internalized from daily experiences? On the other hand, it can be asked how effective methods and activities actually are that are applied to developing intercultural competence (cf. also Casper-Hehne 2008, 310) if the other is usually substituted by a text? If learners are to develop ICC and have difficulty in doing so, how can teachers support them and foster and promote their learning (cf. in Hu 2008, 289)?

This discussion shows that the challenges of assessing cultural competence are visible in four different areas.

(1) the differentiation of performance and competence (knowledge and its practical application),
(2) social desirability,
(3) the interplay of the sub-competences of ICC and their different levels, and
(4) the assumption that intercultural competence develops in similar stages as language competence.

De Florio-Hansen's conclusion from a critical discussion of measuring cultural competence also applies to my argumentation: a valid and reliable evaluation of cultural competence as a complex, demanding, and ethical objective of ELT is hardly possible. Cultural competence is manifested in actual behavior and action in everyday life. In how far learners have gained such competences can best be observed in cultural encounters, processes to which teachers only have limited access and for which they can only interpret indications (cf. also in de Florio-Hansen 2010, 66-69).

The factors that make the assessment, evaluation and measurement of cultural competences difficult serve as a critical outlook to the following chapters. Especially the criticism of the affective and pragmatic level will be elaborated upon in more detail. As a reaction to the literary exemplifications in Part B, chapter 8 suggests different task designs and approaches to developing transcultural competences which help to find solutions for the aforementioned challenges. In this context, I will also refer to the reading competence model that was suggested by Eva Burwitz-Melzer (2007) and which can be transferred to cultural learning (cf. chapter 8.3).

One further aspect that needs to be taken into consideration when reflecting upon the development of cultural competences is the material on which this is based. As the following chapter reveals, this issue is of utmost importance as texts often imply certain assumptions about cultural otherness. Therefore, I argue that the choice of appropriate texts is most essential in order to enable readers to engage in meaningful reflections about otherness and develop ICC.

3. Canadian Literature and Content in ELT Guidelines and Teaching Material

Many scholars have published on the characteristics of beneficial reading material for ELT. Collie and Slater, for example, consider meaningful, enjoyable, interesting and thought-provoking literature to be useful for the English classroom (cf. Collie/Slater 2007, 6-7). Literature read in class should have relevance to the students' life experience, appeal to their emotions and dreams, and be motivating due to high suspense (cf. also in Surkamp/Nünning 2008, 46, 49). When trying to find such texts, Thaler offers rather pragmatic advice and refers to catalogues and brochures of publishing companies in which books are recommended according to the age and reading ability of the learners (cf. 2008, 19). Those catalogues often include short descriptions of the texts which refer to the aspects mentioned by Collie and Slater. Whereas Collie and Slater focus on the texts as such, Thaler rather emphasizes more functional criteria: in how far do texts conform to the curriculum, are methodological material and text-related media available, and in how far are the texts practical for language learning. Also linguistic difficulty, thematic complexity, length, and aesthetic quality (cf. Lazar 1993, 52-55, Surkamp/Nünning 2008, 45, 49, Thaler 2008, 20) are important markers.

In order to argue in favour of implementing Canadian texts in ELT based on their potential for inter- and transcultural learning, it is necessary to have a closer look at texts that are currently used in the EFL classroom. I assume that

- this selection may be sufficient for inter- but not for transcultural encounters and that
- the texts that support encounters with otherness only offer a limited perspective on the culture represented and that this representation reflects a 'minority' position from which the 'other' culture needs to act against a malevolent majority.

With regard to these assumptions, I have a detailed look at the curricula and guidelines of North Rhine-Westphalia, as these provide insights to the kinds of texts that are recommended to be read in class (chapter 3.1). Within TEFL theory and ELT practice it is a well-known fact that curricula nowadays seldom prescribe specific texts that have to be read. These documents rather refer to topics for which teachers and students can choose reading material. Textbooks by educational publishing houses usually recommend reading material which agrees to the demands of the curricula, too. Providing open suggestions for literature is in line with current educational developments that focus on increasing competences: students generally need to be enabled to deal with texts analytically, critically and creatively (cf. Hallet/Königs 2010, 55). The choice of the literary example with which these competences are developed increasingly lies with the teachers and learner groups. Yet, the curricula for higher secondary schools which lead to the school-leaving exam (*Abitur*) include more concrete recommendations as tasks are set by central commissions for each federal country.

The idea that young adult literature entails benefits for language learning, especially on a cultural level is anything but new (cf. chapter 2). Texts have long been the foundation for 'authentic' language input and have been part of classroom discussions and final exams. Yet, with the creation of common school leaving exams and partially drawn from the discussion of a literary canon within the frame of postcolonial debates and changing perceptions of culture, a tendency to prefer specific novels and writers can be identified. However, a critical look at the inclusion of literature in ELT curricula unveils that educators hardly consider Canadian literature for young readers as a source for classroom reflections, despite its huge potential (cf. chapter 3.2). In this context, Merkl's (2005a, 2005b) studies support my argument to include more Canada in ELT as he revealed university students' massive lack of knowledge about Canada. I supplement this by analysing how Canada is implemented in textbooks (chapter 3.3) and how Canadian literature is reflected in current TEFL discourses (chapter 3.4). These aspects not only serve to justify more and other Canadian content in ELT, but also to see selected texts of Canadian literature as an example based on which the concept of transcultural literature can be developed.

3.1 Literary Texts in EFL Classrooms and Curricula

Apart from academic investigations into the complex benefits of literature and the development of ICC, the CEF includes general references to implementing literature in ELT. Furthermore, and as described above, national curricula, especially those for advanced classes, refer to the usability of literature in language teaching. While the references to literature on a European level, i.e. in the CEF are only included on the margins, literatures' potential to function as a means for refuting existing social imbalances, creating imaginative alternative worldviews, and for developing strategies for reintegrating marginalized discourses is carved out more clearly in the new German Standards of Education (2012). The guidelines on a federal governmental level reflect the most holistic perspective on literature in ELT. By reconsidering social and cultural norms that are taken for granted, literature offers students the chance to reassess the self in view of the other that is presented in texts. Thus, literature gains additional value which is essential for intercultural learning (cf. Lütge 2012b, Surkamp/Nünning 2008, 14, Volkmann 2010, 249, Volkmann 2012, cf. above).

Although it is generally true that the CEF refers to using literature, it is astonishing that it does so only in a very condensed way. As Burwitz-Melzer (2007), Lütge (2012b) and Volkmann (2009) observe, "only 11 lines within the

CEFR refer to 'aesthetic uses of language'" (Lütge 2012b, 193) which would be characteristic of and hint at literature. This marginal position indicates a rather pragmatic orientation of language learning and a "neglect of literary learning" (ibid.). Similarly, also the Standards of Education for the first foreign language in secondary schools (KMK-Standards 2003 and 2004) hardly refer to literature (cf. Burwitz-Melzer 2007, 130-132). While both documents ascribe a central position to cultural learning, neither refers in detail to one of the main means through which cultural learning can be achieved.

In comparison, the Standards of Education for the school-leaving exam of 2012 include direct references to texts from the target culture and in the foreign language in the context of ICC (cf. KMK-Standards 2012, 20-22, cf. Burwitz-Melzer 2013b, 46). These, thus, acknowledge literature's potential to give insights to individual, universal and culture-specific views (KMK-Standards 2012, 10). References to literary texts were formerly implied in the communicative competence 'reading,' yet with no differentiation between fiction and nonfiction (Burwitz-Melzer 2013b, 45). However, in the Standards of 2012 reading competence is extended by the newly added text and media competence (cf. KMK-Standards 2012, 22-23, Burwitz-Melzer 2013b, 45). This competence refers to the ability to understand and interpret texts independently, purposefully and in their historical and social context, and to the ability to offer justifications for respective interpretations. Text and media competence explicitly goes beyond basic functional communicative competences (cf. KMK-Standards 2012, 22) and can be seen as a transversal competence (cf. Burwitz-Melzer 2013b, 45). As also Burwitz-Melzer (ibid., 46-47) notes, this competence attempts to include various dimensions such as ICC and communicative competence, and explicitly refers to text analysis and interpretation, changing perspectives and recognizing patterns of the protagonists' behavior. Additionally, students are expected to critically reflect upon their initial understanding of texts which entails that reading understanding is not only a process but could be divided into various stages. On the advanced level, text and media competences also include the ability to recognize aesthetic characteristics of a text and to use these for individual text productions, practically and in critical reflection and reception of processes (cf. KMK-Standards 2012, 23). The inclusion of literature in the new educational standards provides a better foundation for operationalizing competences which are indeed essential for literary reading (cf. Burwitz-Melzer 20103b, 47).

While Burwitz-Melzer praises the inclusion of example texts and tasks,[70] it is worthwhile reflecting upon the two fictional texts in more detail, as especially the implementation of Syal's text seems to be closer to a functional paradigm again.

---

[70] *I am Charlotte Simmons* by Tom Wolfe (KMK-Standards 2012, 44-67), *Life isn't all Ha Ha He He* by Meera Syal (1999) (ibid., 103-145) and Barack Obama's inaugural address (ibid., 68-102).

Two out of four tasks for *I am Charlotte Simmons* are directly related to reading and ICC, when students have to

- analyse texts according to the protagonist's feelings and emotions, incl. settings and characters, use of language, body language (counting 30%)[71] and
- write an email about meeting the new roommate from Beverly's point of view (counting 25%). (KMK-Standards 2012, 45)

The other two tasks focus on mediation and written communication: writing an article about getting a sports scholarship (counting 25%), and on an analyses of cartoons as well as discussing how school prepares for future careers and life (counting 20%). Those tasks not only connect reading, literary and cultural learning, but develop linguistic and aesthetic competences, too. Regarding reading competence, the tasks demand a global and detailed understanding of the text and the ability to filter emotions in relation to different characters. Students also need to use language awareness to differentiate cultural and regional varieties of English and relate these to a social background which both can be located in the broad context of ICC. The mediation task regards ICC, too, as it speaks to the students' cultural knowledge of the target culture. When the demands for the creative writing task combine using a certain register, showing empathy, changing perspectives and applying cultural background knowledge, a connection to important elements of aesthetic language use and ICC is visible. All in all, the text analysis counts 30% for the final grade, creative writing and the mediation task 25% each. Thus, 75% of the final grade is directly connected to literary and cultural competences which can certainly be seen as an improvement compared to the Standards of 2003 and 2004.

In a second example, *Life isn't all Ha Ha He He*, students are expected to

- read the text and match phrases to certain sections (15%) and statements to characters,
- "outline the clichés about Pakistanis and the reality as presented in the text" (20%),
- analyse the narrator's language and its effect (20%) (language analysis),
- relate a statement by the author to Tania's attitude (25%), and
- write a speech for a "festival with music and food from the different neighbours' home countries" as part of a project that "celebrate[s] and improve[s] intercultural relationships" from the perspective of an exchange student (20%) (cf. KMK-Standards 2012, 111).

---

[71] Percentages indicate the extent to which this task counts for the final grade.

An alternative task refers to a role play in which a student is to discuss the benefits of a music workshop to bring "together people from different ethnic backgrounds" with a Member of Parliament who sees this workshop critically (20%) (cf. ibid., 112).

The first three tasks range within close reading and detailed understanding; in order to solve these tasks students need to summarize and interpret the text according to selected aspects. What is surprising, though, is that although this text focuses on cultural issues, the tasks strongly focus on language and style which could be seen as an attempt to balance content and form but which pays less tribute to the cultural dimension of the text. Also in the part that reflects upon the content of the speech, formal aspects are mentioned first and the relevance of intercultural encounters is only referred to as a third aspect. Additionally, hopes for positively living together with other cultures, as they are to be expressed in the speech (cf. ibid., 140), and the focus on music and food as the elements around which the festival is planned, reveal a rather superficial understanding of a multicultural society (cf. chapter 2.2).

Thus, although attempts were made to include literary texts and competences as well as ICC in the Standards, especially the example of *Life isn't all Ha Ha He He* does so on a rather shallow level. Furthermore, it is striking that such competences are expected on this level when the Standards of Education for the lower classes do not refer to their prior development (also noted by Burwitz-Melzer 2007, 128-130 in relation to the CEF); the Standards for the intermediate level of ELT need to be adjusted to these demands and prepare the respective competences at early stages already. Yet, compared to the tasks suggested in the requirements for the school-leaving exam of 2002 (cf. ibid., 135), the tasks in this document allow students to draw from their own experiences and their personal responses to the texts which is in line with the principles of reader-response criticism.

It is remarkable that in relation to those governmental guidelines, the school curricula which are written by groups of teachers and other practitioners do in fact refer to literature and literary learning. In North Rhine-Westphalia, the curriculum for primary schools demands the implementation of authentic children's books (cf. MSW 2008, 9). The Ministry of Education published didactic and methodological training materials for primary school teachers which include one module on children's literature in ELT. This contains information on the interplay of literature and the development of ICC, arguments for implementing literature on a primary English level and criteria for selecting books. Moreover, it offers a list of storybooks which are considered useful in primary ELT. This list, however, is not organized by topic but by author and does not provide information on the books' linguistic level (cf. Bezirksregierung NRW 2008), so that teachers have to look up each book in order to decide whether it fits their teaching objectives thematically and linguistically. However, this list contains books such as Eileen Browne's *Handa's Surprise* (1993) and James Mayhew's *Katie in London* (2003), which have an explicit intercultural focus.

Books like David McKee's *Elmar*-series (e.g. 2007) and Maurice Sendak's *Where the Wild Things Are* (2000) enable children to engage with otherness on levels beyond ethnicity.

The curricula for the secondary school types suggest general guidelines and topics: The curriculum for "Hauptschule", for example, refers to easy readers (cf. MSJK 2011, 20) without mentioning examples. The curriculum for advanced learners (grades 11 and 12) regards changing perspectives as a foundational didactic principle as this supports understanding and experiencing other cultures from different points of view (cf. chapter 2.1). It suggests certain topics for discussions in class and supplements these by specific texts (cf. MSWWF 1999, 25). For reflections upon gender relationships and a changing system of values, the following texts are suggested:

- o Frank Moorhouse's short stories "Five Incidents Concerning the Flesh and Blood" (1972-1976) and "A Person of Accomplishment" (1972),
- o Ian McEwan's novel *The Child in Time* (1987),
- o Armistead Maupin's *Tales of the City* (1978),
- o Arthur Miller's drama *The Last Yankee* (1992), or
- o Harold Pinter's *Moonlight* (1993) (cf. MSWWF 1999, 31)

For the representation of the students' own culture from the perspective of the other culture, as entailed in a confrontation with Germany's past, the curriculum suggests the

- – short stories
  - o "Evermore" by Julian Barnes (1995),
  - o "Nazi Christmas" by Hugo Hamilton (1996), and
- – the novels
  - o *Schindler's Ark* by Thomas Keneally (1982),
  - o *How German is it* by Walter Abish (1980), and
  - o *Out of the Shelter* by David Lodge (1970). (cf. MSWWF 1999, 32.[72]

A similar approach to seeing one culture from the perspective of another is visible within the recommendation of Hanif Kureishi's *Buddha of Suburbia* (1990) and Timothy Mo's *Sour Sweet* (1982) in which students can reflect upon the perception of Great Britain from the perspective of cultural 'minorities' living within Great Britain. Julia Alvarez' *How the Garcia Girls Lost Their Accent* (1991) about Hispanic women growing up in the U.S. and Nadine Gordimer's

---

[72] These recommendations, however, assume that 'German' is the reference for identifying "own culture" and that the members of the learner group share German history. In multicultural societies this cannot always be assumed. The inclusion of such references in curricula unveils a rather German-centric perspective on negotiating otherness.

July's People (1981) about South African conflicts between black and white from the perspective of a white protagonist (cf. MSWWF 1999, 32) offer further insights to cultural groups adjusting to life in the face of certain power structures. Further topics and respective texts, for example, include (cf. ibid., 81-86):

- Oral History, Adolescence, Family Ethics, Racial/Ethnic/Gender Discrimination
  o Mark Behr's *The Smell of Apples* (1995),
  o Sandra Cisneros' *The House on Mango Street* (1984)
- From Rags to Riches: An Irish Success Story
  o Roddy Doyle's *The Commitments* (1987) (*The Snapper* (1990) and *The Van* (1991) as alternatives)
- American Dreams – American Nightmares
  o Sam Shepard's *True West* (1981)
- Understanding African Life Styles, Traditions and Values
  o Chinua Achebe's "Akueke" (1972),
  o Ken Saro-Wiwa's *A Month and a Day: A Detention Diary* (1995, passages)
- Rio and After: Chances for Planet Earth/Global Solutions
  o T.C. Boyle's "Top of the Food Chain" (1994)
- The Broad Spectrum of Love
  o Shakespeare's *Romeo and Juliet* (quarto version 1597)
- From Utopia to the Present – Limits of Liberty
  o Margaret Atwood's *Handmaid's Tale* (1985)

The tasks that the government suggests for the school-leaving exam refer to texts such as
  o Arundhati Roy's *The God of Small Things* (1997) (cf. MSWWF 1999, 126),
  o T.C. Boyle's *The Tortilla Curtain* (1995) (cf. ibid., 141) and
  o Nick Hornby's *Fever Pitch* (1992) (ibid., 144).

Recently, titles like *A Star called Henry* (1999) by Roddy Doyle or *Angela* by James Moloney (1998), which revolve around Irish and Australian culture and history respectively, have been added. Additionally, a number of texts from South Africa and India have been used as obligatory reading material for school leaving exams.

This overview shows that most of the texts that are recommended for ELT are from the 1980s and 1990s, although some are more than 50 years old. Apart from some of the picture books recommended for primary schools (cf. above), none of the texts were published post 1996. What is more, maybe apart from *Fever Pitch*, none of the texts in the curricula for advanced learners are part of young adult fiction. This exclusion contradicts the benefits and potential

of such texts that were discussed in chapter 2, and it confirms the critical observations of a more or less fixed canon of books that are read in ELT (cf. Sur-
kamp/Nünning 2008, 39, Thaler 2008, 19).

Even though Surkamp and Nünning as well as Thaler point at the advantages of a traditional literary canon, they come to the conclusion that current
English literatures offer great potential for ELT, as these would be considered to
be more motivating for students due to their topicality. New English literatures
include formerly marginalized authors and protagonists and refer to issues
which are currently relevant to cultures and societies. These current texts often
make use of postmodern and innovative literary devices like multi-perspectivity,
unreliable narrations, intertextuality and meta-fiction (cf. Surkamp/Nünning
2008, 41-42), which supports the development of literary literacy[73] (cf. Burwitz-
Melzer 2013a, 55-70, Lütge 2012b, 191-202). It goes without saying that the
texts included in the curricula have potential for cultural learning. Nevertheless,
and although the recommendations of literature to be used for preparing the
school-leaving exam reflect a slight turn toward more modern pieces, I would
question in how far these present motivating reading material and accessible
points of references for young learners.

Moreover, in most of the intercultural texts that are read in ELT, *Angela, The House on Mango Street* or *A Lesson Before Dying*[74] (Ernest J. Gaines
1993) for example, a strong connection of coming to terms with multicultural
identity, a struggle for a better life, and the difficult search for a cultural self become apparent. Despite the benefits of contemporary literature as pointed out by
Surkamp and Nünning, I would like to raise critical awareness for the depiction
of otherness in many such texts. As this aspect will be essential in the discussion in chapter 7, I like to signpost here that especially postcolonial texts focus
on a search for cultural identity within a malevolent society and display cultural
identity as issue-laden identity. The (multicultural) protagonists' search for a
balance between differing cultural heritages is presented as a suffering from oppression, a battle which brings them close to their limits. Yet, intercultural and
particularly transcultural learning should not remain on such a level but go beyond this representation of otherness. Therefore, I argue for altering suggested
literature for ELT to include young adult fiction with more balanced representations of othernesses.

While the following argumentation aims at justifying a closer look at Canadian young adult fiction for ELT, its sample character should be emphasized.
This focus is in line with further suggestions of cultural contexts and literary

---

[73] As Lütge outlines, the development of literary literacy is of utmost importance in order to "re-
integrate literature into the competence discourse" (2012b, 200). She summarizes various
scholars' approaches to build a foundation for literary literacy. Hallet's approach is rightly
seen as a promising one as it provides a distinction of stages of literary literacy and goes beyond a mere skill-perspective (cf. Lütge 2012b, 198-199).

[74] *A Lesson Before Dying* was one of the foundational texts of the written school leaving exam
in Niedersachsen in 2012 (cf. Niedersächsischen Kultusministerium 2010).

texts that were formerly pushed to the margins due to a strong focus on the U.S., Great Britain and an established canon of texts in ELT. In *Teaching the New English Cultures and Literatures* (Eisenmann/Grimm/Volkmann 2010), for instance, the contributors focus on cultures beyond the U.S. and Great Britain and unveil the potential of including Canada (Doff in ibid., 3-18), Australia and New Zealand (Grimm in ibid., 19-42), South Africa (Feurle in ibid., 43-58), India (Lindner in ibid., 59-72), the Caribbean (Mitchell in ibid., 72-90) and South-East Asia (Ahrens in ibid., 91-106) and their respective literatures in ELT. These rather theoretic elaborations are supplemented by concrete texts, for example Rau's discussion of Margaret Atwood's *The Handmaid's Tale* (in ibid., 109-124), Eisenmann's discussion of Jane Harrison's *Stolen* (in ibid. 2010, 125-138), Glaap's discussion of plays from Aotearoa (in ibid., 139-150), or Niergarden's reflection upon Caribbean poetry (in ibid., 197-216). Using Canadian texts extends this approach of including new English literatures.

3.2 The Case of Canada

Beyond certain challenges ELT teachers face when including post-colonial literature and widening the scope of teaching English to a global world (cf. Eisenmann/Grimm/Volkmann 2010, vii-xiii), new English literatures and cultures offer the chance to increase the students', and certainly also the teachers' global awareness that English is indeed not only spoken in the U.S. and Great Britain. Additionally, considering an extended frame of reference can trigger processes of "decolonizing the mind" (Ngugi 1986 in Volkmann 2010, xi). The questions "whether a country or an area qualifies for EFL teaching or whether a postcolonial text passes the usual aesthetic norms" (Eisenmann/Grimm/Volkmann 2010, xi) reflect Eurocentric perspectives and a prevalence of Eurocentric aesthetic standards. Therefore asking those questions is seen critically (cf. ibid.)

Yet, especially in the context of transcultural learning and teaching, the issue of using a nationally-defined focus seems pressing, even if it is seen as an example. Certainly, the transcultural concept is based on the argument that "an adherence to territorial notions of culture essentializes individual differences, much in the same way that the category 'race' used to" (Reichl 2013, 108). However, I would still like to ask the question "Why (not) Canada in ELT?" and use the answers as justifications for applying example texts of Canadian young adult fiction within a transcultural frame. Beyond this sample character of this cultural frame, references to students' knowledge about Canada, the in- or rather exclusion of Canadian content in textbooks and Canada's high potential for cultural learning provide further arguments.

In 2002 and 2003, Merkl conducted studies at the University of Wurzburg in which he explored undergraduate students' knowledge of Canada's geography, society, literature and culture. The overall conclusion was that "the image of this country is strongly determined by hetero-stereotypes" (Merkl 2005a, 1) and that students' knowledge hardly goes beyond generalizations and preconceptions. When the students first had to draw a map of Canada, it became obvious "that a considerable number of students do not have the slightest idea of the country's natural features" (Merkl 2005b, 247). For example the students indicated that

- there is only 'one' Great Lake,
- the Great Lakes are at the foot of the Rocky Mountains (with Alaska being in the north-east part of North-America),
- the Rocky Mountains stretch from the East to West and the Great Lakes are somewhere in the (sub)arctic north,
- the St. Lawrence River runs from the Rocky Mountains – which mark the American-Canadian border – westward to the Atlantic Ocean, and
- the Great Plains are in the north-west of Canada next to Alaska. (ibid., 247)

Merkl reveals additional misconceptions within the cultural composition of Canadian society, as students were not aware of the term 'hyphenated Canadians' when they name English, French, Indians, Italians and Japanese as communities within Canada (cf. ibid.). Moreover, the identification of the Maple Leaf as the dominant symbol of Canadian identity and "the Mounties, the beaver, the moose, the grizzly bear, ice hockey and [...] the CN Tower, [...] the enormous size of the country, [...] wildlife [and] the lumberjacks living in log houses" (ibid.) add to the need of including more Canada in order to modify knowledge and assumptions of the second largest country in the world. Merkl relates the causes for such inadequate knowledge about Canada to its marginal consideration in curricula and teaching material (cf. 2013, 15), which I further elaborate in chapter 3.3. In order to deconstruct such oversimplified and stereotypical preconceptions, it is necessary to include more Canadian content in ELT.

In 1990, Groß explained the preference of British and U.S. American content, with

i.   historical: England is home of the English language,
ii. socio-political: Great Britain as a member of the EU and the USA as a political and economic world power are more important to Germany than Canada, and
iii. pragmatic facts: for German students it is more likely to visit Great Britain or the U.S. through exchange programs. (cf. Groß 1990, 174)

Whereas these arguments may have been valid in 1990, it is disputable whether they still are post 2015. Even though "England is home of the English language," it is not clear why this should serve as a reason for focusing cultural teachings on the UK. The great variety of English accents and dialects make it interesting for ELT, especially in connection with other countries and foreign cultures. Besides, it is questionable whether the political and economic status of a country counts more than its social and cultural enrichments for teaching a language. Canada's official multiculturalism and its manifold genres of art add to the high potential for implementing more Canada in ELT (cf. below). Furthermore, Groß's last statement has nowadays lost validity because the homepage http://schueleraustauschweltweit.de lists 37 agencies that support German students who would like to spend a year in Canada, studying at public and private schools (as of November 2014).

Regarding the use of literature, Glaap and Rau (1993) reflect the arguments that were mentioned in chapter 2, but add that literature which seems geographically and culturally further away and does not present options of identification at first sight leads to deeper reflections and a distanced perspective on the subject matter. The less familiar students are with an issue presented through a text, the more likely it is that they are intrigued by it, since the unknown, the other, raises people's interest. Additionally, judgements would be less prejudiced (cf. Glaap/Rau 1993, 107-125). This would especially be the case with Canadian literature as students may not have come across Canadian issues before.

One further and very important argument lies with Canada's policy of multiculturalism which was first presented in parliament by Prime Minister Trudeau in 1971 and was confirmed by the Multiculturalism Act in 1988[75] (cf. Ernst/Glaser 2010, 8) – Canada was the first nation that inscribed politics of multiculturalism into its constitution. In Canada, immigration has played an essential role already long before its establishment as a nation; people especially from Europe and Asia have continuously immigrated to Canada, or moved within its borders. In fact, most Canadians, apart from the Inuit and First Nations, can look back at some kind of immigration history in their families.[76] Throughout the centuries, Canada has become a multicultural nation that reproduces multicultural artefacts such as music and literature. Although multiculturalism faces manifold criticism, positive and negative,[77] this inherent moment of defining Canadian cultures serves as a rich connection to the approach of inter- and transcultural learning and ICC. While new cultures are welcome to contribute to Canadian society, aboriginal cultures play an important role in defining Canadian society as well. In fact, "the Canadian approach to integrating aboriginal societies and their history is often seen as a model by other countries with large aboriginal populations" (Doff 2010, 4). Without entering a detailed discussion about Canada's multicultural society and politics, its advantages and disad-

---

[75] Officially known as Bill-C 93, the "Act for the preservation and enhancement of multiculturalism in Canada" (cf. chapter 4).

[76] Cf. discussion on Canadian national identity in chapter 5.2.1. Tunkel (2012) offers a comprehensive summary.

[77] For a comprehensive summary of this discourse see Ernst/Glaser (2010, 8-13), cf. below.

vantages, supporters and critics at this point (cf. chapter 4.2.1), it should be said that this composition of ethnic groups offers to explore with students both the benefits and challenges of multiculturalism, not only because they might live in multicultural communities themselves, but because Canadian literature provides insights into the different aspects of social and cultural diversity.

Canada's multitude of facets can also be found in further areas. Canada has breathtaking landscapes and vibrant cities, serves as a new homeland for immigrants from all walks of life and is the original territory of First Nation people; Canada is heartland and hinterland, as Glaap and Rau (1993) summarize. The potential of using Canada as a focus in ELT lies with the never-correct answer to a number of questions that can be asked in these different contexts. On a global scale, Canada is moving further into the centre of global issues, be it in reference to immigration policy, multicultural understanding or the protection of the environment, particularly in light of recent debates about the oil industry and First Nations' land rights. Thus, it points out connections to Global Education, too.[78]

The discussion of Canada's potential for ELT has shown that its linguistic and cultural diversity is a rewarding topic for vivid discussions and investigations in ELT. As Doff correctly concludes, Canada "has a lot more to offer than beavers and bilingualism" (2010, 5). When English lessons teach about English-speaking countries and cultures, Canadian examples as points of references should be acknowledged and further explored.

One approach to help students engage with Canada beyond facts and figures, as Merkl (cf. 2005a, 2005b) and Doff (2010) demand, is the usage of Canadian literature in ELT. This agrees to Doff's and Schulze-Engler's notion that New Literatures in English "provide a fascinatingly diverse corpus of literary texts shaped by [...] influences of various origins" and "constitute an enormously productive site for engaging with transculturality." Canadian literature would be one example of such New Literatures in English (cf. 2011, 4, 12). Already in 1990 Korte assumed that an increased recognition of Canadian literature would be especially beneficial for developing intercultural competence.

Apart from the potential of Canada for transcultural learning, a look at current publications in the fields of transcultural and transnational studies indicates that national foci and 'trans'-perspectives are not mutually exclusive. For instance, Tunkel's extended study on *Transcultural Imaginaries* (2012) displays an interdisciplinary perspective on recent Canadian historical fiction from a postcolonial and postmodern viewpoint which also refers to transculturalism. When Tunkel identifies parameters of transcultural features as space, place, time, voices and perspectives, transfer, exchange and resistance in Canadian texts, this supports the perception of Canadian literature from a transcultural perspective, despite a national focus. Furthermore, Ernst and Glaser's *The Canadian Mosaic in the Age of Transnationalism* (2010) sees a strong connection

---

[78] Cf. e.g. Lütge (2012a) for a detailed account.

of Canada and 'trans' as well The contributors to this publication mirror this 'trans' approach in their international and interdisciplinary assembly. They "re-evaluat[e] the concept of the Canadian mosaic in the age of transnationalism" by shedding light on "past and current developments in the realms of Canadian society, politics, literature, and culture, all the while linking national trends to global changes" (Ernst/Glaser 2010, 13). Löschnigg and Löschnigg's *Migration and Fiction: Narratives of Migration in Contemporary Canadian Literature* (2009)

> focus[es] on literary renderings of trans-culturation and the blur-ring of ethno-cultural boundaries in the wake of migration, on ren-derings of the experience of living and writing in exile, as it were, and of living with or in between several languages, societies and cultures (ibid., 9)

which is yet another example that nation and 'trans' offer potential for manifold accounts and investigations.

As reflected in the context of empirical investigations of cultural com-petences, also TEFL publications show that a national focus on literature and a transcultural approach to teaching cultures are not mutually exclusive. Freitag-Hild's study on transcultural learning in the context of British fictions of migra-tion (2010) is framed in national literature just as Fäcke's study on transcultural-ity, foreign language literature and students' mental processes (2006).

Despite the many arguments in favour of including Canada in ELT and in transcultural approaches, the results of Merkl's studies reveal that ELT only pays minor attention to Canadian content. In order to reflect this thesis in more detail, the following chapter looks at the amount and quality in which Canada is implemented in ELT textbooks and additional teaching materials. From Merkl's research results I would assume that it is either not represented at all or that its representation is superficial and evokes stereotypes.

3.3 Canada in Current German Textbooks and Teaching Material

In his study on Canadian 'minority' literature and cultural learning, Merkl also includes a chapter on the representation of Canada in teaching material.[79] He distinguishes four different approaches: the representation of Canada based on facts, based on stereotypes, based on a tourist's perspective and based on negotiations of identity (cf. 2013, 32-39, similar in 2005c). The factual approach aims at providing background information and basic knowledge through comparison and contrast, a procedure that reminds of geography lessons (cf. ibid., 32-33). The approach based on stereotypes reduces complex information to smaller units which are easier to digest for learners. The inclusion of stereotypes could be beneficial because, for example, they connect to students' pre-knowledge (cf. ibid., 34-35). However, stereotypes also need to be seen critically as their shallowness and unification of diversity can be misleading and provoke false assumptions of a culture. The tourist approach functions as a synthesis of facts and stereotypes and sees the learners as tourists who like to get to know the other culture without necessarily wanting or being able to understand it (cf. ibid., 35). The most complex and advanced approach is the identity-based approach which Merkl favours. This aims at teaching culture with respect to its diverse and dynamic identities, including its historical development. Merkl states that this approach is the most difficult one as it is challenging to offer such a holistic image of Canada in English lessons. Accordingly, he concludes from his analysis of teaching material that the representation of Canada does not suffice to provide a differentiated approach to this nation. He states that the identity-based approach tries to support intercultural learning but that 'Canadian minorities' are hardly included in the material he investigated. When these are referred to, an in-depth description of their current life situations and challenges is missing.

For my approach of investigating the representation of Canada in teaching material, I choose a different approach that looks at qualitative and quantitative inclusions of and references to Canada in textbooks for ELT provided by Germany's three main publishers Cornelsen, Diesterweg and Klett. As mentioned, I assume that textbooks only marginally refer to Canada, but that if they do so, the representation is a mixture of the approaches Merkl identifies.

Often textbook to a great extent determine which contexts are included in classrooms (cf. Grünewald/Küster 2009, 96, Henke 1980). Therefore, the following part summarizes an analysis of the Canadian content of textbooks for Grades 7 to 10 and 11 to 13 and the different German school types (Haupt-

---

[79] Merkl uses Rae-Brown's *Canada A to Z* (1994), Glaap and Hartmann-Scheer's *Discover... First Nations Peoples in America. Teacher's Book. Topics for Advanced Learners* (2001), and Rice and Hayhoe's *Writing from Canada* (1994) as references. On the one hand, these are rather outdated materials. On the other hand, these publications only represent teaching material at the margins, because usually textbooks, workbooks, CDs, copy masters etc. are included in the term 'teaching material.'

schule, Realschule, Gesamtschule and Gymnasium) that were available and published until August 2013.[80] I take into account journals and magazines that include lesson plans and teaching ideas, and workshops for advanced learners, which provide ELT teachers with further resources. The analysis shows that the material beyond textbooks seems to substitute the lack of Canadian content; yet, it remains questionable in how far this additional material is actually used.

Canada in Textbooks

The analysis of national and federal curricula revealed that Canadian literature or Canada are hardly mentioned. The same holds true for the content of text-books and teaching material: Canada is only given a marginal position in ELT. A detailed look at

- Klett's *Green Line* series for grammar schools (Weisshaar 2006a-2010), *Orange Line* series for secondary schools (Hass 2005a-2010b), *Red Line* series for comprehensive schools (Hass 2005b-2010d),
- Diesterweg's *Camden Town* series for grammar schools (Hanus et.al. 2004-2008), *Camden Town* (Edelhoff 2006a-2010a) for secondary schools, *Notting Hill Gate* for comprehensive schools (Edelhoff 2007c-2010c) and *Portobello Road* for secondary schools (Edelhoff 2005-2011),
- Schöningh's *The New Summit* for grammar schools and Grade 11 and 12 (Thaler 2007), *The New Pathway to Summit* (Edelbrock 2010) for grammar schools, and
- Cornlesen's English *G21* series for grammar schools and secondary schools (Schwarz 2006-2009c, Schwarz/Rademacher 2010-2011, Schwarz/Whittaker 2010)

confirms that most of the textbooks do not include any references to Canada or Canadian culture at all. If Canada is referred to, it is done by using songs and lyrics by Canadian musicians such as Avril Lavigne (cf. Weisshaar 2007, 88), Shania Twain (cf. Hanus et al., 2005, 20) or Nickelback (cf. Schwarz 2008a, 73), or by references to sports. For example, *Green Line 3* mentions ice-hockey as a Canadian sport in the unit "The World of Sports" (Weisshaar 2007, 9) and refers to the Olympic Games of 1988 in Calgary within a text on Eddie, the Ea-gle (cf. ibid., 16-17). Here and there facts and figures about Canada are included which should support comparisons (cf. Weisshaar 2009a, 10) between Canada and other nations.

---

[80] I do not have any information whether the textbooks are also used in English lessons, but this shall be of minor interest. What is important is that these are published and available and that they are potentially used in current ELT. In total, I included 69 textbooks in this overview (cf. bibliography III.).

Beyond those inclusions, textbooks invite students to learn about Canada's multicultural and multilingual society (cf. Hass 2010b, Hellyer-Jones/Horner/Parr/Parson 2004). In this context, especially the Inuit and their everyday life are focused when students can read and learn about young people's activities in a youth club in Iqaluit, Nunavut. The protagonist Doug refers to things young people like to do in his community, for example to go to discos and film screenings, build igloos, play table tennis or soccer, organize dog races and ride the "ski-doo" (snowmobile with an engine) (Hass 2010b, 20, Hellyer-Jones et al. 2004, 22-33). In *Orange Line 6*, these aspects are included in a unit on English as a world language.

Red Line 6 covers the same topics and also uses references to Inuit cultures (cf. Hass 2010d, 28-31). Students are asked to make comparisons to their own experiences:

> Imagine you have to write an article for the Iqaluit Youth Club webzine about activities in your area/school/club. Collect ideas about how pupils with different cultural backgrounds spend their free-time. Think, too, about differences between boys and girls. Is there a link between culture and activities? (ibid., 31)

Although the text-base is nicely chosen and gives insights to Inuit culture, the task for the students requires a much differentiated view on their own culture if they want to avoid stereotypes and superficial statements.

Textbooks that include units specifically dedicated to Canada are *Red Line New 6* (cf. Hellyer-Jones et al. 2004, 22-33), *English G21 A3* (Schwarz 2008a, 72-93) and *Summit G8* (Thaler 2010, 96-109). Those shall therefore be analysed in more detail.

The peritext of *Red Line New 6* shows a detailed map which indicates the Canadian provinces, but not the territories, and presents Canada as an English-speaking country, ignoring that French is an official language as well. The double page that serves as an introduction to the unit "Canada" offers a variety of pictures presenting urban and rural landscapes, scenes from Quebec, the far North, the Maritimes and sports. Students have to match explanations to each picture. Further words and phrases that have to be put together as sentences are:

> The Inuit – original people of Arctic coast – hunters of seals and whales – contact with Europeans destroyed traditional lifestyle – carvings – now many social problems e.g. unemployment, alcohol, drugs – since 1999 self-government in a new territory Nunavut ('our land'). (Hellyer-Jones et al. 2004, 23)

While these tasks counter Merkl's observation that Canada's 'minority cultures' are not represented or that their depiction lacks references to current challenges, the information given here appear one-sided and inconsistent from a cultural perspective. Traditional lifestyles were not destroyed completely as many Inuit have been able to retain important cultural practices, which is visible in the implementation of Inuktitut in education, for instance. Moreover, the textbooks refers to Nunavut as a territory without including it in the map at the beginning of the book. Students who want to know where Nunavut is located and refer to the map will not find it.

The next double page asks students to read an extract from the Canadian novel *Fish House Secrets* (1992) by Kathy Stinson (cf. ibid., 24-25) in which the two protagonists, Chad and Jill, are at the beach talking about their parents and family problems. The story as such does not have any references to Canada, and the task deals with general analytical skills (character, content, understanding phrases) (cf. ibid., 26). The focus on Canada is only realized through grammar practice: collocations, experiences at a business conference in Calgary, adjectives to express 'big,' Canada as a country of extremes, and idioms in the context of hockey (cf. ibid., 27). The 'focus on language' section continues with practicing reported speech in the context of Quebec as well as Inuit leaders who "fought for their rights for years before they were given their own territory" (ibid., 27). Students are expected to explain the leaders' concerns: apologies for past actions, destruction of lifestyle, treatment as second-class citizens, support in fighting social problems, denial of rights etc. The background information for this task is rather shallow which could make it difficult for students to understand this important and complex political issue properly. Furthermore, it is again inconsistent that Quebec is focused in the unit, while the map does not say that it is Francophone. In another task the conditional perfect is practiced within a story of a man who almost got attacked by a polar bear while eating his pizza, and within a dialog in which Canadians tell a German tourist what she could have done in Canada if she had more time. Expressions of body language are introduced within the frame of travelling through Canada by train and wanting to start a conversation. Students are required to read from the facial expressions of people in drawings whether they would approach them or not. The section 'test yourself' offers a text on the Temagami-area in north-east Ontario which was once home of Grey Owl, one of the world's first environmental campaigners. Compared to the grammar exercises mentioned which utilize Canadian content for functional language teaching, the information and tasks in this section are contextualized in a more motivating manner as the constructed situations are closer to real-life communication.

Cornelsen published *English G21* as the series for grammar schools. The textbook for Grade 7, A3, devotes a whole unit to "Growing up in Canada" (Schwarz 2008a, 72-93).[81] The topics included revolve around aspects such as youth culture, wilderness adventures and dragon boat races. The double page

---

[81] The same unit with less content is included in the grade seven textbooks for secondary and comprehensive schools for both the basic and advanced level.

that serves as an introduction to the unit presents a number of coloured photographs, none of which have a caption (cf. ibid., 72-73). The background pictures show a field with straw bales in front of a mountain range, a row of houses, a city from the bird's eye view and two people in a canoe. In the foreground, partly covering the landscape pictures, four pictures of people and speech bubbles present the protagonist of the unit, Robert Smith from Toronto, who wants to be a DJ and has already done some gigs at parties, Gabriel Leblanc from Montreal, who, in French and English, says that he loves climbing, and Minnie Neeposh from Nemaska for whom hunting, fishing and trapping are part of the traditional way of life of First Nations and for whom this is what life should be like. The fourth picture shows three girlfriends who love sleepovers and "are really into Canadian musicians like Avril Lavigne and Nickelback" (ibid., 73).

On pages 78 to 79, a background file on Canada presents short texts on Aboriginal peoples in Canada, Canadian settlers, immigration to Canada, Canadian sports and two Canadian writers, Margaret Atwood and Frederick Bantin. Each text is illustrated with a picture: an Inuk sitting in front of a hole in the ice, holding a dead fish and a piece of wood in his hands, a bilingual STOP-sign, a group of people from different ethnic backgrounds, girls playing lacrosse, men playing ice-hockey and portraits of the writers. This page also includes a map of Canada indicating the provinces and territories and their capitals, and a chart comparing the head of state, capital, biggest city, official language and number of time zones of Canada and Germany. The background, covering the middle of the double page, shows a red maple leaf.

While it could be criticised that this depiction offers a rather stereotypical image of Canada and specific characteristics, it still opens the view to Canada's cultural, geographic and social diversity. It should not be forgotten that textbook designers only have a few pages to introduce certain cultures and that the more diverse a culture is, the more challenging it can be to make a selection of what to include. Additionally, stereotypes can be a beneficial starting point for further investigating an issue, and certainly for deconstructing an image that is depicted. Yet, this may be the students' first ELT encounter with Canada which could justify a connection to their pre-knowledge and an activation of existing vocabulary.

Schöningh's textbook for Grades 11 to 13 (*Summit G8,* Thaler 2010, extended edition, incl. vocational grammar school) includes one unit on "Distinctly Canadian – I Wonder What They Are" (Thaler 2010, 96-109) followed by a unit on "All in Society – I Wonder Who We Are" (ibid., 113-149). Whereas it is certainly praiseworthy that Schöningh devotes a separate unit to Canada, it is striking that the semantic reference to "Canadian" is the determiner "what," thereby objectifying Canadian, either the nationality or a human. In "All in Society" the semantic reference to "Society" is the determiner "who," which refers to a person. Even though the usage of "what" in the first headline could be understood as a reference to status, it remains debatable whether learners would be likely to grasp such distinct notions of meaning. It also remains unclear why the editors of this textbook include such differentiation.

Within this unit, the learner finds glimpses on various aspects of Canadian culture and identity. Already the introductory double page offers a thought-provoking approach. While it presents four pictures, a landscape of mountains and a lake, a seaside view of Toronto, an ice-hockey game and a scene from a Pow-Wow, which all evoke a rather positive and harmonious atmosphere, the quotes on this page stand in contrast to this. For instance, a Canadian novelist and professor of English is quoted: "If it be true that God turns his back on a people that falls in love with itself, there seems no immediate danger that He will turn his back on Canada," or the aphorism "We've had access to American know-how, British political wisdom and French culture. We've ended up with British know-how, French political wisdom and American culture." Students have to justify whether the pictures "give a visual impression of Canada" (Thaler 2010, 95) and "[e]xplain the views of the Canadians on their nation and their identity. Do you understand their worries?" (ibid.). When students have not heard anything about Canadian identity before,[82] these tasks seem rather difficult and challenging; yet, the contradiction of the visual images and quotes is very provocative and can lead students to question the quite positive reputation that Canada often seems to have. This can be supplemented with a close analysis of Canada's "unofficial anthem" "The Maple Leaf Forever" (ibid.).

An excerpt from Margaret Atwood's *Cat's Eye* (1988) narrates how the main protagonist, Elaine Risley, "returns to her home town Toronto and becomes consumed by vivid images of her mid-20th century past" (Thaler 2010, 96). Through the text the learners can become aware of the British influence on Canadian social and political life, using the example of a school experiences which Atwood reflects in her most autobiographical work. An excerpt from Maria Campbell's *Halfbreed* (1973) is used to have the learners reflect upon the relationship of Métis and "white people" (Thaler 2010, 102, task 1). Moreover, learners are asked to conduct more research on the current situation of "natives in Canada" (ibid.) and to discuss "whether the native population contributes to the construction of a distinctly Canadian identity" (ibid.). Advice on the selection of sources or how to find appropriate material to solve this task would have added an important and necessary point of reference for the students. Especially when it comes to the cultural and historic past and present of the First Nations, Métis and Inuit in Canada, students need to be enabled to distinguish between reliable and unreliable resources and descriptions because information can vary depending on the intentions of the authors.

Another view on Canada's aboriginal past is offered through stills, film posters and excerpts from *Atanarjuat: The Fast Runner* (dir. Zacharias Kunuk, 2001). Here, the tasks demand students to evaluate whether the film poster rais-

---

[82] As schools can chose the textsbooks they work with, it cannot be assumed that students have used the textbook that included a unit on Canada in earlier grades.

es the interest of the potential viewer, to "observe how positive and accurate pictures of the Inuit people are created on the screen" (Thaler 2010, 103) and to discuss whether the praise the film received for "not being some aboriginal folk-art product but an enthralling and sophisticated work that exploits cinema's potential as a visual medium" (ibid.) is justified. Given the small input the learners receive throughout the unit, I apply similar criticism as above. It remains questionable how reflected the learners' answers and opinions could be if the text does not provide sufficient background information.

Apart from the British and aboriginal influences that are said to contribute to a distinctly Canadian identity, the textbook additionally presents a perspective of a "Chinese-Canadian." The excerpt from Garry Engkent's short story "Why My Mother Can't Speak English" (Thaler 2010, 104) focuses on a Chinese immigrant experience and different cultural values of Chinese and Canadian culture. The learners are supposed to get familiar with the process of becoming a Canadian citizen and have to research recent Canadian immigration policy and programs. The year of publishing or an indicator to when the story is set would have been helpful for the learners to see the described events in a particular socio-historical context and relate the text to their own findings. In comparison to the research task given earlier, here the learners do get advice on which sources to use as a link to the governmental page 'Citizenship and Immigration Canada' is provided (cf. ibid., 107).

The unit on Canada closes with a student's report on his experiences during his studies in Toronto. This text should be used to practice mediation and to collect information that are relevant for spending a gap year in Canada. Seeing the teaching unit as a whole, it is worth mentioning that the learners get an insight into various aspects of Canadian culture, especially through the different cultural and ethnic groups that are included. To gain substantial knowledge of Canada, it would be helpful if the students got more advice on how to find reliable information, as the contents from the fictional accounts leave much room for speculation, interpretation and may lead to shallow negotiations of Canadian identity.

Compared to the inclusion of this unit in a textbook for advanced learners, other textbooks for this age group leave opportunities for beneficial references to Canada unused. The textbooks *Context 21* (Schwarz/Whittaker 2010), *Green Line Oberstufe* (Weisshaar 2009b) or *The New Summit* (Thaler 2007) include topics like

- "The Individual in Society" (Schwarz/Whittaker 2010, 80-99),
- "The Media" (ibid., 100-115),
- "Ethnic Diversity" (Weisshaar 2009b, 10-25),
- "Regional Identities" (ibid., 46-61),
- "English Around the Word" (Thaler 2007, 12-27) or
- "Challenges of the 21st Century". (ibid., 180-245)

Yet, in all of these units which would provide interesting comparisons and references to Canada and Canadian society and politics, the U.S. and Great Britain are focused. If Canada is mentioned, it is shortly referred to as an Anglo- and Francophone nation within a language family tree (cf. Thaler 2007, 16) or included through excerpts from Douglas Coupland's *Microserfs* (1995) (cf. ibid., 206-208), which is about a group of Americans who work at the Microsoft headquarters near Seattle, Washington, and entails a critical view on life in a high-speed and high-tech environment (cf. ibid., 206). *Context 21* offers a visual representation of Canada as the opening page for the unit "National Identity and Diversity" shows a picture of two boys with a Canadian flag painted across their faces and an Inuk with a sled dog next to other images of English-speaking cultures. *The New Pathway to Summit Advanced* (Edelbrock 2011) includes a short excerpt of Atwood's novel, *Oryx and Crake* (2003) in a unit on "Science (Fiction) and Technology" (ibid., 273). However, the unit does not offer further references to Canada.

As pointed out, the lack of Canadian content could be explained with the limited amount of content that can be taught in a school year. Yet, this was already rejected above. Why should Great Britain and the U.S. be regarded as the main cultures of reference? A further justification for focusing on the U.S. and Great Britain could be that the textbooks just implement what the governmental guidelines prescribe: The curricula focus on Great Britain and the U.S., so do the textbooks. Yet, this argument has to be rejected, too, because the curricula mainly include suggestions and leave a lot of open space which could be filled and interpreted in favour of Canadian content.

Canada in Additional Teaching Material

Whereas Canada is only marginally included in textbooks, other teaching materials such as texts collections or TEFL journals indeed provide Canadian content for ELT. Already in 1974, Pache published an overview of support material for teaching Canadian literature in *Wissenschaft und Unterricht* (122-133). In the late 1980s and early 1990s, Glaap (1988), Groß (1990), Gulden (1986), Korte (1990) and Rau (1988) contributed to the discussion of introducing Canadian literature into the English language classroom. Gulden (1986) suggests a teaching unit on Canadian identity for upper classes based on the short stories "By a Frozen River" (Norman Levine 2000), "One, Two, Three Little Indians" (Hugh Garner 1952) and "Dancing Girls" (Margaret Atwood 1977). The journal *Der Fremdsprachliche Unterricht,* which aims at providing practical ideas for teaching English, made Canada the topic of its 89th issue (1988), including justifications for using Canada as a focus for teaching English in Germany (Rau 1988, 21-24), and topics like the kite as a symbol in Canadian literature (Franzbecker 1988, 8-12), and the Canadian North (Glaap 1988, 4-7).

Canada's potential for primary schools is unveiled in *Bausteine Englisch* ("Native Americans/Indianer," Müller 2007) and *Grundschulmagazin Englisch* ("Cowboys and Indians," Schmid-Schönbein, 2007) which adapt aspects of Canadian society and identity to playfully teaching English to very young learners. Both journals refer to the issues discussed as "north-American" without defining whether the culture belongs north, south or on both sides of the 52th parallel. Fröhlich's contribution "Native Americans – Hintergrundwissen zum Thema" (2007, 39) points to an U.S.-American context, whereas "The story of the totem pole" (Ertelt 2007, 13) can be contextualized in Canada as well.

In teaching materials for more advanced learners, Canada is commonly related to intercultural learning (cf. Bredella 2008, 2010, Müller-Hartmann 2000), which reflects a gradual inclusion of multiculturalism into didactic approaches (e.g. Nischik 2000). An early example of this is Burford's comprehensive reader *Colorful Canada* (1990), which includes material that depicts a diverse image of Canada. For example, Canada is introduced as home to various cultures like the Inuit in the Northwest Territories, "A Mohawk from the Six Nations Reserve" (Burford 1990, 8) or life in British Columbia from the perspective of a "Chinese-Canadian" (ibid., 9). Additionally, this booklet refers to historical key aspects of "making the nation" (ibid., 10-15), includes information on different regions such as the Maritimes, the Prairies and the North, and introduces famous Canadians, leisure activities, lifestyle, and a critical discussion of Canadian unity.

Also recent TEFL journals for secondary schools have published material about Canada. The July issue of *:in Englisch* (Weisshaar 2007) is titled "Come along to Canada" and offers various teaching ideas for classes five to ten, for instance "A Canadian E-mail Friend" (Piornak 2007, 2-8), "A Canadian Kaleidoscope" (Plitsch 2007, 9-20), "Canada's National Parks" (Schlee 2007, 21-29), and "Town and Country Life" (Gally/Herold 2007, 30-35). *Englisch betrifft uns* devoted one issue to "Canada" (Düwel/von der Grün 2004), focusing on literature (Wauer/Zocholl 2004, 18-27, Atwood's *The Blind Assassin*) and recent trends in Canadian society (Bremicker 2004, 28-32), both of which suggest lesson plans for Grades 11 to 13. Authors usually choose specific aspects of Canadian culture to be discussed in the classroom: the Inuit (Striegler 2004, 37-40), sled dog races and the Yukon quest (Nadolny 2004, 7-11), Canada's national parks (Teepe 2004, 12-17) and the Winter Olympics in Vancouver (Düwel/von der Grün 2004, 33-36).

The issues on "Canada – Country of Superlatives" (*Praxis Englisch,* Lohmann/Schmidt 2011) and "Canada" (*Englisch 5-10,* Kuty 2011), offer a diverse representation of Canada. In both journals, the authors base lesson plans on Canadian literature and art (Alter 2011b, 30-33, Alter 2011c, 14-18, Heidrich 2011, 18-23, Wagner 2011, 29-33), immigration, multiculturalism and indigenous people (Alter 2011b, 30-33, Dreßler/Schmidt 2011, 40-43, Pearson 2011, 39, Schardin 2011, 24-29, Susemihl 2011a, 10-13), nature and the environment (Bretzmann 2011, 4-9), stereotypes of Canada, and the relation to the U.S.

(Litman 2011, 44-45, Susemihl 2011b, 34-39,). Furthermore, the journals present a closer look at Vancouver (Brandl/Kretschmer 2011, 14-17), Canadian schools (Douglas 2011, 9-13) and the influence of the film industry in Canada on British Columbia's and Ontario's economy and culture (Kazaki 2011, 34-38). A special feature provides background information about Canada (Lohmann/Schmidt 2011, 19, 21-28, 44-46). This variety of topics and current aspects allows teachers and students to learn and reflect about Canada beyond stereotypical ideas and develop a differentiated view of this country and its cultures.

Such an approach that aims at raising awareness of Canada's multicultural character is also prevalent in recent booklets which can be used beyond textbooks. Doff's *O Canada! History, Country and Cultures from Sea to Sea* (2006) refers to "Past and Present" (ibid., 6-23), "Country and Peoples" (ibid., 24-37) and "Cultures and Identities" (ibid., 38-64), and gives voice to Canadian authors of various backgrounds representing Canada's multicultural heritage and composition of culture and identity. This is realized by including texts by Margaret Atwood, René Lévesque, David Suzuki, and E. Pauline Johnson, for example. Klewitz' *Canada – Dreams and Realities. Schwerpunktthema Abitur Englisch* (2011) shows a similar but more concrete approach when this booklet for preparing the A-Levels is divided into sections like "Canadian Identity" (ibid., 4-18), "The Canadian Mosaic" (ibid., 19-28), "Education and Lifestyle" (ibid., 29-35), "Ecology and the Economy" (ibid., 36-44) and "Political Issues" (ibid., 45-61). This detailed account appears to be more accessible for points of reference and comparisons, which underlines its potential for intercultural learning. Schwartz' "Canada – Changes and Challenges" (2011) specifically refers to the development of Canada as a multicultural nation, to bilingualism, the indigenous population, oil and its ecological and economic importance, to Canada's immigration policy and to Canada as a country for refugees.

With regard to cultural learning and Merkl's criticism of representing 'minority groups' above, I would like to emphasize the contrast of "coping with the loss of traditional Inuit ways of life" (Schwartz 2011, 3) in reference to Alootook Ipellie's poem "How Noisy they Seem" and "Circus of Life," a video clip about "giving young Inuit a purpose in life" (ibid.). This comparison supports learners in understanding how global influences threaten Inuit lifestyles and perceptions of self, while at the same time Inuit are not solely seen as a vanishing people of the past, but as people who exist in the present and express this in their daily routines and creation of media and art.

Abi Workshop Canada (Horner/Probst 2012) invites students to reflect upon topics like "Identity within Diversity" (ibid., 4-13), immigration policy, education, job situation and teenage life (ibid., 14-25), "Political Voices" (ibid., 26-37), and "Environmental Issues" (ibid., 38-49). In addition, projects on "Famous Canadians," "What makes up Canada," "How English is Quebec?" and "The Canadian Arts Scene" are included which call for further investigations and paint a complex picture of Canada.

Destination Canada (Kisch 2005) appears as a guide to Canadian culture as it covers topics such as government, national holidays, flags and national symbols, Mounties, "Native Peoples," French Canada, geography and wildlife, schools and sports as well as Canadian identity and Canada's future. Notwithstanding the range of topics covered in this booklet which exceeds the range offered in other materials, Kisch summarizes these on one double page only, much of which is used for large pictures and white margins. Therefore, the amount of information on the complex topics is rather limited. Although the vocabulary list at the end of the booklet seems useful for learners, no tasks or activities are included which would enable students to reflect upon and work with the newly gained knowledge. Additionally, the approach taken in this booklet can be questioned when First Nation peoples are included in a short unit on "Native Peoples" in which they are referred to as "Indians" and "tribes" (ibid., 17-18). Of the teaching material considered in my analysis, *Destination Canada* is closest to what Merkl identified as a tourist-based approach to represent cultures (cf. above, Merkl 2013, 35-36).

In the middle of the first decade of the 21st century, a linguistic perspective on Canadian English plays an important role in teaching contexts, too. Benwell (2004), for example, looks at Canadian English as a "linguistic pot-pourri"; Klippel-Mostert (2003) as well as Raith and Möhrle (2006) refer to Canada in their lesson plan suggestions for "Global English" which refers to radio programs from around the world.

Furthermore, short story collections which have been (re)published by German educational publishers pay tribute to formerly marginalized and silenced voices and thus point to the huge potential of Canadian literature for ELT. Müller (1990/2003) and Rau (2005/2011) have put together selections of texts ranging from Margaret Atwood's "Significant Moments in the Life of My Mother," Alistair MacLeod's "The Return" (in Müller 1990/2003) to Thomas King's "Borders," Alootook Ipellie's "Nanuq, the White Ghost, Repents," E. Pauline Johnson's "The Sea-Serpent" or Nancy Lee's "Red Bean Ice" (in Rau 2005/2001). Thus, teachers who like to base their lessons on Canadian literature are indeed able to find suggestions and ideas beyond what is (not) offered in textbooks.

Within this discussion of including and representing Canada in textbooks and additional teaching material for different learner and age groups, didactic reduction resembles one essential case in point. It goes without saying that for each publication of teaching material certain choices have to be made as regards what is included in a textbook or journal, and what is not. Moreover, the information need to be correct and balanced. This is especially true when textbooks are perceived as important documents of social awareness (cf. Thonhauser 1995, 178, Weinbrenner 1995, 25). Therefore, incorrect, one-sided and shallow information about cultures have to be avoided. The need for didactic reduction does not justify the inclusion of false or misleading information, like limiting Canada to provinces in a map and not indicating territories despite mentioning them in one of the units (cf. *Red Line new 6*). Simultaneously, reducing the Inuit to their problems and challenges of the present should not be sufficient as it wrongly portrays people who in the past decades have worked hard to re-establish their language, traditions and pride.

Didactic reduction is sometimes particularly challenging for young learners at primary school. While the content needs to be correct and reliable, it should be motivating and meet the young learners' linguistic and cognitive needs. Although teaching material for them has to be reduced to a lower complexity than for older students, ELT should still try to develop a reliable understanding of Canada and provide young pupils with a differentiated perspective on First Nations, for example. This is particularly striking in the issues of *Bausteine Englisch* and *Grundschulmagazin Englisch* mentioned above, when the lesson plans are labelled "The boys in the cave" (learning English words with Indian names, Vogt 2007, 17-20), "Time to dress up" (fancy-dress parties and Mardi Gras, Waszak 2007, 27-28) and "I'm a happy cowboy" (singing a song about a cowboy, Klein 2007, 29-30). In "Native Americans/Indianer" the pupils are invited to come to an "Indian camp," enjoy "Indian activities" and learn about "Indian names" and "Indian food"; also a crossword and other writing exercises are "Indian" (Müller 2007). Yet, it is not clear why a journal that aims at intercultural education at a primary level uses terms that for long have been coined inappropriate.

This close analysis reveals that some publishers of teaching material about Canada try to present a balanced picture offering basic facts, insights to Canada's various peoples and current challenges of living in a multicultural society. This is especially visible in Schwartz' "Canada – Changes and Challenges" (2011). At the same time, the necessary reduction of content for reasons of time, age and language competence of the students causes stereotypical and simplified representations.

The numerous more recent publications about teaching Canada illustrate that the interest in Canada in German ELT classrooms is rising (cf. Doff 2010, 4). This is evident when noticing the very recent inclusion of Canada as a key topic for the school-leaving exams (e.g. in Hessia[83]) and the provision of the necessary materials by the publishers Cornelsen and Klett. Independent from this positive outlook, it remains questionable in how far those additional materials are acknowledged and used by teachers, since textbooks function as the main point of reference in preparing lessons. One of the core fields in which Canada seems to be represented, though, is in literature. While this is certainly praiseworthy, it is also remarkable to see in how far Canadian literature is reflected in academia, on a research level or as material in tertiary education. The following discussion allows me to link my research more profoundly to current TEFL debates.

---

[83] Cf. "Hinweise zur Vorbereitung auf die schriftlichen Abiturprüfungen im Landesabitur 2014" (2012, 5).

3.4 Canadian Literature for Young Readers in the Current TEFL Debate

In his Canada-focused analysis of German curricula and textbooks for teaching English, Groß concludes that Canada is only given little attention (cf. 1990, 186). As the analysis above shows, I can support this conclusion. Nevertheless, Canada has recently become a point of interest for an academic perspective on TEFL theory and on the tertiary level of education.

In those academic reflections, Canadian literature seems to be the prevalent medium that is suggested for classroom applications. For example, Bredella's (2008) contextualization of Drew Hayden Taylor's drama *alterNatives* (2000) revolves around discussing the existence of irreconcilable cultural differences and conflicts within the construction of identity. Surkamp and Nünning (2009, 114-139) suggest Minnie Aodla Freeman's short drama *Survival in the South* (first performance in 1971) in order to achieve understanding otherness. Their concept uses an authentic drama by an Inuk to challenge stereotypes and evoke changes of perspective as to enable students to develop ICC.

In "Beyond Beavers and Bilingualism: Reasons and Suggestions for Teaching Modern Canada in the EFL classroom" Doff (2010) argues for more Canadian content in ELT in general and turns to aboriginal roots and multiculturalism using storytelling ("Raven finds the first men") and Engkent's story "Why My Mother Can't Speak English." The potential of First Nation literature for the EFL classroom is also discussed by Groß (2004) who suggests reading and analyzing texts like "The White Wampum" (1895) by E. Pauline Johnson (Tekahionwake), trickster stories or modern First Nation texts by Jeanette Armstrong, for example, to deconstruct prevailing stereotypes about the "Indians". The reflections about Canada's multiculturalism based on Canadian literature in ELT is also central in Rau's (2012) analysis of Margaret Atwood's short story "Dancing Girls" and Julia Hammer's (2012a) discussion of Deborah Ellis' *Parvana's Journey* (2002).

These findings indicate that Canada has become a more important topic in recent TEFL discourses and although this is an endorsing development, the discrepancy compared to British or U.S. American content is still significant. In relation to the marginal position of researching the potential of Canadian content and literature for primary and secondary school ELT, Antor (2002) and Merkl (2013) have investigated Canadian literature for procedures of increasing ICC in tertiary education. As both approaches offer extensive insights to the research in this field, I reflect on these in more detail.

Antor has continuously integrated Canadian content and literature in his seminars for advanced students (cf. 2002, 144-163). In these he combined reflections upon intercultural learning and understanding otherness with Canadian auto- and hetero-stereotyping. Interestingly, Antor included fictional and non-fictional texts in these reflections: his students analysed and interpreted the Canadian national anthem (in French and English) and compared it to a video clip that is part of the multimedia presentation *Canadian and World Encyclopaedia* (1998). The students concluded that the national anthem shows great parallels to the images evoked in the video clip, for example nordicity ("The true North strong and free" vs. polar bears and icebergs in the video). Additionally, the students saw their hetero-stereotypes confirmed in how the video presents Canada as a huge country with vast and diverse landscapes of mountain ranges, prairie, and forests, adventurous free-time activities, Canadian Mounties and a multicultural population. Antor's comparative approach agrees to the basic principles of developing intercultural competence and enables students to take a critical perspective. They, for example, noted that the images in the video clip supported Canada's diversity but at the same time presented an ideologically very harmonious and homogeneous image of Canada; the people would be presented as thoroughly happy and free of conflict, which was, however, ascribed to the specific genres of both texts (Antor 2002, 153-154).

Furthermore, the students discovered certain cinematographic techniques which underlined this image, as most of the scenes show the breaking dawn which provokes images of a future-bound nation that is looking at new and innovative days ahead. Many of the protagonists are smiling children which implies that Canada is a young, happy and dynamic nation which mirrors the 'light' metaphor of the beginning of a new day. The scene in which an Inuk child is smiling in front of a Canadian flag that was blended into the picture reminds of the anthem's second line "True patriot love" as it establishes a strong link between ethnic and national identity (cf. Antor 2002, 154). The simultaneousness of Canada's unity and diversity was also discovered in analyzing the pace and cuts of the video clip which revealed that a bird's eye perspective on mountains and passing clouds in fast motion seem like waves on an ocean, an image that is followed by a close up of whales in the waves of the ocean – unifying the natural elements and metaphorically the Canadian nation (ibid., 154-155).

In order to increase a critical viewpoint and give voice to perspectives that are silenced in the video clip, Antor had his students read various titles of Canadian literature such as Joy Kogawa's *Obasan* (1981), Hugh MacLennan's *Two Solitudes* (1945), M.G. Vassanji's *No New Land* (1991), Dionne Brand's *In Another Place, Not Here* (1997), Margaret Laurence's *The Diviners* (1974), Mordecai Richler's *Solomon Gurskey was Here* (1989) and Tomson Highway's *Kiss of the Fur Queen* (1998). Analysing and interpreting these various texts enabled students to develop critical intercultural competence which demands anti-essentialist reflections that focus on differentiation, not only between auto- and hetero-stereotypes but also regarding the images that are processed and the knowledge that is created through media. Antor's progression linked important concepts of current ELT and cultural learning: Deconstructing media images[84] of Canada through a critical reading of Canadian literature provided students with a foundation to establish a thorough and critical understanding of multiculturalism and its implications for Canada's current social, cultural and political state.

Recently, Merkl published a cultural and methodological investigation of identity and understanding otherness in the context of current Canadian 'minority' literature (2013).[85] In this, he tries to establish a synthesis of TEFL theory and cultural studies terminology in order to support students in appropriately identifying and describing cultural phenomena, especially in reference to multicultural and "pluriethnic" societies like Canada (cf. Merkl 2013, 12). The Canadian context, Merkl explains, is important as future teachers have to be able to include lesson plans and projects beyond Great Britain and the U.S. (cf. ibid.); he also points out that new English literatures are only marginally included in ELT.

For his study Merkl uses similar texts as Antor (cf. above) which offer exemplary insights to Canada's multicultural societies. He specifically chooses authors of different ethnic groups who are distinguished representatives of current Canadian 'minority' literature. Merkl sees each text by Asian Canadian and Native Canadian authors (cf. ibid., 64)[86] in a certain light:

- Joy Kogawa's *Obasan* (1981) as "Speaking and Silence" (ibid., 155-172),

---

[84] Media literacy refers to the ability to evaluate "mass media's relationship to democracy, power, social justice, encourage discussions about how media conceptualizes race, class, gender, how it promotes, certain social values through its definitions of such concepts as beauty, prestige, family, love, success, sex, freedom, and consumerism, among others" (Grigoryan/King 2008, 2). Volkmann differentiates between three different levels of media literacy: technological, application-oriented and critical reflexive media literacy (cf. 2010, 216-221). The first refers to using all kinds of media and products in the field of information and communication technology, to instrumental skills which are important to operate different technology adequately and purposefully, to understand their content and structure, and to recognize, choose and use certain media according to communicative needs from a technological perspective. The second refers to receptive and productive skills as well as procedural knowledge and learning strategies and techniques in the field of information and data processing, and the third to the critical assessment of media messages. Further details are offered in Grünewald (2010) and Kellner/Share (2005). With regard to the critical analysis of depicting otherness in literature, students can increase their media literacy, too, because they question what is presented and analyse underlying messages.

[85] Cf. introduction.

[86] Despite not offering the German original to my own translation throughout this work, I consider it to be necessary in this case, as I would like to prevent the mediation of false content. Merkl's original reads: "Die Autorinnen und Autoren sollen unterschiedlichen ethnischen Gruppen angehören und bedeutende Vertreter der kanadischen Literaturszene der Gegenwart sein. Es handelt sich bei den Schriftstellerinnen und Schriftstellern im weitesten Sinne um aus Asien stammende Personen, die der *Asian-Canadian Literature* und der *Native Canadian Literature* zuzuordnen sind" (2013, 64).

- Michael Ondaatje's *In the Skin of a Lion* (1987) as "Unknown Stories of *Silent Voices*" (ibid., 173-194),
- Rohinton Mistry's *Tales from Firozsha Baag* (1987) as "Definition of one's own Hybridity" (ibid., 195-206),
- Sky Lee's *Disappearing Moon Café* (1990) as "Racial Segregation" (ibid., 207-222),
- M.G. Vassanji's *No New Land* (1991) as "Double Migration" (ibid., 223-244),
- Beatrice Culleton's *In Search of April Raintree* (1983) as "Ways of Establishing Identity" (ibid., 245-264),
- Thomas King's *Green Gras, Running Water* (1993a), "How Corporal Colin Sterlin Saved Blossom, Alberta, and Most of the Rest of the World as Well" (1993b) and "Borders" (1993c) as "Alternatives to Dominant Discourses" (ibid., 265-291) and
- Tomson Highway's *Kiss of the Fur Queen* (1998) as "Re-education toward 'high Western culture'" (ibid., 193-310).

Merkl comes to the conclusion that Canadian 'minority' authors reflect issues in their work that result from a problematic relationship between a "dominant white culture," which refers to the Anglo- and Franco Canadian majority, and the 'minorities' (cf. ibid., 313). He qualifies this as a rejection and negation of a romanticized image of Canada as these texts include perspectives beyond Eurocentrism and openly speak to current social problems. In these texts, aspects such as critical identity discourse, critical multiculturalism, the under-representation of 'minorities' in history, dynamic Canadian identity and intercultural negotiations of identity are negotiated. Although Merkl offers a profound analysis of selected Canadian 'minority' literature which he cross-references with postcolonial and intercultural learning discourses, it would have been interesting to see how university students benefit from Canadian 'minority' literature concerning their understanding of otherness and increasing intercultural competences. Such processes could offer intriguing incentives for TEFL research as well.

This debate illustrates that Canadian literature can be integrated in tertiary education in various ways as it provides points of reference for diverse topics of interest like cultural learning and understanding otherness but also reflecting upon ideology or postcolonialism. If Canadian topics are included in university classes and students extend their knowledge about Canadian issues, chances increase that future teachers may use Canadian content in their own teachings or are better prepared to teach Canada as it is included in textbooks and further materials.

Part A of this study investigated the didactic and cultural-theoretical foundations of conceptualizing understanding otherness and developing inter- and transcultural competences. In the context of ELT, chapter 1 looked at different theoretical approaches to teaching cultures, chapter 2 elaborated on key concepts and benefits of using young adult literature, and chapter 3 critically discussed the kind of literature currently used in ELT. I investigated current concepts of cultural teaching and critically reflected upon the opportunities and challenges of using literature as a means of developing ICC. As a result of these discussions, I qualified current approaches to cultural learning and teaching, especially in reference to certain methodology, models of progression of cultural competence and the kind of literature that is applied. It was indicated that current texts only offer a limited perspective on otherness and frame multicultural characters within issue-laden paradigms. I consider this to have undesirable effects on the readers' self-efficacy and perception of self and other. Based on this conclusion I state that a different kind of literature is needed which provides a more balanced perception of othernesses.

This thought is reflected in more detail when the respective novels for young readers have been discussed in Part B. This part introduces Canadian young adult fiction and reflects upon its potential for inter- and especially transcultural learning. In order to justify the text selection, chapter 3 analysed textbooks and teaching material for ELT which unveiled that Canada can indeed be more focused in the EFL classroom, as curricula guidelines, ELT journals and the academic discourse provide space, topics and material. Antor's and Merkl's publications show that Canadian content can be used to increase intercultural competences and understanding otherness on a university level. My research supplements their work in that it transfers and adapts their approach – Canadian young adult fiction in combination with inter- and transcultural learning – to the secondary school level.

To contextualise the three selected texts, chapter 5 is framed by the development of Canadian children's and young adult literature (chapter 4) and a summary of the potential of Canadian young adult fiction for inter- and transcultural learning (chapter 6). As the argumentation above revealed, this body of literature is chosen purposefully, however, it still resembles examples upon which transcultural learning can be based and from which a concept of transcultural literature can be derived.

Part B: Transferring the Reflections on Otherness: Canadian Young Adult Fiction

In order to suggest potential bridges to cross the gaps that were delineated in the previous chapters, I would like to investigate the potential of Canadian young adult literature for furthering transcultural learning. A first section in Part B presents an overview of the development of Canadian literature for young readers. This reflects common characteristics, but specifically focuses on a linkage to multiculturalism.[87] The comprehensive discussion of three selected texts and their depiction of otherness, the transcultural topoi those entail and their teaching implications serve as a basis for drawing conclusions for reconceptualising transcultural competences. The results of Part B serve as a foundation for re-investigating key features of teaching literature in Part C. These will be essential for seeing transcultural learning in a different light and lead to a definition of and justification for using transcultural literature to extend transcultural competences in ELT.

---

[87] Indeed, some of the information provided in chapter 4.1 is rather detailed. Even when the reader may not continuously see a direct connection to the context of inter- and transcultural learning, I consider this to be important in order to frame current developments of Canadian literature for young readers and to be able to qualify the depiction of otherness I will analyse in chapter 5.

4. Canadian Literature for Young Readers

The discussion of the potential of Canadian young adult literature for inter- and transcultural learning at hand focuses on literature that has been published since the year 2000. In order to appreciate the body of literature that has been available since then one cannot but see those recent publications in relation to the historical development of Canadian children's literature in general. Therefore, the following chapter suggests five phases of the development of Canadian literature for young readers. Additionally, characteristics of this literature are summarized. The introduction and discussion of three selected texts results in a detailed presentation of the potential of Canadian young adult literature for inter- and transcultural learning.

4.1 The Development of Canadian Literature for Young Readers

The academic reception of Canadian literature for young readers celebrated its 48th anniversary in 2015, as Stott and Jones regard the year 1967 as the year in which the study of Canadian children's literature reached maturity. According to the two scholars the three milestones of studying Canadian children's literature were laid in this year: Sheila Egoff published *The Republic of Childhood: A Critical Guide to Children's Literature in English* (1967), *In Review*, a journal focusing on Canadian children's books and their authors was first published for the first time, and Tundra Books, the first publishing house devoted to Canadian children's books was founded in that year (cf. Jones/Stott 2000, ix, Saltman 1987, 3-4, cf. Richter 2011).

Surely, and when following Stott and Jones' metaphor, maturity is not reached independent from birth and coming-of-age. Hence, I would like to identify phases of the development of Canadian literature for young readers. To differentiate those phases, publications of Canadian books for young readers shall be taken into account as well as academic research and key events in promoting Canadian children's literature[88] such as the establishment of awards, journals and societies concerned with this field of interest. The five phases that are proposed are:

---

[88] In this and the following chapters the terms 'children's literature' and literature for young readers are used interchangeably in order to prevent a constant repetition and over-usage of either term. Children and young readers are here used to refer to the same readership, although scholarship offers various differentiations (e.g. Coats 2001, Latrope/Drury 2009, Nilsen/Donelson 2009, Nodelman/Reimer 2003, Trupe 2006) (cf. introduction).

- Early Canadian Literature for Young Readers: 1767 to 1900
- Family and Animal Stories, Awards and Popularity: 1900 to 1967
- The Founding of Centers and Publishers: 1967 to 1980
- Awards, Multicultural Orientation and Education: 1980-2000
- Post-millennium Development and Challenges since 2000.

In the following sections these phases are differentiated and described according to the features that were prominent in the respective years.

4.1.1 Early Canadian Literature for Young Readers: 1767 to 1900

In *Children's Literature in Canada* (1992), Waterston discusses different genres of children's literature, styles, motives and themes, and points out what is Canadian about these. Her observation that children's books reflect a geographical and "political evolution of Canada since pre-settlement days" (ibid., 1) is as interesting as it is helpful for understanding the development of Canadian children's literature. Waterston distinguishes between geographical space and literary space; the former explained as the isolated settlement conditions when Europeans arrived: the "impenetrable coastline" of Canada forced early immigrants to settle on islands where "French Roman, Catholics, Irish, Gaelic Catholics, Scots Presbyterians, English Anglicans, Methodists and Baptists" lived in isolation from one another, able to retain their culture in the form of nursery rhymes, folktales, prayers and hymns (cf. ibid.). Amable Bonnefons' *The Little Book of Life* (1777) set in Halifax, Nova Scotia, is an example of such an early literary production (cf. ibid., 1-10).

Waterston's understanding of literary space differentiates various levels, one of which regards the perception of "literature for young people as part of the cultural record of the country" (ibid., 5), which includes collections of Canadian children's literature in holdings of libraries and archives, too. In addition, literary space is created as "many authors read and echo the work of writers from other times and places" (ibid., 6) in common genres as well as in creative innovations. This includes the preservation of past experiences and events, as narratives "hold events in memory," recount and shape them (cf. ibid., 7). Literary space is also occupied by later compilations like McDonough's collection of interviews with Canadian authors and illustrators, published in *Profiles* (1982) or Jones and Stott's *Canadian Books for Children: A Guide to Authors and Illustrators* (1988) (cf. ibid., 8). Finally each "literary work is itself a space, a stage to which the reader brings experience and imagination" (ibid.). Here Waterston refers to major Canadian authors' publications for children such as Margaret Laurence's *The Olden Days Coat* and *Six Darn Cows* which can be related to the adult novels *The Stone Angel* and *The Diviners* (cf. ibid., 7).

According to Saltman, the first children's books that can be called Canadian were written by "visitors to Canada, temporary residents, or new immigrants and were most likely to be published in London, Boston, or New York" (1987, 8). Early children's books mirror the living conditions of immigrants and mainly refer to everyday life and challenges of life in geographical isolation within vast landmasses. Often, the Canadian landscape, with its beauty and dangers, its wildlife and motives of survival in the wilderness, provided the backdrop for early genres like outdoor-adventure stories especially written for boys, and historical romances of exploration and animal stories for girls (cf. ibid., 8-9). Early immigrants used their home stories as a background for these stories, which they often wrote with view of the experiences in the new land. Among those, many stories on British immigration could be found, for example

- Catherine Strickland Traill's *Lady Mary and her Nurse; or, A Peep into Canadian Forests* (1856) or *Canadian Crusoes: A Tale of the Rice Lake Plains* (1852),
- Elizabeth Walshe's *Cedar Creek: From the Shanty to the Settlement* (1863) (cf. Waterston 1992, 1-10), or
- R. M. Ballantyne's *Snowflakes and Sunbeams; or The Young Fur Traders* (1856) (cf. Saltman 1987, 8-9, cf. Waterston 1992, 1-10).

On the one hand, the isolation of geographical spaces preserved the literary variety produced in those settlements. On the other hand, Saltman (1987) and Waterston (1992) characterize later Canadian children's literature as an intertwining of different literary traditions, a European and a Native Canadian, which throughout the years has led to a very specific and modern picture of Canadian children's literature. However, folklore of the First Nations did not impinge on the imagination of the settlers in the early days (cf. Waterston 1992, 30).

Yet, Native stories did exist in "full and rich form." These entail different encodings of viewing time, animals and material possessions as well as male and female responsibility. This is, for instance, visible in storytellers' references to trickster figures like Raven and Coyote "indiscriminately as 'he' or 'she'; without being gender-specific" (ibid.). One of the main differences to European stories lies with the perception of animals, which in the European tradition are rather seen as a threat and an enemy, as for example the wolf in *Red Riding Hood* or the bears in *The Three Bears*, while they are seen as guides, helpers and totems in Canadian (First Nation) stories. In order to offer non-native children[89] stories of the indigenous population, non-native writers began to adopt stories of the First Nations. Examples of such texts are *The Song of Hiawatha*

---

[89] Despite the criticism of labelling something or someone in a negative way, saying what they are not, I am using "non-native" in this context which refers to children who are either immigrants themselves or who are descending from immigrants. The same accounts for writers.

(1858), legends of the "Canadian Mohawk Indians" put together and partly re-written by American poet Henry Wadsworth Longfellow and *The Hiawatha Primer* (1898) by Frances Holbrook (cf. Waterston 1992, 31).

Non-native and Native authors rewrote and retold stories of the other and created a broad variety of legendary and mythological storytelling. Accordingly, those reflect 'traditional' beliefs for First Nation children while displaying extended opportunities for non-native children to learn about other cultures and life in an environment they may perceive as harsh. Oral traditions of different First Nations peoples, French folklore, fairy tales and classical legends were adapted for different audiences to make those available and motivating for Canadian immigrant children (cf. ibid., 30-40). Despite the positive undertone of this development, it should not be forgotten that the adaptation of traditional stories by non-native writers has also raised controversy.

Researchers of the field agree that 'white' retellings of First Nations' stories are oftentimes superficial and distorted, if not simply false (Johnston 1983, Nodelman 1983, McGrath 1983, Stott 1983a, 1983b, Whitaker 1983). Johnston summarizes that First Nations' stories and legends were often "refined, smoothed, edited, made coherent; their foreign, incomprehensible, vulgar, violent, erotic elements were softened, altered or removed" (1983, 82) by 'white' authors for a 'white' audience and were thus adapted to fit 'white' preferences and morals. In reference to Inuit stories, McGrath qualifies these changes as twistings and mutilations, and demands that no substitutes of original Inuit literature should be accepted (cf. 1983, 23). For Stott 'white' retellings and interpretations of First Nations' stories are full of stereotypes, "outright bigotry" (1983b, 15) and inaccuracies, "no matter how sensitive or sympathetic" (ibid.) authors try to be. Whitaker sees one difficulty of transferring First Nations' stories to 'white' audiences in the different understandings of mythological figures such as the Raven (cf. 1983, 46). False representations of First Nations have led to a vicious circle: media, "by which information about Native people have been disseminated have been controlled by non-Native peoples," who produced an image of First Nations under strong influence of European philosophy, politics, and art. This, in turn, has led to "the creation of stereotypes" which found entry to the children's literature about First Nations. Many stereotypes from this European point of view prevailed and non-Native children were exposed to an "erroneous portrayal of Native realities" (Stott 1983, 3). Again, Longfellow's *The Song of Hiawatha* can be used as an example to illustrate this. In the epic poem, he used mainly Ojibwa sources to create a First Nation story but brought it closer to Christian and European standards and morals. For example, "the Indian's 'strength and courage'" was considered within a biblical parallel in order to prevent "tipping into 'savagery and violence' in the white mind." Longfellow also put the Ojibwa people into an agrarian surrounding, bringing them closer to 'white' culture. As a reason for those and further changes, Johnston assumes that the 'white' audience wanted to "see the Indian story as a 'less worthy' or 'materialist' or 'primitive' version" (1983, 87). In general, 'white' versions of

First Nation stories can be distinguished in "radical, and often not acknowledged transformations towards white methods and lessons," "more objective ethnological versions attempting to interfere less with the original," and version which were told "by Natives themselves" (ibid., 82).

However, while images of First Nations people were often distorted, more recent Canadian children's literature was also enriched by First Nation influences. Yet, it was not until the late 20th century and the founding of Theytus, the first publishing house owned and operated by First Nations, that First Nation people could publish stories independently and in their own voices (cf. chapter 4.1.3).

Still, this intertwining of different literary traditions within the creation of Canadian children's literature set the stage for the development of multicultural children's literature. Especially the retellings of traditional tales and legends remained part of the Canadian lore (cf. Waterston 1992, 35-40) with a new (Canadian) touch. For example, Waterston refers to "fresh versions of Hans-Christian Andersen's stories, as in Laszlo Gal's *The Little Mermaid,* and new versions of animal fables, as in *Fox Mykyta,* a Ukrainian story retold by Bohdan Meknyk" (ibid., 40). In its further development, early children's literature written in Canada increasingly tried to establish differences between British and French colonizers and the American neighbour to the South, which Waterston interprets as a "reflect[ion of] a sense of national identity" (ibid., 1-10).

The topic of nature was still popular, too. In line with the earliest children's books written in Canada, the adventure stories of the 19th century reflected the "rugged terrain and intemperate climate and dramatized the northern struggle to survive" (ibid., 1-10). Books like R. M. Ballantyne's *The Young Fur Traders* (1865) and W.F. Butler's *Red Cloud* (1882) focus on hostile confrontations between man and nature as well as man and man. Using close observations of nature and wildlife, Earnest T. Seton and Charles G. D. Roberts established the new Canadian genre of realistic wild-animal biographies with their narratives *Wild Animals I have Known* (1898) or the more poetic tale *The Kindred of the Wild* (1902) (cf. Saltman 1987, 9). Marshall Saunder's sentimental dog-story *Beautiful Joe: The Autobiography of a Dog* (1894) is regarded as a distinctive Canadian contribution to this genre.

"Canadian books document another way of life, similar in basic human desires and fears but different in details, rhythm, and tone" (Waterston 1992, 11). This is foremost a result of multicultural influences. Due to intertwining literary traditions, "Canadian children have access to several streams of traditional tales": First Nation, Inuit and Métis legends, additionally to those of immigration groups such as Ukrainian, Caribbean, Japanese or South African (cf. ibid., 28). According to Barbara Sapergia (interview G.A., August 2011) stories of immigration, arriving and being new to a land have prevailed until today as Canada continues to be open to newcomers from abroad.

4.1.2 Family and Animal Stories, Awards and Popularity: 1900 to 1967

At the beginning of the 20th century an "Edwardian tradition of domestic realism" was visible in stories set in schools or contexts of "child-and-family-life" (Saltman 1987, 9) and gained popularity. This was particularly recognizable in the worldwide success of Canada's international bestseller *Anne of Green Gables* (1908) by L.M. Montgomery; other titles worth mentioning are for example Ralph Connor's *Glengarry Schooldays* (1902) or Nellie McClung's *Sowing Seeds in Danny* (1908). Saltman estimates that until 1975 only a few Canadian titles received international recognition, that "very little Canadian work was written and published for children and even less was memorable" (1987, 9). The few exceptions she mentions cover the genres of outdoor-adventure stories combined with close natural observations, animal stories, and retellings of First Nations and Inuit myths and legends (cf. ibid., 9-10).

E. Pauline Johnson (Tekahionwake)[90] was one of the first to write and publish "poems of contemporary Indian life that gripped generations of children" (Waterston 1992, 31). In 1911, she collected *Legends of Vancouver*, tales from the Squamish people. In *The Shagganappi* (1912) and *The Mocassin-Maker* (1913) Johnson collected and published traditional tales of her father's people – both not primarily aimed at children, but their adventurous style made it popular with readers of all ages.

In 1906, the publishing house McClelland & Stewart was founded in Toronto, which initially focused on distributing foreign titles by authors like Rudyard Kipling and Edgar Rice Burroughs; later they also turned to Canadian titles. Important for the circulation of Canadian children's literature was their publication of the aforementioned Canadian classic *Anne of Green Gables* series and Marshall Saunder's *Beautiful Joe*. (Ing n.y., n.p.). *Anne of Green Gables*, which was already successful in the U.S.,[91] soon became an international bestseller that made the Canadian Maritimes popular and accessible for readers within and beyond Canada's borders and offered glimpses at the lifestyle of Prince Edward Island. While the former period depicted the immigrant experience, the second period rather focused on having arrived at home and established a daily routine in Canada.

In 1936, Governor General Lord Tweedsmuir of Elsfield (also known as John Buchan, author of *The Thirty-Nine Steps* (1915)) founded the Governor

---

[90] 1861-1913, her father was one of the chiefs of the Six Nations. Johnson was of Mohawk and English ancestry, which was also visible in her stories as she combined oral legends of the Iroquois with English Romanticism. She was not only a writer, but also a successful performer touring Canada, Great Britain and the United States (cf. New 2002, 555). In 2000, Gerson and Strong-Boag published *Paddling her Own Canoe: The Times and Texts of E. Pauline Johnson (Tekahionwake)*, an in-depth study on Johnson and her literary and cultural achievements in the context of Canadian literature, women studies and First Nation studies.

[91] *Anne of Green Gables* was first published in 1908 by Page in Boston, U.S. It was only after another two successful Anne-stories that Montgomery left Page for Stokes and the Toronto based firm McClelland & Stewart. In 1971, *Anne's House of Dreams* was the first Anne-book published in Canada (cf. Barry/Doody/Doody Jones 1997, 5).

General's Literary Awards. Since then, the awards have been given out in various categories. They have become and today remain Canada's most prestigious literary awards, which initially included fiction, non-fiction, poetry and drama, and did not regard books in French. Those were only included in 1959 and are awarded in separate categories which supports the acknowledgement of Canadian children's literature in French and recognizes its diversity. While juvenile fiction was already awarded between 1950 and 1959, the Canadian Council Children's Literature Prizes were established in 1975 (cf. Richter 2011, 103). In 1987 this prize was changed to the Governor General's Award for Children's Literature, which still annually honours the best text in English and French and the best illustration of books published in each language. Conclusions about the increasing importance and recognition of Canadian children's literature can be drawn based on the monetary scope of the award as well. Originally, it was a non-monetary prize. In 1951, a prize of $250 was awarded which was consecutively being raised to $15,000 in 2000.[92] In 2014, the winner in the category English text was *When Everything Feels like the Movies* by Raziel Reid (2014) which received a prize of CND$25,000.

In *Creating the National Mosaic – Multiculturalism in Canadian Children's Literature from 1950 to 1994*, Richter (2011) offers a comprehensive and detailed account of the development of "Canadian cultural policy with regard to children's culture and literature" (ibid., 59) which I refer to more frequently as it is the first book-length study of Canadian children's literature and multiculturalism. As I have described elsewhere, Richter "frames her literary observations with a discussion of the larger context of Canadian national identity formation to reflect on the ways in which political, literary, and cultural developments are intertwined, especially as they pertain to multiculturalism" (Alter 2012a, 178).[93] As Richter is able to show, for this stage of Canadian literature for young readers Lyn Cook's *The Bells on Finland Street* (1950) and *The Little Magic Fiddler: The Story of Donna Grescoe* (1951) are especially remarkable. Both fostered multicultural awareness when the Canadian policy of multiculturalism had not been established yet (cf. Richter 2011, 194, also discussed in Petzold 2000). *The Bells on Finland Street*, for example, revolves around Elin and her grandfather who are linked through their mutual fascination for figure skating. Through figure skating, Elin becomes aware of her new home and arrives in Canada, while her grandfather is ensured that Finland remains his home (cf. Alter 2012a). This parallels my earlier descriptions of regarding immigrant stories as a link between old and new home countries.

---

[92] Nowadays, also the publishers of winning books receive $3,000 for promotion, which honours their contributions to the children's book development (cf. Canada Council Homepage).
[93] Within the subchapter of National Identity in Canadian Children's Literature (4.2.3) Richter's account will be regarded in more detail.

4.1.3 The Founding of Centers and Publishers: 1967 to 1980

The third phase of the development of Canadian literature for young readers saw a growing awareness of Canadian national identity. As mentioned in the introduction to this chapter, the year 1967 was a turning point. 1967 was also the centennial of Confederation, which is commonly referred to as a watershed year in the history of Canada's cultural emancipation from its colonial ties and mentality (the 1960s and 1970s are also sometimes called "the Canadian Renaissance") (cf. Alter 2011a, 151). This emancipation had lasting consequences for the development of Canadian children's literature, as awareness rose for the "political significance ascribed to a national canon of literature for Canada's youngest citizens" and for "the impact of children's literature on national identity" (Richter 2011, 124-125). In the 1970s, stories of diverse cultures in Canada gained more attention as other backgrounds than French and English increasingly had access to the public sphere. As Ziaja-Buchholtz notes, "Ukrainians were the first ethnic minority to mark their presence this way" when Victoria Symchych and Olga Vesey published *The Flying Ship* in 1975 (cf. 2002, 68), which contributed to multicultural Canadian children's literature.

It took another ten years until the interest in Canadian children's literature grew to such an extent that the Canadian Children's Book Centre (CCBC) was founded in Toronto. The Centre organized the first Children's Book Festival and started publishing *Our Choice*, a journal which recommends and reviews children's books for young readers. Additionally, the Canadian Society of Children's Authors, Illustrators and Performers (CANSCAIP) was founded in 1977 as part of the National Arts Service Organization (NASO). CANSCAIP is "dedicated to the celebration and promotion of Canadian children's authors, illustrators, performers and their work" (CANSCAIP website). With 450 professional members and more than 500 associate members from across Canada, CANSCAIP is one of the largest organizations bringing together old and new talent in the Canadian children's book sector (cf. Richter 2011, 116).

This development until 1977 had not been possible without numerous new publications in the Canadian children's book market. From 1975 on, Saltman observed significant changes in the stories that were published for young readers. These include an alteration of the traditional male outdoor-adventure story to the inclusion of female protagonists, as well as a shift from a focus on physical survival to more symbolic and psychological struggles in the wilderness which often led to an "integration of the self" (cf. Saltman 1987, 13). Janet Lunn's *The Hollow Tree* (1997), for example, presents a strong and brave female protagonist in a wilderness survival saga, a genre that was usually occupied by males (cf. Saltman 2003, 28). Furthermore, "Native and non-native retellers of indigenous traditional literature have begun to write with the inflections and personalized idioms of the oral storyteller's voice". Oral storytelling then included more "non-native collections culled from the folklore and local legends of Canadian pioneers, settlers, immigrants, and ethnic groups" (Saltman 1987, 13). While influences from the "immigrant experience alter[ed] traditional stories from the homeland" and "illustrate[d] a process of acculturation" (ibid.) this again increased the multicultural image of Canadian children's literature.

However, regarding the representation of multicultural characters, Richter sees a "retrograde step in their handling of Canadian multicultural society" (2011, 235) referring to Jean Little's novels *From Anna* and *Listen for the Singing*, both published in the 1970s. In view of the novels' focus on food, festivals and folklore, I can agree with Richter's estimation that both novels "have not contributed to Canada's national multicultural discourse" (ibid.) but rather reinforced a superficial awareness of Canada's multicultural character. Compared to Little's novels, Frances Duncan's *Kap-Sung Ferris* (1977) reflects upon a protagonist's identity crisis, which is caused by her being born in Korea and adopted by Anglo-Canadian parents at the age of two. Richter interprets Kim's search for identity as actively striving for finding a place and establishing a sense of belonging. The scholar speculates that "Kim's search for personal identity can also be read as representing Canada's negotiation of national identity at a time when the new national anthem and the repatriation of the Constitution were being discussed" (ibid.), as Trudeau's White Paper had only been issued six years prior to the publication of *Kap-Sung Ferris*. However, I have argued elsewhere (cf. Alter 2012a) that Kim's crisis could also be regarded as a result of not being able to share the experience of being othered based on ethnicity, as no one in her surroundings can understand what it means to be non-'white.' As I concluded, multiculturalism can be regarded as a system that both 'others' and includes Kim, as it is the ideology of her surroundings that causes severe uneasiness. While Kim is a member of a social group in which she is accepted for who she is, underlying assumptions about power relations continuously objectify her outward appearance (cf. Alter 2012a, 182).[94] According to Richter, multicultural representation had gained even more attention in the 1980s and 1990s which will be explored in the following chapter.

The important role publishing houses[95] played in promoting Canadian children's books increased in stage three and supported the development of diverse Canadian children's literature. Certainly, one of these publishers is Theytus Books (Penticton, founded in 1980), a First-Nations owned and operated North American publisher for indigenous voices. Theytus is Salish and means "preserving for the sake of handing down," a philosophy which aims at "documenting Indigenous cultures and world views through books" (cf. Theytus homepage). Renown First Nation writers such as Drew Hayden Taylor (*Funny*

---

[94] Such mechanisms of exclusion and inclusion will be reflected in terms of transcultural competence in chapter 7 and 9.

[95] In the 1970s many new publishing houses were founded. For example, Maple Tree Press (Toronto) began publishing under the banner of Owl Books in the early 1970s, Kids Can Press was founded in 1973, Red Deer Press (Markham) and Lorimer Children and Teens (Toronto) were founded in 1975, Groundwood Books (Toronto), Nimbus Publishing (Halifax) and Crabtree Publishing (St. Catharines) in 1978, and Orca Book Publisher (Victoria) shortly afterwards in 1982.

You Don't Look Like One titles, 1998-2004), Beatrice Culleton Mosionier (*Unusual Friendships,* 2002), Alootook Ipellie (*Arctic Dreams and Nightmares,* 1983) and Jeannette Armstrong (*Dancing with the Cranes,* 2009, *Neekna and Chemai,* 1984/2008, *Slash* 1985/2007) have published their work with Theytus. Annick Press, located in Toronto and Vancouver and founded in 1975, publishes the non-fiction "We Thought of It" series which celebrates a variety of cultures and their innovations and inventions. Coteau Books (Regina, Saskatoon), founded in 1975, published the "In the Same Boat" series that specifically focuses on a multicultural scope, and to which two of the titles discussed in chapter 5 belong.

One of the recent Canadian children's publisher, Pajama Press, was only founded in 2011, which indicates that Canadian children's literature still has a lot of potential to satisfy readers' and authors' needs. The work of Canadian publishers has undoubtedly facilitated the thriving of Canadian children's literature and continues to do so as more and more authors send in unpublished manuscripts and look for publishers who support their work (cf. interview with Nik Burton, August 2011). In order to further promote Canadian authors, the late 1970s and beginning 1980s aimed at increasing the implementation of Canadian children's literature in education.

In this phase, the work of illustrators also gained more recognition which was visible through the creation of the Amelia Frances Howard-Gibbon Illustrator's Award in 1971, the first awards for Canadian children's books artist. The first novel to win was Mary Alice Downie's and Elizabeth Cleaver's *The Wind Has Wings* (1968) (cf. Canadian Library Association website). In 2014, Jon Klassen won this award for his illustration of Lemony Snicket's *The Dark* (2013).

4.1.4 Promotion, Multicultural Orientation and Education: 1980 to 2000

In 1982, the Children's Book Festival kit provided by the CCBC included a teacher's guide to using Canadian children's literature in school (cf. Hoyte 2007, 20). This could be seen as a reaction to Jobe and Hambleton's 1981 survey which revealed that "of the 124 titles featured in the 1979 *Our Choice* guide, Alberta, British Columbia, and Saskatchewan teachers had heard of only 35 and used only nine" (Hoyte 2007, 20). As knowledge and awareness of Canadian literature for young readers was still scarce, I suggest that the outreach of people concerned with Canadian children's literature to schools and educational institutions marked the beginning of the fourth phase. This outreach also included the 'TD Grade One Book Giveaway,' a program initiated by the CCBC in cooperation with ministries of education, school boards and library organizations. Since the year 2000 this program has been giving a free Canadian children's book to every child in Grade 1 across Canada. In 2014, this book was

Doors in the Air (Des portes dans les airs), written by David Weale and illustrated by Pierre Pratt (2012) (cf. CCBC homepage).[96]

The establishment of numerous awards for Canadian authors and illustrators promoted and increased the publication of more high-quality literature for young readers, which resulted in an extended international recognition of Canadian children's authors (cf. Saltman 2003, 24). These awards pay tribute to various genres and publications for different age-groups. In total, the CCBC mentions 67 Canadian awards, most of which are awarded annually, and 15 discontinued awards which were given out by the CCBC itself and by national and provincial organizations. Although some awards were established long before 1980, the end of the 20th century witnessed an increasing establishment of new awards, which not only reflect the growing diversity of Canadian children's literature, but its literary and artistic recognition and acknowledgement, too.[97] Remarkably, these awards also include reader's choice awards where students in Grades 4 to 6 pick the winner (e.g. Manitoba Young Readers' Choice Award, The Silver Birch Award).

A further important step in promoting Canadian children's books was the introduction of national chapters, East and West, of the Society of Children's Book Writers and Illustrators (SCBWI) in Canada. Founded in 1971 in Los Angeles as an international organization which supports "people who write, illustrate, or share a vital interest in children's literature," the SCBWI has been having a presence in Canada since 1997, providing "a network for writers, illustrators, editors, publishers, agents, librarians, educators, booksellers and others involved with literature for young people" (SCBWI website). The authors and

---

[96] The books that have been given away reflect Canada's diversity of children's literature, as these include, for example, *Caramba* (Marie-Louise Gay, 2006) given out in 2010, in which all cats can fly but Caramba. When he is accidentally dropped in the water, he discovers his talent for swimming, which the other cats do not have. *The Girl Who Hated Books* (Majnusha Pawagi, 2010) was given away in 2003. The book is about Meena who grows up in a house full of books because her parents are bibliophiles. When she tries to rescue her cat, Max, she falls down a tower of books. As these crash down, the pages fly open and the protagonists escape. Humpty Dumpty, Ali Baba, Peter Rabbit and other literary figures occupy the room. In order to bring them all back, Meena has to read the books to find out where they belong. She needs to open the stories for the protagonists to return home.

[97] For example, the CCBC established the Geoffrey Bilson Award for Historical Fiction for Young Readers in 1988, the 2014 winner was Karen Bass' *Graffiti Knight* (2013) (cf. CCBC website). The Norma Fleck Award for Canadian Children's Non-Fiction was "established in 1999 to recognize and raise the profile of exceptional non-fiction books" in the fields of "Culture and the Arts, Science, Biography, History, Geography, Reference, Sports, Activities and Pastimes," the 2014 winner was Rona Arato's *The Last Train: A Holocaust Story* (2013) (cf. ibid.). New genres were also taken into account. Since 1984 the Crime Writers of Canada use the Arthur Ellis Award for Juvenile Literature to honour the best crime book for young readers. Further awards include The Red Maple Award (1998) for books for readers in Grades 7 and 8 and The Red Cedar Book Award (British Columbia) both established in 1998. In addition, the International Board on Books for Young People through their Canadian section annually honours the best Canadian illustrator of a picture book that was published in Canada with the Elizabeth Mrazik-Cleaver Award established in 1985.

illustrators are supported by conference sponsorings, awards and grants for works in progress and by help in getting published. Thus, the SCBWI contributes essentially to increasing the amount of Canadian children's literature available to young readers.

Apart from organizations that work on an (inter)national level, Canadian Provinces also promote authors and illustrators of texts for young readers. For example, the Young Alberta Book Society (YABS) was founded in 1985 which assists and brings together storytellers, authors and illustrators "to enrich[...] the lives of children and youth through the literary arts" (YABS website). The YABS is committed to inspiring Alberta's children by Alberta's authors, and thus follows educational as well as social integration objectives. Similarly, the Children's Writers and Illustrators of British Columbia Society (CWILL BC) promotes books for young readers by local writers. The Society brings together about 150 members across BC who not only exchange information about creating literature for young readers but who are also available for school or library presentations (cf. CWILL BC website). These measures, the establishment of awards and the foundation of organizations to support Canadian writers, secure the striving for high-quality reading material and allow young readers to have access to Canada's cultural heritage, nationally and regionally.

Between the years 1980 and 2000, further genres became popular as children read more "novels of social history, time travel fantasy, and [...] picture books" (Saltman 2003, 24). The 1990s witnessed an increased publication of (aboriginal) picture books and retellings of folktales, poetry, nursery rhymes, as well as realistic and historic fiction, and novels that tell different kinds of fantasy stories such as animal, revisionist and ghost fantasies.

Toward the end of the 20th century, more and more titles for young readers were published which obtained a deeper and richer consideration of Canada's multicultural population (cf. Saltman 2003, 24).[98] Now, numerous authors of diverse ethnic backgrounds gave voice to their own or their ancestors' immigrant experience. Harvey Chan, Tololwa Mollel, Paul Yee or Luis Garay are some of the writers who enriched Canadian children's literature. Monica Hughes's *My Name is Paula Popowich!* (1983) or Paul Yee's *Breakaway* (1994) (also discussed in Petzold 2000 and Richter 2011) are examples which offer a specific perspective on multiculturalism and its challenges for the individual. Paula, protagonist of Hughes's novel, is of German and Ukrainian heritage and has friends of Italian, Ukrainian, Scottish, and German background. She needs to come to terms with an identity crisis that is triggered by discovering photographs and documents of her unknown father (cf. Alter 2012a, 182). Yet, through this discovery and the help of her grandmother, Paula is able to finally say "my name is Paula Popowich!" As Richter notes, Hughes's novel emphasizes alienation, the importance of a social network and the benefits of multicul-

---

[98] Küster and Keller (2002) offer a concise overview of the increasing ethnicity and multiculturalism in Canadian literature in general.

turalism (cf. ibid., 183, Richter 2011). Yee's *Breakaway* adds another view as the protagonist Kwok rejects his Chinese heritage and favours being Canadian (cf. Richter 2011, 285). However, he is continuously identified as 'other' based on his outward appearance. In my reading of the novel, the existence of a soccer team exclusively for players of Chinese heritage and Kwok's decision not to go to university but to work on his father's farm, reflect a strong separation of both groups which appear as cultural others from each perspective. Additionally, this shows how difficult a practical application of the policy of multiculturalism is in a society of majorities and 'visible minorities' (cf. Alter 2012, 184). Yet, Petzold qualifies these aspects as a rejection of "such shallow ideas of assimilation" and believes that the novel "challenges both the idea that multiculturalism is merely a question of a person being friendly with his or her neighbors and the Eurocentrism of official Canadian policy" (2000, 184).

In this decade the representation of multiculturalism

> moved from the superficial treatment of multiculturalism as a confined issue in the early books of the 1960s and 1970s to a richer examination of life within a variety of cultures. Writers and illustrators of the 1990s tend to address cultural diversity in a broader and more considered exploration. (Saltman 2003, 25)

This indicates that with the turn of the century, Canadian children's literature entered a phase in which multicultural stories gain more popularity, and that, also other forms of otherness are increasingly represented in the literature for young readers. A prime example of a text that has reworked two different literary traditions into one transcultural text of fantasy fiction is Hiromi Goto's *The Water of Possibility* (2001) (cf. chapter 5.3).

4.1.5 Development and Challenges since 2000

The analysis of the development and state of the art of Canadian literature for young readers permits a prediction of a blossoming future, in academics as well as in actual publishing. Both aspects are increasingly present in the post-millennium years. New awards, publishing houses and organization which circulate books contribute to a growing diversification of Canadian children's literature. However, recent challenges have impinged on this impression. At the beginning of the millennium, different journalists, The Canadian Council of the Arts and The Writers Trust of Canada claimed that the publishing industry, censorship, the amount of Canadian children's literature taught in school and a lacking national identity in Canadian literature for young readers have had negative influences on the development of Canadian children's literature. For the context at hand, Canadian children's literature taught in school, the publishing industry as well as the situation in children's book sections in different Canadian bookstores will be considered, as these illustrate the reception of Canadian children's literature in the post-millennium years.

In her article "U.S. demands trample Canadian Kid's Lit" (*The Globe and Mail*, June 1, 2001, M1), Strauss refers to recent incidences which shed a rather pessimistic light on Canadian children's literature. She points out that in order to be able to compete with the children's book market in the U.S., many Canadian children's books are "de-Canadianised" and "Americanized." For example, 'colour' is changed to 'color' and *Kids Cottage Games* are changed to *Kids Summer Games*, because U.S. American children would not be familiar with cottages. Names of places and settings are changed or anonymized in order to appeal to U.S. American readers (cf. ibid.). It would often be difficult for small Canadian presses to publish a larger number of copies of a title, which is why many Canadian authors approach U.S. American presses instead which in turns makes such changes necessary. As Nik Burton, managing editor of Coteau Books confirms, the competition with the U.S. has always been a big issue and will remain one, which is mainly due to the size of the U.S. publishing market and economy, and their subsequent ability to advertise much lower prices than small or medium size Canadian presses. There is "no way a children's book publisher could survive in Canada alone, you have to publish in the U.S. or abroad. Canadian publishers use U.S. spelling in hope to sell more in the U.S., it is a necessity" (interview G.A., August 2011). For a medium publisher such as Coteau Books, different issues of one book are hardly affordable. However, regional identity is essential to their books, and therefore, Coteau Books prefers Canadian spelling and local settings, even if this entails the need to rely on public and governmental, federal and provincial funding (interview G.A. with Sapergia, August 2011).

Currently, one of the challenges of publishing children's books is the competition with new media and the tendency that young people rather read digital media and e-books than paper-based books (Burton, interview G.A., August 2011). The children's book market would be more media-driven than ever before. "There are many publishers in the States which won't even publish a book if it doesn't have a movie tie-in" (ibid.). Again, the competition with the U.S. plays an important role, because smaller Canadian publishers do not "have the budget to compete with novelizations of movies which have a million-dollar advertisement budget" (ibid.). The popularity of personal electronic devices also has a major influence on the book market. "Books are the old world, kindle etc. is the new world; and people are fond of the new" (ibid.). Interestingly, this development is special in the teen division because "it was small to start with: teen fiction is a relatively new category, so any kind of growth is going to be amazing" (ibid.). Burton identifies further reason in the "demographic that can be easily reached with modern media; you can get on Facebook or Twitter and advertise a book to the teen market because this is where they live. The adult market is much more diffused in that; it is easier nowadays to zoom into the teen market" (ibid.).

Despite certain challenges posed by a competition regarding digital media and the U.S. American market, Canadian publishing is able to provide young readers with Canadian content, especially due to strong regional foci, as Burton estimates. This is also visible in the list of Canada-based publishers which includes more than 60 entries (cf. CCBC website), many of which are regional and continuously seek unpublished documents by Canadian writers.

Strauss further estimated that Canada-specific content is about to decrease since the Children's Book Store in Toronto, the largest bookstore entirely devoted to children's literature, had to close as it was no longer able to compete with the offerings of huge superstores (cf. 2001, M1). Indeed, one of the most important entities for distributing books and reading material are bookstores, be those independent or privately owned bookstores, chains that can be found all over the country or online distributors.[99] When Strauss sees bookstores as a means of promoting Canadian children's books, the knowledge of the staff is essential. Visiting various bookstores across Canada, I sampled the staff's knowledge in this field and discovered that the employees' knowledge and stores' selection of Canadian literature for young readers is very different.[100] The employees at Chapters/Indigo in Toronto, for instance, have tried to be most helpful when being asked for Canadian literature for children and young adults, but although one of the employees even mentioned that she had just attended a presentation by Canadian children's publishers, Kelley Armstrong and Gordon Korman were the only Canadian authors for young readers she could mention. When asked for further authors, the employees relied on the symbols of Canadian publishers on the spine of the book to find titles by national authors. Moreover, of the eleven authors of books for young readers featured on the Chapters/Indigo webpage, Kelley Armstrong and Lesley Livingston were the only Canadians (August 2011). Interestingly, their webpage now offers a complete section on "Canadian Books for Teens" (January 2015).

The World's Biggest Bookstore in downtown Toronto, which was opened in 1940 as the first original book superstore by Carl and Jack Cole, houses the largest display of children's books across Canada. The employees have been able and helpful in guiding costumers to Canadian authors for various age groups. The independent Winnipeg-based bookstore McNally Robinson invites young readers to its mezzanine where a wide selection of Canadian picture books and literature for young adults is on display. The reader not only finds separate bookshelves for Canadian titles but also literature by authors from the specific province in the Winnipeg and the Saskatoon store. When asked for advice, the employees were highly helpful and supportive, knowing many titles from their own reading experiences.

---

[99] Online bookstores are left out of the following investigation, as these order books internationally and it is thus difficult to conclude which Canadian titles are actually in stock.

[100] The following is a reflection of personal experiences. Conducting a study which analyses the amount of Canadian children's literature on display in Canadian bookstores would have been highly interesting, but unfortunately this is beyond the scope of my focus in this work.

In sum, the promotion of Canadian titles for young readers depends on the bookstore and the staff members. When looking for Canadian literature for young readers, it is likely to find the most popular books on display; when looking for titles with a special focus or for a certain age-group the reader either has to rely on knowledgeable employees in bookstores or needs to use the internet.

One further aspect in focus is the amount of Canadian children's literature in Canadian schools, which was critically discussed by Harker (1987), Pantaleo (2002) and the Canadian Council for the Arts and Writers Trust of Canada (2002). They generally criticize that although students get a very good education, they too often leave schools without having read a Canadian book, but William Golding's *Lord of the Flies* or Harper Lee's *To Kill a Mockingbird* instead. Johnston conducted a study which showed that in fact only 14% of the texts read in schools are Canadian, which is less than half of the required amount (interview G.A., September 2011). Pantaleo and Canadian Council for the Arts and Writers Trust of Canada state that the majority of literature taught in Canadian schools was written by U.S. American authors, which contradicts and counteracts the measures taken up to promote Canadian literature in school.[101]

Sapergia sees reasons for a decrease of Canadian literature in school in the employment of teacher librarians: "their number has been reduced to save money. You don't have someone in the school who is promoting the reading of Canadian works and who is watching for titles that come out" (interview G.A., August 2011). Burton states that librarians hardly ever buy books that have not received a review from a recognized review journal such as *Canadian Materials* or *Quill and Quire* (interview G.A., August 2011). To improve the situation at schools, many publishers offer free study guides as downloads from their webpages to encourage teachers to use Canadian texts more often. For example, Coteau Books provides teachers with free classroom guides for titles like *Fight for Justice* by Lori Saigeon (2009), a young adult novel on bullying and a number of other books (cf. Coteau website).

Ministries of Education have reacted to this need as well and ascribed Canadian texts a central position in various curricula. For example, the Alberta curriculum[102] demands that

> [i]n each senior high school English language arts course, it is expected that a significant proportion of texts that students study will be Canadian texts. The required minimum proportion of Canadian texts studied is one third of all texts studied in each course. Teachers are encouraged to select Canadian texts for study whenever

---

[101] Cf. Alter (2011a) for a detailed account of the challenges mentioned here.

[102] In Canada, education is a provincial jurisdiction, so each province has its own program of studies and curriculum.

possible and appropriate. (Government of Alberta/Education 2003, 10)

Similar descriptions can be found in the curricula for English Language Arts in the other provinces, for example Manitoba,[103] Ontario,[104] Quebec[105], or British Columbia[106] which demands that "English teachers [...] assign at least one Canadian book per year" (Wigod 2008). While the curricula for Saskatoon do not specifically refer to an amount of Canadian content, these in fact state that cultural and literary competences have to be developed using "First Nations, Métis, and other Canadian and international texts."[107] One spinoff effect of such demands is that Canadian titles inscribed into school curricula increase the amount of Canadian books in bookstores, as these available for longer periods of time (cf. Wigod 2008).

Despite those challenges of the post-millennium years, Canadian children's literature has also moved forward, especially regarding new genres such as cross-media storytelling and the significance it has reached in academic studies. The founding of the Centre for Research in Young People's Texts and Cultures (CRYTC) in Winnipeg in 2006 reflects such growing academic attention. In addition to the hands-on, practical approach of the CCBC which has been promoting Canadian literature for children and young readers since 1977, CRYTC attempts to refine a Canadian perspective on academic approaches to literature for young readers on an international level. CRYTC was established "in order to recognize, organize, and extend the expertise in the study of texts for children and youth that had developed at the University" (cf. CRYTC website). As such, the Centre "supports scholarly inquiry into literary, media, and other cultural texts for children and youth" (CRYTC website). It is also home of *Jeunesse: Young People, Texts, Cultures*, a journal which was first published in 1975. Since then it has been dedicated to "advancing knowledge and understanding of texts produced for children in Canada in a range of media in English, French and other languages" (*CCL/LCJ* website). The change of name from *Canadian Children's Literature/Littérature canadienne pour la jeunesse* (*CCL/LCJ*) in 2009 entailed a change of focus, as *Jeunesse* is internationally oriented while keeping a special interest in Canada. The scope of content has been extended, too: the journal's mandate now is to "publish research on, and to provide a forum for discussion about, cultural productions for, by, and about young people" (*Jeunesse* website). Their special interest lies with "historical and contemporary constructions, functions, and roles of 'the child' and adolescents; and literature, art, and films by children and young adults." This can in-

---

103 Manitoba Education and Training 2000, 98. In order to provide a reader-friendly layout, the following sources are offered as footnotes, references are included in the bibliography.
104 Ministry of Education, The Ontario Curriculum 2007, 16, 35.
105 Ministère de l'Education, du Loisir et du Sport, n.y. 41.
106 Ministry of Education, Province of British Columbia 2007, 17.
107 Ministry of Education, Saskatchewan curriculum, *English Language Arts 10*, 2011, 37.

clude representations of the child and "children's and young adult literature and media" in the broadest sense, also toys and digital culture (cf. *Jeunesse* website). On the one hand, this opening toward an international frame opens Canadian academia to include international perspectives, but on the other hand, this also reduces the academic attention Canadian children's literature had gained until 2009.

Also in the post-millennium phase, several organizations and sponsors have facilitated the circulation and reading of Canadian children's books. For example, Indigo established the "Love of Reading Fund" in 2004 which is now called the "Love of Reading Foundation." This charitable initiative is "dedicated to enhancing literacy and self-esteem in students," to "promoting learning opportunities," and to "supporting teachers and students in high-need schools across Canada by providing new books and resources" (cf. Chapters/Indigo website). Additionally, Indigo launched the Junior Advisory Board in 2004, in which a team of "Canada's best and brightest young readers" offers its opinion on the reading material peers are interested in (cf. ibid.).

The aforementioned establishment of literary awards for children's books has continued, too. The latest of which are the Aurora Awards, founded in 2013, which "honour the best Canadian science fiction and fantasy literary works, artwork, and fan activities" (CCBC website) and pay tribute to the prospering development of new genres within literature and media for young readers.[108] The Burt Award for First Nations, Métis and Inuit Literature was founded in 2013 as well and is given out to authors of excellent First Nation, Métis and Inuit literature who "provide engaging and culturally-relevant books for young people across Canada" (ibid.). As with the previous phases, these new awards continue to support the recognition of high-quality literature for young readers and the diversification of the literary scope.

Topic-wise, books for young readers of the late 20th and early 21st centuries increasingly focus on a struggle for identity and coming-of-age and are set in urban environments[109] which demand the protagonists to handle issues like homelessness, substance abuse and addictions, or struggles with family, peer groups and school as well as global issues. This is, for example, visible in Jennifer Cowan's *earthgirl* (2009), Dennis Foon's *Double or Nothing* (2011), Alma Fullerton's *Burn* (2010), or Eric Walter's *Sketches* (2007a). Currently, vampire stories and stories of supernatural powers have become more popular

---

[108] Other awards that were established in this phase include the Marilyn Baillie Picture Book Award of 2006 to honour outstanding illustrated picture books and the TD Canadian Children's Literature Award of 2004 to honour the most distinguished book of the year (cf. CCBC website). The Canadian Children's Book Centre recently paid tribute to latest developments of genres of literature for young readers. The Monica Hughes Award was first awarded in October 2012 to an excellent book of children's science fiction and fantasy aimed at readers between 8 to 16 years of age; the first winner was P.J. Sarah Collins' *What Happened to Serenity?* (2011) (cf. CCBC website).

[109] As Saltman (1987) and Richter (2011) note, urban environments were already focused in the 1970s as well.

and are also present in Canadian young adult fiction with Kelley Armstrong's *Waking the Witch* (2010), *The Gathering* (2011a) and *Spell Bound* (2011b).

With new media gaining increasing importance in the daily life of not only young people, a few Canadian authors use an intersection of different formats in their fiction (Montgomery 2008, Cowan 2009, Prinz 2009). Books that include lyrics of songs, but also references to an online world either as a part or as an extension of the narration, provide motivating cross-media reading experiences. These are part of 'transmedia narratives' which is a new genre of fiction (cf. Alter 2014, Hallet 2013, Jenkins 2007, Ryan 2010/2013).

This detailed overview shows that despite certain challenges Canadian children's literature is striving, alive and well. Within the past few years literature for young readers, high in quantity and quality has emerged from Canada and it is certainly true that "Canada […] is a storied place [and] a very happening place" (Wynne-Jones in Nodelman 1997, 19). To pull the different stages together, the following chapter offers a summarizing characterization of Canadian literature for young readers.

4.2 Characteristics of (Current) Canadian Children's Literature

"So, what is Canadian about Canadian children's literature? *Everything*. It comes out of us and is the stuff of our living" (in Nodelman 1997, 16). Thus reads Jan Andrews', storyteller and writer who was nominated for the Governor-General's Award in 1996, answer to Nodelman's question what it is that makes Canadian children's literature Canadian. Surely, this is a rather general and inclusive account which is dealt with in more detail in the following part.

From the aforementioned issues of Canadian literature for young readers, it is possible to derive certain characteristics which could help to describe it within a national and cultural frame. The characteristics of Canadian children's literature touch upon various fields, such as Canadian national identity, environment and nature or multiculturalism. In 1997, Nodelman published a survey which dealt with the question "What is Canadian about Canadian Children's Literature?" When answers to this question point to various moments of understanding Canada in environmental, historical, social and political terms, they were just as diverse on a meta-level: "some people loved the idea" (ibid., 15) of such a mindset, while others "objected even to the idea of asking such a question" (ibid.), others

> found it irrelevant and desperately old-fashioned. Some were deeply suspicious about the value of ever doing any thinking at all about literature in terms of issues of nationality. Some were convinced that the project was a conspiracy to promote one particular

view of Canadian identity over others, with upsetting or dangerous political ramifications. (ibid.)

Nevertheless, the responses Nodelman collected refer to categories like images of self, a sense of place, regionalism, heterogeneity, multiculturalism and notions of character; some voices also questioned whether any differences to other literatures for young readers existed at all. Judith Saltman puts the answer to Nodelman's question into a nutshell, saying that "[w]hat makes Canadian children's literature Canadian is its reflection of our history, values, geography, and stories, especially stories. [...] Our books appear to be marked by a spirit of regionalism, diversity, even a quirky deadpan, wonderfully Canadian sense of humour" (in ibid., 21-22).

4.2.1 Reflections on National Identity

Titles like Mandel and Tara's *A Passion for Identity: An Introduction to Canadian Studies* (1987) indicate that Canadian studies, historically, politically, culturally and literary, see identity as a major topic that finds various approaches, suggestions and answers in the respective scholarship. In general and also with regard to Canadian children's literature, Canadian national identity is a central topic. Yet, Canadians seem to be most confident naming what they are not when asked who they are in terms of nationality. They would first of all not be Americans (cf. Doff 2010, 3). However, literature as an artistic expression of a nation's population can be seen as an indicator of what characterises this nation's identity. Northrop Frye and Margaret Atwood are two scholars who critically investigated Canadian literatures and suggested metaphors to describe what unites Canadian literature and Canadian identity.

Frye's identification of a "garrison mentality" (1995, 227) as a defining characteristic of Canadian literature refers to Canada's environment and settlement patterns against a hostile and threatening nature. Both lead to an isolation which in turn determined the character of a country and its people (cf. chapter 4.1.1). Frye characterizes the communities in Canada as "small and isolated [...] surrounded with a physical or psychological 'frontier' [...] compelled to feel a great respect for the law and order that holds them together [...], confronted with a huge, unthinking, menacing and formidable physical setting" (1995, 227). The communities necessarily had to develop a 'garrison mentality' in order to protect themselves and secure the survival of all. This "closely knit and beleaguered society" (ibid.) was already visible in early maps when Canada consisted of forts. However, Frye himself is aware of certain changes as he acknowledges that the 'garrison mentality' lost some of its validity as "writers of the last decade [...] have begun to write in a world which is post-Canadian, as it is post-American, post-British, and post everything except the world itself. There are no provinces in the empire of aeroplanes and television, and no physical separation from the centres of culture" (1965, 848).

One of the most influential attempts to define Canadian identity was suggested by Atwood in her ground-breaking text *Survival. A Thematic Guide to Canadian Literature* (1972), for which she uses Frye's garrison mentality as a foundation. She argues that while "every country or culture has a single and informing symbol as its core" (1972, 32), the Canadian symbol "is undoubtedly Survival" (ibid.), which is "based on numerous instances of its occurrence in both English and French Canadian literature" (ibid.). This notion of survival is visible in Canadian literature and could, according to Atwood, be seen as a unifying symbol of Canadian literary identity. She argues that for the early settlers and explorers, survival was present in facing hostile natural elements and/or the Natives, for the French Canadian it rather meant a cultural survival after the English established a majority and the French had to struggle to keep their religion and language alive under an alien government. In English Canada Atwood sees this survival within a resistance toward the powerful neighbour to the South, the United States.

However, this assumption does not explicitly include Canada's indigenous population or the early waves of immigration. For those, survival was essential as well: for the First Nations as they had to secure their existence against British and French power, and for European (late 19th century) or Asian (beginning 20th century) immigrants in a struggle for acceptance. Interestingly, these struggles were even the topic of children's and young adult fiction, as Richter notices with reference to Lyn Cook's *The Bells on Finland Street* (1950) and *The Little Magic Fiddler* (1951) or Frances Duncan's *Kap-Sung Ferris* (1977) (2011, cf. chapter 4.2.3).

Atwood's and Frye's theories of Canadian literary identity are first attempts to differentiate Canadian from U.S. and European traditions which until then had strongly influenced Canadian self-perception. However, a strong sense of regionalism across Canada and increasing immigration challenged both theories (cf. Bennett 2002, 21-28).[110] This diversity and hybridity, though, was soon seen as the marker that distinguished Canadian identity from the U.S. and their notion of the melting pot.

Through certain political and historical developments, which cannot be discussed here, multiculturalism became Canada's official policy, established in 1971 and legislated in 1988 in the Multiculturalism Act and Bill C-93, the "Act for the preservation and enhancement of multiculturalism in Canada" (cf. chapter 3.2).[111] The Act has originally been thought to constitutionally recognize

---

[110] Tunkel refers to further criticism of Frye's "garrison mentality" and Atwood's "Survival" (2012, 26-28). Both concepts were criticized, e.g. for their attempt "to define a single Canadian identity [and] taking for granted only one specific imaginary and forcing upon the country a constructed national unity" (ibid., 29). This would not agree with the country's changing social and political reality. Furthermore, Bennett (2002) points at certain dividing lines which make it difficult to agree to a unifying Canadian identity (regionalism and a rural vs. urban divide, for example).

[111] Hutcheon (1990) offers a concise overview of the development and recognition of Canadian

Canada's diverse population and promote an attitude of tolerance and understanding for diverse people's individual contributions to Canada's society. However, establishing multiculturalism as an official policy in the phrases used in the Act has caused much criticism, which regard the "mythology of 'two founding nations'" and the failure to "address complex questions of identity" (Johnston et al. 2006, 76). Although the Act intended to secure the same rights to all members of society, Johnston et al. point out that "Canada remains a country in which much of the power rests in the hands of those of European descent" (ibid.). Scholars such as Bissoondath, Bannerji, Kamboureli, and Mukherjee "have [...] expressed dissatisfaction with traditional official notions of multiculturalism" (ibid., 77).[112]

For Kamboureli and Mukherjee one critical aspect was that Frye and Atwood only considered canonical Canadian texts which excluded marginalized voices. Despite being criticized often, these explanations of Canadian identity "have not been replaced yet by more inclusive theories of Canada and Canadian literature" (Mukherjee 1998, 73). In order to get a whole picture of Canadian identity it would be necessary and essential to include "what Aboriginal and racial minority writers tell us about Canada and Canadian literature" (ibid.). Canadian identity cannot be grasped "on notions of Canada's duality and remain[s] profoundly oblivious to Aboriginal and racial minority voices" (ibid.). Kamboureli strongly questions multiculturalism's essentialist attitude:

> while multiculturalism is expected to facilitate the process of decolonizing the inherited representations of Canadian history, the literary traditions, and other forms of culture, it is also seen as essentializing race and ethnicity, namely assigning to racial and ethnic differences, as well as their various expressions, attributes that are taken to be 'natural', and therefore stable. (2007, xxix)

Kamboureli argues that the "unity of Canadian identity is a cultural myth, a myth that can be sustained only by eclipsing the identities of others. We are at the point now where the presumed uniqueness of Canadian identity is only that – a presumption"[113] (ibid., xxvii). Although she refers to some Canadians who may see this Act as a chance for equality and participation, she also mentions that to 'preserve' and to 'enhance' promote stereotypical images of people's culture, "and advocate[s] a kind of ethnocentrism that might further prevent their integration into mainstream society" (ibid., xxix). Based on Canada's cul-

---

multiculturalism with regard to literature in her introduction to *Other Solitudes* (1-16).

[112] In their introduction to *The Canadian Mosaic in the Age of Transnationalism*, Ernst and Glaser (2010, 7-17) offer a recommendable overview of the development of multiculturalism in Canada and its critical reflection. Also Tunkel's (2012) elaborations on multiculturalism, its criticism and development toward transculturality can be recommended.

[113] Kamboureli argues for this position with reference to legislations that limited immigration from certain countries, for example the Immigration Act of 1906 which controlled the influx of Asian immigrants.

turally and ethnically diverse society, for her it is impossible to deduce an all-embracing national identity or an inclusive 'Canadian character.'

When thinking of Canadian national identity at the end of the 20th and beginning 21st century, the comments about Kulyk-Keefer's metaphor of the mosaic can be called to mind (cf. chapter 1.3.2). An interesting case in point for a literary perspective, though, is Atwood's estimation 30 years after the first publication of *Survival*:

> People often ask me what I would change about *Survival* if I were writing it today. The obvious answer is that I wouldn't write it to-day, because I wouldn't need to. The thing I set out to prove has been proven beyond a doubt: few would seriously argue, anymore, that there is no Canadian literature. The other answer is that I wouldn't be able to write it, not only because of my own hardening brain, but because the quantity, range and diversity of books now published would defeat any such effort. (1999, 16)

Regarding Canadian children's literature,[114] Jerry Diakiw took up the challenge to define a Canadian identity inclusive of its diversity. He not only discusses that "shared stories provide a culture with its values and beliefs, its goals and traditions" (1997, 37) and that "schools play a major role in the crea-tion of a national culture" (ibid., 38). Diakiw also ponders the difficulty of de-fining a Canadian national identity that results from formerly mentioned official multiculturalism. He argues that negating a common Canadian culture could re-sult in a "backlash against multiculturalism" and asks whether multiculturalism, on the one hand, and a common culture, on the other, are necessarily mutually exclusive, or whether a "remarkable diversity" (ibid., 39) of Canada could not be able to provide "inclusive commonplaces." His historical view reveals that Canada's diversity has often been named the item that forms the basis of Cana-da's cultural definition (cf. ibid., 39-41).

Despite all difficulty and the complexity of the discourse, and although he is aware of the "temporal character of culture" (ibid., 42) and that "[n]ations are constantly assimilating, combining and revising their national character," Diakiw identifies commonplaces of Canadian culture and identity which refer to

- wilderness,
- a diverse and distinctive nature,
- social determination and a "strong sense of social welfare,"
- a nation of immigrants, English, French and aboriginal roots which are entwined in Canadian culture,
- a strong economy,

---

[114] Bennett (2002) offers interesting insights and multicultural developments in Canadian adult fiction.

- cultural traditions in the arts, sports and popular culture, and
- international reputation as a peace-keeper and partner with all nations. (ibid., 42-43)

While one or more of those commonplaces seem to apply to other nations as well, Diakiw believes and I agree that "the layering of them, one over another, creates a unique Canadian culture" and that the whole is "different from any one of the regional, cultural or ethnic cultures and identities that exist within Canada" (ibid., 43) – those commonplaces are said to be inclusive and relatable for all regions and cultural groups that are part of Canada's multiculturalism.

Diakiw's assumption that stories and literature play a decisive role in sharing and teaching those commonplaces to the next generations is essential. These transmit the foundations of a culture and nation, a statement that reflects and agrees to my discussion of texts in chapter 7. Diakiw supports this thesis by suggesting "a loose list of shared Canadian materials" (ibid., 45) which includes reading material for different genres, topics and for readers of different age groups. For example, for pre-primer alphabet books like R.K. Gordon's *A Canadian Child's ABC* (1931), Erica Rutherford's *An Island Alphabet* (1994) about PEI or Stephanie Poulin's *Ah! Belle Cité: A Beautiful City* (1985) are suggested. Many of the categories like fairy tales and legends, historical novels and multicultural stories include authors and titles that reflect the regional, cultural and religious diversity of Canadian society, including its positive as well as challenging components. Examples of the latter are titles such as Joy Kagawa's *Naomi's Road* (1986), Barbara Smucker's *Underground to Canada* (1978) or Michelle Marineau's *Road to Chlifa* (1992) (cf. ibid., 45-47).

Johnston et al. are convinced that "text[s] written for children and young adults [not only] mirror cultural attitudes [but also] play a part in acculturating young readers" (2006, 76). To investigate the perception of national identity and ideology and the depiction of otherness implemented in Canadian multicultural picture books, Johnston et al. conducted a study with pre-service teachers. This showed that the 40 Canadian picture books included in the study mirror multiculturalism as a central aspect through various means like representing diverse characters and protagonists, diverse regions and environments as well as customs and cultural practices (ibid., 84-86). Thus, they offer links for readers to identify with the books as well as identifying the books as Canadian.

A further remarkable finding of the study regards the perception and imagining of the other (cf. ibid., 86-87). Here, the students' responses to the picture books almost seem surprising when some stated that "[a]s a white, middle-class girl, I felt incredibly under-represented by the literature in the workshop" (ibid., 86). While this student appreciates diversity, she felt that it is "easy to marginalize those who are not concentrated on" (ibid., 86). Other participants responded that they did not see any reflection of 'mainstream' society within the books.[115] The students identified members of different than their own cultural and ethnic background as 'other' and perceived their 'white' middle-class background as 'mainstream' and standard, implicitly labelling multicultural identities as non-standard. For conceptualizing and implementing inter- and transcultural literature in educational contexts this indeed poses a challenge as it is questionable in how far the student's self-perception as 'white middle-class' should also be part of a multicultural frame. As argued in chapter 1 and as will be seen from the choice of novels discussed in chapter 5 and 7, an approach to transcultural teaching of literature cannot be based on visible markers of national and ethnic otherness and identity. As Johnston states "[w]hat once was thought to have been a 'true' story of Canadian identity has become a prism of possibilities: hybrid and heterogeneous, told and retold, imagined and re-imagined in the literatures of its peoples" (2000, online). Within this prism, multicultural literature is supposed to include a multiplicity of cultures.

In *From Nursery Rhymes to Nationhood – Children's Literature and the Construction of Canadian Identity*, Galway (2008) includes Anglophone children's literature written between 1867 and 1911 for an extended study of the formation of Canadian identity. By using British and American roots as a foundation, Galway focuses on aspects such as "Canadian regionalism" (ibid., 33-42), connections to French and First Nation heritage as well as "landscape and environment" (ibid., 145-172) to conclude that diversity and national unity both contribute to defining Canadian identity. This assumption reflects that the negotiation of regional, cultural, ethnic, and linguistic diversity that was visible in the first publications for young readers remains one essential feature of Canadian literature for young readers as well as Canadian identity formation.

4.2.2 Region, Place, Nature, and Environment

Assuming that "Canadian children's literature tends to be concerned less with national than with regional identity – to focus on the attitudes, atmosphere, and issues dominant in the city or province where the action takes place" (in Nodelman 1997, 23), Margot Louis sheds light on another important aspect of characterizing Canadian children's literature. After the millennium this "fascination with the land and its climate" (in ibid., 16) and a "delight in the land and fear of it" (in ibid., 17) has not lost any of its significance. Sapergia and Burton agree that regionalism remains a major issue in Canadian literature for young readers as well as in its publication (interviews G.A., August 2011).

As will be discussed in an example text in chapter 5.1.1, the individual's struggle against a hostile nature (cf. chapter 4.1) still reflects an essential feature of Canadian children's literature. For David Bentley "children (and many of the adults) are nurtured by nature as well as by the society in which

---

[115] In those and further comments the problem of inclusion and exclusion of other people is prevalent, as will be further explored in chapter 7.2.

they grow up" (in Nodelman 1997, 18-19) – a highly important statement for my work as it refers to the influence literature can have on children's perception of the self, but also of others. This linkage is visible in Ruby Slipperjack's *Little Voice* (2001) and Adele Dueck's *Racing Home* (2011). In *Little Voice*, a changing family structure causes 10-year-old Ray to feel less and less comfortable in her home and she enjoys discovering herself and inner strength when she spends time with her aboriginal grandmother in nature. Her teachings of reading the land on and in which they live like a book help Ray to find a balance within herself. Through close contact with the land, beneficial and dangerous, she discovers not only the beauty of the region but also the necessity to be at home on the land, with her mother and step-father, and within herself – all three of which provide a different kind of home she needs in order to be whole (cf. Alter 2010, 2011a, cf. 5.1). In Dueck's story the reader joins 12-year-old Erik on his pioneer adventure of adapting to his new surroundings and of helping his family to establish a home in the Canada when the family emigrates from lush Norway with mountains, water and forests to the dry and flat prairie. Through the hardships of working the dry, almost hostile land, he understands the importance of close family ties and sees that although the place where one lives influences choices of lifestyle, a home can be established almost everywhere if one is able to rely on good will and family relations.

In both stories, the settings are not only used as backdrops against which the storyline unfolds, but rather they are perceived of "as characters in their own rights – living breathing entities that affect the human character in the stories" (Buffie in Nodelman 1997, 18). In both stories, nature and the specific region Ray and Erik come to experience and live in are more than just a geographic condition, but cause both to develop a strong sense of place. Both these books as well as many other Canadian books for young readers reveal a certain "rootedness in particular regions and communities" (Bérard in ibid., 23). *The Hockey Sweater* by Roch Carrier (1984) which "speaks to all Canadians from the rink in the isolated village of Ste-Justine" (ibid.) serves an example. Canada's "finest children's literature proclaims its national character by its intensely local sense of place" (ibid., 24). Tim Wynne-Jones sees a similar connection stating that "[w]riters addressing teen readers seem to find endless inspiration from stranding a youthful protagonist or two in the 'monstrous' wilds" (in ibid., 19).

This does in fact not only apply to fiction in general but also, and to a great extent, to historic fiction, as this genre is usually closely linked to a specific place. In Eric Walters' novel *Save as Houses* (2007b), a fictional account of Hurricane Hazel that roared down on Toronto on October 15, 1954, carries the plot. For eight-year-old Elizabeth the usual babysitting afternoon turns into a matter of pure survival when she and the siblings Suzie and David are left to take care of themselves during this disastrous storm. When it becomes obvious that they are not as save as houses, their survival depends on Elizabeth's maturity, courage and guidance. This novel is a prime example for Margaret Atwood's

Survival in hostile natural surroundings. On the one hand, it is nature's severe storm that sets the house in which Elizabeth and the children first find protection in motion; on the other hand, it is also one of nature's trees in which the children find protection once they are able to leave the house which by then has become an almost deadly trap.

Another factor which supports the regional character of Canadian literature for young readers is the structure of publishing in general. As Lorraine Anderson puts it: "Canadian children's literature is distinctly regional, especially because of small press publications" (in Nodelman 1997, 22). Burton elaborates on this by explaining that for Canadian children's literature, place is indeed an essential moment of defining this literature. Therefore, many regional publishers offer books which reflect the experiences, history and tradition of the people in that region (interview G.A., August 2011). Thus, they contribute to a regional as national identity in Canadian literature for young readers.

4.2.3 Immigration and Multiculturalism

Stating that "the child more recently arrived from another culture is invited to this [Canadian] literary party too," Mary-Alice Downie (in Nodelman 1997) refers to one of the most central aspects of Canadian identity. As could be seen in earlier chapters, immigration and the motif of being new to the land and society while having to make a living and adapt to unknown situations has been a strong leitmotif in texts for young readers since the emergence of children's literature. When Nodelman asked what is Canadian about Canadian children's literature, Vickery "focus[es] on life in a diverse ethnic and geographic landscape and a child's experiences in it" (in ibid., 28). Additionally, "Canadian children's literature welcomes authors and subjects of all races and persuasions into its mainstream[116] by celebrating differences and saluting similarities" (Ware in ibid., 29).

Although this positive estimation is put into a slightly more neutral perspective by Heather Kirk who points to the fact that "[d]espite Canada's [...] increasingly multicultural society, Canadian children's literature continues to be dominated by white, Anglo-Saxon, protestant, middle-class writers [...] despite a few exceptions" (in Nodelman 1997, 35), also Ron Jobe's observation holds true: "there are links which bring them [Canadian children] together – love, a sense of belonging, a feeling of personal competence and a reaffirmation of self-worth" (in ibid., 29). For Jobe, therefore, it is "change [that] is the most common phenomenon in our country" (in ibid., 29), which he underlines with the changing composition of Canadian society. Nevertheless, he also demands a

---

[116] Interestingly, Ware here tries to point to the inclusive approach of Canadian literature to others, but by using 'welcoming them into the mainstream' he remains within a dichotomy of us/them and re-establishes a hierarchy that he tried to neglect.

more visible depiction of this composition, for example according to the various languages spoken in Canada.

Fortunately, Jobe's question "Where is the literature that reflects children speaking [...] languages [other than English and French]" can now be answered with 'in the bookshelves,' his question "How will these children see images of themselves in books?" with 'by reading books by the many authors who have detailed knowledge of their experiences,' and his question "Do we provide images for our First Nations students?" (in Nodelman 1997) with 'yes, indeed.' However, perhaps an insufficient amount of publications may be a justified limitation. But first and foremost thanks to publishing houses such as Theytus Books which since 1980 has published numerous titles by and for indigenous voices and beyond, readers are able to find First Nation images in Canadian literature for young readers.[117] Those include, for example, Jeannette Armstrong's children's book *Neekna and Chemai* (1991) and her bestselling young adult novel *Slash* (rev. ed. 1990), Lee Maracle's *Will's Garden* (2002), or Earl Einarson's and Julie Flieet's bestselling children's book *The Moccasins* (2004). Yet, First Nation writers are not limited to this one publishing option as also other publishers advertise Canada's diverse authorship (e.g. Red Deer Press, Harper Collins Canada); the Association of Book Publishers of BC published a catalogue of "Canadian Aboriginal Books for Schools."

Highly promising for the recognition of cultural identities is the tendency to have literature for children and young adults published in bilingual editions, for example Chief Jake Swamp's *Giving Thanks – A Native American Good Morning Message* (1995), Tomson Highway's *Fox on the Ice/Maageesees Maskwameek Kaapit* (2011), or David Bouchard's *The Drum Calls Softly* (2008). Other titles, for instance Debby Dahl Edwardson's *Whale Snow*[118] (2003) are available in an English and, in this case, an Inupiaq version. Stories like Hiromi Goto's *The Water of Possibility* (2002) or Jamie Bastedo's *On thin Ice* (2006) are in English but include Japanese and Inuktitut phrases and terms, which are sometimes explained and translated in a glossary at the end of the story.

This discussion shows that the political and historical development of multiculturalism in Canada and Canadian literature for young readers have been closely intertwined (cf. Richter 2011). Texts by authors such as Lyn Cook or Paul Yee (cf. above) indicate that a certain multicultural attitude was already present before it became official. Yet, the book market reacted to increasing immigration and social changes and paid more attention to formerly marginalized groups. Certainly, regional publishers played an essential role in diversifying reading material for children and young adults.

---

[117] Those and similar books will be mentioned in a later chapter again in which First Nations books are suggested for inter- and cultural learning (cf. chapter 5.1.2).

[118] As this story represents an Inuit story which transcends national boundaries, it is included in this list, although the author lives in Alaska.

Compared to Richter's account until 1994, in the post-millennium years a new approach to multiculturalism can be identified and characterized as a "balanced appreciation of cultural heritage" (Alter 2012a, 185). As mentioned above, since the 1990s some publishers have increasingly included multicultural works in their programs which present multicultural children as members of Canadian society and not merely and exclusively as strugglers who try to fit in. This could be seen as a reaction to the criticism of multiculturalism in view of dominating references to English and French cultural identity (cf. interview G.A. with Sapergia, August 2011). *The Water of Possibility* by Hiromi Goto (2001) serves as a prime example of this assumption and will be reflected in more detail in chapter 5.3. Nevertheless, a look at recently published multicultural literature for young readers shows that an approach to depicting cultural otherness beyond victim vs. perpetrator and immigrant vs. native dichotomies is recognizable. The respective books pay tribute to cultural heritages, and allow young readers to see beyond ethnic and national boundaries and to perceive and appreciate the other for who they are as humans. Canadian books for young readers which are successful in achieving this will serve as foundations for implementing inter- and transcultural learning in EFL classrooms (cf. chapter 5 and 6). This characteristic will be the central emphasis in defining transcultural literature (cf. chapter 7).

4.2.4 Canadian Children's Literature as Global Literature

Apart from those characteristics of Canadian children's literature, some may argue that an approach to literature that focuses on nationality is not justified – especially in a transcultural context. Rosemary Ross Johnston answers Nodelman's question "What is Canadian about Canadian Children's Literature" with "Not much (beyond *Anne*), I would suspect" and explains:

> National character (whatever that means) is becoming increasingly global, is it not? The issues of conflicting cultures, of an implicit but never quite articulated fear of being consumed by more powerful neighbours, and of general survival (not so much in a wilderness as in a rapidly changing microcosm of family and peer relationships) have become themes inherent in the children's literature texts of other countries [...] they are themes that seem not so much to supersede national identity and character as to make it irrelevant. (in Nodelman 1997, 24)

In a similar sense, Dave Jenkinson states that it is only authorship and publisher which make a children's book Canadian as "the themes of Canadian children's literature address those universal concerns which transcend time and place" (in ibid., 33), which supports the transcultural perspective of my work. Aspects and topics that are depicted in Canadian literature for young readers would not necessarily be specifically Canadian nor would that be an indicator of what makes a good Canadian book. As Barbara Kraus puts it, the "distinction of those [books] I thought to be good, […] was in no way connected to a measurable degree of 'Canadianness,' nor were those that failed the mark in any way lacking this ephemeral substance" (in ibid., 34). When interviewing the employees at *The World's Biggest Bookstore* in Toronto, a similar approach became obvious, as children and parents generally buy books which are gripping because of the story they tell or the extent to which the reader is able to connect to the protagonists. If those books happened to be by Canadian authors or revealed Canada-related content, it was successful for the authors and publishers; if not, young readers may just have a taste for other styles and stories. Children's literature, as Kraus assumes, "is primarily intended for children, for their amusement, their entertainment, their reading pleasure" (in ibid., 34) and "what makes books enjoyable cannot be anchored in political debate."

When John Willinsky mentions that "[m]any of the most important children's books are about a world that has no borders as we know them" (in Nodelman 1997, 34), he may refer to the adventures of Alice, for example, or fantasy fiction in general. Yet, this could also regard titles such as Jennifer Cowan's *earthgirl* (2009) or Jamie Bastedo's *On thin Ice* (2006) which reflect upon global issues. In these titles protecting the environment and global warming contribute to the tension of the stories and the development of the protagonists. Despite their setting in Toronto and the Canadian North, the stories would be transferrable to any other metropolis or circumpolar region without losing any of their meaning or significance. Willinsky's assumption can thus serve as a foundation upon which the perception of Canadian literature for young readers as transcultural or global literature can be based.

Those characteristics confirm that Canadian children's literature has gone "beyond traditional survival themes" (Jobe in Nodelman 1997, 29). Jobe demands "to avoid the exotic and strange approach to culture, and get in touch with the reality of living in Canada today" (in ibid., 29-30). This could be achieved when refraining from focusing on literature which implements cultural stereotypes and turning toward texts which instead offer balanced perspectives on multicultural protagonists.

5. Exploration of Selected Canadian Texts for Young Readers

While the previous chapter analysed the development and characteristics of Canadian children's literature, the following chapter introduces three example texts from the post-millennium phase that I would like to use to suggest a continuum from inter- to transcultural learning and to arrive at a definition of transcultural literature. A justification for the selection of the books is followed by a detailed analysis of the books' depiction of otherness, the transcultural topoi entailed and a discussion of each book's teaching implications. With view of the transcultural topoi and understanding of transcultural competences, these teaching implications refer to students' awareness of perceiving otherness, sensitivity toward perceptions of self and reflections upon their personal experiences with otherness, fear, challenges, and contentment.

With Ruby Slipperjack's *Little Voice* (2001), Eric Walters' *Run* (2003) and Hiromi Goto's *The Water of Possibility* (2001) I introduce three novels for young readers which each depict otherness differently and offer a different approach to cultural learning. This study assumes that inter- and transcultural literature form a continuum, thus, the novels discussed here represent different stages of this continuing development. The analysis of the depiction of otherness in these books results in a reflection upon the general potential of Canadian books for young readers for inter- and transcultural learning (cf. chapter 6).

Little Voice, *Run* and *The Water of Possibility* fulfil the characteristics of Canadian literature for young readers (cf. chapter 4.2) as they contribute to national identity formation, refer to specific regions, places, the environment, multiculturalism and global issues. Although *Little Voice* does not mention specific place names, manifold references to landmarks typical for Canada can be found, for instance the protagonist's encounters with lakes and rivers, a moose and a bear cub. Additionally, she engages very respectfully with the environment, shows detailed knowledge of plants and herbs, and develops environmental awareness when she modestly benefits from nature. At the same time she learns that nature can be destructive; respect is supplemented by caution. In *Run*, many specific place names are mentioned, the Toronto's suburbs and downtown area, Toronto City Hall, and towns in Nova Scotia. From the stretches of road the protagonist Terry runs each day, the reader is able to map his run from St. James, Nova Scotia all the way to Thunder Bay, Ontario. Also the main protagonists' encounters with nature, the dryness of the land and the isolation they face along empty roads account for the awareness of environment and nature in Canadian children's literature. In *The Water of Possibility* the protagonist Sayuri refers to Calgary and her perception of prairie dryness and isolation which stand in contrast to the descriptions of lush forests in Living Earth. Furthermore, Sayuri's active engagement with the destructed environment surrounding the Patriarch's city where she spreads seeds on the barren ground imply this characteristic feature of Canadian children's literature (cf. chapter 5.3.1).

For the main protagonists of all three books, specific places serve as both challenges and the foundation of personal growth: In *Little Voice*, Ray learns about her First Nation heritage in nature and understands that nature can be a healer of her inner struggles; Terry and especially Winston come to terms with their personal challenges and inner demons through their runs in nature; Sayuri needs the encounters of Living Earth as these are foundational for becoming familiar with her new home and self. For all four protagonists, nature, places and environment serve as means to establish a more balanced identity.

Inter- and transcultural learning to a large extent depends on the plot and how the main protagonists are characterized. Therefore, it is of utmost importance to be aware of the perspective in which they are depicted. In contexts of cultural learning, the protagonists are often multicultural characters who are part of a so-called 'visible minority' that is othered based on identity struggles they have to face. Yet, if such texts are exclusively used, this implies the strong notion that 'white' Anglo-Saxon middle class is the standard from which otherness is defined and identified. However, my approach to cultural learning rejects such a power paradigm and supports an understanding of otherness beyond ethnic markers (cf. chapter 7). This approach is reflected in the young adult novels that are selected for this study.

Depending on the readers' perspective and their own background, Terry and Winston can be seen as cultural others, social others or others regarding their mental and physical abilities. Despite representing 'white' middle class males, *Run* is included in a study of inter- and transcultural learning, because it illustrates that otherness does not necessarily have to be defined by national or ethnic markers. Similarly, also the perception of Ray and Sayuri depends on the perspective and background of the reader and their knowledge of and attitude toward First Nation Canadian and Japanese Canadian cultures. If students are experienced in reading First Nation stories, they may be able to understand the close relation of humans and nature beyond a stereotypical and romanticising depiction and may not think that Ray's engagement with herbs and plants is something new. While the tanuki, kappa and oni in *The Water of Possibility* might be familiar to some readers who have knowledge of Japanese mythology, for others those figures may be unfamiliar and, thus, identified as other. It is, however, important to refrain from assuming that readers who share a certain background automatically have knowledge about the myths and stories presented in texts. Therefore, identifying otherness should be seen relative to the readership and perspective of analysis, and not be based on assumptions about or methods of approaching texts.

Due to those aspects and recognizing that the books selected for this discussion address transcultural phenomena such as suffering from cancer, grief for family members and the importance of will-power and personal growth, [119] I believe that they are suitable for introducing a continuum from inter- to transcultural learning. As the discussion indicates, they partly also address global issues and thus go beyond a cultural scope. Therefore, readers from various backgrounds could relate to the adventures narrated in the books.

5.1 "You Can Handle Both Worlds": Ruby Slipperjack's *Little Voice*

From 2001 to 2002, Coteau Books published its children's book series "In the Same Boat" which aims at

> [c]elebrat[ing] the richness of Canada's cultural heritage and the shape of our society in the new millennium. The stories take different forms – adventures, family drama, historical fiction, even fantasy – and include information about a particular culture – its traditions, beliefs, stories, and customs – as background information to the main narrative. This series was motivated by the desire of Coteau Books to do something about the lack of Canadian stories about particular cultural backgrounds. (Lunn in Slipperjack 2001, ii)

Authors like Cheryl Foggo, Larry Warwaruk, or Diana Vazquez followed the invitation to contribute reading material for young readers which tell stories evolving around balanced multicultural protagonists. From this series, *Little Voice* (2002) by Anishinaabeg[120] writer Ruby Slipperjack and *The Water of Possibility* (2001) by Japanese Canadian author Hiromi Goto have been selected for their potential to develop inter- and transcultural competences.

In Slipperjack's novel, *Little Voice*, readers meet 10-year old Ray, a girl whose mother is Anishinaabeg and father is Anglo-Canadian. The story is set between 1978 and 1982 in Northern Ontario. Two, the one and the other, neither

---

[119] These aspects are selected as main topoi in the three novels and are seen line with the transcultural terms that Bredella considers as a foundation for intercultural understanding, e.g. birth, death, love, hate as well as transcultural assumptions about relationships of different genders, of young and old, and between individual and collective identities (cf. 2010b, 122-123).

[120] Ruby Slipperjack is a member of the Anishinaabeg people (Nishinaabe or Anishinini), in English known as Ojibway or Chippewa. Anishinaabemowin is the term describing their language. They form one of the largest and most diverse North American nations. Their traditional territory covers parts of western Quebec, where they are known as the Algonquin, the Great Lakes region, where one subgroup is known as the Odawa, and the prairie provinces, where they are also known as the Saulteaux. New (2002) offers more information about the Anishinaabeg and their culture, esp. concerning literature.

the one nor the other and having to balance twoness of self characterize the four years the reader spends with Ray while she is searching for a balanced sense of identity. In between those years Ray travels back and forth between her home which she shares with her mother and siblings, and her grandmother's house. At each place she learns something new about herself, each journey changes her perception of who she is. She realizes that as an older sister to a newborn child she needs to take responsibility, and as a girl of First Nation ancestry she can be proud of her multicultural background and continue the teaching she received from her grandmother.

Although the plot sounds very similar to 'typical' multicultural coming-of-age realistic fiction books (cf. chapter 7.2), Slipperjack tells a story which is different to these as Ray's struggle for identity is represented through personal challenges and not through discrimination and disregard from her surrounding environment and society (cf. Bushman/Park 2006 in chapter 7.1.1).

5.1.1 Otherness and Transcultural Topoi

Little Voice includes various depictions of inter- and transcultural topoi.[121] These lie with Ray's multicultural family, as she grows up with Anishinaabeg influences from her mother and, more importantly, from her grandmother, as well as with Anglo-Canadian culture exemplified through her community. These also refer to her inner struggle for identity and wish of belonging and being content with the person she is.

At the beginning of the book, the reader meets a young girl who is facing different challenges that cause uneasiness and a lack of self-esteem. Despite the death of the father when Ray was a little girl and the family's financial problems, her mother is able to provide a warm home for Ray and the two younger siblings; the family never goes hungry and the children always have clothes to wear to school. While Ray is aware of the problematic situation and the help the family receives from neighbours, her reflections do not emphasize this. The family's mutual support and love are more important than their lack of money.

The situation in school seems to be more worrisome. There, Ray often feels uncomfortable because her schoolmates comment on her appearance and make fun of her green eyes, long black hair and dark skin (cf. Slipperjack 2001, 9).[122] She often remains silent because the other children could laugh about wrong answers (11) or because her teacher talks down to her (16). Her strategy of dealing with the difficult situations and disrespectful attitudes at school is to try to avoid confrontations.

At home Ray is also silent most of the time, she stopped talking much when her father died, which allows the reader to see Ray's lack of speech not

---

[121] A similar discussion of this book can be found in Alter (2010) and Alter (2012b).
[122] If not indicated differently, in this chapter the number in brackets refers to the page number in Slipperjack (2001).

only related to the teasings at school, but to transcultural features such as death, anger and grief as well. This silence only changes when her grandmother comes to visit. The girl sees a source of relaxation and comfort in her despite the fact that the two could hardly talk to each other. Ray's "Ojibwa language wasn't all that good" (11) and the grandmother "grudgingly answered […] in her broken English" (11). However, the lack of a common language does not prevent both from developing a strong and loving relationship. While Ray enjoys the silence, her wish to talk to her grandmother and her inability to find the right words also make her realize how much she actually misses out by not being able or willing to speak.

One essential feature that causes comfort and simultaneously worries Ray is her name, because her schoolmates think it is a boy's name (4-5). Yet, she enjoys hearing the story of why she is called Ray (18-19). When the girl was born, her grandfather expected his first grandchild to be a boy and wanted to name him Raymond, after himself. He was slightly disappointed that the child was a girl, [123] but he "said he'd call you Ray anyway" (19); additionally, she was "born at the first ray of sunlight in the early morning" (18). The title of the book derives from her grandmother who calls her 'Naens', because "there was no "R" in the Ojibwa language, so an "N" was used instead. Ray became "Nay," and "Little Ray" became "Naens," and "neans" means "little voice" in Ojibwa" (13). Although she faces some struggles with her name, she sees a very strong family connection and regrets that she never had a chance to meet Grand-father Raymond.

Within the first couple of pages, the reader is introduced to a setting which can be characterized by poverty, isolation, disrespect and a sense of being misunderstood, while strong family ties, love and harmony, for instance preparing food on an open fire and storytelling, simultaneously paint a positive and pleasant, yet no romanticized, picture. It is remarkable that a particularly significant aspect of First Nation culture, storytelling, through which culture is inherited and the younger generation is educated, is interrupted by chores around the house (7-8). These force Ray to stop being a child and to take on the role of an adult, caring for her siblings and cleaning the house. The short encounters with storytelling are not sufficient for Ray to establish a stronger connection to this part of culture that has been neglected for so long. It is, therefore, her wish to spend a few months with her grandmother to escape the struggles at school and the tight situation at home. When Ray returns to her family for good, she recognizes that being with her grandmother has enabled her to become familiar with a traditional Anishinaabeg life style and develop a more balanced identity as a girl of Anishinaabeg ancestry. Leaving and returning to her family's home established a sense of belonging at home and an arrival at her new sense of self.

---

[123] This passage would certainly call for a gender specific reading. Yet, in First Nations cultures this topic is highly complex and a discussion could here only touch upon selected aspects. Therefore, the interested reader is referred to Barker (2015).

While staying with her grandmother, Ray swims in lakes and the river, picks berries, cooks and comes to celebrate a close connection to nature through adventurously befriending a moose calf and a black bear cub. Compared to her other home, Ray sees herself in surroundings which offer her the possibility to establish a self that re-learns to use her voice (cf. Alter 2012b). One main foundation of this process is Ray's grandmother who becomes a provider of knowledge and an excellent teacher and guide. As a midwife and healer, the grandmother knows the effects and functions of herbs and plants, she knows about the secrets of childbirth and recognizes that Ray is able to inherit her knowledge. Ray is eager to learn from her grandmother who supports her in reconnecting to Anishinaabeg heritage.

Mobility and migration have been established as markers of the development of global societies (cf. above.). In a very concrete way, this can also be seen in *Little Voice* as Ray is constantly traveling back and forth between her mother's and her grandmother's house. She not only crosses generational borders but geographical and cultural borders, too, a process through which she is able to leave the insecurity from the beginning of the novel behind. After spending a longer period of time with her grandmother, Ray not only gains a voice and a language with which to speak about herself, she also gains knowledge of her ancestors and is able to close the gap of missing self-confidence. By travelling back and forth between her mother's and her grandmother's home, she builds a solid bridge between the cultural identities both places represent and establishes a hybrid sense of self within a 'third space' which is "not based on exoticism or multiculturalism of the diversity of cultures, but on the inscription and articulation of culture's hybridity" (Bhabha 1994, 56). Ray personalizes Bhabha's hope that it is in this space that one finds words with which one can speak of oneself and others (cf. Alter 2010). She is able to combine aspects of her identity which she formerly regarded as incompatible, if not exclusive of each other.

Compared to the beginning of the book, belonging to two differing cultures no longer poses a challenge for Ray. On the contrary, as her grandmother assures her that

> [y]ou are someone who can handle both worlds – the Native and non-Native, the old and the new. Someone who can learn the knowledge of the past and carry it forward into the future. (Slipperjack 2001, 245)

Through her grandmother's teaching and the new positions she finds within her family, Ray transcends the challenging binary of neither belonging to one world nor the other and develops an identity which shows traces of both. She understands that she is not only capable of inheriting two cultures but that she needs both in order to be whole. Her newly gained voice and her education further strengthen her self-esteem. This process which leads to a new self-perception contains high potential for classroom reflections that focus on the development of inter- and transcultural competences.

5.1.2 Teaching Implications

Little Voice's usability for inter- and transcultural learning derives from Ray's personal development as well as her relationship to family members, classmates, the environment and herself. Yet, as was explained in chapter 3.1, implementing original literature in ELT poses a challenge regarding an appropriate language and content level. Books written for native speakers of a certain age are sometimes difficult to use with English learners of the same age because their level of English could not be sufficient enough to understand the original text. As a solution, some scholars suggest that graded readers or simplified versions of the original texts can be used instead (cf. Hermes 2007, 105-126). In *Little Voice*, 10-year-old Ray has to deal with an absent father, struggles at school and finding her way within two seemingly different cultures. Students of a similar age attend primary school; when finishing Grade 4 they usually reach a language level of A1 (cf. MSW 2008, 14). This prescribes that students can read and understand short and simple texts which mostly entail familiar vocabulary (cf. MSW 2008, 16), or that students "can understand familiar names, words and very simple sentences, for example on notices and posters or in catalogues" (Council of Europe 2001, 26, 68-71). Thus, the whole book cannot be read in the same age-group for which it is originally intended. As the topics of struggling with school and family and enjoying one's freedom in nature are relevant and interesting for slightly older students as well, extracts from the book could be used with students between 12 and 14 years of age. Accordingly, the following section presents scenes in which the potential for inter- and transcultural learning becomes especially apparent.[124]

At the beginning of the novel, the reader learns that Ray does "not like school very much. In fact, I hated it!" (Slipperjack 2001, 2), because the other students "just picked on me all the time" (3, see also 11, 15). One way of avoiding such treatment is that Ray makes sure she gets the answers to her teacher's questions right because "they [her classmates] would make fun of me if I got [one] wrong" (3). After Ray spends time with her grandmother, she returns to her home and school and has gained new strength in that she "didn't care what the kids called [her]" (60). As this is one of Ray's essential personal developments, it is worth discussing this proof of courage and self-esteem with students. They can try and understand Ray's feelings and reactions, but also try and find reasons why the other classmates make fun of her beyond the ones given in the text, and talk about appropriate reaction to such teasings.

---

[124] This chapter, and also 5.2 and 5.3 only refer to a content level of possible reflections. Methods and procedures for each text are suggested in chapter 8. This will also take a certain language barrier and privacy issues into account.

Throughout the book, engaging with the environment supports Ray's formation of a balanced identity. While Ray spends time with her grandmother, she swims in lakes and rivers, goes canoeing and builds a fire, and befriends a moose calf and a bear cub. Those encounters allow her to spend time with herself, away from all the struggles she faces at home. That nature has a healing effect for her inner turmoil is also visible when Ray starts speaking once she is outside. Students can reflect nature's influence on the girl and examine how they perceive nature, and whether being outside carries any meaning for them.

Ray's growing awareness of nature and the environment can also be explored using scenes in which the grandmother asks her grandchildren to leave some of the berries "for the bears" (11) and in which "each plant she released from the soil was replaced with a pinch of tobacco" (224). Both mirror a very respectful approach to nature. Students can investigate their own relationship to nature and how they try to protect the environment. Additionally, Ray's grandmother teaches her about the different plants and their effects on health which could motivate students to explore some of the plants in their surroundings. Apart from nature, Ray's social environment contributes to her identity formation, too. Similarly, students can regard the influences that have an effect on their personality and have contributed to their identity. Despite the students' young age, such questions can be very thought-provoking and lead them to astonishing insights about themselves.

What makes Ray's struggle for a balanced identity so challenging is her multicultural background. For her, this binary is ever present because she has "dark skin and black hair like Mama, but [...] green eyes like my father" (9). Students could use this scene to have a closer look at themselves and see who they resemble more, their mother's or their father's facial features.[125] They could investigate whether there are any resemblances according to their traits of character. What do those similarities mean to the students? Do those have any effect on their personal lives? For Ray, her outward appearance means more than just an uneasy feeling and her schoolmates making fun of her as this is also a constant reminder of being part of two worlds: her mother's, which is filled with love and care, but also financial struggles, and her father's whose "family members decided we did not exist" (18). This experience of rejection is further increased by her school community. For students it would be insightful to put themselves in Ray's situation and examine whether they have been trapped in between two seemingly opposing poles and how they acted in such a situation. This could be an initial consideration to change perspectives and understand Ray's challenges.

In *Little Voice*, students can learn more about the Ojibwa people. As it can be assumed that they have not had much contact with a First Nation culture, it is worthwhile reflecting upon it in more detail. Lutz (2002), Krebes (2002)

---

[125] Of course, if such an activity is implemented, teachers need to apply highest sensitivity to their students' family situation and consider whether such a task is appropriate.

and Susemihl (2008) investigated German children's and university students' knowledge of First Nation peoples and uncovered that children grow up with a highly distorted and stereotypical image of the 'Indian': the standardized and idealized images depict mounted warriors and hunters who ride through the endless prairies, who are decorated in war paint, wear feathers, quietly crawl through the grass and woods, spend a fair amount of time on one leg dancing around fires, and gracefully smoke the peace pipe (cf. Susemihl 2008, 122). The results of Susemihl's and Krebes' study (2002/3) show that

> [t]he vast majority of the students associate with the Indian "hunting buffalo with bow and arrow" (82%); "living in tipis in the prairies" (81%); "unfair suffering" (71%); "adventure" (68%); "stories at the camp fire" (61%) and "brave warriors riding on horseback" (60%). (Susemihl 2008, 123)[126]

Characteristics like "long black hair" (97%), "friendly and civilized" (52%) and "brave, courageous and heroic" (51%)" (ibid.) are deeply rooted in children's and students' knowledge of First Nations. When 81% of the students involved in the study claim that they base their understanding of Native Americans on Winnetou or other feature films (75%), Karl May novels (69%), television documentaries (62%), and non-fiction (54%), one can conclude that those false images are produced and implemented through media. I believe that reading about Ray and her experiences in nature, and supplementing this with other fictional and non-fictional texts by First Nation authors which meet the students' linguistic needs, could challenge the existing stereotypes and prejudices and develop an awareness of First Nation cultures.

Additional fictional reading material for younger readers that can be used for further investigating First Nation cultures on an intercultural level could include

- Jeannette Armstrong's *Enwisteetkwa* (*Walk in Water*) (1982),
- Chief Jake Swamp's *Giving Thanks – A Native American Good Morning Message* (1995), the original Thanksgiving Address of the Haudenosaunee,
- Tomson Highway's *Fox on the Ice/Maageesees Maskwameek Kaapit* (2011),
- Anne Renaud's *Missuk's Snow Geese* (2008), or
- Jan Bourdeau Waboose's *Morning on the Lake* (1997).

These offer the chance to discover similarities or intertextual references which Hallet identifies as one element of ICC (cf. 2002, 2007a, 43). One concrete example of such a similarity is Armstrong's picture book *Neekna and Chemai*

---

[126] Percentages indicate how often a certain answer occurred in the tests and questionnaires.

(1984) about two girls and their exploration of the seasonal life pattern of the Okanagan people of the interior of British Columbia. From Neekna's grandmother the two friends learn about the tasks their people had to fulfil during each season which secured their well-being and a sustainable usage of nature. Similar to Ray, Neekna and Chemai also learn about the healing powers of certain plants and herbs for specific illnesses, and how to be respectful and pay tribute to nature's offerings. Both books feature a powerful figure of a grandmother who functions as a source of knowledge for the girls and as a guide to their ancestors' wisdom.[127] As the picture book is intended for child readers, it should not be problematic to implement it in primary English classes or also parallel to reading excerpts from Slipperjack's *Little Voice*.

For advanced learners, short stories and plays by Drew Hayden Taylor (as for example suggested by Bredella 2008, cf. chapter 4.1.3) present negotiations of First Nation identity in an often humorous way, whereas Armstrong's young adult *Slash* (1990) reveals the harsh reality of being First Nation in a hostile society in more serious tones. Jamie Bastado's *On Thin Ice* (2006) tells the intriguing story of Artic teenager Ashley, whose frightening dreams of a singing and drumming bear-man increase her obsession with Nanurluk, the legendary spirit-bear of the Inuit. Further elements interwoven in the story of discovering cultural heritage are messages of global warming and consequences of human encroachment into animal habitat. As this story for older readers and more advanced learners revolves around Inuit people and life in the North, it adds to establishing an awareness of the diversity of First Nations people in North America.

Ray's struggles in *Little Voice* are rooted in her insecure ethnic identity and her search for a balanced sense of self. This frames the novel in an intercultural scope. However, the book does not emphasize this part of Ray's story, but focuses on her school experience, family relations and engagement with nature which reflect a certain transcultural perspective as well. Although closer to the intercultural, *Little Voice* can be applied to inter- and transcultural learning and seen as an example of inter- as well as transcultural literature, depending on the perspective with which the book is read. A differentiation of both will be discussed in detail in chapter 7.3.

---

[127] For a more detailed and exemplary account of the role of grandmothers cf. Anderson's account in *Nlakapmux Grandmothers' Stories: How Generations of Indigenous Grandmothers of British Columbia Carried out their Responsibilities to Transmit Knowledge* (2012).

5.2 "A Road (Not) Taken": Eric Walter's *Run*

Eric Walter's biographic fiction novel *Run* (2003) for young readers tells the story of Terry Fox, born on July 28, 1958, who became one of the most famous and popular Canadian heroes. After the amputation of his leg, the 18-year-old decided to run across Canada to collect donations for cancer research. Until then he had been a successful basketball player for the Simon Fraser University team. On the evening before his operation, his coach visited him and gave him an article about a young man who ran the New York marathon despite his leg amputation. After the operation, this man should become Terry's inspiration. What became known as the "Marathon of Hope" lasted 143 days during which Terry ran 5373 km, from St. John, Newfoundland, to just outside Thunder Bay, Ontario, where he had to interrupt his race because cancer had affected his lungs.

It was his dream to collect one Dollar from every Canadian in order to help other patients who suffered from cancer. On February 1st, 1981, his dream was fulfilled as the Canadian population reached 24.1 million people and the donations in Terry's name increased to 24.17 million Dollars. Terry was able to witness his success, but died in June 1981. Until today, the Terry Fox Foundation organizes the Terry Fox Run every year and has collected more than 550 million Dollars.

5.2.1 Otherness and Transcultural Topoi

In *Run*, Terry's quest is framed within the fictional story of 14-year-old Winston McDonald, a boy whose parents are divorced, who continuously plays hooky, is suspended from school for drinking alcohol, and has a difficult relationship with his mother. This relationship is mostly characterized by a lack of communication. The novel's opening scene describes how Winston is brought home by the police, handcuffed, after two days and nights wandering around Toronto. While Winston's mother is unsure whether to be worried or angry, Winston enjoys making her even more furious by not "say[ing] a word. She could make me do a lot of things, but she couldn't make me talk if I didn't want to." He knows that "say[ing] as little as possible [...] drove her crazy" (Walters 2003, 6).[128] When she sees herself unable to cope with her son, she sends Winston to spend some time with his father, Winston Sr., who works as a journalist and is sent to Nova Scotia to cover Terry's "Marathon of Hope." Having to focus on his work, he does not want to deal with his troublesome son either.

Winston arrives in Nova Scotia, he and his dad hire a car and follow Terry and his friend Doug in their van. Neither father nor son are very fond of this. Winston Sr. spends time working on his coverage, Winston Jr. spends time

---

[128] If not indicated differently, in this chapter the number in brackets refers to the page number in Walters (2003).

being angry at the world and boredom around him. He thinks that running across Canada on one leg is ridiculous, but is taken aback when he meets Terry on the road. He is immediately impressed by the small young man who looks like his own age. Winston, who does not seem to care about anything or anyone than himself, suddenly pays a lot of attention when his father interviews Terry and is almost brought to tears when he reads the resulting article (67). He finds Terry's quest more and more amazing and simultaneously difficult to understand. When he sees Terry running along never-ending stretches of tarred roads he cannot understand how someone can be that determined and follow his goals, no matter what. This is even increased when Winston sees that Terry is in a lot of pain because the stump has developed severe blisters, none of which would ever cause Terry to stop running.

In the course of Terry's marathons, Winston decides to give it a try and starts running along – first steps toward facing his own demons. He often gets the chance to spend time with Terry, to talk about his ambitions and dreams and thereby reflect his own faults and missed chances. Winston realizes that his angry attitude caused him to run away from home: dissatisfaction with his family situation, a lack of talking about it, and the frustration with his mother have led to his discomfort and attempts to find an easy way. In the face of Terry's determination he is increasingly embarrassed about his past and has "no intention of telling him about getting suspended. It wasn't something [he] was proud of" (85). Spending time with Terry and getting to know him better, Winston reflects that "now, it didn't seem like something that could ever happen to me. I used to be good student... well, I guess before" (ibid.).

One night, Terry is woken up by Winston playing basketball in the parking lot outside their motel. He joins Winston and challenges him to a game. Winston reluctantly and carefully plays against the 'disabled' until Terry demands some serious moves and wants Winston to forget about the artificial leg. Winston does so, pushes Terry to the ground and sincerely apologizes. Yet, Terry does not want to hear any apologies and tells Winston to continue the game. Winston is in awe of Terry's courage and strength of mind. While Terry runs along lonely stretches of Canadian highways to collect money, Winston uses the time to reconsider his own life. He begins to understand that one can only lose if one gives up.

Besides learning about Terry and what it means to follow a dream, Winston also learns about justice, ethics and honour when he comes to discover that some of the journalists who follow Terry's run misuse their job to publish stories that are misleading and shed a negative light on Terry's quest. When Winston recognizes that his own father tries to meet the public's need for more exciting news and some hidden scandalous stories by writing an article questioning Terry's truthfulness and friendship to Doug, the outlet for his anger is running away again. Winston's solution, as with his mother back in Toronto, remains to flee from conflicts and find shelter in the apparently easy way out. This time, Terry finds Winston and tells him that his father has been looking for him all over the place and that he has dropped the article Winston got so angry about. Winston sees that he has been successful in preventing his father from printing the story, but this does not provide a solution for the problematic relationship to his dad.

When Winston returns to Toronto, he follows each and every media coverage about the "Marathon of Hope" until Terry reaches Toronto and the two meet again. Terry is thrilled to hear that Winston finally managed to stay in school and that not only the relationship to his mother has improved but also the relationship between his parents. Terry's determination, strength and endurance sparked in Winston the power not to give up but to reach a point where he can be proud of his achievements and develop enough self-confidence to face his own struggles and deal with them other than by running away. When Winston later hears that Terry has died, he is comforted by his parents and sees that they are there for him when he needs them most.

The transcultural potential of the book lies with its many references to phenomena which are not culture bound but entail a transcultural notion, for example loyalty, heroism, perseverance, abilities and disabilities, prejudice, equality, hope, endurance, working toward and achieving a goal, integrity and friendship, as well as cancer (similar to the transcultural aspects mentioned in Bredella 2010b). Additionally, Walters' *Run* offers a depiction of otherness that transcends ethnic identity. Here, otherness is represented through a prosthesis-wearing protagonist and his unlimited courage. Instead of giving up and lamenting about his devastating destiny of having his leg amputated or being singled out by the surrounding society, Terry's desperation serves as a solid source of strength and determination. The amputation of his leg provides him with a new quest and challenge. He turns it into something that makes his life meaningful and gains agency. What is usually regarded as a destruction of a sportsman's career is reinterpreted as a task to support the fight against a disease that threatens thousands of lives each year. Terry confidently states that "[m]y run is about ability and not disability. [...] I was a survivor of cancer and not a victim" (172).[129]

---

[129] One could argue that *Run* nevertheless tells an 'overcoming story' (cf. Rembis 2013), a genre that has been debated in disability studies because on the one hand it shows how impairment does not have to be a negative life sentence, but on the other hand it focuses on the individual, medical aspects of disability only. Disability and impairment "are not synonymous [...]. Terms such as 'disablism' and 'disablememt' [are used to] acknowledge the marginalization of people with impairments" (Goodley 2011, xi) and not the structural, cultural, and social features that make life with a disability oftentimes more difficult. However, I do not read Terry's story as such, as Terry does not aim at making the amputation of his leg invisible, he does not "engag[e] in a complex form of passing" (Rembis 2013, 116). Goodley states that disability studies has undergone a paradigm shift from "disability as personal predicament to disability as social pathology. If we locate disability in the person, then we maintain a disabling status quo. In contrast, by viewing disability as a cultural and political phenomenon, we ask serious questions about the social world" (Goodley 2011, xi). Yet, one needs to be aware that *Run* is a biographic fiction story about Terry's life experiences. Therefore, the depiction of an impaired person notwithstanding the social and cultural constructedness of 'disability' needs

Within Winston's story transcultural topoi can be identified, too. As mentioned, he has severe problems at home and at school. His trouble is mainly caused by the dissatisfaction with himself, by not knowing how to deal with it and how to voice his feelings to his parents. It can be assumed that his uneasiness started when his parents separated about two years prior. Similar to his father who left the family when their problems increased, also Winston runs away in order to solve his problems. But just as Winston Sr. is unsuccessful in finding solutions for the challenges of his marriage, so does Winston Jr. fail in escaping his problems by running away from home and school. In this line of thought, Winston could be identified as a social other with whom students can engage. This form of otherness refers to one of the characteristics of transcultural literature which will be further established in chapter 7.

If following assumptions about cultural learning that focuses on the inclusion of other identity markers to meet the requirements, demands and expectations of a readership in a multicultural society (cf. Kramsch 1993, 206), *Run* can realize transcultural learning. The novel introduces one of Canada's most heroic figures; in addition Winston's struggles with school, parents and feelings of being misunderstood are struggles that are recognizable by young people beyond national and ethnic borders. The following section discusses the novel's teaching implications in more detail and, similarly to *Little Voice*, offers points of reference for intertextual readings.

5.2.2 Teaching Implications

Run is recommended for native speakers of 13 years of age and older. As the text mainly consists of everyday language, describes general events, expresses wishes, fears and personal opinions, an English level of about B1 should be sufficient for understanding excerpts from the text (cf. Council of Europe 2001, 26, 68-71). According to national curricula, students at the end of Grade 8 are expected to be able to read texts about familiar topics; they can apply pre-knowledge to texts that are suitable for teenagers regarding topic and language (cf. MSW 2007, 30). With an appropriate language level to understand the content

---

to be seen in this specific context. The Terry Fox Foundation and Fox family were initially cautions as they are the "guardians of Terry's name, legacy and dream" (Walters 2003, 196) and did not want any fiction to be published about him. Thus, they made sure that Terry was portrayed as the young man he was. Disability studies is an interesting and wide-ranging academic field that offers further points of references in this context, which cannot be discussed here in detail. The *Canadian Journal of Disability Studies* offers insights to the field from a Canadian perspective. Goodley's *Disability Studies: An Interdisciplinary Introduction* (2011) and Titchkosky and Michalko (2009) offer a concise introduction. Mitchell and Snyder (2000) discuss disability in literary contexts. Truchan-Tataryn (2011) offers an elaborate analysis of disability in nine Anglophone Canadian novels published between 1823 and 1974. Aho (2013) offers a concise overview about the developments in the field within the past 40 years. For the context at hand, Rembis' "Athlete First: A Note on Passing, Disability and Sport" (2013) is especially insightful.

analysed above, the text is suitable for learners from the end of Grade 8 on; as the book tells an incredible story it is very well readable with more advanced learners, too.

The aforementioned aspects that serve as points of reference for transcultural learning can be identified in specific passages. With each, the students can practice changing perspectives and try and develop empathy and understanding for Winston's and Terry's situation by relating the boys' experiences to their own.

– "It seemed like my mom was working hard to get rid of me, while my father was working just as hard not to take me. It felt special to be so wanted." (Walters 2003, 14)

Throughout the novel it becomes clear that Winston has severe difficulties dealing with his parents' divorce. He runs away from home and his mother is eventually desperate enough to ask for a break in space and time. At the same time, his father is busy with work and concentrates on his career, a concept where a troublesome son does not really fit in. However, when a solution is found and Winston Jr. joins his father in Nova Scotia, the time on the road gives Winston a chance to come to terms with his demons. This turns out to be harder than he thought, as "[i]t wasn't like I knew why I kept running off and just wasn't telling [anyone]. I was still trying to figure it out myself. It just seemed like the only time anybody noticed me was when I wasn't there" (ibid., 91). It is possible that students have made similar experiences and are able to understand and relate to Winston being trapped in his own indefinable emotions. As it turns out, he wants to be part of something and belong somewhere. Terry's quest offers him just that. Talking to him and witnessing his determination, Winston is able to establish a more balanced self and relationship to his parents. When Terry runs into Toronto and Winston is treated as a special guest, he knows that he finally is "part of something so much bigger than anything [he] could imagine" (ibid., 183). Even after having lost his guide forever, he is still able to be content with himself and his family. It could also be the case that students cannot understand Winston's situation, but rather see it critical. They then have the option of reflecting how they themselves would have reacted differently. As chapter 6.3 reveals not identifying with a protagonist can lead to elaborate and indepth negotiations of plots and character developments as well.

– "Then it's probably wise to stay quiet." (ibid., 18)

Winston is annoyed at everyone and does not want to talk with his father when their flight departs to Nova Scotia. His father's reaction surprises Winston, as his mother always wanted to make him talk and never accepted his unwillingness to do so. But here, Winston is allowed, almost told to better remain quiet if he does not have anything to say. Students can reveal why this would be a good advice for Winston Jr. and in which situations remaining silent could indeed be the better choice. This is especially remarkable when Winston's attitude changes and he does talk to Terry and his parents a lot more as the narration proceeds. Students can draw conclusions about Winston's personal development throughout the novel by analysing the way and amount he talks as well as the topics of his conversations.

– "The only people who don't make mistakes are those who are too timid to try new things. Stay bold, take chances . . . Little people make little mistakes. Big people make big mistakes." (ibid., 26)

Winston Sr. does not seem to be too astonished that Winston got suspended from school. In one of their first conversations Winston learns that his father dropped out of school and actually never got his high school diploma (ibid., 27-28). When his father says that he only went to university one afternoon to pick up his degree, Winston questions whether he has actually earned it. His father explains that he earned the honorary degree "from the school of hard knocks" (ibid., 28). But when this topic gets too uncomfortable, he asks what kind of career his son has in mind. "[I]f I keep skipping school maybe I could become a journalist" is Winston's answer. Here, students can discuss the value of education, as well as the risks and chances of going one's own way and doing things differently. If Winston Sr. had not skipped school, he may have never become a successful journalist. However, many who skip school end up in back alleys. Students can reflect upon what it takes to make it and what kind of lessons cannot be taught in school.

– "By running like this I let people know that cancer can be beaten... that life can go on... that you define people by their ability and not their disability." (ibid., 49)

This is Terry's answer to Winston Sr.'s question why he is running across Canada. In the EFL classroom it is worth looking in more detail at this scene, as it not only mirrors Terry's self-perception but also a general attitude with which society encounters physically variant people. Terry does not think of himself as a victim, but rather as a survivor. Although his leg had to be amputated, he was still able to get up from his hospital bed and walk away (cf. ibid., 45). When Winston first hears about Terry's mission, he meets him with the same ignorant and sarcastic attitude he shows toward his parents. He is almost offensive when he is convinced that this young man must be simply 'insane.' Winston does not think that Terry can actually accomplish the goal of running a marathon a day and suggests that instead of "Marathon of Hope, Cross Canada Run in Aid of Cancer Research" "Trying to Run Cross Canada Run" (ibid., 42) should be written on the side of Terry's and Doug's van. Winston identifics Terry as disabled and sees his missing leg as the feature that defines Terry's identity. Through getting to know him better, Winston is able to look beyond the surface and to recognize the personality within the frame of the body. As Winston learns, Terry is much more complete and balanced than himself and that the shape of the body has nothing to do with someone's strength, will-power and determination.

> – Terry says to Winston, "Besides, we both know that you can't run away from your problems." (ibid., 141)

As analysed in the sections above, *Run* is a story about facing challenges and having enough self-esteem to overcome difficulties. For Terry, and finally also for Winston, this attitude is essential as it determines Terry's ability not to give up. Even when his leg is amputated, he finds a way of facing this apparently devastating operation and seeks strength in his abilities. Students can discuss situations in which they thought running away was the easier way out, situations in which they maybe did just that and reveal in how far running away could be justified. The question "What does it take not to give up?" is as interesting as it is difficult to reflect upon.

> –"I know I don't have one friend who would give up half a year of his life or more to take care of me, to help me chase one of my dreams. Do you have a friend who would do that?" (ibid., 101)

Having covered Terry's story for a while, Winston Sr. thinks that there is nothing more to the story than what has already been said. Yet, his editor wants him to stay with Terry and find a new angle to the story and write things that readers might find exciting. Thus, he starts looking for some sensational news. Maybe Terry skips a few kilometres or keeps the money he collects for himself? Winston Sr. knows that "[t]he only thing the public likes better than building a hero is tearing one down. Tragedy sells more papers than triumph" (ibid., 69). In this context, Winston Sr. begins to question Doug's motives of being there with and for Terry. He and his son are reminded of their own circle of friends and realize that although they have friends, they could not think of someone who unconditionally supports them.

As friendship is one of the central topics in the book, it is worthwhile reflecting upon with students as well. Reading about Terry and Doug, students could ponder their own experiences and friendships, elaborate on the traits of character they value most in their friends and on situations in which they needed a friend or needed to be reliable for somebody else. In those considerations, students can reflect Winston's and Terry's experiences in their own light and personally connect to the story.

Since Terry is seen as one of Canada's most famous and popular heroes, students can additionally examine the question of what makes a hero and whether there are different types of heroes. This is addressed in the first newspaper article Winston Sr. writes for his magazine (Walters 2003, 62-67). Heroes such as Terry Fox can be found in many cultures. Students could suggest and present people who they consider to be heroes and engage in debates in which they justify their choices.[130]

Beyond these scenes the book offers further incentives for investigation. The attentive reader may have recognized the intertextual reference within the headline of this chapter. Indeed, Robert Frost's poem "The Road not Taken" (1916), shows thought-provoking parallels to Terry's and Winston's story.

> Two roads diverged in a yellow wood,
> And sorry I could not travel both
> And be one traveler, long I stood
> And looked down one as far as I could
> To where it bent in the undergrowth;   *5*
>
> Then took the other, as just as fair,
> And having perhaps the better claim,
> Because it was grassy and wanted wear;
> Though as for that the passing there
> Had worn them really about the same,   *10*
>
> And both that morning equally lay
> In leaves no step had trodden black.
> Oh, I kept the first for another day!
> Yet knowing how way leads on to way,
> I doubted if I should ever come back.   *15*
>
> I shall be telling this with a sigh
> Somewhere ages and ages hence:

---

[130] Tasillo's essay on "Heroism: What Does It Mean to be a Hero?" (2006) offers more example texts for intertextual references.

Two roads diverged in a wood, and I—

I took the one less traveled by,

And that has made all the difference.   *20*

Similar to the protagonist of this poem who decides to take the unused road, Terry took a road never travelled before. An amputee's run across Canada was a new form of raising awareness of cancer and collecting donation; even such a run in itself has hardly ever happened before. Winston, too, takes a road he has not taken before, one of reflecting upon himself, talking to his dad and reconciling the relationship with his mother.

Although the last two lines "I took the one less traveled by / And that has made all the difference" (l. 19-20) carry the notion of a rather individualistic adventure, for both Terry and Winston taking their roads has strong social and communal implications. Terry collected millions of Dollars for cancer research and his run emotionally connected Canadians across the country. Winston's road leads to personal reflections about his self which allow him and his parents to re-establish connections they thought to be lost. Similarly to the voice of the poem, Winston has to make important decisions regarding his future and develop the urge to come to terms with his struggles. Before meeting Terry and spending time with his father, Winston's solution had often been to run away from his problems. His experiences, however, make him recognize that this is not possible and that he needs to face his challenges. Using this poem as a parallel text, students can explore the metaphorical meaning of running and choosing between different directions.

A further text that can be used for an intertextual analysis is Alan Sillitoe's *The Loneliness of the Long-Distance Runner* (1968) in which parallels to Winston Jr. can be identified. It tells the story of Smith who is sent to Borstal, a home for delinquent youths after he is caught robbing a bakery. While he is there, he starts long-distance running to find solitude from the aggressive atmosphere at Borstal. Similar to Winston Jr., also Smith soon recognizes that while running he has time to think about his life and future. For Winston running is a distraction from the boredom of a monotone landscape and it offers him a break from his father's presence. For Smith it is a distraction from the brutal atmosphere at school. While running himself and experiencing Terry's "Marathon of Hope" first hand support Winston in dealing with his problems and improving the relationship with his parents, Smith's running first functions as a physical and emotional escape from his desolate working-class home and predictable future, but it takes a different turn. The authorities of his school-prison guarantee him early release if he participates in and wins a cross-country race against a prestigious public school. Although this is initially tempting for Smith, he also feels exploited for improving the name of his school. During the race Smith is far ahead of the other runners, showing them that they do not stand a chance against him. Yet, he stops a few meters short of the finishing line. By allowing the other runners to finish the race before him, Smith express-es his unwillingness to be instrumentalized for the Borstal authorities' plan to improve their reputation and to become part of their repressive system – an act that can be interpreted as a demonstration of his free spirit and independence. The aim of Borstal is to turn the boys into honest young men. For Smith, refus-ing to win the race for those authorities is the most honest act he can perform, as he stays true to himself. It resembles an act of self-confidence as he gets "a bit of my own back on the In-laws by letting them sit up there and watch me lose this race" (Sillitoe 1968, 67).

While Winston frees himself of his personal dissatisfaction, Smith can-not reconcile his past and will not be released early but has to return to Borstal. His manual work leads him to contemplate about his behavior and to conclude that he does not regret anything, including "losing the race on purpose" (ibid., 77). In his mind he is as free as he can be. When he is released for good, he is diagnosed with pleurisy, a disease which causes water to collect around the lungs (cf. ibid.) and which prevents him from having to join the army. As he is again able to escape authorities and heteronomy, this is a second win for Smith. In the end, Smith is back on the road, stealing money and pulling crimes again.

As a link between *Run*, "The Road not Taken" and *The Loneliness of the Long-Distance Runner*, students can reflect upon the image of finding or choosing a path. In Sillitoe's short story this is present in that Smith contem-plates "You should think about nobody and go your own way, not on a course marked out for you by holding mugs of water and bottles of iodine in case you fall and cut yourself so that they can pick you up – even if you want to stay where you are – and get you moving again" (ibid., 64).

In Sillitoe's and Walters' texts, the readers encounter 'angry young men'[131] who run away and toward their goals in different dimensions, with dif-ferent motivations and consequences. While Winston used to run away from his problems, meeting Terry who himself is running for curing cancer leads him to run toward a whole sense of self. Smith first runs to escape the hardship of Bor-stal but soon realizes that he is being exploited for a system he rejects. There-fore, his final run becomes a run toward independence and self-determination, although this entails a return to Borstal and eventually to a criminal life. Simi-larly to Winston, also for Smith running entails notions of coming to terms with himself and his past experiences, which for him mainly surround the memory of

---

[131] Angry Young Men is also known as a literary movement of the 1950s during which a group of British novelists and playwrights expressed their dissatisfaction with the established socio-political order of Great Britain. Being members of the working class or lower middle-class, their scorn was mostly addressed at the hypocrisy of the upper and higher middle-class and the postwar welfare state. Examples of this movement are John Wain's novel *Hurry on Down* (1953) or Kingsley Amis' play *Look Back in Anger* (1956). Usually, the work that emerged from this group centers around rootles, lower-middle or working class male protagonists who have conflicts with authorities but still try improve their living situation (http://www.britannica.com/EBchecked/topic/25251/Angry-Yo ung-Men). This literary and historic background could also be included in classroom reflections.

how he found his father after he committed suicide at their home. Smith has not thought about his incident since it had happened but while running also his thoughts run free and repressed memories return. For students, this image and the different realizations and interpretations can be highly thought-provoking and invite them to reflect upon their own approach to personal challenges and risks they may take to change the prospects for their future.

5.3 "What a Great Story You Have Travelled": Hiromi Goto's *The Water of Possibility*

Similar to *Little Voice*, Hiromi Goto's *The Water of Possibility* (2001) was published in Coteau Books' "In the Same Boat" series. In this novel, Japanese mythology empowers the Japanese Canadian protagonist Sayuri to re-define her identity as a young girl who faces different challenges of growing up. Her journey begins when she discovers a parallel world beyond the walls of the root cellar of the family's new house in which Japanese mythology has come to life. Thus, Goto creates a 'third space' which enables Sayuri to grow beyond her wisdom, strength and courage to finally be brave enough to face her deepest fears. Eventually, when Sayuri and her brother Keiji return from their journey, she is able to leave behind her shadowy self.

By having the children move through the earthy walls of the root cellar, the author uses a mysterious image that provided the title of Janet Lunn's novel *The Root Cellar* (1981). Sayuri and Keiji follow an adventure similar to that of Lunn's protagonist. Yet, while twelve-year-old Rose encounters historic events like the American Civil War, the siblings discover Living Earth, a place inhabited by figures of Japanese mythology which they have so far only known through their parents' storytelling (cf. Alter 2012a, 185). The adventures Sayuri has there pose challenges for her decision making and maturity. However, through applying knowledge about Japanese mythology, approaching the inhabitants of Living Earth respectfully and making wise choices, she is able to develop an identity as a young, confident and balanced girl entering puberty.

5.3.1 Otherness and Transcultural Topoi

The Water of Possibility entails specific potential for transcultural learning, which is grounded in the story's depiction of otherness. This can be identified in

- the relationship of siblings and parents,
- environmental issues,
- the importance of friendship, and
- quests of self-discovery.

Referring to intercultural learning students can focus on the setting of the story in the Canadian prairies as well as the representation of Japanese mythology and folklore. Both the novel's complex intercultural dimension and the transcultural perspective on otherness make this story the most multifaceted of the books selected for this discussion which justifies a more detailed analysis.

The opening scene of *The Water of Possibility* introduces the reader to Sayuri, a sad girl who is on her way to the family's new home in Ganola. Accompanied by "[d]rying canola, sweet-smelling hay, small herds of black Angus, red-and-white Herefords" (Goto 2001, 1),[132] this is nothing but a trip "toward eternal boredom and prairie isolation" (2). With a sigh she remembers "maybe not the most glamorous city in the world [...], but [...] her home" (2). Based on descriptions such as "Memorial Park Library, the Lindsay Park pool" (1), this could be Calgary. Sayuri's repeated sighing, a missing reaction from her parents and the disgust with her younger brother Keiji picking his nose set the main conflict situation. She does not want to move to Ganola, she is annoyed by her younger brother, and she is mad at her parents for making her leave her friends behind. This personal and familial struggle is further intensified when the reader learns that Sayuri is suffering from her changing body and that Keiji does not understand that she, as a growing woman, needs some privacy (36-37).

At the beginning of the book, the reader encounters Sayuri as a young girl who is overwhelmed with the effects of puberty and her quickly changing emotional state which she finds difficult to classify. Sayuri seems fragile and self-centred, while nevertheless grateful for loving parents. They, however, often embarrass Sayuri; especially her mother, a writer of horror stories who "parade[s] T-shirts with logos that would be banned in any school" (4). For Sayuri, the first impression is very important, which makes it difficult for her to accept her mother's appearance at their first meeting with swim coach Donovan:

> "Don't you dare say anything embarrassing when we get there!" Sayuri warned. "Promise?"
> "Have I ever embarrassed you?" Kimi raised her eyebrows. Sayuri stared at the theatrical eyeliner and the pink T-shirt with a snail decal. "Eat My Slime!" was scrawled beneath it. Toes with black toenail polish peeped out of sparkly platform shoes. She sighed.
> [...]
> "It took me a long time to be proud of who I am. You take your own path. But always be proud of who you are." Kimi's lips smiled, but her eyes were serious. (44)

---

[132] If not indicated differently, in this chapter the number in brackets refers to the page number in Goto (2001).

Although initially one of the girls of the swim team seems to be distant toward Sayuri and has difficulty correctly pronouncing her name, this is explained with Sayuri thinking that being the "'new kid' was simply awful" (49). Goto refrains from relating Sayuri's uneasiness to her ethnic background, but rather points at teenagers usually being hesitant toward newcomers. Although the author does not ignore ethnicity, she does not put this aspect of identity into the spotlight either. Sayuri's incompleteness stems from her being lost, geographically as well as personally, not ethnically.

Once the family arrives in Ganola, Sayuri initially feels uncomfortable: as a swimmer and lover of water, she immediately recognizes the dry land and strange new house: it is dusty, empty, and smells weird. One evening Sayuri and Keiji have to cater for themselves because their parents have to work late and forgot to prepare dinner. As the kitchen cupboards are empty, the only option the children have is to go downstairs into the root cellar where the supplies are stored. It is dark, dry and functions as a natural refrigerator. Looking for the light switch, the children accidentally move through the walls of the root cellar and discover a parallel world. Sayuri and Keiji are transported through a "portal of secrecy" (West/Harris 2003, 84) into a strange, mysterious, and also dangerous Living Earth.

In Living Earth, the children encounter figures of Japanese mythology they know from their parents' bedtime stories. The first figure they meet is Yamanba. From her mother's story Sayuri knows that Yamanba is the great mountain woman who lived in the dark forests of Mount Aso where she is "keeper of the fires in the volcano" (40). To honour Yamanba's important work, each autumn the people in the village had a "Festival of Fires"; Yamanba in turn controlled the volcano and only allows the beast to erupt every few decades to feed, "for all living creatures must eat" (ibid.). Thus, Yamanba controlled life and death. But as time passed, the people forgot about Yamanba, she became weak and the beast got hungrier. The neglected honour made it difficult for Yamanba to keep the volcano quiet. She finally vanished and the volcano erupted violently, destroying everything that stood in its way. It was only when the people remembered Yamanba and prepared a new "Festival of Fires" that the volcano was calmed down and Yamanba returned (cf. 39-41): "And from beneath the soil, there was a movement. The earth heaved, shuddered, and a loud wail filled the night air. For Yamanba had been born anew" (42).

In a similar way, at the end of the book Sayuri is born anew when she, together with Keiji, her newly gained wisdom and the assurance that she saved Living Earth, re-emerges from underneath the soil through the root cellar. By moving to Ganola, a hopeless place for a girl whose life belongs in the city, Sayuri faces destruction but also rebirth, symbolized by her journey through Living Earth, saving this place and her new friends and returning home with a new sense of self. Just as Yamanba's rebirth rebalances life and death around Mount Aso, Sayuri's re-emergence from Living Earth enables her to balance her new life in Ganola. Yamanba's farewell greeting "Your life spiral will take you to many wondrous places" (167) thereby has manifold meanings regarding her further adventures in "Earth As I Know It" (146).

Living Earth resembles a space in which sensible and mature decisions turn the 12-year-old whiny adolescent into a mature young woman. The space where the children are caught forms a space of personal growth. For example, when she is imprisoned and has a chance to flee, Sayuri frees all the other prisoners before saving herself without knowing how dangerous they might be (149). In a different situation she saves the Patriarch despite his cruel oppression of the inhabitants of Living Earth (cf. below).

Apart from her choices, also Japanese myths and stories are essential for Sayuri to find a balance within herself and to escape dangerous situations. When Sayuri cannot fall asleep, it is the story of Great Yamanba in the evergreen forest of Aso mountain (39-42, cf. above) that Kimi tells her and that calms her down. In this scene, Japanese mythology serves as a means to provide comfort and ease of fear in unknown surroundings. Similarly, when Sayuri faces the very hungry oni in Living Earth, it is a story that helps her to not only find comfort but also to avert his first attack by impressing him with heroic tales. When the oni re-appears in the village of the tanuki (158), her mother's stories are supportive as Sayuri remembers a "little manling who grew bigger with the magical double-headed mallet! Pounding on one side of the mallet made things bigger, but pounding in the other side of the mallet made things smaller" (159). Sayuri uses this trick to prevent him from attacking a second time; she makes him smaller and reduces his hunger. As one of the main principles of the tanuki says that "[c]ruelty calls cruelty and kindness calls kindness" (160), the tanuki welcome the oni into their village. In return, the oni later helps the tanuki to fight the Patriarch. Familiar stories in unfamiliar surroundings help Sayuri to base her behavior on this knowledge and to act wisely.

In Sayuri's quest, Yamanba becomes a guardian in uncovering and relating the stories the girl knows from her mother and Yamanba's very own story. This "combination of the guide and the unfamiliar – or defamiliarized – physical space within which [she] operates, opens up the stunted potential of the protagonist to a new possibility of growth" (West/Harris 2003, 78). In this sense, Yamanba not only guides Sayuri's journey through place, space and time, but also toward self-understanding by leading her to self-discovery and encouraging her to face her greatest fears. Through Yamanba's influence, the protagonist is able to "move away from an unhealthy introversion […] towards a more vigorous openness – a vital new psychological space" (West/Harris 2003, 78). It is Yamanba who supports Sayuri in transcending the constrictions imposed on her inner life which were caused by the dissatisfaction of leaving her friends and swim team behind, by moving into a remote area, and by a lack in self-confidence. The encounters with the mountain woman facilitate a process of self-discovery through which Sayuri achieves a more complete identity; not necessarily an ethnic identity, but her personality as a 12-year-old girl.

After their ordeal in Living Earth, the children stand in front of the basin that holds the Water of Possibility. Yamanba explains that the children have to reach into the Water before they can return home. Both children are scared because they have to "receive both the good and bad [they] carry within [them]selves" (301), as good and bad always come together and the one can only exist with the other. Sayuri and Keiji are left alone, hold hands and reach into the Water. Their hands pull out a globe which shows visions of their longings: Sayuri sees her family enjoying a day by the ocean, she and her father are swimming, her mother and Keiji are sitting at the shore and starting the picnic (303). When they reach for the bad Keiji pulls out a clown, his greatest fear of all. Sayuri finds the hand of a child, another Sayuri whose "teeth shone too bright, silver-pointed razors that overlapped, row upon row, in her monstrous mouth, teeth that were meant to raze and destroy" (306). The girl realizes that the monster she pulled out is herself, representing the bad and evil that is part of her identity equal to the good and honourable traits of her character. She is reminded of the Patriarch who earlier said that Sayuri's good and his evil are twins (270, 306) and understands that she has to be brave and accept the good and bad in herself.

Throughout the book, constant references to the environment and nature point at a further reference for transcultural learning.[133] While the lush surroundings in Living Earth are taken for granted, Sayuri is shocked when she sees Living Earth as

> dead landscape all around them, razed into an unnatural flatland. […] The countryside dotted with piles of drying stumps and branches. No birds. No chattering insects. Nothing but the sound of pounding feet. It didn't make any sense. The land wasn't being used for crops or even construction. What was the purpose of razing the land and leaving nothing in its place? What kind of lunatic destroyed his own home? […] The dry wind swirled dirt against their faces and stung their cheeks. (185-186)

As Sayuri later learns, the electric supply of the Patriarch's city is based on organic material. After the Patriarch is defeated, he takes on his old name, Haru, and understands that he has done wrong to the creatures around him and to the land; he decides that "[f]irst, I must replant the blasted lands with saplings and seeds" (290). Additionally, Sayuri and her friends replant the earth as they take "pouches of seeds: wildflowers, grasses, wingpods of maples, sticky burrs, and fruiting seeds" (293) with them when they leave the city in the hope that these take root and revitalize the land. Here, Sayuri not only shows responsibility for her friends but also for her natural surroundings. Remarkably, her scattering of

---

[133] Basseler (2014) and Bartosch/Grimm (2014) have recently investigated environmental education and ecodidactics from an ELT perspective and offer interesting points of references in the frame of global education.

those seeds resembles the image of Grimm's *Hansel and Gretel* who leave crumbs of bread on their path in order to find their way back home. The last scene of *The Water of Possibility* describes that the root cellar in the family's house is no longer a concrete floor but that there is movement

> [b]eneath the surface. A small nudge, nudging through aeons with the small magic of hope and compassion. A pale green shoot pushed through the dark dirt, twining upward from aged roots long thought dead. The verdant stem stretched upward, unfurling three small leaves. (314)

This emerging plant mirrors an established connection between Sayuri's home and Living Earth, and metaphorically also to her balanced personality. The seeds she scattered have indeed taken root and found a way into Sayuri's world. Thus, she may also be able to find a way back to Yamanba and her new friends, and apply her development to a more confident girl in her real world and new home. She will be able to retain her new personality in Ganola.

When Sayuri and Keiji return home, they spend a wonderful evening with their parents, during which Sayuri asks whether she could join all kinds of clubs in order to learn rock climbing, orienteering and yoga which will keep her in balance. She suggests "to consider a fish-only non-meat diet" (312) out of respect for other beings. When they all sit together after dinner, Sayuri just watches her family, "the miracle of their expressions, the emotions which played on their faces" (312). Sayuri is content with herself and with her surroundings. While Keiji has been a nuisance in the past, Sayuri now acknowledges that he has achieved something great by facing his fears. The fear of losing him changed how she now sees her brother. This feeling of content culminates in asking her mother whether she would like to sleep in her room, for this time the daughter wants to share stories.

Remarkably, in *The Water of Possibility* the perception of otherness is counteracted by the inhabitants of Living Earth as these mythological figures are the real 'people' and Sayuri and her brother are seen as fictional. To the talkative creatures like the oni and tengu, the frog-like kappa called Echo, tanuki raccoons, mischievous foxes, and a big, purple cat, Sayuri appears as the strange creature from "Earth As I Know It"; Sayuri and Keiji as humans are the others, as one tanuki comments "'I have oft heard tales of mythical humans, but have never cast my eyes on such a creature'" (145).

While the novel refrains from depicting Sayuri as the ethnic other, for the reader otherness is created in the vibrant descriptions of the figures of Japanese mythology. Including Japanese folkloric creatures in the plot in a very imaginative way, Goto enables these to move from merely mentioned beings that add exotic flavour toward vivid and memorable characters that enrich a fast-moving plot. Moreover, those mythological figures, for instance the kappa and the shape-shifting fox, combine important aspects of Japanese and Canadian culture – both of which are fundamental for Sayuri to rescue her brother and Living Earth.

Sayuri's successful personal development is founded on her adventures in Living Earth, on her brave decisions, and on her ability to solve heroic tasks during her journey. A new position emerges: She now is a brave young girl who is ready to live in Ganola. These incidents contribute to her becoming a young and reflected, self-confident and well-balanced girl. At the beginning of the novel the reader encountered a rather egoistic girl who could only think of her life in the big city, her friends, and being a competitive swimmer. After Sayuri's adventures and looking back at all the good deeds she accomplished and friends she found, she prefers taking Yoga classes together with her mother and learning about herself. In order to fully arrive in Ganola and accept her new life in the prairies, she needed to leave home, struggle through a world of mythological figures, challenge the Patriarch, and return home again, having formed a new sense of self and having overcome some of her greatest fears. This reveals that Sayuri has grown as a young girl in general, not as young girl who needs to find a balance between two or more ethnic influences on her personality (cf. chapter 7). Young readers of various backgrounds are provided with multiple points of reference and identification that go beyond ethnic boundaries. As Sayuri is depicted as a girl, not a Japanese Canadian girl, a focus on the 'ethnic other' is transcended.[134]

5.3.2 Teaching Implications

As is visible in the depiction of otherness and the reflections upon transcultural topoi, *The Water of Possibility* includes manifold teaching implications for inter- and transcultural learning. While the book is intended for native speakers between 9 and 12 years of age, it could language-wise be too challenging for English learners of the same age. But when choosing excerpts that are most interesting and that offer food for thought, the text can well be read toward the end of Grade 8. Yet, it is advised to refrain from tasks that demand a detailed analysis of content and language because learners may lack the advanced linguistic tools which would be necessary to complete these successfully. Rather, learners should be allowed to reflect their knowledge, impressions and similar experiences in view of the situations and challenges Sayuri and her friends face.

From an intercultural perspective, discussions of aspects that present a rather strong notion of otherness to most students can be used as a first encounter with the text. Japanese mythology is probably new to the students and the descriptions of figures such as the oni, tengu, tanuki, Yamanba and kappa, as well as a shape-shifting fox entail potential for exciting discovery learning. While the aforementioned figures can be placed in a Japanese context, shape-

---

[134] Cf. chapter 7.1.2 in which I critically reflect upon a different approach to the depiction of ethnic otherness.

shifters are common figures in Canadian, especially First Nation stories as well. Students can learn about the myths and stories revolving around these figures and enjoy Sayuri's encounters and adventures with them. Sayuri's respect and her honorable behavior toward the mythological figures can be a model for the students' own approach. What is more, students can think of similar mythological figures which have special powers or around which adventurous stories exist from their backgrounds.

While reading the text, students can relate to several of Sayuri's experiences. They may have moved from a place they called home to a new city, leaving friends and familiar and beloved places behind and having to adjust to new surroundings. They may have been new to a class in which they did not have any friends yet and could understand Sayuri's uneasiness in the new swim team. They may have encountered situations in which their siblings were annoying or their parents were embarrassing.

For Sayuri, stories carry essential meaning, because they are comforting and provide knowledge and awareness of how to approach figures of Japanese mythology in Living Earth. This can be included in classroom discussions by having students think about stories that were told or read to them when they were younger. Using fables, for example, students could reflect upon the relevance of morals included in those specific stories. They can compare whether similar stories exist in different cultures and which traits of character are ascribed to which animals and figures. The folk story of Yamanba could serve as an example and foundation (cf. Goto 2001, 39-41). This approach speaks to interdisciplinary teaching, as fables are part of the curriculum in German classes (e.g. MSW 2011, 19, 20).

Beyond these aspects also transcultural topics like friendship and justice can be focused (cf. Bredella 2010b, 122-123).

A.   In Living Earth, Sayuri has to rely on the support of her newly found friends. They are the only ones who help her to find Keiji and try to right the wrongs the Patriarch has brought over the land. As Sayuri, Echo and Machigai quickly establish a very close relationship to strive for their common quest, Sayuri is very disappointed when she learns that Echo has apparently betrayed his friends. Yet, Sayuri is about to do the very same when she escapes from the soldiers. After being captured by a group of kappa soldiers and marched toward the city, the soldiers demand a break before entering the city (cf. Goto 2001, 173-187). Assuming that Machigai is smart enough to help himself, Sayuri decides to escape when she sees that the kappa are too tired to follow her. Although she is successful, she realizes that while she may be free, Machigai is still captured. Sayuri sees that her friend would be lost without her help as his snout is chained and no one "would give Machigai water" (ibid., 187-189). She just repeated what she hated in Echo: she betrayed her friend. Thus, instead of seeking security in the forest, she returns to Machigai and her kidnappers and prefers remaining in captivity to leaving him behind.

This incident can be used for students to reflect upon the importance of friendship and to think of situations in which they felt deceived by their friends or maybe saw no other option than betraying them.

B. When Sayuri and her friends have destroyed the amplifying machine that had supplied the city with energy, her remaining task is to save her brother. She is able to end the fight between Machigai and the Patriarch, but sees that the Patriarch still has a chain fixed to Keiji's heart with which he has captured his memories and has started to drag the unconscious boy over the stones toward him. In this moment

> [y]ellow fire roared through Sayuri's body and blinded her vision, the katana a blaze of light. She leapt high, the sword held above her head, and swung with a scream, the blade of fire cutting through the Patriarch's wrists, the inhuman hands falling off like wooden stumps. (ibid., 272)

She freed her brother. Some time later, Sayuri and the Great Mother Tanuki sit together and contemplate what has happened. Sayuri learns that the Great Mother Tanuki and the Patriarch used to be companions and that although he has turned her into stone for hundreds of years, she still forgives him. Sayuri cannot believe that the Great Mother is actually friendly to the Patriarch, as he has done a lot of evil. Sayuri "scowled fiercely" and wonders whether "murder count[s] for anything in this place?" (ibid., 278) "'In my world,' Sayuri stated, 'we punish criminals [...], we put them in prison'" (ibid.). With Momo's[135] interrogating questions, Sayuri ponders what is actually entailed in processes of healing, and realizes that she herself performed a great act of violence when she cut of the Patriarch's hands to protect her brother. Taking "[t]he hardest steps she'd ever taken" (ibid., 279), Sayuri approaches the Patriarch and uses the remaining healing water to replace his hands with his original paws. She understands that he needs those to begin his own healing, and that she needs to do this to come to terms with her experiences in Living Earth and to return home as a whole person herself.

---

[135] Momo is an apparently stuffed cat that Keiji and Sayuri discover in one of the attic rooms at the beginning of the book. When the children approach the stuffed animal, it turns out to be alive and it jumps through the wall. For the children, it is the first encounter with the new house as a mysterious place. Momo reappears in Living Earth and turns out to be Yamanba's pet.

This central scene of the book can serve as a basis for debates about friendship, justice and forgiveness. Students can try to understand Sayuri's hesitation of forgiving the Patriarch and think of other possible solutions for her difficult situation. It would not be surprising if students were of the opinion that Sayuri should not have forgiven him but that some other form of punishment should have been found for the Patriarch. Would it not be fair to punish him for all the suffering and death he has brought to Living Earth? Why does Great Mother Tanuki forgive him? Would Sayuri be satisfied knowing that she cut of his hands and that he will forever be reminded of the wrongs he did? Those and other questions in reference to the book and the students' individual experiences with betrayal, forgiveness, punishment and (in)justice can be included in this context.

This chapter provided a detailed discussion to three Canadian texts for young readers and their different representation of otherness. The analysis of intercultural references and the transcultural topoi entailed in each reveals that all three books for young readers offer interesting and useful points of reference for inter- and transcultural learning outlined in the teaching implications for each title. The following chapter offers a more general perspective on the benefits of Canadian young adult fiction for inter- and transcultural learning in ELT.

6. Canadian Young Adult Fiction and Cultural Learning

Based on the discussion of the books above, I see one of the central benefits for cultural learning in their different approaches to otherness. With view of the reflections of inter- and transcultural learning, I would like to carve out and suggest a continuum from inter- to transcultural learning and literature. The following chapter also summarizes the potential of Canadian texts for cultural learning in ELT.

6.1 From Inter- to Transcultural Awareness

As elaborated in detail in chapter 1, intercultural learning, simply put, assumes that members of one culture increase knowledge, awareness of and respect and tolerance for members of another culture. This concept entails that two differing cultures exist between which meaning and understanding can be negotiated. On the surface, Ruby Slipperjack's novel *Little Voice* is an example of an intercultural text with which intercultural competence can be increased. It is the story about Ray's development of a balanced identity as a multicultural child of First Nation and Euro-Canadian background. Torn between the worlds represented by the community in which her mother and siblings live and her grandmother's house, she tries to find her own way and come to terms with who she is. Her grandmother's teaching of Anishinaabeg traditional knowledge of plants and herbs and the time she spends in and with nature serve as a healing process of the struggles she faced at home. This constellation accounts for a search of ethnic identity which is a common motif in intercultural literature (cf. chapter 7). The narration focuses on an individual overcoming story rather than on a structural critique of what causes Ray's unhappiness. However, beyond this level, Ray's struggles at school and her uneasiness with the new family situation when her mother remarries and has a new baby also entail transcultural notions, as those cannot be limited to a child's experiences within a certain culture. In this sense, *Little Voice* offers points of references for both inter- and transcultural reflections and, thus, the development of awareness in both spheres.

    The main argument for including Eric Walters' *Run* lies with challenging the assumption that in most TEFL research the other is almost exclusively reduced to 'ethnic minorities,' and with questioning the common practice of including only these in cultural reflections. Both, I believe, entail a strong notion of seeing 'white middle class' as the norm, as described in the introduction to chapter 5. In *Run*, though, two young 'white' middle class males are seen as others[136] based on their social behavior and physical and mental abilities. This

---

[136] I am aware of current disability studies which argue that the separation between able-bodied

establishes a difference to what is commonly understood as intercultural learning. With Terry and Winston Jr., students engage in debates of otherness which can result in recognizing that the other is not necessarily the ethnic other, but that otherness can be perceived along various lines. This can also lead to questioning otherness in general. Additionally, Terry proves that physical particularities can play a minor role in identifying otherness and that exceptional strength of mind and determination are features which contribute to seeing someone as other. Referring to transcultural issues like cancer and human traits of character that distinguish people, *Run* offers approachable alternatives to reflect upon othernesses and can thus, in my view, be seen closer to a transcultural scope.

Finally, Hiromi Goto's *The Water of Possibility* depicts otherness beyond ethnic identity and issue-laden contexts altogether. This novel is therefore seen as a prime example of a novel that raises transcultural awareness and represents transcultural literature (cf. chapter 7.2). Sayuri is of Japanese Canadian background, but her issues are age specific and she becomes a heroine because of her personal development, not because of her (lack of and successful search for) ethnic identity. In-class reflections of this book can lead to questioning definitions of otherness and becoming aware of a normalcy of the other (cf. Hunfeld e.g. 1991, cf. chapter 8.3).

While Ray seems to be caught between two cultures and her otherness is one of ethnic identity, Terry and Winston Jr. represent other othernesses of social struggles, ability and will-power. With Sayuri, otherness is present on yet another level, as the multicultural character becomes the heroine of the story based on her courage and development of sense of self. All of the four protagonists are somehow other, but each with view of different features. This perspective on the protagonists' depiction reveals a continuum from inter- to transcultural representation, in which Ray can generally be located on an intercultural level, because despite her other adventures, her search for a balanced ethnic identity takes center stage. Sayuri can be located on a transcultural level as her search transcends issues of ethnic identity; the multicultural protagonist rather deals with transcultural struggles such as puberty, a lack of self-esteem and an annoying brother. Winston Jr. and Terry can be placed in between as they represent other others, social and physical, and thus reflect transcultural notions. However, Winston is nevertheless caught in identity struggles, which is a motif that often seems to be ascribed to intercultural negotiations. Both young men

---

and disabled bodies is a cultural construct. "[C]ulturally generated and perpetuated standards as 'beauty,' 'independence,' 'fitness,' 'competence,' and 'normalcy' exclude and disable many human bodies while validating and affirming others" (Garland-Thomson 1997, 7). Cultures and other collectives, such as age groups for example, identify such deviation differently, which points at the social constructedness of a seemingly neutral, natural, and physiological basis. Despite being aware of the connotation of labeling a prosthesis-wearing protagonist as other, I would like to use this differentiation with regards to Terry in order to shed light on the depiction of other others in the context of inter- and transcultural teaching in which ethnicity is often the main distinction.

are members of a 'white' Canadian middle class and, therefore, the inclusion of *Run* also contributes to widening the scope of transcultural reflections.

In cultural learning, a perspective on self and other seems to be prevalent which often considers the self to be 'white.' This estimation is grounded on the observation that inter- or transcultural negotiations are often based on other literatures, i.e. literatures from other cultures and countries. As will be discussed in more detail in the following chapters, this perspective is no longer justified as the perception of otherness and processes of othering are relative to an audience and, thus, highly subjective. In increasingly multicultural classrooms, one cannot assume that learners identify otherness along similar lines or based on ethnicity. When putting all four characters, Ray, Terry, Winston and Sayuri next to one another it would be interesting to see who is 'outstanding enough' for students to be identify as the other. In such a constellation it could well be that Winston and Terry are identified as other, as they are 'white.' This short reflection causes further debates of distributions of power and Eurocentric perspectivity, which also furthers the concept of transcultural literature (cf. chapter 7.2.3).

6.2 Mirroring of Balanced Multicultural Identities

The three novels discussed in chapter 5 offer a new perspective on otherness and ethnic identity. In *The Water of Possibility* Sayuri does not fall victim to intercultural challenges she needs to overcome by fighting against a malevolent mainstream society. She is not turned into the other because of her ethnic background but because she begins to recognize that she herself develops into someone other than her childhood self. Her ethnic identity is seen as matter-of-fact. Instead of struggling for it, she is caught in an adventure story, set out on a mission to save a mysterious Living Earth and her brother. She is a girl filled with passion, courage and the need to support her new friends. In order to be successful she needs to trust herself, overcome her critical self-perception and the challenges of puberty and rely on her knowledge of Japanese mythology which she gained from her parents' storytelling. Yet, she is not depicted as a mere positive character, but displays egoistic and arrogant traits as well, which portray her as an ordinary girl on an exciting adventure beyond ethnic identity formation.

Similarly, in *Little Voice* Slipperjack creates a character who strives for ethnic identity, but who cannot be reduced to this dimension. Engaging with nature, cautiously and prudently interacting with the environment and self-confidently reflecting her schoolmates' comments, Ray establishes a complex identity as a child of multicultural background who faces a multitude of challenges that go beyond ethnic issues. Similar to Sayuri, Ray not only entails positive traits of character; rather, she could also be seen as self-centered when she is unable to cope with her mother's new partner and the new baby.

Furthermore, the author uses a very subtle narrative approach to convey Ray's experiences. Situations in which Ray is being discriminated against are to a large extent not related through direct dialogues between the children at school but rather indirectly through Ray's memories. Although her accounts are rather drastic at times – for example she says that "I did not like school very much. In fact, I hated it!" (Slipperjack 2001, 2) – readers only receive vague hints at the reasons for this as "[t]he other kids always made fun of me" (ibid.) or "[t]hey just picked on me all the time" (ibid., 3, cf. 11, 15). Yet, readers do not learn in what particular way because the text refrains from echoing the expressions that offend Ray. It could be assumed that the words caused too much pain to be remembered. However, Ray's development and the framing of those incidents do not provide any cues for such interpretation. Although Ray's story focuses on a child's struggle for identity, this struggle is embedded in story of discovery, filled with colourful descriptions and balanced images without romanticizing it. Issues that cause suffering, such as her family's poverty or the death of her father, are mentioned but do not dominate the narrative. Readers can engage with a fully developed character with a multitude of facets, not one reduced to the role of a suffering victim. Her grandmother's teachings help Ray to understand who she is and where she as a representative of two cultures may belong within the multicultural kaleidoscope of Canadian society. This differing focus will be central in the critical discussion of Bushman and Park's recommendations of literature for cultural learning in chapter 7.1.1.

In *Run*, Terry's personal growth is caused by the amputation of his leg, but is accomplished by his willingness and determination to run in order to support others who suffer from cancer, too. His struggle is not related to this amputation but rather to raising awareness for cancer research, serving as a role model and helping Winston to get back on track. His otherness is not defined by his artificial leg but is seen in his outstanding strength. A balanced representation is especially visible in Winston's depiction. At the beginning of the story he is characterized as a selfish troublemaker who is unable to talk to his mother. Winston is unwilling to understand her worries for her son and enjoys making his mother even more furious. Through meeting Terry and reflecting upon his experiences, he changes into a considered young man who is able to unbuild the walls around his inner life and allows his parents to comfort him when Terry dies.

In *Little Voice* difference is part of the story, but does not take centre stage; in *Run* and *The Water of Possibility*, difference is acknowledged. Especially in these two books, the characters' ethnic background is of minor importance; what is important is who the protagonists are as young people. Light is shed on main characters who independently make decisions and are active in pursuing their goals. In this understanding "multicultural literature can act as an iconoclastic force that replaces stereotypes with an understanding of the actual people who have inspired a literature and a way of life" (Maillet 2003, 51-52). For cultural learning in ELT this entails a perspective on inter- and transcultural learning that transcends issue-laden ethnic identities and widens the frame to reflecting upon multicultural protagonists as heroes and heroines, as balanced identities, not as objectified others.

6.3 Non-Identification as a Basis for Perceiving Otherness

The extended notion of other others that was introduced with Eric Walters' *Run* can be taken one step further by considering other examples of Canadian novels for young readers. The discussion of the following books shows that the perception of otherness in transcultural learning should indeed include diverse depictions of otherness*es* and offer students in increasingly multicultural classrooms the option to widen and thereby also question their perception of otherness. As Haun suggests

> Canadian adolescent literature, created out of the postcolonial discourse surrounding transcendental hybridity, is a powerful tool for modelling how to actively, consciously choose to coexist in […] diversity, creating from that diversity a national vision of cultural plurality. A third space can be created […] a space of communication, negotiation, and translation – a space of hybridity. (Haun 2003, 43)

In the following examples, this is illustrated by exploring the potential of unreliable protagonists and processes of non-identification as an additional way of perceiving other othernesses.

The potential of such non-identification, which could also be ascribed to Winston and his unwillingness to be sensitive toward his mother, can for instance be further explored with Colleen Sydor's *My Mother is a French Fry and Other Proof of my Fuzzed-up Life* (2008), which tells Eli's coming-of-age story. Eli is constantly mad at and highly embarrassed by her mother's behaviour, style and personality. In her perspective, her mother has a lack of inhibition and a very individual way of having things done around the household. For example, the mother earns money by wearing a foam rubber French fry suit in the favourite diner of Eli's classmates and uses the neighbors' thrown out furniture and household trash as the newest decoration items in her own home. Hence, Eli avoids spending time at home, not to mention being brought into connection with her mother in public.

The mother-daughter-conflict is caused by mis- and non-communication, which had reached an extreme level after Eli's sister, Elizabeth, died only a few months after she was born. Eli had no understanding for her parents, when they named the new-born Elizabeth as well. Although her father tries to be as understanding as possible, he also avoids conflicts by all means and hardly offers any support in problematic situations. Eli's only source of comfort is her best friend Grace and her two dads. They have a loving family life and their cozy and welcoming home makes Eli envious. Sydor's references to this homosexual couple as mere side remarks add to the book's transcultural perspective on gender and sexuality, as they are presented as members of society and not problematized or turned into an issue. By referring to them as nothing unusual and mentioning them matter-of-factly, Eli's family and the problems she is facing are 'othered' – not the homosexual couple.[137] Here, students can reflect upon the question of what actually makes a family different. They can investigate Eli's attitude toward her mother and reflect upon the depth of their problematic relationship, too.

An approach to teaching this young adult novel could be based on tasks which ask the students to try and understand Eli's anger and embarrassment, and to identify with her. Yet, it is likely that students rather distance themselves from Eli, seeing her behavior and comments as very egoistic, rude and disrespectful. Reflecting upon the main protagonist could in this case lead to non-identification which nevertheless contributes to the excitement of and investment in reading this story. A certain hesitance to identify with Eli makes the story thought-provoking and appealing. Certainly, this also contributes to the development of literary competences: When meeting such characters in texts, tasks that aim at changing perspectives could be processed in more detail because the characters' traits could be more challenging to comprehend.

This challenge could be even more difficult in Deborah Ellis' *True Blue* (2011), a story about the strong friendship between Casey and Jess which changes drastically when Casey is accused of murdering a little girl. At the beginning of the story, Casey and Jess are enjoying the summer holidays as counselors at a children's camp. One of the members of their group is Stephanie who is annoyingly spoilt, never wants to participate in group activities and does her best worrying everyone with her constant disappearances and bullying of other children. Casey is tired of the girl and comments that she could kill her if she continues to act like that. When Stephanie's body is found after a night camping out in nature, Casey, a grade-A-student who has received a scholarship for studying insects in Australia, becomes the prime suspect. It does not take long until the town turns into a media circus, Casey's plan to become an entomologist is suddenly portrayed as sinister, and her home is vandalized by a group of teens. Yet, Casey's role model position at school and in the community and her high achievements make it difficult for the reader to believe that she could actually be the murderer. Which story is true: Casey insisting on her innocence or the investigations and coverages of the media and police? This becomes more severe when the story constantly implies that Jess, Casey's best friend, actually knows what had happened but remains silent instead of helping.

---

[137] An in-depth analysis of this issue is offered in chapter 7.2.1, when this novel is read as an alternative to ethnicity-based problem-novels/realistic fiction.

Non-identification increases the appeal of the story as the reader may find Jess' lack of loyalty toward her best friend difficult to understand, if not unbelievable. Jess knows what really happened but does not even interfere when Casey is imprisoned. On the contrary, Jess' motives are highly selfish because she realizes that as long as Casey is in prison she will not use her scholarship to go to Australia to study biology and leave Jess behind. The analysis of Casey's and Jess's justification for their behavior provides material for fruitful classroom discussions about the topoi of friendship, trust and (in)justice.

The protagonists' intriguing representation in each novel could indicate a new perspective on otherness and identification as key features of including young adult fiction in the EFL classroom (cf. chapter 2.1). In both novels readers meet characters whose behavior and attitudes cause rejection rather that empathy. In *True Blue*, Jess' inability and unwillingness to tell the truth likely leads to a growing distance between protagonist and reader. In *My Mother is a French Fry and Other Proof of my Fuzzed-up Life*, Eli's egoism and her reluctance to try to understand her mother may make it challenging for students to sympathize and empathize with her. As the depiction of the protagonists causes processes of non- or only limited identification and essentially add to the special appeal of the young adult novels, (non-)identification and identity formation will be further explored in a reinvestigation of key features of using literature in ELT (chapter 7.1.3 and 9).

Additionally, both novels do not reveal the ethnic background of the protagonists and other characters which supports their transcultural potential. Readers can create images of the protagonists and analyse the clues within the plot on which they base these images. They can then question in how far their conclusions about the protagonists' ethnic backgrounds are justified or in how far these may just be assumptions in critical discussions. Similar to the inclusion of Walters' *Run*, this aspect involves a debate in how far 'whiteness' is included in a multicultural scope and which consequences this could have for (re)considering a formerly fixed and criticised canon. Chapter 9.4 will pose this as an open question for further research.

6.4 Mechanisms of Exclusion and Integration

When reflecting upon literature that negotiates multicultural identities, it is worth having a closer look at mechanisms of cultural, social and personal exclusion and integration and discussing those in class. Again, all three books of chapter 5 offer a different perspective on such mechanisms.

In Slipperjack's *Little Voice*, mechanisms of cultural exclusion can for example be uncovered in the opening scenes in which Ray remembers her experiences at school. A closer look at those memories can help learners understand how people base exclusion on certain characteristics of a person, and that exclusion often develops in dynamics in which a majority of people (the school-mates) identifies a common other (Ray). Singling out Ray and directing chants at her is easy for the other students as there "weren't many Native children going to that school" (ibid., 15); they create a collective power and can hide behind each other. The teacher's non-interference with the classmates' bullying directed at Ray and his impersonal address to his student as "You!" (ibid., 16) enables learners to discover how discrimination can run through different social layers, can be institutionalized and become part of a public sphere.

Moreover, students can explore how interpersonal and institutional discrimination differ in terms of power and options for resistance. While Ray does not have the power to withstand her teacher and uses her knowledge to prevent being singled out, she uses silence as a form of escaping her schoolmates' bullying. However, and more importantly, Ray's personal development under the influence of her grandmother leads to increased self-esteem and courage which also reflect a form of (private) resistance against suffering from such exclusion. This, however, needs to be seen in a critical light, as learners should be made aware that neither the classmates' nor the teacher's behavior is rejected – the book does not take a stance against this discrimination, but lets Ray work through it individually. Learners need to understand that it is actually Ray as the victim of discrimination who needs to actively change in order to avoid being victimized, and that the book neither implies that the offenders change their discriminatory behavior against Ray nor that they are punished. Using *Little Voice*, more advanced learners can reflect upon the distribution of power and responsibilities and the cultural and social implications of exclusion and inclusion.

A similar approach is possible to Walters' *Run*. As a consequence of his parents' divorce, Winston Jr. is caught in a web of despair and feeling lost. His way of coming to terms with his changing family dynamics culminates in him being brought home by the police. As outlined in chapter 5.2, his personal social exclusion is a result of his and his parents' inability to talk about their family problems and to communicate personal feelings, hopes and fears. Remarkably, it is through Terry who does not allow himself to be excluded from society or society to exclude him after losing his leg to cancer that the family starts to reflect and reconcile their inner struggles. Through experiencing Terry's courage and will-power, Winston Jr. is able to be part of his family again and to regain trust in the social net his parents provide. His social and familial exclusion and integration are based on the personal struggles of a teenager who fears being lost and his engagement with a role model who encourages him and the surrounding society to acknowledge and be aware of cancer and death.

In Goto's *The Water of Possibility* exclusion and integration is reflected on a personal level, as Sayuri feels uncomfortable with herself, which has effects on her social and familial environment. She suffers from her physical age-dependent changes and cannot come to terms with the fact that she is starting puberty. As a consequence she keeps to herself, and is never really sure about the relationship to her younger brother Keiji and her parents. During her adventurous journey through Living Earth, Sayuri needs to develop strength and courage in order to save her brother and new friends – all of which contribute to her growing as a person and becoming a strong and responsible, brave and caring girl. Back at home she is able to accept herself the way she is; in essence, she manages to include her true self into her personality. What is remarkable and what contributes to *Run* and *The Water of Possibility* as prime examples of transcultural literature is that mechanisms of exclusion and integration are not related to and directed at ethnic identity, but at 'trans' markers of identity formation.

The different references to mechanisms of cultural, social and personal exclusion and integration in *Little Voice*, *Run* and *The Water of Possibility* reveal important conclusions to differentiate inter- from transcultural literatures (cf. chapter 7.2) and, thus, also inter- from transcultural learning as it was indicated in aforementioned chapters. While in inter- or multicultural literature mechanisms of cultural exclusion are often made visible and focused in the multicultural protagonists' quest for ethnic identity and coming to terms with different influences, transcultural literature, as I will suggest, includes protagonists beyond ethnic and national identity and detaches them from problem-identities.

The overview of Canadian literature for young readers and the detailed discussion of three example texts regarding the depiction of otherness, transcultural topoi and their teaching implications delineated the potential of Canadian young adult literature for inter- and transcultural learning in ELT. The different representations of the protagonists have been identified as a central feature of differentiating between both concepts. As a result of the preceding investigations, key concepts of teaching literature have to be re-evaluated when the development of transcultural competences is specifically taken into account. Part C focuses on those re-evaluations in more detail and suggests that transcultural literature is needed if transcultural competences are to be developed.

Part C: Transcultural Perspectives on Using Literature in ELT: Identity Beyond Dichotomies

In the previous chapters I closely looked at selected Canadian titles for young readers which, as examples, offer potential for developing inter-, but especially transcultural competences. Apart from this potential, the analysis revealed that some of the concepts touched upon throughout Part A need to be reconsidered, because their validity was partly challenged. This regards the depiction of otherness in fictional texts and some of the justifications for using young adult literature in contexts of cultural learning.

Based on the discussion of Canadian literature for young readers in Part B, Part C sets out to re-evaluate some of the underlying assumptions that were presented in Part A. Teaching literature and culture in ELT classrooms is framed by certain conditions, of which the fact that reading takes place in a constructed context with non-native speakers is central. Reading literature in ELT not only aims at establishing a generally positive attitude toward reading, fostering it as a life-enhancing experience and developing language skills and competences, but at increasing inter- and transcultural communicative competence, too. This entails changing perspectives, identification and empathy which should culminate in understanding otherness. However, teaching literature and culture in ELT also involves challenges such as making decisions about what to teach about cultures and how teachers can assess and evaluate the cultural competences students have gained (cf. chapter 2).

I re-investigate this issue and discuss my claim that certain books which are implemented in ELT and are suggested for developing cultural competences only marginally allow students to sufficiently reflect upon otherness in chapter 7. As a consequence I suggest the concept of transcultural literature as a foundation for transcultural learning. In chapter 8, I continue the reflection on challenging classroom procedures that were indicated in chapter 2 and offer solutions. Finally, I pull the different lines of argument together and propose identity competence and awareness of alterity as extensions of the existing competence cluster of cultural learning in chapter 9.

7. Re-investigation of Key Facets

As Part B revealed, certain key facets of enhancing inter- and transcultural learning appear in a different light. This especially regards empathy and processes of identification. As I elaborated in chapter 2, one of the benefits of using literature in contexts of intercultural learning is the development of empathy. Yet, while it is described as showing tolerance and acceptance, acknowledgement and respect, those terms are not interchangeable, but refer to distinct concepts of perceiving the other. Furthermore, the selected texts in chapter 5 offer new perspectives on the depiction of ethnic identities and understanding otherness compared to texts recommended for and used in ELT (cf. chapter 3.1).

Consequently, the following section engages more critically with common concepts of developing cultural competences with literature. It is assumed that a limited representation of otherness also limits options for identification and confines protagonists and readers to certain spaces. This argument is supported with studies about reading literature and perceptions of self. Eventually, this chapter demands an extended understanding of otherness, awareness of the intersectionality of othernesses and attentiveness to how ethnic otherness is depicted in realistic fiction. This line of argument culminates in a definition of transcultural literature.

7.1 Ties that B(l)ind Cultural Representations and Identification?

In most publications about the value of ICC, there is a tendency to understand culture in terms of different ethnic and national backgrounds; inter- and transcultural learning and teaching literature aim at understanding otherness that is usually and mainly seen in this frame. However, as elaborated in chapter 5, otherness does not only unfold along those lines. Following the previous discussion, I consider it useful to extend otherness to include further degrees of alterity and thus pay tribute to heterogeneity and multidimensional formations of identity of both parties involved in transcultural learning processes – the self and the other.

Identifying the other as an ethnic other does not agree with past and current processes of globalization, including mass migration, modern means of communication and a growing intracultural diversity. Already in 1988, Clifford noted that

> [t]his century has seen a drastic expansion of mobility, including tourism, migrant labor, immigration, urban sprawl. More and more people "dwell" with the help of mass transit, automobiles, airplanes. In cities on six continents foreign populations have come to

stay -- mixing in but often in partial, specific fashions. The "exotic" is uncannily close. Conversely, there seem no distant places left on the planet where the presence of "modern" products, media, and power cannot be felt. An older topography and experience of travel is exploded. One no longer leaves home confident of finding something radically new, another time or spaces. Difference is encountered in the adjoining neighborhood, the familiar turns up at the ends of the earth. (13-14)[138]

Therefore, depending on the experiences of the readers, someone from the same ethnic background could be identified as other when other diversity markers are more decisive for this individual. Beyond ethnicity and nationality, othernesses can be perceived as different constructions of gender and sexual orientation, family structures, perceptions of age, religious beliefs or questions of ethics. Furthermore, it is possible that various features intersect in one person. This needs to be reflected in the literatures educators and students encounter in cultural learning environments as well.

That otherness could also have positive connotations became visible in Walter's *Run*. There, Terry Fox could be seen as the other when focusing on his illness and the amputation of his leg. But more importantly, his perseverance despite pain and despair are far more significant for his character and thus define him as someone whose physical variation actually *ables* him to achieve greatly; exceptional determination renders him other. If the 'trans' in transcultural learning is emphasized and students are to explore formations of identity beyond narrow ethnic boarders, such an approach to developing cultural competences needs to offer reading material which goes beyond an understanding of diversity in ethnic and national terms, but needs to include social, psychological, physiological, religious and sexual diversity as well.

An underlying assumption for this investigation is that classrooms are becoming increasingly diverse and transcultural themselves. Terminology such as 'hybridity' and 'third space' can be applied to the protagonists that are encountered in narratives, but also to the diverse individuals of the readership of such texts. Especially in the concept of transcultural learning which entails a broader perception of self and other, the understanding of what constitutes both needs to be taken into consideration as well. Both need to be recognized in their diversity and alterity:

> [n]o one today is purely one thing. Labels like Indian, or woman, or Muslim, or American are not more than starting-points, which if followed into actual experience for only a moment are quickly left behind. Imperialism consolidated the mixture of cultures and iden-

---

[138] Despite this statement still being valid, Clifford's explicit focus on "Western visions and practices" (1988, 9) nowadays needs to be relativized as such processes have certainly extended globally even when to varying degrees.

tities on a global scale. But its worst and most paradoxical gift was to allow people to believe that they were only, mainly, exclusively, white, or Black, or Western, or Oriental. Yet just as human beings make their own history, they also make their cultures and ethnic identities. No one can deny the persisting continuities of long traditions, sustained habitations, national languages, and cultural geographies, but there seems no reason except fear and prejudice to keep insisting on their separation and distinctiveness, as if that was all human life was about. (Said 1993, 407-408)

Here, Said refers to different layers of identity and to their dynamic and hybrid character, an account that is mirrored in my approach to transcultural learning, too. Additionally, this diverse understanding of othernesses also points to the fact that processes of othering and perceptions of othernesses are a matter of perspective and power. Defining someone as an ethnic other, for example, implies that he or she is not part of a certain group and exercises power over the other. As Bishop notes

[t]he label [the Other], then, is inadequate as a descriptor. Identifying multicultural literature as literature of or about 'The Other' – people other than white middle-class citizens of the Unites States – helps to reinforce and maintain old social patterns by setting up the American white middle class as the norm, and all others as 'multicultural,' an obvious misuse of the term. (1997, 3)

For my approach this implies that the terms 'multi'- and 'transcultural' need to be unfolded in various directions because for a European reader a story of a Mexican-American hero may count as a multicultural story, while for the Mexican-American reader it could be a story about a German-Jewish heroine. Therefore, the scope of othernesses included in cultural learning needs to be widened. What has been regarded as a Eurocentric point of view in literature needs to be re-included in a multicultural scope or, depending on the content, as representing othernesses as well.

In this sense I agree with Bishop in asking for literature defined in a "comprehensive and inclusive manner" as books which reflect the racial, ethnic, social, and religious etc. diversity of increasingly pluralistic societies. This perspective is of central importance for transcultural learning and the choice of material in multicultural classrooms. Therefore, questions of ascribing power and agency to certain characters and of implied readership become highly relevant. Reactions to these aspects call for a further analysis of ways in which to identify with protagonists, to experience empathy and to form identity. If this should culminate in reading for pleasure[139] and life-long reading, the depiction of otherness is even more important.

In reference to this perspective on othernesses, investigating markers of otherness that are dominantly perceived by students in ELT presents a promising issue of research which has not yet been realized. However, I would question whether especially younger children who grow up in multicultural societies such as Germany, the U.S. or Canada, perceive otherness based on different ethnic backgrounds or whether otherness is rather seen in terms of gender, class or physical impairments. What constitutes otherness and when does the other become the Other? Studies that were conducted in this field often focus on children's perception of sex, race and ethnicity (Ausdale/Feagin 2001, Eggers 2008, Phinney/Rotherman 1987, Ramsey/Derman-Sparks 2006, Ramsey/Myers 1990, see below). Empirical studies about the perception of other markers of identity have so far not been conducted, and certainly not in ELT contexts. Yet, this topic is highly interesting, and the following section, therefore, reflects some of the existing studies and their implications for choosing literature in ELT.

In order to reflect upon aforementioned issues, a look at developmental psychology research is helpful. Various scholars have focused on processes through which young children acquire ethnic identity and differentiate between ethnicities:

---

[139] Reading for pleasure is also termed 'extensive reading.' Academic discourses on the benefits of extensive reading (Biebricher 2008) and opening curriculum space for reading for pleasure in order to increase reading motivation and language acquisition have reached a wider audience, as is, for example, visible in the publication *Children's Literature in Language Education - From Picture Books to Young Adult Fiction* (Bland/Lütge 2013). The methodological approach of extensive reading in ELT aims at developing communicative competences by means of engaging students in a variety of texts from which they can choose and of which they read as many as possible (cf. Carrell/Carson 1997, Bamford/Day 2008, 2). Within extensive reading programs, it is essential that students read texts for pleasure (Bamford/Day 2008, 2): the reading process is not preceded or followed by tasks. This kind of reading is close to everyday reading as it does not involve an externally guided selection of information from the text. This concept is connected to intrinsic motivation for reading and increasing a global understanding of texts. However, empirical research remains open as to whether extensive reading is able to increase reading competence or whether this is mainly achieved through the application of post-reading activities (cf. Biebricher 2008, 9). Evidence can be found, though, for the fact that extensive reading in a foreign language increases learning vocabulary, and that it supports language acquisition, reading skills and world knowledge (Lütge 2013c, 220). At the same time, Thaler's "vicious circle of the good reader" shows that students who read a lot, understand better, read faster and, thus, enjoy reading (cf. 2008, 53 and 2012, 191) – a common assumption that is generally not disputed. Bamford and Day describe a number of factors that should be followed when extensive reading is to be carried out successfully (2008, 2-3). These refer to the language level and topics of the books, silent and individual reading of texts, and to the teacher who is seen as a role model. They also mention that the "teacher orients and guides the students" (2008, 3) which should not be seen as a contradiction to the earlier neglect of pre-, while- and post-reading activities. Rather, this aims at making students familiar with this new classroom practice, offering books and keeping track of what and how the students read (cf. Nodelman/Reimer 2003).

- In the late 1980s and early 1990s, Ramsey published several studies about young children's perception of racial and ethnic differences (e.g. Ramsey/Myers 1990).
- Ramsey later extended her study to anti-biased multicultural education (Ramsey/Derman-Sparks 2006).
- Phinney and Rotherman investigated *Ethnic Socialization of Children* (1987);
- Ausdale and Feagin explored *How Children Learn Race and Racism* (2001).
- Devine, Kenny and Macneela (2008) investigated Irish primary school children's construction and experience of racism.
- Devine and Kelly (2006) explored dynamics of exclusion and inclusion regarding ethnicity and gender in multiethnic Irish primary schools.
- Most recently, Eggers published on the racialization and children's perception of social power (2008).

The scholars all come to the conclusion that race is indeed a decisive factor that influences children's categorization and preference of others. Ramsey and Myers reveal that "whites showed stronger same-race preferences than their black peers" while on the other hand "black children's patterns reflected more cross-race acceptance" (1990, 64). For both this suggests that social attitudes play an important role and lead to white children's own-race preferences, "whereas black children's are contradicted by the higher social value placed in whites" (ibid.). The scholars also investigated the salience of sex in cross-reference with race and noted that "race was equally more salient than sex in their categorization of themselves and others" (ibid., 65). They suggest that the social context could explain the "direction, intensity, and consistency of racial attitudes and that white children are at greater risk for developing early and fixed cross-group prejudices" (ibid.). Ausdale and Feagin argue that even young children are able to cognitively apply derogative terms and attitudes which do not solely imitate a social model but require forethought (2001).

Krajewska-Kułak et al. conducted a study on the "Perception of Disabled Persons held by Children and Adolescents based on their Artwork" (2012), in which sick, healthy and children with special needs in hospitals, recreation centres, schools, and art studios participated in a contest titled "My disabled friend." Most of the children and adolescents drew children in wheelchairs. The authors conclude that the "children's drawings show their positive attitude towards people with disabilities. Children are aware of the need to help and support people with disabilities. In the imagination of children, a disabled person can fully participate in society" (Krajewska-Kułak et al. 2012, 124). Although using children's artwork for qualitative and quantitative empirical studies should not be underestimated, I believe that the context in which this study was conducted had a strong influence on the results. When children participate in contests they usually know that a reward is included, which for me leads to a certain critical stance toward the researchers' conclusions as the pictures may present what is socially desired.

The results of Smith-D'Arezzo and Moore-Thomas's study on fifth graders' perception of peers with disabilities, in which they used books that feature a main protagonist with a learning disability and applied small-group activities (cf. 2010, 5) indicate that "perceptions of students with learning disabilities were not significantly, positively affected by the presented books and accompanying discussions" (ibid., 12) – an issue that will be critically mirrored in chapter 9. Yet and similar to the study by Krajewska-Kułak' et al., it does not provide a foundation for drawing conclusions about how children learn to identify otherness in terms of disability.

These few examples and their limitations show that children learn to differentiate people for their skin color and sex already at a very early age. Although it can be assumed that opinions transferred through media, families and peer groups play a major role in influencing children's perception of others, such processes need further research. These studies focused on the perception of race and sex, but did not include children's differentiation of other forms of identity as they are visible in societies today. Therefore, extended research is necessary which also applies an extended view of otherness. Children's awareness of race and sex differences and the resulting discrimination[140] support my demand to use children's books and young adult fiction which offer balanced representations of ethnic otherness, but more importantly mirror societies' diversity beyond ethnicity. Additionally, to my knowledge no studies exist about the perception of otherness in the context of cultural learning in second language acquisition in Germany. This could be beneficial for designing inter- and transcultural learning environments as these would provide a diagnosis and starting point for developing the respective competences.

From the perspective of reader-response criticism, the reader is actively involved in the process of reading by filling empty spaces, by allowing the text to affect the reader. Through literary contact with different kinds of othernesses, readers have the chance to re-consider their existing assumptions about others. It is possible, however, that reading a text causes fear of the other when it questions the readers' values, norms, life styles, and/or individual orientations (cf. Scheller 1998, 19). Here, the development of transcultural competences has the potential to allow students to reflect upon these effects and turn them into active negotiations of self and other. In this process, otherness leads to othering the self, as readers engage with and are affected by the content of texts; they elaborate on the effects and may see previous assumptions in a different light. This process is essential in transcultural learning and needs to be taken up in the

---

[140] The aforementioned researches repeatedly encountered three- and four-year olds who said things like "I'm really glad that I'm white" (Ramsey/Derman-Sparks 2006) or "I need to move this [bed] because I can't sleep next to a n***" (Ausdale/Feagin 2001).

classroom in order to help students understand the self in reflection of the other. Once processes of understanding othernesses and re-interpreting the self are initiated, students need guidance, for example by certain methods or forms of communication, to re-establish a balanced self and to avoid the risk of being lost in between the (de)construction of self and other.

The complexity of the argumentation behind the debate I just hinted at would justify presenting the following chapters as a hypertext. The different lines of thought mutually influence each other so that it is challenging to argue in a straight line without referring to information that is given in a later chapter. In chapter 7.1.1 I show that the majority of multicultural texts recommended for young readers presents multicultural protagonists as struggler identities and as characters who need to fight against a malevolent society. This marginalizes multicultural protagonists and reinforces ethnic otherness as the dominant and prevailing form of otherness. To this discussion chapter 7.1.2 adds a critical perspective in view of developing empathy and tolerance, arguing that realistic fiction which limits multicultural protagonists to these problem-laden identities is likely to cause limited identification of reader and protagonist. On a more general level chapter 7.2 investigates in how far the genre realistic fiction is suitable for transcultural learning, which further (sub)genres could serve as alternatives and, finally, draws conclusions from this discussion by suggesting a definition for transcultural literature.

7.1.1 Blind Spots of Transcultural Representations

Multicultural literature gives space and voice to members of societies who have often been ignored in public discourses. It is, therefore, considered to have beneficial influence on students' personality and on their perception of the world around them. Scholars who (still) argue in favour of a literary canon make sure to include titles not about but rather written by culturally diverse authors. Multicultural literature represents a genre that focuses on

> the social realities of cultural groups, based on ethnic, religious, or national heritage. What the culture is, in relation to traditions, beliefs and worldview, plays a significant part in the work. Often the cultural group is under-represented and unassimilated, as opposed to Euro-American groups. (Watson 2001, 497)

Moreover, multicultural can be understood as 'cross-cultural,' referring to children of various cultures and ethnicities who are immigrants, refugees and travelers in other countries (cf. ibid.). In this sense multicultural literature also includes works in translation.

On the surface, multicultural texts as they were referred to in chapter 3.1 and as they are mentioned and recommended in curricula, invite students to meet (fictional) members of other cultures. Through the protagonists' life experiences, students can engage in intercultural encounters and negotiate meaning. These texts might be very beneficial for the development of *inter*cultural communicative competence, however, I see two difficulties in the context of *trans*cultural learning:

- Texts suggested in curricula and used in ELT depict national or ethnic others in issue-laden contexts fostering victim and struggler positions from which they have to fight for their right to be accepted by a majority.
- Although curricula include references to transcultural concepts, they do not clearly differentiate these from an intercultural scope. Despite differences between inter- and transcultural learning, also in TEFL scholarship the body of literature mainly remains similar.

Transcultural learning focuses on features which are present beyond national boundaries such as gender relations, or appeals to topics in which students reflect upon the representation of the other in the mirror of their own culture(s) (cf. chapter 1.3.1). References to these transcultural aspects are included in curricula, too (cf. e.g. MSWWF 1999, 31-32). From what is indicated there and an impression that can be gained from looking at empirical research of transcultural learning (cf. chapter 2.3.2), teachers are expected to pursue intercultural learning objectives with transcultural notions based on similar texts. However, I state that the concept of transcultural learning not only needs a strong theoretical foundation, but also practical applications which are distinguished from an intercultural scope. The necessity to follow such a differentiation becomes apparent in the influences literature has on processes of identity formation in young readers (cf. below). The following reflections support this perspective in that I juxtapose the demand of cultural learning with the effects certain depictions of multicultural protagonists have on readers. This contributes useful insights and justifications for defining a different kind of literature for transcultural learning.

In the early 1990s, Hall (1992a, 1992b) critically reflected upon how media reproduces limited options for identification of multicultural people. He summarized that non-representation is essential, as it reflects a society's value system. Excluding certain people from public media reveals that these members of a society are marginalized and made invisible from the public screen (also in Norton/Pavlenko 2007, 675). Apart from not representing certain members of a society, limiting their representation to certain spaces can have severe consequences for their self-perception as well.

In 1999, Yeoman conducted a study in which she analysed the influence of texts on the self-perception and belief system of students in Grade 4 and 5 in a public urban school in Canada. The children of 9 to 11 years of age were part of a diverse school body regarding their national and ethnic origin and their socio-economic status (cf. ibid., 428). In the six-month study, the students read disruptive stories, which "challenge and go beyond conventional and limiting traditional storylines about race, gender, and class through presenting unexpected characterizations, plots, outcomes, or details; for example, feminist fairy tales, or stories where the protagonists belong to visible minorities" (ibid., 427). Students were expected to base their interpretations of texts read in class on their previous literary experiences.

Having heard a Cinderella-like tale – San Souci's *The Talking Eggs* (1989), a story about a child of color who discovers a magical world set in the American South – the children were asked to draw the main character using their knowledge of the classic *Cinderella* and *Mufaro's Beautiful Daughters* (Steptoe 1987), an African Cinderella-like tale presenting an African heroine. Yeoman reports that the children "almost invariably drew White characters no matter what colour they were themselves" (1999, 437). When asking her students why they chose the respective skin colour, an African Canadian student answered that she "mostly thought [the protagonist] would get married and live happily ever after," a student of Chilean background "imagined her dark, but I'm drawing her blonde" and "drew her yellow [haired… because …] she was good, so I wanted to make her pretty" (ibid., 437-438). From those and further results Yeoman concludes that "white images of goodness and beauty are still vastly more pervasive" and that

> such ubiquitous cultural forms, blondeness (especially for females) and certain kinds of bodies, clothes and so on, maintain [the students'] powerful associations with goodness, beauty, comfort and romances. Darkness, on the other hand, is still equated with the exotic, the occult, and, often, with evil. (ibid., 438)

I agree with Hurley in considering the implications of only seeing 'white' as good, living happily ever after, and pretty (cf. 2005, 222) highly disturbing.

One can argue that the relation of white/good and dark/bad presents an old religious motif; but from a social and literary perspective this reflects a pervasive discriminatory value system which children have been exposed to, which they have internalized – to a large extent, but not exclusively, supported by the Disney industry, for example[141] – but which needs to be challenged if children are to develop positive images of self and if stereotypes are to be overcome. Yeoman's study shows that although young readers may have found various options for identifying with the characters in the books, reading these African tales only contributed to the children's identity formation in that they equated white skin colour with positive character traits. Their former reading (and media) ex-

---

[141] This issue has been researched extensively, cf. Beres (1999), Craven (2002), Dundes (2001), Gooding-Williams (1995), Hurley (2005), Martin-Rodriguez (2000) and Towbin et al. (2003).

periences have established a strong link between white and right, and an extended reading phase which tried to counter such images was not sufficient to challenge these. This was not only present in an imagined world, but also within "their practical understanding of the real world" (Yeoman 1999, 439) – an argument that calls for the need to challenge media exposure of young children, and that also emphasizes the close link between reading literature and identity formation (cf. chapter 9.1.1).

As a second line of argument, recommendations of literature for multicultural education are to be reflected. According to Norales multicultural education is "an education for life in a free and democratic society. It helps students transcend their cultural boundaries and acquire the knowledge, attitudes, and skills needed to engage in public discourse with people who differ from themselves" (2006, 3). In Bushman and Haas' chapter on "Diversity in Young Adult Literature" (2006, 186-204) this aspect is mirrored when the authors state that

> it is important to provide all of our students with literature that would be somehow diverse to its reader. We must not stereotype our students by the reading we recommend and assign. It is important to provide students with literature that features characters like them and familiar situations. (2006, 194)

This approach to multicultural literature shows parallels to what has been established as the aims of transcultural learning in chapter 1.3 and can therefore be applied to my larger argument.

Yet, when the authors continue to recommend specific texts that are said to be beneficial for multicultural education, the almost exclusively negative contexts around which the stories of protagonists of various ethnic backgrounds evolve are highly striking. Almost all of the books entail the protagonist's desperate need to fight against discrimination and their struggle for a better life: African American protagonists have "dialogue[s] with therapists," they have to deal with an "absent father" and "survive after the death of both their parents," they are "accused killer[s]" or have to endure the "hopelessness of [their] neighbourhood" (Bushman/Haas 2006, 195-196). Latin American narrations evolve around problems like being 15 years old, pregnant and having to deal with the disapproval of the father or "self-doubts," and stories set in Asia evolve around protagonists who face an arranged "marriage with an ill boy" who dies and the girl being left to take care of herself, or a girl who "masquerade[s] as a boy to feed herself and her family" (ibid., 197-198). [142]

This perception and depiction of multicultural protagonists as strugglers is further extended when Norton identifies multicultural literature as "[b]ooks for older children and young adults [which] often have the characters face se-

---

[142] It needs to be added that this chapter also refers to other forms of feeling and being different, such as gender, sexuality and illness (187-188) and suggests titles accordingly. However, also these to a large extent focus on 'other' identities as problem-laden identities.

vere personal and social conflicts" (2011, 379) and suggests example texts accordingly (cf. ibid., 379-386). Likewise, Clarke and Miller include books in which "a young person of color is often aware of his or her inability to fit mainstream society's ideal of physical attractiveness" and books about "some of these adolescents [who are] being discriminated against because they are of mixed racial origins or appear 'different'" (2000, n.p.).

I would challenge the extent to which educators can achieve the proclaimed multicultural education if representations of otherness remain in establishing ethnicity as otherness and limiting these protagonists to problem-laden environments. Instead of trying to go beyond a dichotomy of self and other, Clarke and Miller's selection re-implements this by referring to books in which "people of color" also perform acts of discrimination:

> The pain of prejudice and discrimination is experienced in varying degrees by the main characters in each of these stories, and the books show how judging people on the basis of race or ethnicity puts obstacles in the way of crosscultural understanding. Although many of the books focus on how people of color experience racism, in an ironic turn several point out how prejudice toward white people or those of mixed racial heritage negatively affects relationships. (2000, n.p)

I find it difficult to understand how an article about "exploring cultural identity" can only refer to titles which actually underline oppressive relationships of ethnic identities. If the formation of identity is influenced by such media, it should not come as a surprise that Ramsey identified stronger same-race preferences in "white" children than in "black" peers (cf. chapter 7.1). The stories mentioned above include broken families, physical, psychological and structural violence, and cause the 'visible minority' child to be (dis)placed to the bottom of the social ladder. While Sims tries to establish a "traditional awareness of the ties that bind" (1982, 70) in reference to young-old relationships in African American children's books, I would rather suggest that these raise a traditional awareness of 'ties that *blind*' because none of the diverse readers are given the chance to perceive the other beyond certain social and ethnic categories by which they seem to be divided.

Furthermore, I question in how far these recommendations agree with Bushman and Haas' demand of avoiding stereotyping. The suggestions offered by the scholars tend to reduce the ethnic other to negative contexts, which "denies the possibility of personal growth or change, or of different but equally valid ways of being black or Jewish or Asian or Native American" (Nodelman/Reimer 2003, 171-172). Essentializing and stereotyping are equally difficult "for children whose parents belong to different ethnic groups and who therefore must be perceived by essentialists as somehow incomplete or fragmented rather than as the whole individual beings they are" (ibid., 172). I would like to question what students learn if literature that is highly praised for cultural learning mainly depicts multicultural protagonists who have to negotiate ethnic identity in the face of an unwelcoming and hostile society that has caused the character's problems in the first place.

In contrast to this close link of ethnicity and problem in certain children's and young adult fiction, Saltman states that "children's literature of a nation [is] a microcosm of that country's literary and socio-cultural values, beliefs, themes, and images, including those of geography, history, and identity" (2003, in Bainbridge/Carbonaro/Green 2005, 311-312). Which microcosm is visible in the recommendations above? Which values, beliefs, and images are transported when the 'visible minority' is reduced to the struggler and the fighter against society? It becomes obvious that social spaces are not only reinforced by politics and economy, but by literature available to young readers, too. Nodelman estimates that "whether we are conscious of it or not, illustrations always convey information, not just about what things look like, but how we should understand and what we should feel about the things depicted" (1993, 6). This can also be extended to the quantity and quality in which multicultural characters are depicted in young adult literature.

Even though these contexts might represent 'real-life struggles'[143] – whereas it is disputable what these are –, the question remains whether children do not deserve positive reading experiences which may prevent processes of identity formation that lead to seeing the self as less worthy than what is depicted as mainstream (cf. above). Which images of self can young people develop if fiction that offers a "sense of belonging" ascribes certain groups to certain social and cultural spaces? What do they see when they "need to see themselves reflected so as to affirm who they and their communities are" (Botelho/Rudman 2009, 1)? Rather than deconstructing spaces of the dominated, the powerless and the inferior, narrations like the ones mentioned above reinforce white vs. non-white dichotomies. The conclusion that these "textual representations of race and ethnicity [reflect] Eurocentric normative ideals" (Saldanha 2000, 165) seems to suggest itself.

"The images used usually replicate the popular social values and moral attitudes of the times and of the culture, often without the realization that the child is unconsciously absorbing these values and attitudes from the images presented" (McKenzie 2003, 201-202). Therefore, it is especially important that children, in general and especially in cultural learning, get to read literature that refrains from re-establishing and implementing victim and struggler positions pre-occupied by protagonists who represent and thus define 'minorities,' and from re-constructing a society that supports second-class citizenship. Educators

---

[143] The term 'reality' is equally challengeable as 'authentic' and 'authentic reading material.' Readers need to be aware that each representation of reality is a selection, a picture taken through a specific lens with a specific purpose. Therefore, fictional writing could only be realistic to a certain extent. As the novels suggested by Bushman and Haas belong to the genre of realistic fiction, it is can be asked which lens they used.

need to understand "how the public texts of everyday life construct our understanding of the world, and position persons to take up various social, political and cultural identities" (Luke 1997, 20).

When young readers encounter characters of different ethnic backgrounds in literature, it is of utmost importance that they develop a critical understanding that it is not the protagonists' ethnic background that makes them inferior per se, but rather their discursive positioning as a 'minority' (cf. chapter 6.4). Literature that re-establishes dichotomies of 'minority' vs. 'majority,' 'coloured' vs. 'white', victim vs. perpetrator and thus implements these binaries, severely limits transcultural learning and teaching and causes readers to perceive certain people within certain roles.

> One of the purposes of literature is to help us understand our lives and the human condition. What message do youngsters receive when their image and world are absent from the literature they study? They learn that they are insignificant – and that books and literature have nothing to do with them. (Hansen 1998, 14, similar remarks in Sutherland 1997)

Yet, I would additionally question the quality of how multicultural protagonists are depicted. Especially for the development of transcultural competences this paradigm is highly significant (cf. chapter 9).

To revise missing literary spaces of balanced cultural identities from a psychological perspective, Bandura's "triadic reciprocality" (1986, 22-30) offers important insights. It explains that "behavior, cognitive and other personal factors, and environmental influences all operate interactively as determinisms of each other" (ibid., 23). Applied to teaching literature, this reciprocal determinism is remarkable because it helps to show why a balanced representation of multicultural characters gains such high meaning: When the multicultural protagonist is constantly represented as the struggler for equality at the bottom of the social ladder, it is likely that readers believe this social positioning and act accordingly, assuming this positioning of others as natural or inheriting it themselves.

Within many of the multicultural novels taught in ELT, the members of the so-called 'minority group' face a multitude of struggles in their attempt to form identity and it is usually this pool of challenges which is focused. The analytical and creative tasks that are applied usually demand the students to see the plot and experiences from the perspective of the main protagonists and to identify with them (cf. Fäcke 2006, Freitag-Hild 2010). Yet, processes of negotiating meaning that are limited to such issue-laden contexts are likely to cause pity instead of understanding and to re-implement rather than challenge the social and cultural structures represented in the text.

Besides this critical perspective, I should also mention that the texts usually have a positive ending. The protagonist's successful development and often powerful strive for a better situation can be seen as a role model for the reader. Nevertheless, as mentioned, the focus of the books usually lies with the struggle; the positive ending is only reflected on the last few pages. It remains open whether the struggle or the solution are mainly reflected in ELT and which conclusions are applied to both. If the stories depict and focus on a protagonists' ethnicity as the cause for their struggle, this link of ethnic identity and problem is also likely to be established in the students, reflecting the notion that *although* those protagonists have these issues, they *still* live a good life. Yet, from a cultural learning perspective it could be asked in how far it would be more beneficial to see how the good life is lived, i.e. to get to know multicultural protagonists who do not have to struggle that hard in order to be happy, or to read stories which start at the point where their lives improve. Here, readers would encounter (multicultural) protagonists whom they could see as role models beyond ethnic struggles.

Hoffman (1996) uses a similar line of argument stating that the multicultural protagonists' search for identity is often overemphasized in young adult literature. She sees a strong connection of culture and issues, and of culture and self-esteem, too:

> For one thing, not all minority cultures are as a rule prone to producing individuals with poor self-esteem, and it is certainly dangerous to assume that there is inherently any link between minority cultural status and low self-esteem. This perspective insidiously privileges the majority culture by defining it as the norm – the standard of high self-esteem toward which the minority should strive. (1996, 561)

Hoffman agrees that readers disregarding their background deserve an optimistic view on protagonists beyond an issue-laden paradigm with whom they like to identify (cf. email to Grit Alter 2011). She adds another level by questioning in how far the good life that 'minority protagonists' can live after overcoming all problems is a good life at all and who establishes this life as favourable. This would again present the perspective of the majority which sees its own status as the way life needs to be in order to be good and an ideological construction of the other as fiction "of the marginal, the deviant, the disaffected, and the underclass" (Crawford/McLaren 2003, 144).

Whereas one can ask what is left out and whose voices are silenced in classrooms, I would rather pose this question from a different angle: Which voices are put in which stereotyped contexts, and what do they actually get to say? When students become critically aware of such mechanisms and are offered counter examples like in *Run* or *The Water of Possibility*, they are enabled to discover otherness beyond problem-laden paradigms which allows them to decolonize their minds (cf. Ngugi 1986) from prejudices that may be prevalent in their surrounding societies.[144]

For inexperienced readers it is often challenging to detect a subtext which tries to establish a certain social, moral or political opinion. Such subtexts can be intentionally created as conscious manipulations of young readers or (un)intentional reconstructions of common social beliefs of a society that label and identify the other as Other. In this context, Hollindale's (1988) elaborations about ideology in literature for young readers can help to identify modes of power and agency or racism. Ideologies are

> the systems of belief which are shared and used by a society to make sense of the world and which pervade the talk and behaviors of a community, and form the basis of the social representation and practices of group members. Literary discourse, on the other hand, serves to produce, reproduce and challenge ideologies more self-consciously; thus, all aspects of textual discourse are informed and shaped by ideology. Texts produced for children seldom thematize ideology, but either implicitly reflect its social function of defining group values or seek to challenge received ideologies and substitute new formations. (McCallum/Stephens 2011, 370)

In *Ideology and the Children's Book*, Hollindale (1988) identifies three levels on which ideology can be implemented in literature for young readers. As this has increasingly come to be seen as texts that involve politics rather than offering a purely enjoyable reading experience (cf. ibid., 5-6), Hollindale regards ideology as an "inevitable [...] factor in the transaction between books and children" (ibid., 10). McCallum and Stephens agree that "[n]o narrative is without an ideology" (2011, 370). Hollindale's first identification of how ideology is included in books for children is "surface ideology," (1988, 11) which becomes visible through "the explicit social, political or moral beliefs of the individual writer, and his wish to recommend them to children through the story. [...] Its presence is conscious, deliberate and in some measure 'pointed'" (ibid., 10-11). The second level can be detected through a closer reading which reflects a rather passive ideology included through the authors' "individual [...] unexamined assumptions" (ibid., 12). On this level, authors rather unconsciously include in their narratives values and societal conventions that are taken for granted and widely shared by the society that surrounds them. Hollindale refers to unquestioned and accepted values a society carries, which in turn carry the greatest potency with unreflected readers, who may read humorous or ironic passages literally (cf. ibid., 13, cf. Nodelman/Reimer 2003, 151-152). The "private, unrepeatable configurations which writers make at subconscious level from the common stock of their experience" (Hollindale 1988, 15), the authors'

---

[144] In a later chapter this aspect will be recognized in close proximity to transcultural literature's potential for an emancipation of protagonists, writers and readers (chapter 7.2).

world which also becomes visible in their choice of words and rules of language, establishes the third level on which features of a certain ideology are seen as "natural." According to Hollindale, a certain set of truths of a society as a whole defines how literature is understood and what kind of meaning an expression entails. Thus, ideology of this kind is still one level beyond the unconscious inclusion mentioned above.

With a view to teaching objectives of ICC and developing students' critical cultural awareness, it is especially important to unveil the underlying ideologies entailed in multicultural literature for young readers.[145] Teachers could guide students in detecting the underlying contexts and morals, the societal and ideological sub-themes a text entails as they need to "learn to understand and negotiate the various signifying codes used by a society to order itself. The principle code is language, since language is the most common form of social communication" (McCallum/Stephens 2011, 360).

Xie offers yet another interesting case in point:

> Children are perhaps most victimized and most urgently need to be postcolonialized, not so much because they are the most colonized as because they are most violently subjected to colonialist ideas of racial-ethnic Otherness at the most formative years of their life. If children's literature and the criticism of children's literature take upon themselves to decolonize the world, they will prove the most effective postcolonial project in the long run, for the world always ultimately belongs to children. If today's children grow up with postcolonial education, and if they are encouraged to understand and appreciate racial/ethnic difference, that would tremendously expedite the progress towards a globalized postcoloniality. (2000, 13)

Although literature is surely not the only medium that influences identity formation, understanding the other and forming opinions about the other, the significance of the link between social factors and cognitive processes (cf. Carducci 2009, 426) should not be underestimated as it can lead to a negative perspective on one's personality. Yeoman's, Ramsey's and other research (cf. above) illustrates the problems associated with depicting people from ethnic backgrounds in connection with stereotypical behavior. The analysis of texts suggested for ELT shows that curriculum developers and educators have tried to pay tribute to a changing notion of culture by searching for texts that value other

---

[145] From my teaching experience at the Universities of Hildesheim, Mainz, Muenster and Innsbruck where I read Bushman's and Haas' chapter "Diversity in Young Adult Literature" with about 140 students, I can conclude that they were totally unaware of the paradigms entailed in multicultural texts. Also critical readings of Disney, e.g. from a feminist perspective was eye-opening to the majority of them. This indicates the implications critically reading academic texts in the field of cultural education can have for tertiary students and in teacher education.

perspectives and that resonate with students' own experiences and backgrounds. Still, texts which provide a positive reading experience and a more balanced depiction of an other protagonist are missing in curricula guidelines and also in TEFL theory and practice.

The discussion in the previous chapters emphasizes the relevance of selecting literature for cultural learning. Apart from a non-stereotypical depiction of otherness, I state that if texts offer a more balanced image of alterity, students may reflect upon protagonists differently as they do not have to focus on the other's cultural struggle but can engage with the other as a whole person beyond ethnic determination. This could offer a solution to the problematic issue of social desirability of students' answers, as was described in chapter 2 and as will be solved in chapter 8. Expressions of empathy and tolerance could be brought to a more serious level when students can investigate charismatic and complex protagonists beyond ethnic identity struggles. However, as explored in the following chapter, empathy and tolerance remain critical features of cultural learning.

7.1.2 Revisiting Empathy and Tolerance

The willingness, ability and disposition to show empathy is seen as a foundation for social behaviour and for understanding other people and cultures. Therefore, empathy takes center stage in cultural learning (cf. chapter 2, e.g. Surkamp/Nünning 2008, 28). Whereas this aspect is included in manifold publications in the scholarship of literature didactics, it is seldom presented in more detail, especially in view of an empirical grounding of its central position. Therefore, the following section offers more insights to and a critical reflection of empathy in view of the results of my study so far. I discuss that the concepts 'tolerance' and 'empathy' as they are currently discussed in TEFL theory and cultural learning need to be altered in order to be beneficial for transcultural learning.

The term 'empathy' was coined by experimental psychologist Edward Titchener in 1909 as an attempt to translate into English the German term "Einfühlungsvermögen," a concept that was introduced by Theodor Lipps. Already in 1915, Titchener mentioned that literature can touch readers on an emotional level, stating that

> [w]e have a natural tendency to feel ourselves into what we perceive or imagine. As we read about the forest, we may, as it were, *become* the explorer; we feel for ourselves the gloom, the silence, the humidity, the oppression, the sense of lurking danger; everything is strange, but it is to us that strange experience has come. (1915, 198)

As readers we have the "'feeling' of our own concernment in the imagined situation." Titchener identifies "this tendency to feel oneself into a situation" as empathy (1915, 198; cf. also Keen 2006, 209).

Since then, the concept has been explored and discussed by various scholars. Suzanne Keen, for example, explores whether reading novels can cause empathy and provoke a feeling of altruism in the reader. In sum, her results reveal that especially character identification (cf. 2007, 216-219) and the narrative structure (cf. ibid., 219-220) contribute to emotional resonances to fiction and feeling empathy toward characters and their development. Nussbaum's approach leads in a similar direction: "As we tell stories about the lives of others, we learn how to imagine what another creature might feel in response to various events. At the same time, we identify with the other creature and learn something about ourselves" (in Harmon 2002, 177).

Keen understands empathy as "a vicarious, spontaneous sharing of affect," which "can be provoked by witnessing another's emotional state, by hearing about another's condition, or even by reading" (2006, 208). She further states that people who have established empathy "feel what [they] believe to be the emotions of others" and that empathy is "by definition other-directed" (ibid.). In this respect, empathy needs to be differentiated from sympathy, as the former is understood as "I feel what you feel" and the latter rather entails a notion of "I feel a supportive emotion about your feelings" (ibid., 209).

As these approaches indicate, empathy lies at the foundation of understanding otherness, identification and identity formation, because its emotionality serves as an opener to the experiences of the protagonists. Consequently, and as it is the foundation for intercultural encounters, scholars focus on empathy as one justification for and objective of integrating literature in teaching languages and developing ICC (cf. Surkamp/Nünning 2008, Bredella e.g. 2002, 2002a, 2010c, Volkmann 2010, Brown/Stephens 1998, Willis et al. 1998, Oliver 1994). Such references broaden the scope and complexity of empathy and its interrelation to further key terms of this field.

While Mar et al. (2008, cf. chapter 2.1.2) were able to show that people who read fiction expressed more empathy, it is certainly challenging to identify which competence is cause and which is effect of such expressions. Negotiating meaning, changing perspectives, understanding otherness and identification are closely intertwined and it is difficult to determine whether empathy is a basis for such engagements or a result. Empathy contributes to these, but certainly already needs to be established in order to initiate open encounters with otherness in the first place.

Moreover, in contexts of cultural learning, empathetically engaging with otherness in literature is supposed to function as a vehicle for active and respectful participation in intercultural encounters in real life. However, this could not be proven in Keen's study (2007). Scholars can only draw limited conclusions about the consequences this empathy has for changing a readers' behavior on a pragmatic level. While participants in the studies expressed empathy, it is challenging for scholars to define which further influences determined such expression (cf. chapter 2). Similar reservations apply to students' performances in cultural learning contexts in ELT (cf. chapter 2.3). Yet, these observations extend the aforementioned understanding of empathy (cf. "other-directed") to include the role of the self in the process of developing empathy.

Next to these limitations, the central position of empathy in cultural learning can be seen critically with a view to further terminology that is involved. For example, "tasks to take a critical stance" are demanded because intercultural encounters shall be based "upon mutual acceptance and tolerance of their members, and overcoming the barriers raised by ideology and prejudice" (Candlin 1987, 17, cf. Müller-Hartmann/Richter 2002, 5). Acceptance and tolerance are mentioned as central objectives, although they really are two different modes of appraisal. To tolerate certain behaviours does not mean that one accepts these as well. Tolerance, as suggested by Candlin and as it appears in a number of other publications on intercultural learning (cf. Bredella 2010a, 2010c, Haß 2006, 159, Surkamp/Nünning 2008, 27-28, Volkmann 2010, 250), is only a very thin distinction to ignorance. As Nussbaum explains:

> Toleration is a grudging half-way house. When people 'tolerate' others, they give them grudging acceptance, but they don't think of them as equals, with fully equal rights. Indeed, toleration is often compatible with a condescending top-down attitude: these people are not really as good as we are, but we'll graciously put up with them anyhow. (2008, 100)

Thus, tolerance hardly leads to overcoming barriers but rather to noticing without the need to challenge these. If this kind of empathy is developed in ELT, the approach is rather superficial and egocentric. Also Baumann sheds a more critical light on the term and concept of tolerance:

> [It] would be no more than just another of the many superiority postures; at the best it would come dangerously close to snubbing; given propitious circumstances, it may also prove an overture to a crusade. Tolerance reaches its full potential only when it offers more than the acceptance of diversity and coexistence; when it calls for the empathy admission of the *equivalence* of knowledge-producing discourses; when it calls for a *dialogue*, vigilantly protected against monologistic temptations; when it acknowledges not just the *otherness* of the other, but the legitimacy of the other's interests and the other's right to have such interests respected and, if possible, gratified. (1992, xxi-xxii, emphasis in the original, also in Bredella 2002, 324)

These qualifications of tolerance point out how complex the concept is and how closely it is connected to empathy and understanding otherness. Its original meaning, however, does not reach far enough for being simply mentioned in the general discourse of cultural learning and understanding otherness. Tolerance needs to be extended and altered in order to include a more profound approach beyond egalitarian notions of opinions and individuals merely standing side by side. After all, the Latin origin *tolerare* merely means 'to endure' or 'to bear.'

If the understanding of tolerance remains unspecific, educators can neither follow critical cultural awareness nor inter- or transcultural learning objectives seriously as this runs the risk of causing in students either universalist or reductionist attitudes toward the other. If the understanding of tolerance remains in the frame of 'enduring', students have no incentive to engage with the other, as the other's otherness does not demand action. Furthermore, if the depiction of ethnic otherness in victim positions (cf. chapter 7.1.1) is tolerated, this positioning of constructed ethnic otherness will not be questioned, as tolerance does not imply a critical perspective on the other or a deconstruction of the dichotomies presented. Adding the concept of empathy to this scope, it becomes clear that the empathy students feel and express could likely be as shallow as tolerance.

This argumentation reveals that scholarship should define which term of tolerance is applied, or refrain from using tolerance as such a central concept altogether and rather reach a higher conceptual level by referring to respect, acceptance or awareness of otherness. Acceptance and respect have a different connotation and entail an active negotiation and acknowledgement of alterity. Both are based on approaching others on an emotional level and feeling empathy for their experiences and behavior.

This is especially essential when asking how processes of transcultural learning, understanding otherness and developing empathy should be encouraged. Scholars have suggested that readers identify with the protagonists of a narration in order to follow their experiences through their perspective. Within ELT specific publications, identification with a protagonist is said to positively contribute to students' identity formation.[146] Yet, also identification is often left without further explications despite its complexity. Therefore, I consider it necessary to present this aspect in more detail before drawing conclusions from aforementioned observations.

---

[146] Cf. Blell (2013), Burwitz-Melzer (2013b), Bredella (2010c), Bredella/Christ (2007), Bredella/Meißner/Nünning/Rösler (2000), Bredella (2002a/2010b, 2010c), Bredella/Delanoy (1999) and Byram (1997).

7.1.3 Re-evaluating Otherness and Identification

Reading theory understands identification as "the conscious alignment of one-self with the experiences, ideas, and expressions of others" (Alsup 2010, 9). In their empirical study on students' responses to culturally diverse texts, Jordan et al. conclude that "the pattern of needing to identify with the text in order to comprehend it is still evident" (1997, 29-30). However, identification is a complex endeavour as Holland conceptualizes:

> our so-called 'identification' with a literary character is actually a complicated mixture of projection and introjection, of taking in from the character certain drives and defences that are really objectively 'out there' and of putting into him feelings that are really our own, 'in here'. And, needless to say, we do not just incorporate a character's drives and defenses – we incorporate the whole character, clothes, features, manners, physique, and the rest. (1968, 278, cf. partly also in Alsup 2010, 10)

In this view, identification can be seen as a process of self-exploration, as well, since readers identify aspects in the protagonists they reject or agree with. By identifying certain features in the protagonists, readers focus on aspects that are relevant to themselves, thus, identification with otherness enables them to draw conclusion about the self. Such a balancing of inner and outer influences is an active process of negotiating meaning to which the reader applies emotionally, mentally and cognitively determined decisions. These remarks imply that the underlying processes of identification are multifaceted and deserve a more detailed consideration.

One starting point is to acknowledge that the self consists of a number of identities (cf. Stets/Burke 2003), which are determined partly through the social roles a person inherits and the expectations of a society. Based on this common assumption, certain aspects of identification with protagonists in literary texts that are continuously brought forward in TEFL theory and the resulting teaching methodology could be relativized and seen in a more critical light. While a detailed account of identity theory needs to be provided by experts from psychology, I would like to trace selected assumptions about identification which will support my suggestion of identity competence as an extension of cultural competences (cf. chapter 9).

For the re-evaluation of otherness and identification I continue referring to Keen's "Theory of Narrative Empathy" (2006) and follow her argumentation using Miall (1988) and Gerring (1990) to qualify the novels I discussed in chapter 5, especially *Run* and *The Water of Possibility*. I also draw on Alsup's insightful research on adolescent identity and teenage fiction (2010). In respect to other scholars' praise of using literature in educational contexts and their preference of young adult fiction (cf. chapter 2), I raise the question how worthwhile the objective of identifying with protagonists is when this kind of literature is written for this specific readership. It purposefully offers a plot that is similar to the readers' experiences in that it tries to meet their interests and discusses problems similar to their own. Alsup addresses a similar question and wonders "how readers can learn more about themselves by reading about characters just like them? How exactly does persistent textual identification lead to individual growth?" (2010, 10)

Alsup's more general question, which is also thought-provoking for my account, is whether "a reader [can] learn and grow through vicariously experiencing a character's trials and tribulations?" (ibid., 9). Although a readers' identification with a fictional character is likely, it is important that readers learn to step back from the text and distance themselves from the piece of fiction, recognizing it as such (cf. ibid.). If readers manage this differentiation, they become "holistic" or "autonomous" readers who can merge response, analysis and eventually social criticism (cf. ibid.). The scholar uses this claim to argue in favour of texts that "create some dissonance in the teenage world" (ibid., 11) and lead readers to discuss similarities and differences more profoundly. Based on Alsup's assumption and the general demand to offer material which is closely linked to students' everyday experiences, a paradox of perceiving texts and offering identification can be unveiled. On the one hand, readers should be provided with texts that reflect their own experiences; on the other hand, they should be offered texts about otherness to expand their perception of self, society, culture and the world.

Alsup's critical view on texts that mirror young readers' experiences and lives is indeed remarkable as is visible, for example, with Doug in *Run* who committed more than one year of his life to help Terry with the "Marathon of Hope." When students reflect upon such a proof of friendship they may reveal that the friendship between Terry and Doug must be larger than life. Doug's investment in Terry's quest is characterized by such affection that he almost forgets about his own life and is completely devoted to Terry's dream.

In this sense, *Run* presents characters who may not be similar the readers themselves, but characters who cause a certain distance to the reader. Reading about Terry and Doug's story and finding limitations to identifying with Doug, students start reflecting upon their personal attitude toward friendship, may see themselves in a new light and can extend their understanding of friendship and trust. Additionally, Terry is a character who performs exceptional strength and courage to such an extent that some readers may not be able to see themselves in him. This novel, thus, corresponds to Alsup's criticism and provides opportunities for more reflected processes of identification.

In view of Alsup's approach to identification and her proposition of using additional literature with protagonists who are not like the readers but cause dissonance, I suggest that there is a certain pleasure and fascination to the limitations of identification (cf. chapter 6.3). This can be brought to the extreme by offering controversial characters with whom readers may not like to identify. With such books, discussing characters and plots may even be more intense and less biased because the protagonists act so very differently than readers may expect. Such stories could also have a more profound influence on identity formation (cf. chapter 9.1.1) as students negotiate traits of character they do not want to inherit and are offered anti-role models from which they may delimit themselves.[147] Commonalities may make identification easier, but difference can make it more fascinating and does certainly not make it impossible. The ability of putting oneself into the position of someone who is rather different than similar may also reflect a higher level of cultural competence as a wider distance needs to be bridged and rather unfamiliar aspects of personality need to be taken into consideration.

As I established in the previous chapter, identification with a character is very closely linked to empathy (cf. Keen 2006, 216). According to Keen aspects such as "naming, description, indirect implication of traits, reliance on types, relative flatness or roundness, depicted actions, roles in plot trajectories, quality of attributed speech, and mode of representation of consciousness" (ibid.) and the narrative situation (cf. ibid., 219-220) are factors on which the intensity of character identification and therefore empathy depend. However, Miall (1988) qualifies this by putting the characters' motives first and assuming that these rather than character traits account for the affective engagement and self-projection of readers onto characters: "motives explain behavior [...] what characters do as actants and why; and traits are the relatively enduring style, the how, of what is done. But in the last analysis it is motive which is more important than traits" (ibid., 270). For Bortolussi and Dixon "'transparency' or the judgement of characters' behaviour as sensible and practical" contribute to identification (cf. 2003, 240 in Keen 2006, 218) with protagonists. In the following sections, these assumptions are qualified and put into perspective with the novels discussed in chapter 5.

I agree with Keen who concludes that these references taken together could set aside some of the common convictions about identification techniques. For example, a critical preference of a round character does not preclude empathetic responses to flat or minor characters. On the contrary, flat characters may play a greater role in readers' engagement with novels than is usually expected.[148] Keiji in *The Water of Possibility* can serve as an example of such a character. His development does not take center stage; in fact, he is held captive and therefore absent from most of the story. When he is present, he is depicted as the little brother who is insecure and whiny, needs help and a lot of encouragement. His characterization is not as multilayered as Sayuri's, which is justified because he is a minor character in the book. Due to the little information the novel offers, a closer analysis of his character is worthwhile, because he leaves more space for interpretations, assumptions and speculations. Sayuri, on

---

[147] Further examples, also beyond a Canadian focus are Jay Asher's *13 Reasons Why* (2007), J.M. Coetzee's *Disgrace* (2000), John Green's *Looking for Alaska* (2006), Jamaica Kincaid's *A Small Place* (2000), and Janne Teller's *Nothing* (2010).
[148] Burwitz-Melzer (2007, 154) indicates the potential of flat characters, too.

the other hand, is the girl who experiences all the adventures. In Bortolussi and Dixon's sense, she is more transparent, simply because she is focused on. Therefore, emphatic responses to Sayuri and identification with her could be easier, but at the same time, also more homogeneous as readers are offered the same kind of information and not much space for imagination is left.

In addition to the distance-approach to Doug, this aspect can be applied to him as well: He is mainly left in the background with minor attention which offers more gaps to fill and points of reference for creative explorations. Yet, Doug's traits may not offer that much food for thought and evoke responses, but rather his motives for supporting Terry. In fact, much has been speculated about Doug's reasons for joining his friend, and Terry has used every option to express his gratitude for him, as can also be read in Walters' novel. Doug thus mirrors Miall's assumptions that motives can be a central reference for empathy and (non)identification.

This line of argument on differentiating characters' motives and their traits, general description and ascribed roundness or flatness set an important background for the choice of books offered in ELT. Both Keiji and Doug illustrate an extended perspective on empathy and identification in that they invite readers, and certainly teachers who design tasks, to pay more attention to minor characters. As argued, these processes of identification and developing empathy may trigger more varied responses than a focus on main characters only. Protagonists like Keiji and Doug may appear flat, but they carry higher potential for in-depth reader responses.

Despite the continuing advancement of the argument of identification, I add a further critical stance from a different perspective. A lack of identification could also be seen as a "point of entry into the question of cultural (or racial) distinction" (in Sommer 1999, x). When reading texts in which a 'white' teenager is struggling through adolescence and is thereby facing obstacles such as peer-pressure, first love or a problematic relationship with his or her parents, it is disputable whether a young adult from a different cultural background is prevented from identifying with this protagonist. What would inhibit a young American girl of African descent to identify with a 'white' teenage girl who is trying to come to terms with being pregnant? (cf. also in Nodelman/Reimer 2003, 171). This aspect may be controversial and an answer to this question may not be as easy as it may seem. On the one hand, this and similar issues reflect deep and individual, yet transcultural experiences and human desires, and identifying with these is not necessarily linked to a cultural background. On the other hand, some scholars involved in children's literature (cf. Hansen 1998, cf. below) report that certain youngsters do feel excluded from enjoying books and cannot identify with the protagonists as the narrative world does not relate to them. Thus, the cultural background of protagonists is indeed seen as a central aspect and often the first marker for describing the content of a book. Furthermore, a non-representation of multicultural identities in (young adult) literature would further marginalize them (cf. above). Apparently, the two different discourses mentioned here, identification with human experiences and literary and social exclusion and marginalization seem difficult to find a common ground. However, this line of thought leads to interesting questions and answers.

In view of the problems readers face in understanding texts from and about a culture other than their own, the questions Jordan et al. asked in their study are highly relevant:

- Is the process of reader identification with the text modified by either the culture of the text or the culture of the reader?
- Does the pleasure of reading a text vary depending on the distance of the text from the reader's culture? (1997, 10)

One result of their empirical study is that students identified with a certain character "because she's Black like me" (ibid., 29-30), which relates identification to race, whereas other students identified with a protagonist's experiences, which means that "a common history was the connection" (ibid.). Therefore, a general answer to the issue of identification and a lack thereof based on the cultural identity depicted in fiction cannot be given.

Yet, it should be the aim of transcultural teaching to have students discover pleasure in reading texts based on the themes and topics depicted. They should read and discuss *Run* because of Terry's achievements and Winston's personal growth, not because it is a story about two young 'white' Canadians, one of which is an amputee and the other a school drop-out. *The Water of Possibility* should be enjoyed because of Sayuri's courage and her loving way of helping others, rescuing her brother and forgiving the fox for his misdemeanors, rather than as a story about Japanese Canadian children that facilitates intercultural teaching. Nevertheless, such reasoning should by no means ignore the socio-political dimension of excluding certain identities from the literature that is recommended for classroom readings.

Transcultural education needs to support open attitudes toward otherness and help young readers to find themselves in books because of the topics these touch upon beyond the skin color of the protagonist. Therefore, increasing transcultural competences can reveal itself to be of utmost importance, as a lack of identification with other protagonists could indicate a lack of transcultural competences. Simultaneously, certain modesty should be applied to the objective of identifying with others. This implies that students may encounter protagonists who show traits of character they see critical or reject. However, they may experience protagonists who cause non-identification to be especially fascinating and therefore engage with them more profoundly.

Sommer observes that

> [a]bsences can incite the fill-in work that keeps a reader self-important, but they also interfere with comprehension (which still means grasping, seizure) to release readers from the exorbitant (and unethical) but usually unspoken assumption that we should know the Other well enough to speak for him or her. Released and relieved from that obligation, we may wonder at the persistence of our desire to overtake otherness. (ibid.)

This can be applied to another dimension when asking in how far we can know the other enough in order to identify with him or her. "A variety of rhetorical moves can hold readers at arm's length or joke at their pretence of mastery, in order to propose something different from knowledge. Philosophers have called it acknowledgement. Others call it respect" (ibid., xi). This aspect needs to be considered when applying methods to developing transcultural learning with texts and when evaluating the results (cf. chapter 8). Sommer not only draws attention to the significance of limitations in reading and understanding cultural texts, but also points to the fact that through a construction of boundaries otherness is given space (cf. ibid., xii), and that this space constructs boundaries itself. Thus, cultural difference should be seen as a value in itself.

Within a theory of transcultural learning, this paradoxical conjunction of identification and the perception of the other that remains the other is difficult to solve (cf. chapter 1.1). As a consequence, I believe that identification with an othered protagonist could be too high an objective to be reached and that students may be more likely to reach a reduced form of empathizing with the other. This teaching objective will be described as an 'awareness of alterity' in chapter 9.1.2. This also entails the advantage of viewing narrations and protagonists' behavior more critically, as will be further elaborated in reference to tasks and methods (cf. chapter 8.1).

From the discussion in the previous and present chapters, I can draw two different conclusions: First, the depiction of different degrees of other othernesses invites readers to negotiate alterity more profoundly. The respective books move beyond problem-laden paradigms which ascribe multicultural characters certain social and cultural positions. This, in turn, provides for deconstructing similar stereotypes in students' daily experience, which could also increase critical media literacy in general. The development of transcultural competences thereby includes a strong notion of critical cultural awareness, as students learn to read multicultural texts critically with regard to the positioning of ethnic otherness. I hold the view that such readings are beneficial as students have the chance to feel empathy for otherness beyond shame, guilt and pity. This echoes the representation of Terry Fox in *Run*, a physically variant person who is mentally exceptionally strong and Sayuri in *The Water of Possibility*, who does not stand out because she searches for belonging and a whole sense of self as a Japanese Canadian child, but because she is a girl growing up for whom the trials and tribulations of adolescence and family relations are challenging, whereas her ethnic background is not.

Second, empathy and identification need to be reflected more profoundly as both processes are highly complex. Feeling empathy for protagonists depends on various factors that are intertwined and it could be fruitful for classroom discussions to explore the limitations and challenges of identification with and empathy toward protagonists as well. Additionally, flat or minor protagonists leave more space for interpretation and speculation. Protagonists with features that contradict students' expectations or that cause readers' dissociation from the text may trigger more creative and genuine negotiations and discussions as the students have to engage more closely with them. Moreover, with considering other others, the development of empathy and processes of identification gain new qualities, which compared to intercultural learning extend the perspectives of transcultural learning. There, identity and alterity take centre stage, not ethnic differences which are projected onto others.

One reaction to such qualifications of the value of identification and empathy and their practical implementation in classroom procedures could be a call for altered methods and approaches (cf. chapter 8). Another reaction could be a call for a certain type of literature for transcultural learning which is in the following defined as transcultural literature.

7.2 Approaching Transcultural Literature

In order to link the rather critical discussion of identification and the careful selection of books, which culminates in a definition of transcultural literature later in this chapter, I shortly reflect upon using books as bibliotherapy. This introduces the criticism of certain types of realistic fiction[149] (cf. below) as a base for increasing ICC on a rather broad foundation which is useful for further reflections in this chapter.

Bibliotherapy goes beyond any concepts of reading motivation or the development of ICC in TEFL contexts as it addresses a personal involvement in and experiences through a text from a psychological perspective. Depending on the readership and classroom members, reading fiction could lead to responses that are not free of risks if teachers are not prepared to appropriately react toward these. For the context at hand, the risks entailed in bibliotherapy support

---

[149] This could also be true for other genres but as realistic fiction is most commonly used as a literary base for cultural learning, the following chapters focus on this genre. Of course, this does not generalize the assumptions that are made to include all kinds of realistic fiction or exclude other genres from this critical perspective.

the sensitivity applied to selecting literature for classrooms, especially within the genre of realistic fiction.

Tunnell and Jacobs argue that bibliotherapy which "is any kind of emotional healing that comes from reading books" (2008, 3) can function as a kind of reward of engaging with literature. This therapy falls into three different categories:

1. The broad therapeutic feelings of recreation and gratification experienced by an individual reader,
2. The sense of connectedness felt by members of a group who read and share books together, and
3. The particular information and insight books can provide in dealing with specific personal problems. (cf. ibid., 3)

In educational contexts and classroom readings, the first two categories seem to be present most visibly. Readers may experience recreation when they engage in books, when they "discover the deep satisfaction, stimulation, and comfort that books can bring" (ibid.). Readers can experience connectedness when reading books with a larger group, a class or together with a teacher, and thereby share laughter and thoughtfulness, or exchange impressions and experiences based on the text. Though these imply that readers may benefit from literature, underlying challenges and limitations need to be taken into consideration as well.

While scholars and teachers usually assume a positive learning atmosphere for their theoretic descriptions and practical applications, it should be kept in mind that bullying, for example, has become a major issue in many schools (cf. e.g. Ellis 2010). Although some students may use the opportunity to speak about personal experiences as a result of reflecting a fictional text, there are at least as many who do not want to participate in certain discussions out of fear of humiliation and of being the focus of the issue-laden reflections. Therefore, teachers need to be very aware of the classroom situation and their individual students, and they need to carefully select literature to be read in class and certainly involve the students in this decision. Whether or not students benefit from the reading sessions certainly depends on the teacher's and classmates' sensitivity toward certain topics.

Compared to the first two, the third category mentioned above has the deepest impact and should therefore be treated with special care. Plots that outline a protagonist's personal problems may also speak to students' deep-seated personal issues which an untrained audience may have difficulty dealing with and which should therefore be reserved for professional therapists and psychologists (cf. Tunnell/Jacobs 2008). Whereas the authors point to the positive outcome of such readings, such as offering personal insights, comfort, and finding answers to troubling questions, teachers should be aware of the complications that could arise from including certain texts in their lessons and the task to identify with the protagonist.

Many of the texts suggested for in-class readings belong to the genre of realistic fiction and problem novels in that they represent a young individual who faces issues of growing up, coming-of-age, and dealing with family matters. Including these books in classroom readings is justified as these offer manifold points of references and incentives for classroom discussions. Additionally, students have the possibility to see their own struggles mirrored in a fictional text and to find hope in the way a protagonist deals with the hardships of becoming an adult and of life in general (cf. chapter 2.1).

While this could be true, students could also find themselves facing issues that are personally too severe to be brought to the surface in classrooms. This is especially important when keeping the depiction of multicultural protagonists in certain examples of realistic fiction in mind. When choosing books to be read in class, teachers need to be aware that they are not therapists but teachers and should know their limits. Aims of in-class readings are to increase cultural competences and support understanding or awareness of otherness, to teach reading competences, to motivate students to discover a secondary world that lies hidden in books, to encourage a positive attitude toward reading and pleasure for reading. This should not be mistaken for helping students with their potential personal issues.

As the discussion of current texts in the EFL classroom (cf. chapter 3) and the suggestions of young adult literature for cultural learning have shown (chapters 5 and 7), multicultural literature is predominantly used to enhance cultural learning and understanding othernesses. Almost all of the titles mentioned are examples of the genre of realistic fiction. Yet, based on the aforementioned criteria, my approach holds the view that such realistic fiction in which multicultural characters exclusively fight against prejudices and injustices of their surrounding society is not suitable to increase transcultural competences in ELT. Rather, those texts, which I see closer to an intercultural scope, implement an (already existing) link of a certain culture to certain social and personal issues and do not allow the multicultural protagonists to move beyond those issue-laden spheres. In those examples, the genre realistic fiction has connotations that could be misleading and result in misinterpretations of cultures and individuals (cf. chapter 7.1).

Lynch-Brown and Tomlinson point out that children's literature is appealing to young readers because they "can often see their own lives, or lives much like their own, in these stories" (1999, 133). Yet, in view of the aforementioned connection of multicultural protagonists and conflict-laden paradigms I see this critically. Within this kind of literature, identity formation is restricted to a bias of ethnic identity in terms of experiencing struggle, conflict, and prejudice. In those contexts a quick conclusion could be drawn that the underlying message of multicultural realistic fiction includes the notion that 'something is wrong with you.' As Hoffman pointed out, the idea of identity struggle is overstated in realistic fiction. Yet, when children are supposed to see "lives just like their own," they deserve books with a more balanced view. This leads to challenges and limitations of using such realistic fiction for developing transcultural competence.

7.2.1 Countering Realistic Fiction

> Children's lives are sometimes sad and harsh. Realistic stories of today openly address these situations as well as the happy and humorous situations of life. Children of all ages appreciate stories about people who seem like themselves or who are involved in familiar activities. These realistic fiction stories have appealed to children for many years and continue to do so today. (Lynch-Brown/Tomlinson 1999, 129)

Thus reads the introductory paragraph to Lynch-Brown and Tomlinson's chapter on realistic fiction (cf. ibid., 129-148) in which they define, describe and suggest realistic fiction for young readers. Despite its usage in cultural learning scenarios, I would like to voice concerns regarding the assumption that multicultural realistic fiction is beneficial for developing cultural learning objectives.

According to Lynch-Brown and Tomlinson, realistic fiction can take different subject matters, most of which usually evolve around the relationships of self(s) and other(s). Realistic fiction for young readers often involves teenagers, their families and peers, and refers to adolescent issues, survival, adventure, and cultural diversity; sub-categories are sports stories, mystery and animal stories (cf. 1999, 136-139). Generally, those are stories about "familiar situations with which children can readily identify," they "often reflect contemporary life, and portray settings not so different from the homes, schools, towns, and cities known to today's children" (ibid., 139). Whereas the protagonists of these stories are fictional, their actions and reactions are very close to those of people in real life. "Realistic fiction [...] is the 'real' story, it is what we perceive reality to be" (Hillman 2003, 185, similar approaches in Gamble/Yates 2008, 130-136, Norton 2011, 357-406). Realistic fiction can include different components of realism:[150]

---

[150] In general, authors of the literary era realism aimed at depicting ordinary life as it is in differentiation to a romanticized display of an idealized reality. In Canada, F. P. Grove is most prominently associated with realism. Writing often revolved around the portrayal of humans and their threatening exposure to reckless nature or their resistance to give in to nature. However, within realism one needs to be wary of the circumstances of such publications: Who writes what kind of realistic novels and in how far does that construct a certain episode of reality (cf. New 2002, 457/938).

- factual realism, which entails descriptions of actual people, places, and events,
- situational realism, which refers to stories that revolve around situations that are quite likely and possible, for example survival stories,
- emotional realism, which includes believable feelings and relationships among characters and for which coming-of-age stories are an example,
- social realism, which entails an honest description of society and its conditions (cf. Lynch-Brown/Tomlinson 1999, 130), and
- contemporary realism, which refers to stories that take place in the present and include references to and attitudes and morals of present cultures. (cf. ibid.)

Lynch-Brown and Tomlinson point out that realistic fiction often focuses on current social and individual problems such as alcoholism, racism, poverty, and homelessness. Even when more recent stories include happy childhood experiences, they would also refer to the harsh and unpleasant realities of children, to "child abuse and neglect, peer problems, the effects of divorce on children, drug abuse, physical and mental disabilities, disillusionment, and alienation from the mainstream society" (ibid., 130). Realistic fiction novels could also be sub-categorized as problem novels in which the plot and characterization of the protagonists are determined by a problem. The authors estimate that these stories are usually used to lecture or to "capitalize on whichever societal problem [...] currently [is] at the forefront" (ibid.).

This description of the problem novel and realistic fiction identifies the genre's high potential for offering reading material and guidance for (troubled) teenagers. Young people who may be caught in similar challenging situations may read realistic fiction and find solutions for their problems and personal questions by seeing the protagonists' struggle as a model for a way out of their own misery. For others it may present life as it could be and offer enjoyment in reading about someone's successful handling of challenging situations. While I relativized identification and empathy above, scholars and educators focus on the benefits of realistic fiction for identity formation and understanding others. What seems to be striking, however, is in how far such personal reflections may take place when this kind of literature is read in foreign language classrooms, and in how far students are willing and able to engage in respective discussions in ELT. As mentioned before, I would also like to ask in how far teachers are prepared for such procedures (cf. chapter 7.2).

Additionally, and especially in the context of transcultural learning, the relation of realistic fiction and the depiction of multicultural characters is highly interesting. It is astounding that realistic fiction seems to be the preferred genre for stories that depict multicultural characters and negotiations of ethnic identity. This also became obvious in the recommendations of multicultural literature in chapter 7.1.1 when the majority of the suggested books which are supposed to offer multicultural readers a sense of belonging do so in realistic fiction that renders ethnic identity as problem identity. From Bushman and Haas', Clarke and Miller's as well as Norton's suggestions it seems as if multicultural protagonists predominantly move in spheres of neglect, struggle and complications. In these stories it is not so much the case that the teenagers are "frequently testing themselves as they grow toward adulthood" which may cause young readers to empathize with them and gain insights to their own predicaments (cf. Lynch-Brown/Tomlinson 1999, 139), but it is rather the surrounding society that tests them. None of the protagonists in the novels recommended by Bushman and Haas face their struggles voluntarily; in all of these stories it is the multicultural character who needs to change in order to establish a balanced identity, not the malevolent society.

In such titles, a close connection of ethnic background and problem functions as a devoicing that deprives multicultural characters of power and performance of agency which can only be overcome by an intense struggle to regain voice and power. Building on Foucault's understandings of discourse, knowledge and power (cf. 1972, 1995), Botelho and Rudman identify "four positions, which [...] form a continuum of how power is exercised" (2009, 117) in literature for young readers. This continuum ranges from domination to collusion to resistance and, finally, to agency. It exists because of "structural power inequities" (ibid., 118), as people "live in raced, classed, and gendered hierarchical arrangements" (ibid., 118). The following scheme is an adaptation of their continuum:

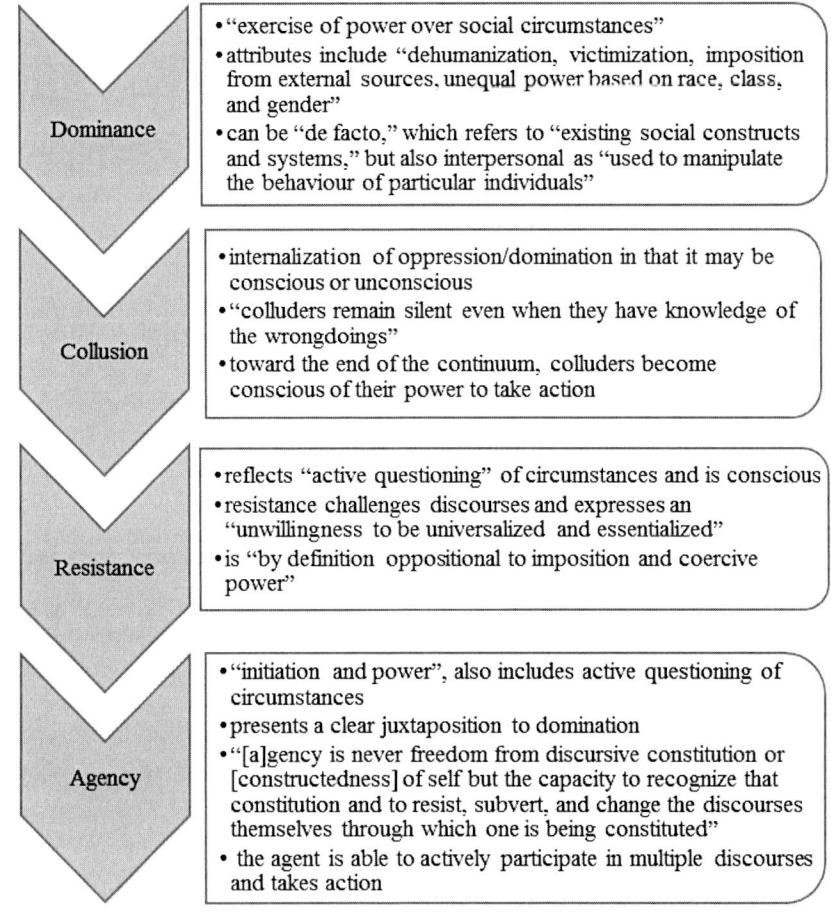

Dominance
- "exercise of power over social circumstances"
- attributes include "dehumanization, victimization, imposition from external sources, unequal power based on race, class, and gender"
- can be "de facto," which refers to "existing social constructs and systems," but also interpersonal as "used to manipulate the behaviour of particular individuals"

Collusion
- internalization of oppression/domination in that it may be conscious or unconscious
- "colluders remain silent even when they have knowledge of the wrongdoings"
- toward the end of the continuum, colluders become conscious of their power to take action

Resistance
- reflects "active questioning" of circumstances and is conscious
- resistance challenges discourses and expresses an "unwillingness to be universalized and essentialized"
- is "by definition oppositional to imposition and coercive power"

Agency
- "initiation and power", also includes active questioning of circumstances
- presents a clear juxtaposition to domination
- "[a]gency is never freedom from discursive constitution or [constructedness] of self but the capacity to recognize that constitution and to resist, subvert, and change the discourses themselves through which one is being constituted"
- the agent is able to actively participate in multiple discourses and takes action

Scheme 1: How power is exercised (cf. Botelho/Rudman 2009, 117-119)

The development of (multicultural) protagonists in realistic fiction moves along a similar continuum of power and agency: In some texts they find themselves caught in positions in which certain forces dominate them, on an external and social level (e.g. family structures, classmates, peer-pressure), or on an internal level (e.g. addictions to substances, mental oppression, trauma). Throughout the narration, the protagonists try to free themselves from this force, from this entity that dominates and limits their actions. Through a sphere of collusion, the protagonists reach a position from which resistance is possible; they reach a point where they are able to and it becomes essential to resist the external or internal force in order to secure their individual well-being and survival. Only when the protagonists have been able to successfully transcend the dominating force will they regain agency over their determination and exercise power over themselves – a process that can be identified in Ray in *Little Voice* (cf. chapter 5.1). However, the power they exercise is often a 'power against' and directed at a certain force and no 'power for' the protagonists themselves, independent from the force. As such, gaining this power is seen in close connection to the struggle that lies behind the protagonists and not as a power they may possess beyond ethnic identity struggles.

Lynch-Brown and Tomlinson's criteria to select and evaluate realistic fiction include "well-developed characters who manifest change as a result of significant life events, a well-structured plot with sufficient conflict and suspense to hold the reader's interest, a time and place suitable to the storyline, and a worthy theme" (1999, 131). The authors' more detailed account of these criteria includes references to positive outcomes in order to provide a more optimistic view, as children need to be encouraged and should be allowed to trust that "this world can be a good place in which to live and that it can be made a better place through the efforts of the individual. Children [...] need to understand that problems can be overcome" (ibid.).

Although the titles of realistic fiction mentioned above usually offer an ending in which protagonists overcome the hardships of life and thus present positive role models, the impression of a positive reading experience remains doubtful. From their selection of titles Clarke and Miller conclude that the "protagonists frequently encounter challenging situations related to race, social status, and origins. Several of these realistic novels end with hope or resolution of conflict, but all bring to the fore issues of culture and cultural identity" (2000, n.p.). The multicultural stories they describe exclusively evolve around the "experience of being caught between two cultural worlds" and the "characters struggle to preserve their cultural heritage against forces that seek to undermine it" (ibid.).

This close connection of realistic fiction, culture and problem deprives multicultural protagonists of power and ownership of individual decision-making. The protagonists usually face abjection; their chances for gaining voice are often limited to the sphere of oppression in which they are caught. Despite the "feeling of comfort that comes from being part of something larger than oneself [a]s an important experience for many of the characters" (ibid.), it is striking that the protagonists almost only find comfort in 'their minority group' and not the larger society they often long for. For example, Clarke and Miller mention that "Deirdre longs for her Baltimore African-American community because she perceives herself as isolated in the new school" and that

> Chinatown is presented as a kind of cultural fortress that protects and nurtures the Chinese traditional heritage. Stacy's opportunity to visit the people and places of her family's past provides her with a sense of what it means to have a cultural home. (ibid.)

Such stories ascribe ethnic protagonists to a frame in which they can find comfort and support at home, they need to turn to their cultural roots in order to be happy, and those roots are 'there,' not 'here' – and apparently also not part of a constructed 'mainstream.' Likewise, Clarke and Miller emphasize that "[t]hese novels recognize the importance of establishing relationships and making connections with people who share similar cultural backgrounds, beliefs, and attitudes" (ibid.) – rather than with the diversity of people in the culture and society in which they actually live, buy food and go to school. They remain in spheres of dominance and collusion even when their struggle is overcome.

As a conclusion, I believe that for developing transcultural competences in ELT such realistic fiction should be seen critically. As was established earlier (chapter 7.1.1), scholars agree that contemporary realistic fiction[151] for young adults accurately portrays a young protagonist's life now or in the recent past (Latrobe/Drury 2009, 70). Yet, my analysis of recommended multicultural texts for young readers and the close connection of multicultural novels and realistic fiction revealed that multicultural protagonists tend to be over-represented in this genre. Teachers and students need to be aware of the kinds of 'realities' that are depicted in those stories. In this view, Saltman's assumption about literature as a microcosm of a country's literary and socio-cultural values (cf. chapter 7.1.1) can be re-evaluated, not only in how these stories end but also regarding their underlying message. In order to unveil this microcosm and the underlying values, advanced ELT classrooms can approach such texts with a mindset that questions the depiction of culturally othered protagonists, their positioning and the frame in which they can act as role models for readers. Asking the following questions is especially important when texts are meant to enhance inter- and transcultural learning: [152]

- What kind of reality is represented?
- What kinds of stereotypes are depicted in those books?
- Are those stereotypes challenged or being re-implemented?
- Who is held responsible for changing the critical situation of the protagonist?

Further questions for reflecting this issue on a meta-level can be:

- In how far can it be justified that multicultural readers, assuming they want to read books with characters who are just like themselves, whatever that means and entails, find the majority of titles within the genre

---

[151] Yet, one needs to be careful not to generalize realistic fiction as such. Latrobe and Drury limit their assumptions to contemporary realistic fiction and indeed one cannot generalize this multifaceted genre. I emphasize throughout this chapter that my criticism refers to the kind of realistic fiction that is mainly suggested and currently used in TEFL theory and practice, and which depicts multicultural protagonists in problem-laden paradigms.

[152] Doff and Schulze-Engler draw a similar conclusion: Intercultural learning which uses "more or less absolute cultural difference" as a starting point and sets up "essentialist binary oppositions between one's own culture and 'strange', 'alien' or 'other cultures' […] reproduces stereotyped notions of cultural difference that are hard to reconcile with the social and cultural realities that teachers and learners are faced with in an increasingly globalised world" (2011, 1).

of realistic fiction where they can read how a suppressed teenager tries to make a living *despite* a harsh and threatening social environment?

– Why are multicultural characters deprived of the right to be heroes and heroines of the stories as who they are: children, teenagers who grow up and encounter human challenges?

Putting both strings together, a) children's and young adult literature as a representation of how a society perceives of itself and b) education as young people's preparation for participating in social life, the consequences for the perception of others are severe. When only such texts as mentioned above are read in ELT or school in general, society re-constructs its own 'mainstream' as the standard and deprives not only the protagonists in the novels of balanced identities and a whole sense of self, but also the readers. They are denied multicultural protagonists beyond problem identities, but almost only meet protagonists that are othered because of their ethnic identity struggle. Thus, the image of the other, in fiction and real life, is constructed in students, and not challenged. In reference to Botelho and Rudman's continuum of power exercise, neither the protagonists of such stories nor the respective readers have options to move beyond the stages of dominance and collusion.

In this context, the discussion of ideology (cf. above) is essential because on a social level ideology functions as "defining and sustaining group values" and on a cognitive level as "supplying a meaningful organization of the social attitudes and relationships which constitute narrative plots" (McCallum/Stephens 2011, 360). When "both racism and anti-racism are ideologies," they may "serve to establish or maintain social dominance, as well as to organize dissidence and opposition" (ibid.). As such, young adult fiction in which multicultural characters are depicted beyond problem-laden paradigms carries the potential to evoke an extended perspective on the diversity of people in societies. This potential was unveiled in the discussion of *Run* and *The Water of Possibility* (cf. chapters 5.2 and 5.3), as both young adult novels, historic and/or sports fiction and fantasy, present otherness beyond ethnic challenges.

The section about the appropriateness of realistic fiction revealed that TEFL theorists and practitioners need to be aware of the (limitations of) power and agency that a text ascribes to certain protagonists and of the contexts from which this *de*-scribes others. When selecting literature to enhance cultural learning, the perspectives on the multicultural protagonist are as essential as the assumptions that are imbedded in the closure of a narration. Students and teachers should be sensitized for the way in which literature reconstructs and also constructs reality (cf. Botelho 2004, 95).

I discussed that stories which a) re-implement ethnic binaries and which b) focus on issue-laden problematizations of other identities are only marginally useful for fostering transcultural competences. In order to develop transcultural competences, multicultural protagonists should be presented as whole personalities with positive as well as negative characteristics, strengths and weaknesses, making decisions the readers can follow and those they are likely to reject. Based on the imbalances of such depictions of multicultural protagonists in realistic fiction, the following part suggests other sub-genres which lead to an understanding of transcultural literature.

7.2.2 Offering Alternatives to Negotiate Transcultural Identity

> In a world in which race and color still play such an important part in defining the experiences of individuals, books by and about people of different backgrounds are bound to offer access to a vast spectrum of ways of being human. Experiencing that spectrum is one of the pleasures of literature. (Nodelman/Reimer 2003, 171)

When establishing an environment for inter- or transcultural learning based on multicultural literature that is beneficial for all students disregarding their ethnic backgrounds, I have argued that teachers should refrain from only using such realistic fiction in which multicultural characters are presented as strugglers, as the ones who need to fight external forces in order to live a fulfilled life. In chapter 5.1, I discussed Ruby Slipperjack's *Little Voice* which is an example of a realistic fiction story that depicts such a paradigm – Ray is not accepted by her society and is the one who needs to change in order to live a balanced life whereas the surrounding society does not change. She has developed enough self-confidence to move beyond being hurt by her classmates' comments. This kind of realistic fiction only marginally contributes to a reflective transcultural competence as certain roles for certain members of a society are written into their ethnic background and not challenged. Therefore, this novel is closer to an intercultural scope.

Instead of re-implementing such binaries, teachers should select fiction in which multicultural characters are represented as who they are, balanced characters who have negative and positive traits they share with other humans. Moreover, competences that refer to culture should address different aspects of culture and not limit people to their ethnic identity. This understanding justifies including Eric Walter's *Run* and the detailed elaboration of Hiromi Goto's *The Water of Possibility*.

The 'negative and positive traits they share with other humans' indicate a trans- rather than an intercultural approach to questions of identity and aim at selecting topics and issues young readers can relate to indifferent of their ethnic background. The genres and stories in which such connections can be found are, for example, adventure stories, stories of survival, fantasy, sport stories, and mysteries as well as animal stories. Compared to the depiction of multicultural protagonists in the kind of realistic fiction described above, in these sub-genres they are often enable to be part of a story based on their value as humans.

As could be seen in the example of *The Water of Possibility*, fantasy novels offer great opportunities for presenting multicultural characters beyond contexts of searching for ethnic identity. These invite readers to join protagonists on their adventurous journey to unknown mystical places where they meet strange beings and dangerous challenges.[153] "Fantasy allows us – even forces us – to become greater than we are, greater than we could hope to be" (Nilsen/Donelson 2009, 216). A much repeated definition of fantasy was suggested by Goodwin:

> Classic fantasy is centered around quests. The quest may have any number of different motives – spiritual, political, sexual, material – but its presence in the text is essential. The quest expresses the desire to accomplish a thing fraught with difficulty and danger, seemingly doomed to failure. It also enables fantasy writers to deal with rites of passage; the central figure grows in stature as the quest evolves. Typically, the journey will be full of magical, symbolic, and allegorical happenings which allow the hero to externalize his or her internal struggles […]. Fantasy also deals with flux. The central characters operate in a world turned upside down, amid great wars and events of a cataclysmic nature. The possible outcomes are open and endlessly variable; the responsibility carried by the hero is enormous. In fantasy, the imagined world is always a global village. No action can take place in isolation. Every decision taken by the hero affects someone else, and sometimes the fate of nations. It is a deeply social genre. (1993, 32)

Heroes and heroines are often "fumbling or unsure about themselves and their quests" (Nilsen/Donelson 2009, 217) in the beginning, but they soon have to prove worthy of their quest. During these "meaningful quest[s] or journey[s] […] the main character matures, gains wisdom/insight, or comes of age" (Cunningham 2010, 113). In *The Water of Possibility*, Sayuri is on such a journey and quest as she has to develop strength and courage to overcome insecurity and fear in order to save her brother and Living Earth (cf. chapter 5.3). In differentiation to the depiction of multicultural protagonists in the titles mentioned in chapter 7.1.1, I would like to draw special attention to the fact that the quests in fantasy narrations are often defined beyond a connection of ethnicity and issue-laden paradigms and that, on the contrary, fantasy can allow multicultural protagonists to be child heroes and heroines based on their achievements. In *The Water of Possibility* the ethnic background plays a subordinate role; Japanese

---

[153] Cf. Norton (2011, 263-266, 307) for descriptions of fantasy's specifics of plot, characterization, setting, themes, and point of view.

mythology serves as a background from which the protagonist benefits to help others.

The moral in fantasy fiction is established through "identifying and revealing [what] is good and evil, brave and cowardly, just and unjust, noble and treacherous" (Cunningham 2010, 113). Fantasy excels as it develops a moral that takes as its starting point an "internalized concept of the world as it *should* be" (emphasis in original), not as it is. The focus is on action and the kind of behavior it takes to right the world in those aspects in which it differs from an ideal (cf. ibid., 114). In these stories, multicultural protagonists have the chance to be the heroes and heroines who right the wrongs. I agree with Cunningham in seeing special potential for (cultural) education in fantasy fiction, as these narratives often provide readers with different perceptions of the world. While multicultural realistic fiction is often framed by negative emotions, heroes and heroines in fantasy fiction need to trust themselves and be self-confident to face magical or mysterious forces, quests which cause them to grow as whole persons, not as ethnic identities.[154] In this sense, fantasy "engages [the readers'] imagination and takes [them] on a journey with tough moral choices and battles around every corner, and ends up returning [them] to [their] own troubles with a fresh set of tools to deal with them" (Cunningham 2010, 116).[155]

Mystery novels are another example of enjoyable readings beyond ethnic boundaries. These stories usually entail a complex character who has to solve a puzzle. Characteristic for mysteries is the strong element of suspense which creates the enormous appeal and interest in young readers. There are numerous novels for young adults available that revolve around multicultural characters and their mysterious adventures, for example

---

[154] However, fantasy can also present a positive perspective on the bad and evil. Just as any other genre, fantasy per se is no hallmark for beneficial literature for young adults. Additionally, one can object that fantasy does not encourage students to face real world challenges, "real-life scenarios, moral dilemmas, and social and cultural dynamics" (Cunningham 2010, 115-116). Cunningham further asks "how do you expect children to grow up and deal with the harsh realities of life when their heads are filled with fluff and nonsense like unicorns, magic wands, and moving castles?" (ibid., 116) Surely, fantasy should not be the only genre present in classrooms and students' reading careers, but it deserves a place in young people's reading experience and education because it can provide encouragement and challenge the perception of and focus on otherness.

[155] Cunningham reflects her own reading experiences to describe this process on a personal level: "Give me a story that is close to my own experiences (a teacher who moves to a small, Midwestern town to pursue graduate studies), and I will immediately start looking for ways in which my story differs from that of the teacher in the story. I will start evaluating whether the author's style and description are true to life or lack authenticity. However, by the same token, give me a story about a princess who lives in another world and is imprisoned against her will because she teaches birds to talk and become spies for her kingdom, and I will immediately start looking for ways to connect my understanding of the world with hers. Fantasy creates that space between us and the world that allows us to rediscover ancient truths and see old things for the first time" (2010, 117).

- Drew Hayden Taylor's *The Night Wanderer* (2007)
- Zetta Elliot's *A Wish after Midnight* (2008)
- Leah Bobet's *Above* (2012)
- Eden Robinson's *Monkey Beach* (2002), and
- Welwyn Wilton Katz's *False Face* (1987)

In a similar sense, sport stories, which are defined as stories in which protagonists struggle for special achievements in sports, offer young readers options of seeing themselves reflected in the story, independent of their own ethnic background. Determination and will-power are not related to ethnicity but rather to reaching individual goals.[156] Although the need and opportunity to achieve in sports depend on social and cultural circumstances, and sports can certainly be one essential means of social upward mobility,[157] the examples below illustrate that the fight to be a successful sportsman or sportswoman is not necessarily and explicitly related to ethnicity. In this selection, readers can identify with simply 'making it':

- Sandra Diersch's *Home Court Advantage* (2011),
- Mauree Ulrich's *Power Plays* (2007) and *Face Off* (2010),
- Michele Martin Bossley's *Jumper* (2006) and *Kicker* (2007),
- Sigmund Brouwer's *Absolute Pressure* (2009),
- Erin Thomas' *Boarder Patrol* (2010), or
- Jeff Ross' *Powerslide* (2011)

In these stories protagonists could serve as idols for young people who want to succeed with their diverse talents. None of the titles state a specific ethnic background of the protagonists[158] and most of the covers depict the protagonists either from a distance or dressed in their sports gear. Thus, ethnicity plays a minor

---

[156] With this suggestion I assume that even readers who are not interested in sports still find pleasure in the exciting plot and character development. The challenges the protagonists face are e.g. related to essential decisions regarding doping or choosing success over friendships.

[157] Beyond this literature perspective, it is very revealing to further investigate, also with learners of English, the relationship of race, ethnicity and sports in more detail. On the one hand, this could relate to the role of so-called minorities in national sports, e.g. Jackie Robinson and major league baseball in the context of desegregation and the Civil Rights Movement, or on the other hand, to ascriptions of special achievements in popular media, when the success of 'white' athletes has often been contextualized with character, culture, discipline, and organization, and the success of athletes of African descent often with their biology, nature, social needs, and physical abilities. For more details refer to e.g. Carter/Cheuvront/Harrison/Proctor/Myburgh/Brown/Malina (2010), Miller (1998), Rasmussen/Esgate/Turner (2005), and Jarvie's *Sport, Racism and Ethnicity* (1991).

[158] Some of the covers show 'white' protagonists. On the one hand, however, this does not indicate a specific ethnic background; on the other hand, this would not counter my concept of transcultural literature. As mentioned earlier, 'white' cannot be excluded from a transcultural scope, as this would re-establish a certain power dichotomy which 'trans' tries to transcend.

role in these novels, the focus lies with the protagonists' skills and abilities. In this sense, I understand sports fiction as transcultural.

Despite those suggestions of alternatives to realistic fiction, this section does not aim at establishing a dichotomy between realism and fantasy, mystery or sports novels. Certainly, the genre realism has a strong socio-critical dimension as the depiction of life is not blurred by romantic glamorizations or transfigurations, but is rather shown the way it was and is, including harsh, cruel and unsettling realities. Realistic fiction is not per se less worthy for increasing cultural competences as it is a complex genre with manifold characteristics and sub-genres. Rather, the reflection above unveils some of the underlying paradigms of the roles in which so-called 'minority' protagonists appear and how their agency is allowed to develop. I raised awareness for the selection of texts for ELT and pointed at alternatives that I believe are necessary for transcultural learning.

7.2.3 Toward Transcultural Literature

The aforementioned considerations argue in favour of different kinds of literatures to support a non-essentialist and balanced perception of cultures, which is, according to my point of view, important for increasing transcultural competences. Based on the discussion in chapter 7.2.1, one could ask whether it is possible, necessary or even obvious to define a new kind of literature that is specifically useful for implementing transcultural teaching objectives.

Whereas multicultural literature seems to be a common phrase, for my account a differentiation to transcultural literature is highly interesting. In the argumentation so far, the main term of reference has been multicultural literature which refers to texts that represent groups and perspectives which "have, until recently, been absent or misrepresented in books for children and remain underrepresented today" (Lynch-Brown/Tomlinson/Short 2011, 217). This refers to main characters from "racial, ethnic, religious, and language minorities, those living with physical or mental disabilities, gays and lesbians, and the poor" (ibid.). The authors assume that these books can be instrumental in developing in all children a new understanding and appreciation for others as well as providing characters with which minority children themselves may more readily identify (cf. ibid.).

Being aware of the close ascription of multicultural characters and problem-laden identities in realistic fiction (cf. above), it is indeed challengeable whether those books truly help young readers to gain "new understanding and appreciation of the others" or offer 'minority children' protagonists with which they can identify. It could be assumed that young readers want to see that they are not alone with their struggles and need to be given hope for a positive future through the books they read. Moreover, inter/multicultural literature in the form of realistic fiction opens the literary discourse to experiences of discrimination against and racism toward 'minorities' and provides inscription into literary visibility. Yet, if students in their reading career, in ELT and in general, only listen to stories that establish closely knit webs of ethnicity and issues, this does not help readers who share this background nor the 'out-group' reader of a different background to extend their perception of self and others. These essentialist narrations rather implement stereotypes and preconceptions and may put the multicultural reader in a spiral of self-fulfilling prophecies.

Although there is no clear-cut definition of multicultural literature, Pratt and Beaty see in it a "potential as an agent for positive change" (ibid., 3). The authors refer to Bishop who states that "multicultural literature should include books that reflect the racial, ethnic, and social diversity that is characteristic of our pluralistic society and of the world" (Bishop 1997, 3). For Tunnell and Jacobs defining multicultural literature as literature "about people of color [...] is far too narrow" as a "diverse population includes a variety of cultural groups that often cross color lines, such as religious groups" (2008, 188) or individuals with intellectual and physical challenges. The authors also point out that the protagonists in multicultural literature shall be represented in an "honest, positive way" (ibid., 189). I understand multi- and intercultural literature in line with Bishop's explanation. However, in order to distinguish inter- and transcultural literature more clearly, I see titles which refer to other aspects of alterity beyond ethnicity closer to transcultural literature which I further define below.

For Pratt and Beaty *Transcultural Children's Literature* invites children to "begin personal odysseys of learning about different peoples and cultures" (1999, v). The chapters in this book are differentiated according to various regions[159] of the world like Asia, Canada, the Caribbean, and Central America. An introduction to each area examines the specific cultural region and patterns of selected children's books. The authors establish their understanding of transcultural literature according to "two distinct categories: (a) books [that] were geographically or culturally centred in the United States and (b) those that were not" (ibid., 2). The geographic region and cultural milieu of the reader is crucial. Hence, Pratt and Beaty identify transcultural children's literature as

> children's books that portray peoples, cultures and geographic regions of the world that exist outside the reader's own country. Thus, which books are deemed to be transcultural is relative to the reader's own home culture and geographic region. (1999, 2)

---

[159] When having a closer look at the books Pratt and Beaty suggest, the first impression is that these hardly go beyond a stereotypical representation of the single countries. Austria is included through a book about Beethoven, France through a book about Vincent van Gogh, Germany through books about castles and Johannes Gutenberg. Each choice of children's books can of course only offer a selected view of a culture and authors may transcend their own cultural boundaries when writing stories for children. But still, and especially in transcultural educational contexts, diverse representations shall take center stage and be seen as core elements when selecting books.

For Pratt and Beaty the phrase "of the world" determines what they understand as transcultural literature, as they believe that "children's books about peoples and cultures existing outside the reader's culture and geographic location constitute a body of children's literature different from multicultural children's literature" (ibid., 3). If their introductory assumptions that the world is shrinking and that "citizenship is extending beyond traditional borders of individual countries to the global community" (ibid., 1) were holding true, this would indicate that their inside/outside dichotomy of geographic and cultural spaces is no longer credible. The distinction of inside and outside the U.S. and multi- and transcultural respectively, entails a strong ethnocentric notion which, according to the introductory statement and common understanding of global citizenship, should not be the core aspect. According to Welsch (1999, cf. chapter 1.3), transcultural rather aims at understanding areas of cultures as overlapping and losing clear linguistic, communicative, economic and ethnic boundaries. In this perspective, transcultural literature would rather include texts that deal with common issues which invite and allow readers to identify with protagonists and plot indifferent of their cultural or ethnic background. Therefore, my definition of transcultural literature shall less be based on an inside/outside perspective of one certain culture or nation, but rather on a perspective that encourages people to discover similarities and to re-apply the transcultural ideas to the readers' understanding of self. In this view, Pratt and Beaty's approach could also be labelled 'international' literature. From the term 'transcultural' one would expect literature that transcends cultures and gains validity by being applicable to readers of various backgrounds.

Pratt and Beaty additionally do not seem to pay tribute to the fact that the U.S. itself is a multicultural society and home to many peoples from around the world. Would children's books about Asia (ibid., 63-108) serve as a transcultural reading experience for Asian American children? Would children's books about Canada (cf. ibid., 109-132) be a transcultural reading experience for children from Montana, or for children who are members of Native American peoples whose cultural roots may stretch beyond the 52nd parallel? Furthermore, it remains questionable whether children's books "about" the different regions offer balanced insights into those cultures compared to books 'by' respective authors.

For van Dyck, transcultural literature is literature that is written with more than one language in mind. It is written in one language which is influenced by and uses a second language to express something it could not do without this second language (cf. 2012, 267). Thus, the readership is invited to inhabit a world that is neither exclusively one nor the other, but both. With this approach, van Dyck argues "against dividing literature in terms of national borders: homeland, new lands, ethnic communities" but rather looks at "literature for how it moves between languages and cultures, how it includes one language in the other" (2010, 3). Applying this reading to otherness, transcultural literature represents and facilitates an understanding of what "lie[s] between and outside the opposing poles of source and target, foreign and familiar" and moves beyond "transnational and transethnic modes of belonging that do not fit the established patterns of separatism or assimilation" (ibid., 12). The argumentation at hand speaks in favour of avoiding an inside/outside dichotomy which is in line with van Dyck's linguistic level of transcultural literature.

Hallet suggests the concept of "transcultural fiction" which he "conceptualise[s] as the formation or emergence of a textually pluralised, at times multimodal and culturally diversified, though integrated narrative" (2011, 51). It is "concerned with problems of ethnic difference, cultural orientation and interpersonal relations that transgress cultural borders" or "events [...] that allow for or enhance intercultural encounters" (ibid., 53-54). Especially the part of "transgressing cultural borders" can be seen in close proximity to the term of transcultural literature that I would like to suggest. Yet, for my understanding the direct reference to "problems of ethnic difference" is too close to an intercultural paradigm. My understanding of transcultural literature rather focuses on a depiction of alterity, and thus extends van Dyck's emphasis on language and Hallet's intercultural notion.

For the purpose of developing transcultural competences, which aim at reflecting similarities of one culture within the other and using this reflection as a point of reference for further explorations of the self, I suggest to use literature in ELT which reflects negotiations of identity beyond ethnic determinations and identity issues; these are not presented as prevalent in certain people only, but could occur in a global frame. In this sense, transcultural literature should transcend cultural boundaries and an essentialist perspective on plot, setting and ethnic identity. From this derives the idea that transcultural literature has the potential to invite young readers to experience alterity based on similarities. Transcultural fiction is built around well-rounded characters whose journey focuses on developing identity rather than ethnic identity; it represents alterity rather than an ethnic other. This entails the notion that the ethnic background does not carry any central meaning as such but supplements the narration and allows the protagonist to benefit from diverse cultural resources. Transcultural literature refrains from establishing a close link of ethnic background and issues or problems with which the member of this certain group has to deal. It rejects the stereotypical and symbolic markers of ethnicity which stigmatize a person's ethnicity in terms of religious practices, social and cultural traditions (cf. De Luca 2009, 71). In that respect, the protagonists entail trans- rather than multicultural identities. My suggested understanding of transcultural literature for young readers carries the potential of offering alternative views of 'other' identities which transcend a perception of otherness in a limited perspective on stereotypes, generalisations and shallowness.

This view on selecting literature for the development of transcultural competences entails references to enlightenment and emancipation, both of which have been established as essential paradigms of intercultural pedagogy (cf. Borrelli 1991, 278) but which have moved into the background in cultural didactics. However, in the understanding of transcultural I suggest in this work, criticism of ideology (cf. chapter 7.1.1), "questioning political, social and economic realities and the legitimation of power" (Borrelli 1991, 278), is recovered. Enlightening people through education is closely linked to liberating people from former mindsets and ideological convictions. The emancipation of 'othered' people "from a status as political minors to the subject of the historic process" (ibid.) – from being socially marginalized to gaining voice and participating in the public sphere – is one objective of transcultural learning. Thus, this also needs to be reflected in the literature and methods implemented in transcultural teaching. In intercultural pedagogy, emancipation processes are especially, but not exclusively, aimed at immigrant or multicultural identities who face a more powerful majority. Out of fear of a shift in power, both groups tend to find themselves in situations marked by structural violence. Yet, in transcultural learning this emancipation has an essential and slightly altered function, as it allows both the othered and non-othered identities to move beyond their given space.

Volkmann applies the concept of emancipation with a slightly different notion referring to a positive attitude toward hybridity which entails an emancipatory gesture (cf. 2010, 26). This indicates an empowerment of the individual toward the constraints of a cultural and linguistic implementation of norms (cf. ibid.). In addition, my application of emancipation points at empowering multicultural protagonists with regard to their continued depiction as individuals deprived of balanced identity, which they have to search for and which, once gained, automatically seems to imply happiness ever after. In this sense, transcultural literature facilitates revising established stereotypes and social relations. Protagonists no longer only struggle for voice, but for new subject positions which enable them to speak and act both in and on the world (cf. Crawford/McLaren 2003, 152). The aforementioned connection to "de-colonizing the mind" is also present in this understanding.

In my understanding of transcultural learning this focus on an emancipating and enlightening moment of cultural pedagogy is essential. Through transcultural literature that I suggest for transcultural learning, cultural pedagogy gains a humanizing and democratizing perspective. In *Run* and *The Water of Possibility* the protagonists emancipate themselves from the surrounding pressure, be it experiences of parent's divorce and holes in a social network, expected suffering from a terminal illness, or the effects of puberty on one's psyche and self-esteem. On a meta-perspective, the authors of those books enable protagonists who represent various degrees of otherness to emancipate from almost inherited victim positions and to establish balanced human identities. This, in turn, encourages readers to question an implied correlation of a certain ideology that is transported through fiction and social reality: "Education strives for humanity in two different ways, one being an individual act of liberation towards oneself, the other as a collective act of liberation towards the societal whole, towards the human as species" (Borrelli 1991, 282).

Transcultural literature is literature that addresses common issues beyond the protagonists' ethnic background. This background and a certain ethnic identity formation is not the focus of the protagonists' struggle; it does not define their character, but supplements their decisions and frames the story. In transcultural literature, protagonists are self-reliant and active agents who come to terms with their personal development as human beings. It invites children to experience various forms of othernesses based on identifying with aspects that are common across cultural boundaries. Yet, the discussion of the three selected texts has also shown that a clear-cut differentiation of inter- from transcultural literature is not possible. Therefore, my conclusion suggests a continuum from inter- to transcultural literature which reflects a continuum from inter- to transcultural learning as well.

Of the texts that I discussed in chapter 5, *Little Voice* is closest to an intercultural frame, as Ray's search for balanced identity against her classmates' and teacher's hostility and difficult family situation, which can both be traced to ethnic identity struggles, take centre stage. Yet, this novel still needs to be differentiated from the type of realistic fiction that was analysed in chapter 7.1.1 and 7.2.1, because Slipperjack refrains from repeating the derogative terms that are used against Ray but focuses on how she establishes a balanced ethnic identity and not on the malevolent society.

Run is part of transcultural literature as it offers a different perspective on otherness. The novel depicts a prosthesis-wearing young man not as a victim but as someone who takes action and stands out for his courage and will-power. It also tells Winston's story who comes to terms with his parents' divorce through meeting the young man who lost his leg to cancer. Encountering otherness is applied to a physically variant person whose exceptional strength of mind has turned him into one of Canada's most prominent heroes and to a surrounding society which encourages a single man's fight against cancer. *Run* can thus be seen as an example of transcultural literature as it transcends ethnic boundaries, presents a different kind of alterity and therefore extends the current concept of transcultural learning.

The fantasy novel *The Water of Possibility* likewise fits into this concept. In this novel, Hiromi Goto largely draws from Canadian and Japanese cultural images to allow the protagonists to move between and use both to solve mysteries and find answers to questions of identity. Sayuri's cultural background frames the story and supports her success, but it does not determine her identity formation. Her development is rather age-related. Therefore, this title represents transcultural literature as it moves beyond ethnic boundaries, and, most essentially, does not ascribe the multicultural protagonist a certain problem paradigm based on her ethnic identity. Because my understanding of transcultural literature avoids implied standards and power perspectives from which otherness is ascribed to certain protagonists, authors and plot developments, Hiromi Goto as a Japanese Canadian writer is included in the transcultural frame, just as Eric Walters, a white male Canadian of European ancestry.

Despite the advantages an understanding of transcultural literature contribute to the critical reflection of inter- and transcultural learning, texts alone do not guarantee a successful development of transcultural competences. Additionally, activities and methods have to be applied which facilitate a critical reflection of self and other. Yet, even if those reflections are carried out, their assessment still poses challenges. Both aspects are elaborated upon in the following chapter.

8. Procedures of Developing Cultural Competences

In order to elaborate on the challenging issue of teaching and assessing cultural competences, I would like to call to mind decisive aspects of the previous discussion. First, inter- and transcultural competences were described as multifaceted competences which include cognitive, affective and pragmatic dimensions (cf. chapter 1). As was analysed in chapter 7.1, some of the underlying concepts of teaching literature in ELT do not easily translate into classroom discourses as identification and developing empathy, for example, are complex processes which demand profound negotiations of cultural meaning. The value of the objective of developing tolerance can also be challenged because in the original sense tolerance indicates a result of noticing something without the need to change or question what is noticed because it does not concern the individual (Nussbaum 2008). Additionally, as was initiated in chapter 5 and discussed chapter 7.2, a certain kind of literature can be more beneficial for facilitating reflections upon othernesses and increasing awareness of alterity.

One pivotal element regarding the methodological approach to increasing cultural competences is an insecurity that resonates in drawing conclusions about learners' cultural competences based on their performances in normative and institutionalized classrooms. I believe that social desirability can limit ascriptions of cultural competence when students know what kind of opinions are expected from them (cf. chapter 7.1.3). Nevertheless, if cultural competences are to remain anchored in ELT, the discourse of developing cultural competences needs to include this aspect in the critical discussion of methods and assessment.

The approaches to methods and tasks I suggest and explore in this chapter attempt to pay tribute to the transcultural frame by foregrounding identity and alterity, and by abstaining from putting the protagonists' ethnic identity struggles into focus. As I pointed out in chapter 1.3.3 and 7.1.1, I consider the prevailing understanding of the transcultural element in TEFL research to be too narrow. I propose a more profound understanding of 'trans' that goes beyond the perception of an ethnic other but offers perspectives on various degrees of alterity and takes the self stronger into consideration.

From this line of argument I derive that an extended approach to transcultural learning should also refer to an extended approach to methodology and outcome description. I would like to bring forward tasks of personal involvement and tasks of negotiating otherness that result from the texts discussed in chapter 5, and suggest methods which could prevent students' reactions influenced by social desirability. I label the example methods "Fold Your Answer," "Agree and Disagree," "The Other Person" and "Focus Groups." In view of extended objectives, chapter 9 will elaborate on identity competence and awareness of alterity. As a foundation for the following discussion, the methods and classroom scenarios applied in Freitag-Hild's and Eberhardt's studies (cf. chapter 2.3.2) are reflected in more detail.

8.1 Methodological Considerations

As soon as cultural learning reaches a point where students have to express empathy, respect and positive attitudes toward others, and teachers have to evaluate and assess this, cultural learning faces criticism that branches out to different directions and to different agents: toward the teachers' perspective as they set tasks and assess results, and the learners' who react to questions, attempt to solve tasks and, usually, prefer good results. From both points of view the development of cultural competences is problematic when taking factors into account which influence teachers' decisions and learners' responses. Besides, as discussed above, also the interpretational openness of the text base can play an essential role. In chapter 2.3.3 I elaborated on the challenges of evaluating cultural competences which were summarized as

(1) The differentiation of performance and competence,
(2) Social desirability,
(3) The interplay of sub-competences of ICC and the different levels, and
(4) The assumption that intercultural competence develops in similar stages as language competences.

In her empirical study on British fictions of migration in contexts of teaching inter- and transcultural literature, Freitag-Hild (2010) suggests a typology of tasks, their function and format as well as examples for intercultural learning. This typology includes

– tasks of attunement which aim at a willingness to negotiate cultural otherness and are usually used in a pre-reading phase (forming hypotheses about protagonists and plot or discussing central topics that appear in the text),
– tasks of self-perception which aim at becoming aware of and reflecting one's own perspective and which entail articulating, discussing and reflecting experiences during the reading process (reading log/diary, personal statements about protagonists and plot, critical reflection of one's own perception of the protagonists and plot),
– tasks of interpretation and empathy which aim at differentiating, coordinating and taking over perspectives, these are usually applied in a while-reading phase to develop images of the protagonists, and to cognitively and emotionally reconstruct the protagonists' perspectivity

and their relationships (elaboration and comparison of attitudes, values, motives and protagonists' identity, characterizations, transferring the text into a different medium, drama transformations),

- tasks of analysis and reflection which analyse the fictional model of reality, e.g. literary device, their meaning and function in understanding the text; these could also be product-oriented (constellation of characters, point of view, focalization, constructed images of self and other, influence of literary device on the perception of the text),
- tasks of negotiation and participation, e.g. dialogic negotiation of meaning and difference, e.g. discussions about the reception and interpretation of a text, discussions to compare individual and cultural perspectives, experiences and interpretations,
- tasks of contextualization and transfer, e.g. research tasks, tasks to explore links to one's own cultural frame of reference, tasks to discover intertextual references and discourses in and about other cultures, and
- reflection tasks which aim at coordinating perspectives, reflections of the self, reflections on a meta-level (one's own (inter)cultural learning process), and reflections about prerequisites and problems of understanding otherness (critical reflection of origin, reasons and justifications of the perspectives of the self and others, changes of these perspectives and the significance of texts and tasks for increasing competences, the significance of changing perspectives and cultural knowledge for understanding otherness). (cf. Freitag-Hild 2010, 120-121)

Freitag-Hild's task typology is directed at advanced learners in Grades 11 to 13. Indeed, most of those tasks not only demand increasingly complex text reception but also increasingly complex text production; additionally, learners need to be prepared for the high level of literary analysis. When reading texts with younger learners, similar task can be applied, yet those tasks need to be adjusted to their analytical and linguistic competences. [160] As the texts and classroom applications that I discussed in chapter 5 aim at middle school learners, I suggest tasks and methods that are suitable for this age group, and which hence can be performed on a B1 level of English.

Freitag-Hild's elaborate task typology for intercultural learning in advanced classes allows to draw conclusions for teaching objectives of cultural learning based on literature. Yet, I believe it is difficult to derive certain conclu-

---

[160] Fäcke (2006) and Eberhardt (2013), among others, are open to using one's native language for negotiating cultural meaning in foreign language teaching. This agrees to concepts of 'informed monolingualism,' which implies teaching languages with mother tongue support as proposed by Butzkamm (e.g. 1973, 2003, 2008, 2009). However, the complexity of negotiating cultural meaning of self and other can also be challenging in students' native languages. Therefore, the teachers need to pay close attention to the demands of such tasks (cf. chapter 8.2).

sions about their impact on the development of inter- and transcultural competences. On a methodological level, it can be assumed that students find some of the tasks to be predictable or repetitive, for example phrasing a hypothesis about certain characters, the topic or the plot, or also changing a passage to a different genre. Furthermore, the tasks explicitly refer to an intercultural level and it remains open whether the same tasks can be applied or whether it is necessary to design a separate typology for developing transcultural competences.

In view of my earlier elaborations, it is striking that on a content level, the scholar repeatedly refers to cultural otherness and to the affective level of cultural competences. The multicultural texts she uses for increasing cultural competences exclusively depict the ethnic other as a person who struggles for equality or is a victim of social circumstances (Hanif Kureishi's "My Son the Fanatic" (1994) and Qaisra Shahraz' "A Pair of Jeans" (1988, 1991), cf. Freitag-Hild 2010, 122-138). Regarding content and perception, both aspects can be seen critically because it remains questionable in how far tasks that demand a change of perspective or developing empathy[161] enable students to reflect upon cultural issues beyond what is socially desired and beyond concernment if the protagonist is caught in such paradigms (cf. chapter 7). Even when emphatic statements toward the protagonists are expressed, a reliable assessment of such affective performances is limited. Moreover, it is debatable in how far such activities increase intercultural competences which students can beneficially apply outside the classroom.

Eberhardt's study aimed at investigating learners' personal experiences with and attitudes toward cultural otherness. He did this by asking students to comment on culturally laden photographs and intercultural dilemmas, and to describe their own experiences with members of a different culture and language. Students were also exposed to film clips, which were followed by interviews (cf. chapter 2.3.2, Eberhardt 2008, 282). Although this procedure is not based on literature, it still entails manifold moments in which students have to reflect their intercultural competence (e.g. changing perspectives or expressing empathy). As Eberhardt's focus lies with the students' reactions in culturally laden situations in which no protagonist is othered, more concrete conclusions about the students' cultural competences could be drawn. It could be assumed that particularly the perception and interpretation of photographs is beneficial for inter- and transcultural learning, as these are relatively easy to approach; students are familiar with photos and reactions to photos do not necessarily involve statements about a specific protagonist. Photos could emanate from the learners' experiences and are framed in a very individual and personal space. Therefore, students' reactions are likely to move beyond social desirability. Yet, this should not imply that literature per se is not useful for developing inter- and

---

[161] E.g. transformations of the original text from a different perspective, writing letters from the point of view of the main protagonist, or reflections of the other from an attempted inside perspective.

transcultural competences. As the elaborations show, the choice of texts and an appropriate approach influence its success.

However, as Eberhardt qualifies, it should not be ignored that the photos he uses depict national hetero-stereotypes[162] (cf. 2013, 467). The extent to which answers and reactions toward tasks that relate to those photos can be used as a foundation for evaluating cultural competences, therefore, remains disputable. From a methodological and evaluative perspective, the following questions are highly relevant:

- What kind of answers are students supposed to give who may not have had any personal contact with French cultures beyond classrooms?
- What kind of answers are students supposed to give whose opinion about France stems from social and political issues they do not agree with, and which overshadow other, more positive aspects about French cultures?
- Can personal experiences be assessed?
- Can emotional reactions toward pictures and the verbalizations these provoke be evaluated?

These questions indicate that on the one hand, students should be given the chance to reflect upon their attitudes toward a certain culture beforehand. This helps to diagnose their general knowledge and feelings about a culture and unveils how their attitudes may influence their cultural learning process. On the other hand these questions point out that the assessment of the affective and pragmatic level of cultural competences faces limitations.

I propose a similar critical stance in reference to one specific task format. In cultural learning students are often asked to write diary entries or further personal texts from the perspective of a specific character. A diary entry is a very personal and private document. I question in how far students seriously and profoundly analyse and reflect upon their reading impressions when they know that they will either have to read their texts out loud or that these are read by a teacher and possibly even graded. This is especially the case when the text base entails individual suffering and trauma related to discrimination and racism. I would like to emphasize this objection under the spotlight of social desirability as I doubt that one can derive conclusions about a student's cultural competence based on such diary entries written for educational purposes. Yet, I am not in favour of completely avoiding such tasks, but raise awareness for their limitation in cultural learning. If these are frequently applied, I suspect it is likely that students' results rather reflect their ability to write texts in a specific

---

[162] E.g. a military parade on Avenue des Champs-Élysées, street cafés, baguettes and berets. Eberhardt finds it unproblematic to use these because he believes that the students' responses to these pictures represent subjective knowledge (cf. below). He conducted his study in French lessons, therefore examples refer to French culture.

genre and their sociocultural awareness about the morals and values a society supports than their cultural competences.

Students are highly aware of socially desired patterns of opinion and behavior so that it is difficult to derive from their answers whether they have acquired respect or feel empathy for others, especially when their answers are given in an artificial space such as institutionalized classrooms. From grammatically correct sentences and consistent essays on cultural topics only limited conclusions can be drawn about a learner's attitudes toward otherness. No matter whether used for the development or assessment of cultural competences, Schulz (2008) and Dervin (2010) agree that traditional tasks like multiple choice, question and answer, essays, reports, analysis of literature, and role plays do not lend themselves easily to the assessment of cultural competences as they often provoke stereotyping (Schulz 2007, 17, cf. Dervin 2010, 164-165). Sercu (2004/2010) and Schulz (2007) have put forward further objections which extend the challenges of assessing cultural competence discussed in chapter 2.3.3. These include

- the possibility of scoring students' answers objectively (Sercu 2004, 78 and Sercu 2010, 27),
- the interpretational character of cultural learning material and tasks; culture is always subjectively experienced and constructed (cf. Sercu 2004, 78, Atkinson 1999, Sercu 2010, 27),
- the validity of students' personal interpretations of cultural phenomena (cf. Sercu 2004, 78 and Sercu 2010, 27),
- the application of problem-solving strategies that were maybe not taught in class (cf. Sercu 2004, 78, Sercu 2010, 27),
- the justification of assessing learners "with respect to particular attitudes or personality traits. Does education want to be prescriptive about the intercultural attitudes learners should develop and can learners be punished for not having particular desired personality traits, such as 'interest in cultures' or 'positive self-image,' which have been identified as characteristics of the effective intercultural person?" (Sercu 2004, 78, Sercu 2010, 28),
- the quality of the material used in the classroom: Do teachers need a "checklist of the sort of situations one is likely to need to deal with […]" and apply these to classrooms "before one can deal with intercultural situations adequately" (Sercu 2010, 30),
- the awareness of a certain degree of "interdependence between the different dimensions of intercultural competence" and awareness that the "extent of a learner's culture-specific or culture-general knowledge may affect the learner's learning skill" (ibid., 28),

– the likelihood "that difference in communicative competence in the foreign language may cause assessees with the same level of intercultural competence to perform differently." (ibid., 28)

Furthermore, similar challenges that were unveiled in the context of teaching cultures (cf. chapter 2.2.1) also apply to the assessment of cultural learning. This regards, for instance, that cultures are multilayered and form hybrid constructs that are fluid, flexible and open to change.

Additionally, Sercu sheds light on the problematic distinction of different phases and levels of cultural competences asking "whether learning interculture can be viewed as a quantifiable step-by-step process from one level to the next" (ibid., 28, cf. chapter 2.3.3). She also questions whether the development of cultural competences culminates in full competence, which "once acquired will remain acquired" (ibid., 30). The author's critical discussion of the objectives of increasing cultural competences in the classroom indicates that "school learning without direct contact with other cultures cannot lead to the development of intercultural competence" (ibid., 31). Yet, although direct contact can indeed be beneficial, it does not guarantee cultural competences either – a catch-22 situation which underlines the complexity of this topic.

Whereas learners can present certain opinions, reactions and answers in the classroom, it is very difficult to draw conclusions from these about the learners' attitudes, emotions and willingness to apply them outside the classroom. As elaborated above, it is simply not possible to say whether certain answers to tasks that ask for a change of perspective are given because of the learners' vivid imagination, their high linguistic competences, their awareness of what is socially desirable, or whether they have truly understood the cultural implications of the topic discussed and were able to see the other from a reflected inside perspective. Even if the learners' answers are based on such reflected intercultural competence, it cannot be said in how far this was actually developed during English lessons specifically and in how far this competence is applied to negotiations of meaning in intercultural face-to-face encounters.

When transcultural teaching and learning is taken seriously, it is necessary to enable students to form opinions they truly have – also in test formats. But "[w]hat test formats can be used to elicit data on the cognitive, competence and affective dimension of intercultural competence?" (Sercu 2010, 24). Sercu states that apart from language skills,

> holistically, one would also have to assess to what extent learners can be viewed as intercultural beings, assessing the presence or absence of intercultural values and attitudes (e.g. be intrinsically interested in understanding cultures from within) and recognising demonstrations of such attitudes or values in particular student attitudinal behaviours. (ibid.)

Although no systematic operationalization of cultural competences is used as a foundation for assessing cultural competences yet (Eberhardt's study of 2013 could be a starting point, cf. below), attempts have been made to develop a respective framework. For example, Bartz and Vermette suggest 16 prototype formats for assessing intercultural competence (cf. Bartz/Vermette 1996, 75-83, also in Sercu 2010, 25-26, Schulz 2007, 17). Yet, a closer look reveals that all of the activities they suggest refer to the cognitive level of cultural competence. Activities that entail an affective notion evoke answers which are speculative or generalizing, for example descriptions of typical behavior (cf. Bartz/Vermette 1996, 79), photos or drawings of situations depicting social behavior in an unknown culture, audio or video documents for observing sociolinguistic behavior, and organizing and making sense of one's cultural observations (cf. ibid., 82-83). One of their activities asks students to create a list of opposing adjectives "in two columns; those characterizing a people favourably in one column and those characterizing them disparagingly in another (e.g. lazy/workaholic, beautiful/unattractive, outgoing/shy)." Students then have to put an 'A' for American, an 'F' for French or an 'FC' for French-Canadian next to each antonym indicating for whom it applies (cf. Bartz/Vermette 1996, 77). This activity is highly disputable as it re-constructs (existing) stereotypes, even when these are discussed critically afterwards. Therefore, those formats only offer limited insights to students' development of cultural competences and intercultural awareness.

Eberhardt's study with 10th graders learning French offers an empirical foundation for suggesting a competence model for ICC. In this he differentiates Byram's indicators of intercultural competence on horizontal and vertical levels. This competence model establishes the three horizontal categories precision, complexity and abstraction, which are each vertically categorized into a basic, intermediate and elaborate level. For example, 'knowledge about characteristics of culture' is one sub-competence of Byram's main competence *savoirs*. On the basic level of precision of *savoirs*, students document vague and relatively shallow knowledge about characteristics of a culture which often includes stereotypes. On the intermediate level, this knowledge is more precise, more detailed and only partly stereotyping, already showing simple differentiations. On the elaborate level of precision, students' knowledge about cultures is precise, detailed and generally differentiated. Eberhardt offers a similar differentiation for the complexity and abstraction of this and Byram's other main- and sub-competences (cf. 2013, 412-415).[163] I mention Eberhardt's typology of the *savoirs* because it help to illustrate how challenging the endeavor is to develop such descriptors for all of Byram's 27 categories of intercultural competence[164] according to their conceptualization and to their transfer to foreign language

---

[163] For details about the horizontal level cf. Eberhardt (2013, 335-343).
[164] As Eberhardt notes it was not possible to describe a three-fold development for 5 out of Byram's 27 items. He could not consider the main category *savoir apprendre/faire* (cf. 2013, 458).

teaching, i.e. their applicability to assessing and evaluating cultural competences.

The iceberg and onion models of cultures (cf. chapter 2.2) help to illustrate that in this model, the cognitive category of cultural competence could be the easiest to assess. Compared to facts, figures and observable cultural phenomena located on the visible part of the iceberg and outer skins of the onion, phenomena that are placed at the lower part of the iceberg or inner skins of the onion are more difficult to assess. These involve more complex concepts which increasingly need to be approached affectively. However, this cognitive level is challenging as well.

A main difficulty is to assess whether stereotypical and generalizing comments could be regarded as culture-related knowledge. Eberhardt qualifies a truth-based term of knowledge because this would either mean that stereotyping, generalizing and culturalizing statements are true, or such statements are regarded as false, which would, however, ignore students' subjective perspectives (cf. 2013, 425-429). Both options do not agree with dynamic and differentiated culture terminology (cf. chapter 1 and 2); in both cases knowledge not only depends on a certain context but also on the individual. As a solution, Eberhardt favours an understanding of knowledge which pays tribute to the individual character of knowledge and simultaneously to consensus-orientation. This entails that stereotyping and generalizing statements about cultures are considered as auto- and hetero-stereotypes and as culture-related knowledge. Such an understanding would agree to a dynamic and fluid culture term which can be culture-bound and does not assume objective and shallow cultural realities. This kind of knowledge is based on individual knowledge that is shared by a community, in Eberhardt's study a group of students (cf. 2013, 427), and as such, it has to be recognized as a subjective perspective.

Eberhardt's differentiation of precision, complexity and abstraction for a basic, intermediate and elaborate level for Byram's main and sub-competences is a first reflective attempt to investigate the development and evaluation of intercultural competences. His model of intercultural competences is highly complex and an important step toward operationalization. Based on the students' answers and empirical data he collected, Eberhardt was able to identify their knowledge of and tolerance toward other cultures as well as a willingness to negotiate cultural meaning on certain levels. Eberhardt could also conclude and prove that cultural (sub-)competences are highly intertwined and linked. This makes their assessment even more challenging as German Standards of Education are usually designed to assess competences separately.

However, I believe this model is only convincing if one assumes that students responded to tasks disregarding the institutionalized circumstances under which the study took place. One also needs to take into consideration that Eberhardt's results were collected based on certain tasks, specific material, and a certain relationship of students and teacher. Additionally, this elaborate and detailed study does not allow to draw conclusions concerning the students' intercultural competences and the pragmatic application of these competences outside the classroom (cf. Eberhardt 2013, 457, 479).

As a consequence of this critical reflection, I conclude that it may be useful to differentiate between tasks for the development of inter- and transcultural competences and tasks for their assessment. Tasks of negotiation and participation, transfer, contextualization and reflection allow students to engage with inter- and transcultural issues, provide incentives for changing perspectives and expressing empathy. Students can reflect upon the other and express their ideas and opinions. Yet, as soon as they know that their answers are assessed, it can be questioned in how far those expressions are sincere and based on their honest opinions. Therefore, I believe that whereas methods and activities applied in cultural teaching and learning could reach the affective and substitute the pragmatic level, it is highly difficult, if not impossible, to include these levels in assessment processes. These levels are too complex and their pragmatic application cannot be ensured. Therefore, teachers either need to limit assessment to the cognitive domain being aware of certain restrictions, or have to describe transparent criteria that facilitate a justified evaluation of students' statements that refer to an affective and pragmatic level. As mentioned, reasons for these limitations lie with the framing of cultural learning in normative classrooms, with a socially desired and benevolent approach to others, and with the limited options of drawing conclusions about a pragmatic application based on students' correct answers and coherent essays.

Despite all criticism, the development of cultural competences is the central and general objective of foreign language education. Transcultural learning is just being introduced to English language teaching and saying that its evaluation is not possible negates further research of and discourse in the field. Thus, I would like to suggest alternatives and options for tasks and methods that are able to withstand the criticism mentioned above. These suggestions relate to the texts discussed in chapter 5 and are based on their potential for transcultural learning as summarized in chapter 6.

8.2 Classroom Procedures of Understanding Self and Other in Classes 7 to 10

Zydatiß sees the reduction of the Standards of Education to basic functional competences highly critical and warns of the consequences of disregarding general education and concrete output orientation, respective tasks and assessment for literary and cultural learning (Zydatiß 2005a, 279, 2005b).[165] Those Stand-

---

[165] "Die sogenannten „Bildungsstandards" der KMK (2993) richten den Fremdsprachenunterricht auf funktionale Basiskompetenzen aus, allerdings ohne jedes Moment von Bildung" (Zydatiß 2005a, 279).

ards would neither refer to the poetic-imaginative dimension of language, which is foundational for fictional and humoristic language use, nor to the dimension of general education, personality development, cultural understanding, orientation in the world, and self-reliant critical thinking (cf. ibid., 278). Therefore, he demands a skeptic approach to the sustainable development of the quality of foreign language teaching[166] (cf. ibid., 279). However, the Standards for the school-leaving exam indeed include references to those aspects of language acquisition (cf. chapter 3.1). Yet, Zydatiß additionally states that literary didactics and didactics of understanding otherness have to adjust to output orientation if both would like to keep their current position in the curricula. Tasks would have to be designed which withstand the evaluation of aspired objectives, and both fields should try to empirically show that the usage of demanding fictional texts and topics allows students to learn more in comparison to trivial texts and topics[167] (cf. Zydatiß 2005a, 279).

Yet, just as the complexity of using literature in ELT and cultural learning should not be underestimated, also the complexity of the underlying methodology needs to be acknowledged and reflected. The discussion of key facets of increasing cultural competences revealed that certain processes are far more complex and multidimensional than often assumed. Yet, cognitive processes and selecting literature for ELT are only two of the many factors that influence successful cultural learning, as the teachers' personality and methodology certainly are decisive as well. A text can neither be perfect, nor does a text automatically work in cultural learning environments, but successfully developing cultural competences depends on both content and procedures.

In the current practice of teaching English it is common knowledge that action-oriented and learner-centered approaches facilitate productive learning processes (cf. Hammer 2012b, 301). While productive tasks such as completing a text, ordering tasks and changing the style of texts support creativity, these cannot, however, be sufficiently completed without a preceding analysis of the text. Thus, analytical tasks are essential for dealing with texts; not only because they ensure the development of declarative knowledge and procedural understandings of texts, but also because they secure creative negotiations of meaning. In many publications (e.g. Volkmann 2010, 228-230, Nünning/Surkamp,

---

[166] "Da hinsichtlich der Implementierung der Standards bisher die Überprüfung fachbezogener Leistungen von Schülern im Vordergrund steht, ist massive Skepsis angebracht, was die nachhaltige Qualitätsentwicklung des schulischen Fremdsprachenlernens betrifft" (Zydatiß 2005a, 279).

[167] "Ich fürchte, die Literaturdidaktik und die Didaktik des Fremdverstehens müssen sich sehr bewusst auf das output-orientierte Denken einstellen, wenn sie ihre bisherige Rolle im fremdsprachlichen Curriculum halten wollen. Sie sollten zum einen Aufgaben entwickeln, die der Überprüfung der angestrebten Lernziele standhalten; und sie sollten sich über empirische Forschungsprojekte auf die „Ertrags"perspektive einlassen – sprich, sie sollten versuchen zu zeigen, dass über anspruchsvollere fiktionale Texte und belangvolle Themen „mehr" gelernt wird als mit vergleichsweise trivialen Inhalten und expositorischen Texten (und das darüber hinaus auch noch etwas „Anderes" gelernt wird)" (Zydatiß 2005a, 279).

2006, 21) tasks take center stage that enable students to apply theoretical knowledge to decode words, sentences, and plots, to recognize rhetorical figures and genres (bottom-up processing), and tasks which support students in recognizing extra-textual references (psychological schemata, literary conventions (top-down processing) (cf. Hammer 2012b, 301-302). The following reflection, however, refrains from describing and analyzing such tasks in detail. I also refrain from entering the discourse of 'complex competence tasks' since an adequate discussion would far exceed the limits of my work.[168] I rather shed light on formats which focus on a more holistic approach to working with texts and developing competences of dealing with alterity.

The reflection of selected Canadian young adult fiction and their potential for inter- and especially transcultural learning (chapters 5 and 6) are in the following mirrored regarding certain methodology and tasks that evade the challenges described in the previous sections. While the following subchapter offers suggestions for concrete tasks and classroom procedures for reading *Little Voice*, *Run* and *The Water of Possibility*, my concluding remarks will point to certain general characteristics of tasks for transcultural learning. These need to be seen in close connection to the understanding of transcultural literature that was established in chapter 7.2. In principle, this discussion reflects approaches to cultural teaching as suggested by Freitag-Hild and Eberhardt. Yet, my suggestions differ in that I specifically try to avoid a focus on ethnic otherness but rather use the self as a starting point for reflecting upon self and alterity. The tasks and methods I would like to put forward can be seen in close proximity to a character-centered approach. These focus on the "reader's imagination of the characters and their textual world" (Hallet 2011, 55), wherein the protagonists' as well as the learners' personality, behavior, relation to others, their interests and developments take center stage.

In addition, as mentioned, Freitag-Hild's and Eberhardt's studies were conducted with more advanced learners of English or French. Therefore, my example tasks specifically address younger learners. When they are asked to engage in complex discussions of cultural issues based on literature and other media in higher secondary ELT, such skills and competences need to be developed and initiated with young and intermediate learners already. This is particularly important with view of multilayered constructions of cultural identity and intricate representations of cultural issues.

As was indicated in chapter 2.3.3, linguistic and cultural competences are closely connected, albeit they not necessarily correlate (cf. also in Sercu 2010, 27). It can be the case that learners are lacking the appropriate language

---

[168] I am aware of the current discourses of 'complex tasks for competence development' ("Komplexe Kompetenzaufgabe") (cf. Hallet 2012a, 2012b, Siepmann 2012, Surkamp 2012) and 'tasks to support learning processes' ("Lernaufgabe") (cf. Vollmer 2010, Tesch 2013, Bär 2013) and their relevance for TEFL theory and praxis. Both are central discourses which have gained increasing significance and attention with the reform of education toward output-orientation. However, these discourses are too complex to be reflected here in detail.

material to voice certain ideas that would reflect their actual cultural competence. It cannot be assumed that cultural competences develop in similar stages as linguistic competences and it is important to be aware that younger learners mainly focus on processes of language acquisition. As a consequence, similar to Fäcke (2006) and Eberhardt (2013), I believe that they should be offered the alternative to express their ideas in German – an approach that follows the principles of teaching with mother tongue support ("Aufgeklärte Einsprachigkeit") (cf. Butzkamm 1973, 2003, 2011, cf. above). This of course does not mean that learners will not improve their linguistic competence so as to be able to negotiate cultural meaning in English, but it offers them the chance to express cultural competences where linguistic skills may not yet be adequate.

8.2.1 "Fold Your Answer": Tasks and Methods for *Little Voice*

The following tasks aim at familiarizing students with the text and involving them personally in Slipperjack's *Little Voice*. These tasks use Ray's experiences as a point of reference, but focus on the learners' self and reflect upon their own experiences and personality.

Example Tasks of Personal Involvement

- Ask family members (or search the internet) about the meaning of your name.
- Do you sometimes feel that you and your parents/family/friends speak different languages or that they simply do not understand you? In which situations? Can you name reasons?
- Do you have a place where you go when you need to get away from home for some time? If you do, which place is it and how does it help to make you feel better? If not, what kind of place could it be? How would you characterize it? How would it make you feel better?

Older students can reflect upon the following task:

- At the end of the book, Ray's grandma assures her that she is "someone who can handle both worlds" (Slipperjack 2001, 245). Can you imagine to whom this might apply as well? How about yourself? Would you see/Have you seen yourself in a position where you had to manage two different worlds? How would/did you bridge the gap?

Teachers can use these tasks to involve learners in the text they are going to read or when students have read the first pages and met Ray already. The aspects touched upon reappear in the book and the learners can compare their thoughts to Ray's situation. It would be possible that the students take notes in a chart so that they can write down the equivalences of Ray's experiences when they continue reading.

Those tasks refer to very personal issues and learners may not be willing to discuss them in the classroom. To offer students a chance to nevertheless reflect upon personal impressions and experiences, wishes and desires in written form, it would be possible to use the methodological approach "Fold Your Answer:" Students fold a piece of paper in half. On the inside they take notes only for themselves, these can remain private and should not be read by anyone else unless the student gives permission. On the outside of the folded paper, students write answers they would like to share with their classmates and teacher, aspects and ideas they are willing to read out loud or discuss openly. This method could ensure that students reflect upon personal, emotional and also cultural issues that are discussed in class more seriously and honestly, while it gives them the option of not sharing, but still becoming aware of what they think and feel. With "Fold Your Answer" students thus carry high ownership of their comments as they decide who reads their hidden opinions.

In addition, this method pays tribute to conflicts of identity and role confusion that were identified by Erikson (1968), for example. "Fold Your Answer" also refers to Goffman's dramatization of behavior and his distinction of "front" and "back" behavior: "front" behavior tends to conform to certain standards that need to be complied with in certain situations (1959, 22-23), individuals act as if playing a role and acting out a ritual (cf. ibid., 24) while the "backstage may be defined as a place, relative to a given performance, where the impression fostered by the performance [may be] contradicted" (ibid., 69). Activities in which part of the students' reactions are kept "backstage" allow them to be more honest, they could be themselves and act contradictory to the performance they want their classmates and teachers to see and believe.

In the process of forming two opinions the objection of social desirability can be relativized, too. When writing down two different opinions students can become aware of these two levels and consciously reflect why they have these two opinions, one of which they would rather not share (cf. chapter 8.3). Apart from that, my own and my colleagues' teaching experience revealed that students often grew more confident during classroom discussions and after a while unfolded their papers and openly discussed those aspects they originally wanted to keep private. I assume that this was prompted by having the students write down what they really thought in the first place, through which they voiced their opinion in writing. As the discussions in class proceeded, they became more conscious of the relevance of their contributions and began to be more profound in reflecting critical matters.

Neither Ray's experiences with her name, her inability to communicate with people who are close to her, nor needing a place where she finds comfort are culture specific. As the aforementioned tasks refer to these aspects, they also refer to the transcultural level of the book. Students do not reflect upon the protagonist but focus on themselves in similar situations and see the protagonist as a point of reference. In transcultural literature, conflict situations do not necessarily need to be caused by the protagonists' ethnic identity but rather by their life situation as teenagers who grow up and who are maybe torn between various influences. Thus, seeing the other as an ethnic other is avoided, and transcultural aspects of identity formation are moved into the foreground.

Beyond this transcultural level, *Little Voice* can also be read interculturally as the book offers references to negotiate ethnic identity as well. In order to engage with Ray on an intercultural level, the following tasks could be applied:

Tasks of Negotiating Alterity

- Why does Ray feel uncomfortable at school?
- Read the classroom scene at the beginning of the book. How would you react in Ray's, the teacher's, and her friend's position?
- Compare Ray's home to the cabin where she lives with her grandmother. Describe and characterize both places. Draw conclusions about Ray's feelings at those places. How does Ray's environment support her feelings at both places?

Older students can reflect upon the question

- In how far is Ray able to form a hybrid identity when travelling between both places?

Other tasks could focus on Anishinaabeg traditions and lifestyles as represented in the book and on reading other texts by First Nation authors. Using additional children's books and young adult fiction allows students to further explore First Nation cultures (cf. chapter 5.1.2). For example, *Neekna and Chemai* (Armstrong 1984) can be used to reflect the protagonists' encounters with nature and the role family plays in both texts. In a more global perspective, advanced learners can also engage in parallel reading activities and investigate other indigenous peoples as represented in texts, for instance finding links to James Moloney's *Angela* which is set in an Australian Aboriginal context. These tasks show an intercultural implication as they focus on the other culture and ask students to negotiate otherness based on ethnic identity. They take ethnic influences on identity formation into account and aim at learning about First Nation cultures. These tasks do not transcend cultural boundaries but ask students to consider the protagonists' ethnic identity from an outside perspective as well as from within their cultural frame. They remain with in a separate perception of different cultural frames, therefore, rather agree to an intercultural sphere.

8.2.2 "Agree or Disagree": Tasks and Methods for *Run*

As was discussed in detail in chapter 5.2, I regard Eric Walters' *Run* as an example of a text that is beneficial for inter- and transcultural learning as it represents a Canadian national hero as well as otherness beyond ethnic problem identity. In the frame of intercultural learning, the following elements can be reflected upon in more detail:

- the story of Terry Fox and the legacy of the "Marathon of Hope" which takes place each year all around the world[169]
- similar heroes or heroines from the students' culture/society
- a closer look at the map and distance Terry ran in order to collect donations and the landmarks he passed, and
- a transfer of the distance onto Europe (5300km).

The interview Winston Sr. conducts with Terry can be used for an explicit development of communicative competences when students are required to transform the interview into an article for a local newspaper (cf. Alter 2011c). Hallet's approach to generic learning provides useful insights to using generic models as a base for students' product-oriented and creative writing processes (cf. Hallet 2009a, 2009b, 2013).

Within the frame of transcultural competences, *Run* offers a multitude of references, for example to the characters themselves, but also to certain topics and issues (cf. chapter 5.2). Based on the plot and Winston's and Terry's experiences, students can reflect upon transcultural issues such as trouble at school, with parents and/or relatives and friends, cancer as a global issue, ability and disability as well as the question of what makes someone a hero or heroine. Students can, for example, compare Winston and Terry according to their 'run:' what are their different reasons to be on the road? What caused their run? What are their goals? Which troubles do they try to solve? When this is done in a chart, students can add a column and fill in their personal responses to the protagonists' challenges. These aspects can also be reflected using the quotes that were discussed within the teaching implications of this book (cf. chapter 5.2.2):

- "It seemed like my mom was working hard to get rid of me, while my father was working just as hard not to take me. It felt special to be so wanted." (Walters 2003, 14)
- "Then it's probably wise to stay quiet." (ibid., 18)

---

[169] The homepage of the Terry Fox Foundations offers a list of international runs (cf. Terry Fox Foundation homepage).

- "[T]he only people who don't make mistakes are those who are too timid to try new things. Stay bold, take chances . . . Little people make little mistakes. Big people make big mistakes." (ibid., 26)
- "By running like this I let people know that cancer can be beaten... that life can go on... that you define people by their ability and not their disability." (ibid., 49)
- "Besides, we both know that you can't run away from your problems." (ibid., 141)
- "I know I don't have one friend who would give up half a year of his life or more to take care of me, to help me chase one of my dreams. Do you have a friend who would do that?" (ibid., 101)

Students' responses to these aspects can be very personal; therefore, the method "Fold Your Answer" as explained above can also be applied here to offer students more private space. The quotes can be used for an activity that can be called "Agree or Disagree," as these can provoke approval as well as rejection. Students are expected to find justifications for agreeing and disagreeing with the statements, a task that implies a change of perspective and developing empathy, but that could also cause a critical view. For example, there can be certain situations in which speaking up against authority and running away from problems could indeed be appropriate.

Another method that ensures a more private discussion among students is "Focus Groups," in which it may be more likely that students openly discuss topics such as trouble at school or with parents. Students get together in groups of four or five, pick one of the quotes, respond to it individually, one after the other, and then engage in a discussion about their opinions and experiences. When reflecting their group discussion with the class, they can decide which aspects they would like to share and which they would rather keep to themselves.

8.2.3 "The Other Person": Tasks and Methods for *The Water of Possibility*

Hiromi Goto's *The Water of Possibility* was identified as a transcultural novel that offers specific potential for transcultural learning (chapter 5.3). In comparison to *Little Voice* and *Run*, this text is different in that it represents the multicultural character as the heroine of the story beyond a problematic ethnic identity. The text focuses on issues that are likely to be relevant for other teenagers her age, too, like the importance of friendship, relationships among siblings and parents, trust and forgiving, the challenges of puberty, and global issues such as protecting the environment. In my understanding, transcultural learning is promoted as Sayuri's challenges are not directly determined by her ethnic background. However, this can be focused when students, for example, further investigate the figures of Japanese mythology or the Japanese stories that are told. Reflections could also sensitize students to intertextual references to stories they may know and encourage them to find similar morals in these. Despite the critical remarks about the cognitive level of intercultural learning and factual learning (cf. chapter 8.1, cf. Eberhardt 2013), such activities are based on developing knowledge about Japanese culture and further texts. In view of reliable assessment of cultural competences, this foregrounding of the cognitive dimension points at a re-evaluation of factual knowledge (cf. below). However, this also implies a respectful reading and developing students' openness toward these stories.

As the following example tasks illustrate, also on a transcultural level are students asked to change perspectives, express empathy or be critical toward Sayuri, but – and this is essential for the understanding of transcultural learning supported in my work – not focusing on Japanese Canadian identity, but on 'child-becoming-adolescent-identity.' This remarkable depiction offers various options for a transcultural reflection of the book as students can focus on transcultural aspects of life and can personally be involved beyond feeling pity for an ethnic other. In chapter 5.3.1 I analysed selected scenes on which such reflection can be based, for instance the incident of the embarrassing T-shirt, Sayuri's awkwardness at her first training in the new swim club, or the strange, unwelcome feeling at her new home. Students can reflect upon their own reactions in situations like these by putting themselves in Sayuri's position.

An activity that can be called "The Other Person" is applicable in the scene in which Sayuri first cuts off the Patriarch's hands and later uses the healing water to replace them with his original paws (cf. Goto 2001, 272-279). While students can reflect upon justifications and objections of forgiving others for their deeds, they can also see this decision from the perspective of other protagonists. What would Kimi's reaction as a nurse have been, or her mother's? Would Keiji, who was the Patriarch's captive who stole his memory, have replaced the paws? Additionally, students could evaluate Sayuri's decision to show this level of kindness and reflect upon this plot development on a meta-level: Why did the writer decide in favour of healing the Patriarch? In "The Other Person" students regard one scene from a multitude of perspectives that are present in the text, as well as from the perspective of the writer. Moreover, they could invite other characters to certain scenes and extend the text by their reactions. In this de-personalized reflection, students can go beyond socially desired concepts but speak with the voice of other characters and thus transcend a personalization of their opinions.

Advanced students could be engaged in more abstract and analytical tasks. When negotiating otherness, a further interesting aspect to analyse is how texts as fictional literature create otherness – what happens in the texts that makes the reader aware of the protagonists' otherness? How is otherness established, described and negotiated? By comparing the depiction of otherness in different books the students have read, they can draw conclusions regarding the construction of otherness, reflect how the protagonists are presented, how their actions and behavior are contextualized and which spaces they (are allowed to) occupy. However, these analytical tasks demand not only advanced linguistic competences, but advanced awareness of discursive negotiation of alterity, too. When older students are supposed to perform these, foundations need to be built in their earlier school career already. Only then can one expect students to be able to reflect upon the respective consequences that were outlined in chapters 6 and 7.1.1. In order to raise teachers' awareness for such positioning, similar reflections could also be integrated into tertiary education.

The methodological consequences of the critical reflection of transcultural learning and teaching can be summarized as follows:

- Transcultural learning needs a different kind of literature: Multicultural protagonists are not to be presented as problem-laden identities only but as human individuals who face human opportunities and challenges.
- Transcultural learning needs to be supported with specific tasks and methods: These could be de-personalized in order to withstand objections such as social desirability.
- Transcultural learning demands a critical negotiation of meaning. Therefore, also critical voices need to be encouraged in ELT. It should be possible to argue beyond an often pursued obligatory harmony by justifiably rejecting a protagonist's decision.
- For the assessment of cultural competences in general, the extent to which factual knowledge and a cognitive level contributes to cultural learning needs to be reconsidered. Cultural learning that refers to the affective and pragmatic level cannot be sufficiently assessed in normative classrooms. Simultaneously, awareness needs to be raised for the dynamic character of cultures, and essentializing attitudes need to be avoided despite a focus on facts (subjective knowledge).
- The objective of "cultural" learning needs to be reconsidered as an often implied focus on ethnicity does not meet the demands of a transcultural paradigm. Here, identity competence or the ability to deal with alterity in general could be more appropriate and promising for the development of transcultural competences.

Methods and classroom activities that are specifically applied for transcultural learning

- encourage personal involvement,
- allow students to voice opinions from different perspectives, and
- allow students to keep parts of their reflections to themselves.

The example tasks suggested in this chapter mirror the differences between an inter- and transcultural scope which I discussed on a more theoretical level in chapters 1, 5 and 7. While intercultural learning often aims at reflecting upon the ethnic other in order to develop empathy and respect for and understanding of the other in their cultural settings, transcultural learning focuses on aspects beyond ethnic settings and ascribes the self a more central position. Transcultural learning goes beyond establishing the ethnic other as otherness and takes into account various degrees of alterity. This applies to the composition of multicultural societies more realistically, as students learn together in multicultural classrooms and a stigmatization of ethnic otherness constructs rather than deconstructs a stereotypical perception of others. This also leads to a critical stance toward the term otherness (cf. chapter 9.1.2). Yet, from the discussion so far, certain consequences for new approaches to teaching and assessing cultural competence become visible.

8.3 New Approaches to Teaching and Assessing Cultural Competences

In the previous chapters I discussed the challenges of and alternatives for developing cultural competences which reflect the complexity of cultural learning in reference to the methodological and content level. More generally, these challenges and alternatives indicate that certain, be it slight, changes in the approach to increasing cultural competences can be beneficial for ELT which focuses on transcultural learning.

One consequence of a shifting focus away from the inter-paradigm of cultures is the inclusion of different degrees of alterity in ELT, not only to extend the frame of cultural and ethnic representation in the classroom but also to enable students to deconstruct prevalent stereotypes and problem ascriptions to othernesses. Scholars like Freitag-Hild (2010), Eisenmann (et al. 2010), Sommer (2001), and Volkmann and Delanoy (2006) have recently looked at literatures from cultural frames beyond the U.S. and Great Britain, and widened the scope to invite further English-speaking cultures into the classroom (cf. chapter 3.1). Delanoy and Volkmann's *Cultural Studies in the EFL Classroom* (2006) additionally offers a perspective which includes so-called small-c and small-l topics such as *Harry Potter* (Hestermann 2006, 313-322), *The Lord of the Rings* (Honegger/Honegger 2006, 323-336) or comics and graphic novels (Vanderbeke 2006, 365-380).

However, my work suggests that the selection of literature for ELT needs to be further extended, not necessarily according to the cultural background but rather according to the image of alterity these entail. The value of literature for developing cultural competences is not to be questioned (cf. chapter 2). But what is striking is that investigations into transcultural competences apply the same kind of literature as is used for intercultural learning and also the same approaches to discuss these in class (cf. Fäcke 2006, Freitag-Hild 2010). As I argued, when inter- and transcultural learning differ in their conceptualizations, also the literature, methods and approaches could be distinguished.

Additionally, the methods and tools of academically investigating cultural competences cannot be excluded from a conceptual reflection of classroom procedures. In many studies, researchers refer to cultural competences – be it within the results of empirical studies, in defining models for their description or proposing task typologies for the development of cultural competences. However, I suggest that those studies need to apply a differentiation of competence and performance. I believe that these studies rather investigate cultural performances as the conductors cannot describe students' potential behavior in actual cultural encounters.

As a solution, one could apply the term 'performance' instead of competence, although this seems to be one step back from what has been suggested in the debate about outcome orientation and competence models. However, 'performance' is able to withstand certain criticism that distinguishes in-class behaviour from a transfer to daily life. Furthermore, in-class performance could indeed be assessed. Although this argument may lead the empirical study of cultural competences into a cul-de-sac, it cannot be neglected but needs to be taken into account. Appropriate conclusions need to be drawn for further developing empirical research tools in the context of cultural teaching methodology.

Moreover, the objectives of teaching and learning English gain a deeper level in that the concept of the "intercultural speaker" (cf. Byram/Zarate 1996) can be extended to a "cultural mediator." Burwitz-Melzer states that learners are supposed to use English as a lingua franca to be able to talk to all members of the respective countries (cf. 2003, 52). A near native language competence which was supported before Byram's 'intercultural speaker' became popular can therefore be challenged anew, as it remains a "myth" (cf. in ibid.). For Risager, the ideal objective of ELT is to develop a mediator's competence. The term 'mediator' was already encountered in Byram's descriptions of ICC and is here extended to using the foreign language as a contact language in all kinds of situations characterized by cultural and linguistic complexity; among others also as a lingua franca in international and interethnic communication (cf. Risager 1998, 249, also in Burwitz-Melzer 2003, 52). Kordes considers a "cultural mediator" to be someone who is able to recognize, work on and overcome sociocultural interferences which would hinder successful intercultural communication (cf. Kordes 1990, 296, also in Delanoy 1995, 289). On the one hand, cultural mediation refers to a mediation between a learners' pre-knowledge and the experiences with the other in intercultural encounters; on the other hand, cultural mediation also refers to understanding the other in terms of intercultural hermeneutics (cf. in Delanoy 1995, 289). On a pragmatic level, cultural mediation entails interactions in which partners attempt to understand each other's cultural meanings (cf. ibid.) – the broader a learners' understanding of culture and alterity, the more they are likely to engage successfully in encounters with alterity. Mediation, therefore, needs to be understood on a linguistic and a cultural level.

Setting tasks for intercultural learning has proven to be difficult as especially the affective and pragmatic levels can hardly be reliably reached in institutionalized language education and standardized classrooms. As the critical discussion of applying cultural learning in classrooms revealed, extended methods and approaches to reflect upon alterity can be beneficial for engaging students with alterity more profoundly. Freitag-Hild's typology of tasks for intercultural learning (cf. 2010, 120-121) is useful for this scope, but in my line of argument it is rather difficult to be applied to transcultural learning. A typology of tasks for transcultural learning needs to withstand criticism such as social desirability and a focus on an ethnic other. As the examples show, tasks and methods are needed which allow students to reflect upon their ideas honestly and without fear of negative consequences. Classroom reflections are needed during which students can become aware of their opinions and decide which of these are to be made visible and which responses they would rather keep to themselves. I believe that when meeting these demands, it is more likely that students develop a sense of alterity and self beyond pity and stereotypical assumptions about otherness.

I also believe that using methods like "Fold Your Answer" has beneficial consequences for students' identity formation. When they note down different opinions on the inside and outside of their folded papers, they become aware that they have these differing opinions, and that for certain reasons they do not want to share the opinions on the inside. They are likely to think about reasons that prevent them from sharing this hidden opinion – moral, personal, political etc. – and to reflect upon these critically.

Similarly, students could begin to reconsider these opinions once they formulated them in writing. The approach of this method to identity formation reflects a tendency toward recognizing non-participation as features of identity construction. As Wenger argues

> [w]e not only produce our identities through the practices we engage in, but we also define ourselves through the practices we do not engage in. Our identities are constituted not only by what we are but also by what we are not. […] what we are not can even become a large part of how we define ourselves. (1998, 164)

When the secret reflection of literary texts and otherness is seen as a form of non-participation, then one could argue that such tasks even need to be integrated in language teaching as this invitation to non-participation offers a direct chance to support identity formation.

However, it is also possible that this leads to undesired consequences for and directions of identity formation and that this method may not cause hidden opinions to be revised. Yet, such a procedure offers a thought-provoking perspective on in-class reflections and food for thought for engaging classroom discussions. "Fold Your Answer" could turn uncertainty about socially acceptable reactions into a central element of ELT as this method facilitates processes of acknowledging personal and socially desired opinions and reflecting upon their evolution.

Despite the advantages of these methods, they do not offer a solution for the assessment of cultural competences. I still believe that tasks that speak to the affective and pragmatic level of cultural competences, indifferent whether 'inter'- or 'trans,' can only offer limited information about students' cultural competences, because students are aware of public opinions that are accepted in a society. Therefore, the assessment of cultural competences needs to identify a certain scope of expectations and competence descriptions. If these are to be reliable, I assume that the respective tasks should be based on analytical procedures as these tend to be more objective. Additionally, although tasks that focus on the cognitive level of cultural competence need to be seen critically, as otherness and other cultures are dynamic, fluid and undergo constant processes of construction, de-construction and re-construction, I have argued that these are the most reliable sources of valid assessment.[170] Whenever affective and pragmatic levels of cultural competences are addressed, a certain distance to drawing conclusions about the learner's competence development is necessary. Moreover, an assessment of cultural competences should be based on a diagnosis (cf. chapter 2.3.3), which, however, faces the same limitations as tasks for developing cultural competences.

This differentiation of assessing cultural learning and aspects of diagnosis are also included in Burwitz-Melzer's suggestion of a reading competence model, which became necessary because literary and cultural competences play too minor a role in the CEF, educational standards and further national guidelines (2007, 127-136, cf. chapter 3.1). In this model, reading competence is divided into five sub-competences:

- motivational competences,
- cognitive and affective competences,
- intercultural competences,
- competences of communication about the text, and
- reflexive competences. (ibid., 138)

Although these are distinguished in the model, Burwitz-Melzer emphasizes that the different fields overlap and are highly intertwined (ibid.). For each of those

---

[170] Despite the central role of the affective and pragmatic level of cultural competence, cognitive or declarative knowledge could be ascribed certain validity. When students know about certain cultural procedures and apply this knowledge in intercultural encounters, this could prevent misunderstandings and conflicts in the first place.

areas, she describes objectives for seven task domains of working with texts in the classroom:

- building up and keeping expectations,
- individual and inter-individual construction of meaning,
- aspects of literary analysis (rhetoric, characteristics of narrative and genre),
- developing cultural and intercultural competences,
- developing research competences,
- text production, and
- presentations and performance. (ibid., 139, 144)

The resulting matrix[171] is not only highly complex, but can also be seen as an important step to answer the need for a more concrete representation of literary and cultural competences in official guidelines and classroom practices (cf. also in Lütge 2012b, 197).

As literary and cultural learning can hardly be clearly differentiated and the model could be extended to cultural learning, I consider this model very useful for further explorations of operationalizing both fields. Furthermore, the model is open and dynamic in that it does not set an order or hierarchy of certain areas or assumes to be complete (ibid., 138, 139). It offers various advantages such as basing competences on psycho-linguistic skills in dealing with literary texts (ibid., 138) and making learners' and also teachers' evaluation of competence development possible (ibid., 139). I believe that the formulation and operationalization of learning and teaching objectives (ibid., 138, 139), and especially the usability of this model as a basis for assessing literary and cultural competences (ibid., 138) are the most significant advantages.

Within the reading competence model, Burwitz-Melzer points out that the cognitive and affective sub-competences and the competences of communication about the text can usually be evaluated and graded. For those, manifold objective criteria can be found (cf. ibid., 143). In comparison, motivational competences cannot be graded as these include personal dispositions; some students may not be used to literary texts and motivation to read is, therefore, a rather high demand. Nevertheless, teachers can support and praise motivation and

---

[171] For example, the matrix describes the sub-competence 'motivation' for the domains of constructing meaning and literary analysis as 'The learners should be able to independently remain motivated even when the reading and working process is not linear and demands various intense readings of the text. In this and further reading phases they should understand that they are able to decode literary texts based on their world knowledge and their personal experiences' (Burwitz-Melzer 2007, 141-142). The sub-competence 'intercultural competence' for the domain 'research competence' is described as 'They should be able to independently find further material of specific cultural information about the other culture in the text in the foreign language' (ibid., 142).

give feedback so that students' motivation could increase (cf. ibid.). Similarly, also reflexive sub-competences should be excluded from grading but should rather offer students the chance to evaluate their individual reading and learning processes (ibid.). For intercultural competences Burwitz-Melzer offers a similar distinction as I suggest, stating that it is relatively easy to assess and grade cultural knowledge,[172] while the assessment of changing perspectives is more challenging because it includes a certain level of social and moral maturity. While this level should be acknowledged, its assessment is not advisable (ibid., 144). Yet, personal opinions, especially when they are politically incorrect or morally questionable, should be reflected and commented in the classroom but should not be evaluated with a grade (ibid.).

This complex, dynamic and open model of reading competence can be transferred to cultural learning as it describes similar areas and domains. Therefore, it offers a beneficial foundation for classroom procedures. Still, the model needs to be extended in order to be applicable for lower classes and all language levels.

Even though transcultural learning focuses on similarities between self and other and negotiates meaning based on identity features that are common for both, this approach should not lead to an assimilation of the other or to assumptions that negate differences between both. Perceiving of the other as the other should not be overcome; rather, the other should be experienced as enriching the self. In order to engage in "fusions of horizon" (cf. chapter 1.1), the other needs to be preserved as the other who can respectfully be approached and approach the self. If ELT leads to universalizing or ignorant attitudes in students, transcultural learning has missed its objectives. This understanding of otherness should also be included to new approaches to teaching cultures. Hunfeld labels this approach "the normalcy of the other" as he explains that in modern Europe (and beyond, I would add), the other is no longer the stylized exotic, the exaggerated ideal, the reduced inferior, the exploited, the enemy or the subjected colonized. Rather, the other has become a daily experience. Self and other are dynamic and open for mutual influences (cf. Hunfeld 1997, 2, Hunfeld 1991, 1992, 1997, 2004).

However, if students are to recognize this, labeling the other as other could already be problematic as it establishes a boundary and distance that clearly differentiates the self from the other. Although this is necessary to encounter others and negotiate meaning in the first place, I believe the terms 'alterity' or 'difference' as they were used time and again throughout this chapter are more useful for developing transcultural competences. 'Alterity' opens the scope to shades of otherness beyond ethnic and national frames that often seem to be assumed in TEFL research.

---

[172] As mentioned earlier, this also finds limitation in view of the complexity, hybridity and dynamics of cultural knowledge.

This reflection about renegotiating alterity rather than otherness also leads me to renegotiate selected objectives of cultural learning (cf. indicated in chapter 7.2.2). In chapter 9, I suggest extending the competence cluster of cultural learning to incorporate 'identity competence' and 'awareness of alterity.' These could help to clarify processes of identity formation and understanding alterity, setting tasks and assessing outcomes. Although it seems to appear as a lowering of the current objectives of cultural learning, I argue that EFL classrooms can reach this level of education more realistically.

9. Critical Discussion and Perspectives

Based on the discussion of understanding otherness, its complexities, potentials and challenges for and in ELT, I suggest a different focus on the teaching objectives for the broad field of cultural learning. As analysed in chapters 7 and 8, some of the common assumptions of cultural learning appear in a different light when certain perspectives from philosophy, psychology and teaching methodology are taken into consideration. In the context of developing cultural competences based on young adult literature, this has specific consequences for identification, the depiction of otherness and respective classroom procedures. It also implies that ICC as a main objective of ELT needs to be re-evaluated and altered. Therefore, I would like to suggest 'identity competence' and 'awareness of alterity' as additional objectives of ELT.[173]

As a starting point, one could step back from the complex concepts mentioned above and ask more basic questions:

- In how far are students who search for identity and try to come to terms with themselves able and open to encounter and understand othernesses to the extent current TEFL scholarship indicates?
- What do students gain from transcultural perspectives, when they are in a phase of their lives in which they try to transform their adolescent identity to adult identity and sway between being different from others and being part of larger groups and subcultures?

Young people who are confronted with developing ICC and understanding otherness are often caught in a binary of establishing their own self independent and in separation from others while simultaneously wanting to be part of a group identity: "[i]dentity is about belonging, about what you have in common with some people and what differentiates you from others" (Weeks 1990, 88). Possible reactions to this issue could include statements that move beyond inter- or transcultural competences and take competences more directly into account which help young adults to develop their personality while facing a multitude of different local and global influences.

As students need to be prepared for a reflective and enlightened membership in multicultural societies, I believe that understanding otherness needs to be supplemented with an awareness of the general norms and values of societies which would enable them to critically participate in creating their individual futures. This in turn makes it possible for learners to create satisfactory communal life worlds. While this seems to sound similar to current notions of inter-

---

[173] Such alternative perspectives are anything but new in TEFL research. One recent development, for example, regards a global lens through which language education is seen and which is increasingly introduced to TEFL discourses (cf. Antor et al. 2010, Delanoy 2012, Flechsig 2000, Hammer 2012b, Lütge 2012a, Volkmann 2010).

and transcultural competences, I reflect upon identity competence and awareness of alterity in broader terms. I argue for specific sub-competences for both based on previous elaborations on the depiction of otherness in literature in ELT and its effects on students. This discussion is rounded off with reflections upon a conceptualization of cultural learning that is suitable for the 21st century, an outlook to teachers' competences and desiderata for future research.

9.1 Potential and Consequences of Teaching Culture: Identity and Alterity

Self and other are characterized by diverse social, physical, gendered, ethnic, racial and ability-based formations of identity. As the reflections upon inter- and transcultural learning revealed, especially transcultural approaches take the self more strongly into consideration and open new perspectives on various degrees of alterity. Compared to current conceptualizations of transcultural learning, I would like to put more emphasis on the learner's perception of the self in relation to alterity and describe this additional sub-competence as 'identity competence.'

Additionally, it is striking that transcultural learning aims at raising awareness for the dynamic, hybrid and heterogeneous character of cultural identity on the one hand, but on the other hand hardly goes beyond perceiving the other as an ethnic other. In contrast to understanding otherness, this aspect leads to suggesting 'awareness of alterity' as an extended set of competences within a transcultural scope. Yet, both identity competence and awareness of alterity are connected to established objectives of cultural learning.

The exploration of cultural literacy (cf. chapter 1.2.2) has indicated that cultural competence in the 21st century needs to be seen in more complex ways than it currently is. Still, even in this concept the underlying perspective on culture can be criticized and challenged for its separating notion and implicit limitation to ethnicity and nationality. Yet, for the transcultural focus that I suggest, culture needs to be understood in broader terms to include various forms and realizations of identity.

9.1.1 Identity Formation and Identity Competence

Some scholars[174] assume that reading literature has the potential to enrich read-ers' personality and to beneficially contribute to their identity formation. In ELT, such processes are often supported through reading multicultural and postcolonial texts based on which students are asked to develop empathy for the protagonists and to understand their identity struggles. It is assumed that by changing perspectives and experiencing protagonists' challenges, learners take some of these in, learn from these challenges and apply the newly gained in-sights to their own lives. Narrative texts are especially accessible for such pro-cesses as these include protagonists' involvement in plots, different points of view, conflicts on various levels, and negotiations of identity issues based on which readers may fill empty spaces and interpret and understand texts (cf. Iser 1994, chapter 2). Yet, as I critically reflected earlier, such procedures find limi-tations, for instance, regarding the text base (cf. chapter 7) and, as the following elaborations show, also regarding further details of identity theory and devel-opment.

Identity and identity formation are interdisciplinary fields which have caused various debates and discussions, for example in structural (Erikson, Freud, Mead) or narrative psychology (Sarbin). In foreign language research, one of the early and detailed accounts is provided by Fäcke (2006) who ap-proaches this topic in view of philosophical accounts of subjectivity. She elabo-rates on the construction of the subject and its dependency on and integration in contexts (Descartes) and the dissolving of the subject in discourse (Foucault), as well as a differentiation of self and other (Lévinas e.g. 1987). From this en-gagement with subjectivity and context one can derive that the subject only be-comes the subject through active and critical negotiations of meaning with other subjects and contexts (Fäcke 2006, 32, also in Bredella 2010d, 32 in reference to Nothdurft 2007, 111). This is particularly interesting for cultural learning, as a certain other is necessary, not only as a partner of constructing meaning, but also as a point of references for self-awareness.

Although I will hardly be able to present a concise account of identity research of the past decades, the following section aims at reflecting upon se-lected insights as to point at some of the foundations and challenges of identity research in connection to foreign language teaching and learning. I first reflect upon some of its key positions from neighbouring fields and TEFL theory which will then lead to a relativization of the current position of identity for-mation in TEFL research. This discussion results in critically arguing for identi-ty competence as a new part of the competence cluster.

Identity can have individual and collective connotations. It refers to a person's awareness of his or her differentiation to other people or to another

---

[174] E.g. Bredella (2002, 2010b, 2010c), Bredella/Christ (2007), Bredella/Meißner /Nünning/Rösler (2000, ix-lii), Burwitz-Melzer (2003, 2013b), Löschnigg/Löschnigg (2009), Reichl (2013), Surkamp/Nünning (2008), and Thaler (2008).

group. In a different distinction, Norton refers to "social identity" and "cultural identity," whereas the former "refers to the relationship between the individual and the larger social world, as mediated through institutions such as families, schools, workplaces, social services, and law courts" (1997, 420), and the latter "to the relationship between individuals and members of a group who share a common history, a common language, and similar ways of understanding the world" (ibid.). In both it is important to emphasize the heterogeneity and the dynamic character of the groups and individuals (cf. ibid.). Thus, I believe that identity needs to be understood in the plural. As described earlier, forming identity is a lifelong process that varies according to differing influences and negotiations across boundaries of space and time, and that identity cannot become "a forced issue, a stance to be taken or a choice to be made" (Hoffman 1996, 558). The difficulty of dealing with some students' lack of awareness of identity and other students' multiple identities should be taken into account when developing inter- and transcultural competences.

Identity formation describes processes of establishing a concept of self which offers psychological stability and orientation for social performance. The individual is "the product of [his or her] unique personal biography." Simultaneously, identity can vary according to the individual's company, social situation and the motivations one has, although being "by no means free to choose how [one is] defined" (Buckingham 2008, 1). Following his detailed discussion of identity as a key construct of social sciences, Block understands

> identities as socially constructed, self-conscious, ongoing narratives that individuals perform, interpret and project in dress, bodily movements, actions and language. Identity work occurs in the company of others – either face-to-face or in an electronically mediated mode – with whom to varying degrees individuals share beliefs, motives, values, activities and practices. Identities are about negotiating new subject positions at the crossroads of the past, present and future. Individuals are shaped by their sociohistories but they also shape their sociohistories as life goes on. The entire process is conflictive as opposed to harmonious and individuals often feel ambivalent. There are unequal power relations to deal with, around the different capitals – economic, cultural and social – that both facilitate and constrain interactions with others in the different communities of practice with which individuals engage in their lifetimes. Finally, identities are related to different traditionally demographic categories such as ethnicity, race, nationality, migration, gender, social class and language. (2007, 27)[175]

---

[175] A detailed analysis of the different categories that Block mentions at the end of this paragraph is followed by the essential addition that these do not "stand independent of one another in the larger general identity of a person" (2007, 42).

Post-structuralists' conceptualizations of identity and subjectivity in terms of "multiple, non-unitary, and dynamic" characteristics which "leave[s] room for the view that individuals need not be locked forever in particular positions" (Norton/Toohey 2001, 417, Block 2007 offers a similar approach) decisively contribute to the current discussion of identity formation. A fluid and dynamic understanding of identity as it is visible in Bauman's *Liquid Modernity* (2000), is relevant in my argumentation, too. As "society is being transformed by the passage from the 'solid' to 'liquid' phase of modernity" (Bauman 2005, 303), identities need to be perceived as dynamic relationships with one's cultural and social environment. Stable and invariable identities can no longer be assumed because individuals are no longer bound to certain places and inherit certain positions (cf. Castanheira et al. 2007, 173, also Hall 2000, 17). Buckingham (2008) and Hall (2000) also underline the dynamic character of identity formation when they use the term "identification" rather than identity which reflects an ongoing process of negotiation, invention and change. Certainly, such processes are complex and develop over long periods of time. In the context of postcolonial theory, Anderson describes the concept of "imagined community" which states that "the members of even the smallest nation will never know most of their fellow-members, meet them, or even hear of them, yet in the minds of each lives the image of their communion" (1991, 6).[176] As will be reflected later, this concept has also been adapted to foreign language education.

Identity refers to "how people understand their relationship to the world, how that relationship is constructed across time and space, and how people understand their possibilities for the future" (Norton 1997, 410, cf. below).[177] This understanding defines identity as a social construct that is influenced by negotiations of the self and its environment; its variability makes shifts and alterations possible. Norton's statement includes the notion that identity is directed toward a certain ideal which can be unfolded individually and in exchange with one's surroundings. However, whether this ideal can actually be reached is disputable, especially in view of sociocultural changes and challeng-

---

[176] While I believe that Bauman's and Anderson's remarks on identity formation in the 21st century are beneficial for my conceptualization of identity competence, also these can be seen critically. Whereas this globalized, postmodern and post-structural thinking of identity formation sounds reasonable, one should not underestimate the level of liquidity of former identities and societies. A detailed discussion of this issue goes beyond the focus of my work, yet, I would like to mention that humankind has always been searching for new horizons; travel and trade have for long influenced people in different parts of the world and offered insights to other cultures and lifestyles. Stressing how liquid, fluid, dynamic and in fact also multicultural societies and individuals have recently gotten should not neglect the developments of the past and the experiences of former societies. Additionally, societies such as the U.S. and Canada have been multicultural even before they were formed as nation states. If scholarship stresses the social and cultural heterogeneity of relatively recent decades, this tends to ignore that identities should have always been thought in dynamic relation to their cultural and social environment. Certainly, these developments were intensified by what is called globalization; however, they were only initiated by it to a certain extent.

[177] Norton's approach will be qualified later in this chapter.

es of the post-industrial era, and influences of power structures which are prevalent in societies and which influence options of choice, resistance and accessibility. These options are in turn characterized by a growing fragility of biographies, a reduction of stable social relations, and an increasingly multicultural and multilingual environment (cf. Küster 2010, 108).

From a transcultural perspective, Welsch conceptualizes "transcultural identity formation," which entails that

> [w]henever an individual is cast by differing cultural interests, the lining of such transcultural components with one another becomes a specific task in identity-forming. Work on one's identity is becoming more and more work on the integration of components of differing cultural origin. (1999, 199)

Yet, apart from changing markers of identity, one could also argue that identity does indeed include certain "defining constituents," which remain the same, such as "specific pictures, symbols, songs, smells, languages, myths, [or] memories" (Tunkel 2012, 116). These are considered to mark traditions and "constructed differences of communities and cultures" (ibid.). Interestingly, Tunkel sees a close connection of the transcultural and identity formation:

> To be aware of the transcultural, means to accept the flexible, fluid conception of cultural constructions that define one part of present day individual and collective identities – while the other, possibly even stronger part might well strive for at least temporary identitary stability, emotional security (however it may be achieved), and the fulfillment of (moral) values. (ibid.)

In Welsch's account individuals face manifold points of references which offer them various options for their further development based on personal attitudes, approaches and opportunities; individuals may have to negotiate various influences, take these in or reject them. Mathews labels this availability of a range of models a "cultural supermarket" (2000)[178] in which international media, advanced technology and peer groups can be considered as main references for identity formation.

Those few insights to identity formation from post-structuralism, post-colonialism and transculturalism reveal that identity work has become increasingly challenging as especially young people are exposed to numerous influences and have several possibilities of identification and alternatives from which to choose. Therefore, it is important to support and guide students in selecting from this offer and in forming identity. Foreign language education has

---

[178] Block correctly qualifies this metaphor indicating that this supermarket is no free market as not all individuals of a society have the right to make free choices, e.g. societies in which strict roles are ascribed to men and women (cf. 2007, 22-23).

specific potential for increasing identity competences, because students encounter other cultures and are therefore offered the chance to actively reflect upon different negotiations of self and other. Bonny Norton has been highly influential in this field as she, for example, adapted the concept of "imagined communities" to second language acquisition transferring it to "imagined identities":

> There is a focus on the future when learners imagine who they might be, and who their communities might be, when they learn a language [...]. Such communities include affiliations, such as nationhood or even transnational communities, which extend beyond local sets of relationships. Such imagined communities may well have a reality as strong as those in which learners have current daily engagements, and might even have a stronger impact on their investment in language learning. [...] a lack of awareness of learners' imagined communities and imagined identities could hinder a teacher's ability to construct learning activities in which learners can invest. (Norton/Toohey 2011, 422)

Lütge (2013a) refers to the potential of this concept for the theoretical foundation of language learning and identity quoting that

> [t]he theoretical constructs imagined communities and imagined identities contribute usefully to understanding SLA, because a learner's hopes for the future (or their children's future) are integral to language learner identity. For many learners, the target language community is not only a reconstruction of past communities and historically constituted relationships, but also a community of the imagination, a desired community that offers possibilities for an enhanced range of identity options in the future. An imagined community assumes an imagined identity, and a learner's investment in the target language can be understood within this context. (Norton/Toohey 2011, 415, also in Lütge 2013a, 168)

Research like Norton's often focused on second language learner identities, on identity in terms of investment and took the relationship of learner and teacher or learner and learner into account.[179] Yet, also beyond assumptions about investment in language learning and identification with a future language community, identity and identity formation is an upcoming and diverse field in TEFL theory. This can, for example, be seen in the recent publication of *Identität und Fremdsprachenlernen – Anmerkungen zu einer komplexen Beziehung* (Burwitz-Melzer/Königs/Riemer 2013). Of the articles relating to different as-

---

[179] Cf. Alsup (2010), Block (2007), Castanheira/Green/Dixon/Yeagerb (2007), Grimm (2009), Kramsch (1993, 2009a, 2009b), Mercer (2011), Norton (1997, 2000, 2001), Norton/Toohey (2011), and Toohey (2000).

pects of identity formation in ELT, Blell's (2013), Burwitz-Melzer's (2013b) and Lütge's (2013a) are of special interest to the context at hand as these refer to literature and identity in the English classroom specifically (cf. below).

Kramsch's scholarship on language learning and forming an identity in a 'third space' between the culture of the self and the target culture is one foundation for the current approach to identity formation and reading literature in ELT. Yet, certain implications like describing a 'culture of the self' are not free of challenges. Hoffman, for example, questions in how far people possess a certain culture (cf. 1996, 557, cf. chapter 7.1.1). She agrees with post-structural perspectives, too, which emphasize identity as contextual rather than property of the individual (cf. email to G.A., July 31, 2011). Apart from the conceptualization of "every student has a culture" in terms of power and control that derive from ownership and property rights, Hoffman challenges the

> one-to-one relation between self and culture characterized by a clear, fixed, commitment to a particular cultural or ethnic identity. In this model, gaps or points of nonconformity, degrees of distance, freedom, or flexibility that do in fact characterize identity in the real and infinitely more complex world of culture as it is lived are absent. (1996, 557)

Notwithstanding the relevant connection of literature and identity formation, I believe that there is a tendency to automatically assume that using literature in ELT influences learners' identity formation as a matter of course and that the complexity of this issue tends to be underestimated (cf. above). Certainly, identity formation is a highly complex field, especially because it draws from various interdisciplinary fields and scholarships such as sociology, philosophy, social science, postcolonial studies, cultural studies, feminist studies, queer studies and recently also TEFL theory (Burwitz-Melzer/Königs/Riemer 2013). Still, more detailed insights into some of these fields provide a new perspective on identity formation in connection with literature in ELT.

The elaboration above reveals two aspects important for identity formation in ELT: a) identities are constructed in the presence of a certain company and certain contexts, and b) identity formation is a process. When literature is read in ELT classrooms, both aspects need to be taken into account and are included in my argumentation. In the previous sections I raised critical awareness for identification and identity formation as central objectives and principles in ELT, both of which are seen as justifications (but not functionalizations) for using literature in ELT.[180] Yet, despite these statements, teaching objectives that impinge on identity formation can be reconsidered based on the discussion of selected titles in chapter 5, the reflection upon balanced multicultural identities

---

[180] Cf. introduction to Part C for a relativization of a certain functionalization that could be read into such a statement.

and upon other others (cf. chapters 6.2 and 6.3). The main questions regard in how far one can assume a genuine process of identity formation in a student and whether the timely limited exposure to narrative texts may already contribute to the student's formation of identity.[181] With view of applying literature in cultural learning in ELT, it could be an over-estimation to assume that texts discussed in the EFL classroom have a direct effect on students.

In this context it is revealing to ask which features, which experiences, and which motives contribute to one's identity, what constitutes identity and what causes changes. These are thought-provoking questions, especially with regard to a pre-structured, planned and institutionalized reading of literature in ELT lessons that usually last for 45 or 90 minutes. It is challenging to conclude that even when students encounter various texts in school, a change or alteration of identity can be ascribed to the exposure to and discussion of literature as it is often proposed (cf. above). It cannot be denied that the 'third space' in language teaching gains significance as a mental space in which learners negotiate individual and collective identity in the presence of a certain other which broadens, alters or confirms horizons of the self (cf. Hallet 2002, Kramsch 1993, 2009a). Yet, it is disputable in how far the results of such negotiations also become visible as identity formations in classrooms, in how far these are rather negotiated "backstage" (cf. Goffman 1959 above), or which other experiences contribute to identity formation respectively.

Consequently, one should not disregard the difference between student and private identity, which is mirrored in the approach that I would like to apply in my suggestion of identity competence. Based on the discussion above and the limitations of empirical research (cf. chapters 2.3.2 and 8), I believe that when identity formation is focused in ELT, it is first and foremost the student-identity, the identity within the social role of being an ELT learner that is developed. Although it is difficult to strictly separate student and private identity, I assume that identity formation needs to be limited to this frame as educators cannot know which influences and lesson-contents are processed on a private level and are applied holistically; just as they cannot know whether students' cultural skills are a matter of performance or competence.

This also supports the argument to carefully draw conclusions about the success and development of identity related competences as these may not be visible in ELT. What is visible, though, is a certain performance (cf. chapter 2.3.3). Furthermore, reflections upon the self and identity formation are rather private processes, and it is questionable in how far it is ethically justified that teachers take part in, observe or even assess such processes (cf. chapter 8).[182]

---

[181] As the results of Yeoman's (1999) study with young children and their pictures of princesses revealed, even reading other texts for an extended period of time could not challenge their preference of 'white' and blond princesses and ascriptions of a good and successful life exclusively to this appearance (cf. chapter 7.1.1).

[182] Using students' expressions of empathy as a foundation to ascribe cultural competences (cf. chapter 7.1.2) can also be included in this line of argument. Byram and Zarate suggest "self-

Therefore, the central position of identification and identity formation as educational goals in ELT are put in a different light.

Despite such critical remarks, ELT does indeed offer options for identity work and certain possibilities are not to be negated. Gabriele Blell (2013) understands identity and identity formation as the development of a subjective cultural and linguistic self-concept which is dynamic but simultaneously offers psychological stability as well as continuous social and linguistic orientation for behavior by emphasizing a difference between the self and the prescribed social roles (cf. 2013, 30, in reference to Assmann). Her approach to the specifics of language learning and identity in the context of literature and culture in ELT thus echoes Lütge's (2013a) process dimensions of identity formation. Blell's reference to Keupp's "Identitätsarbeit" (identity work) reflects the difficult and complex task of identity formation for young people in a post-industrial and increasingly multicultural world. In order to integrate identity work into ELT, Blell suggests process- and product-oriented approaches to narratives. She notes that young adult fiction is beneficial because students can trace the development of the protagonists' identity and see how they deal with conflict situations and personal challenges (2013, 31-32). Additionally, ELT can offer learners the possibility to share their own narrative products and reflect upon and discuss these with their peers (ibid., 34-35).

Blell also refers to narratives as a means of identity formation in the context of portfolios in which learners document their personal development and progression (2013, 31-32). Despite the critical view that was applied to portfolios earlier in this work, in this context they may be beneficial. On the one hand, they allow students to engage with this rather personal topic as portfolios are usually kept for the learners themselves and should not be used as a base for assessment. Moreover, a number of studies have shown that students use a foreign language as a mask behind which they can hide and, thus, may participate differently in conversations and classroom discussions (cf. Dewaele/Nakano 2013, Wilson 2013).[183] Therefore, reflecting upon identity formation in a foreign language and in a private sphere may cause students to reflect upon identity formation differently than in their native language. This could also be applied to reflecting upon cultural issues in the foreign language as students may, through the other language, also feel a certain distance to their reflections. Such links could be especially fruitful for tasks in which students are allowed to keep some of their statements to themselves (cf. chapter 8).

Pluralization, fragmentation and increasingly dynamic processes of identity formation which have been pointed out in reference to Anderson, Nor-

---

assessment on the part of the learner" (1996, 242) as a solution to this ethical problem, e.g. through portfolios (Byram 1997, 93). Yet, one needs to be aware that self-assessment "presupposes a high degree of self-awareness, the ability to reflect on one's own learning and achievement, which suggests in turn a particular mode of learning and teaching" (ibid., 102).

[183] Again, this research is highly illuminating and would certainly deserve more space. The interested reader may refer to the Dewaele/Nakano (2013) and Wilson (2013).

ton and Bauman above, need to be recognized and established in ELT as well (Lütge 2013a, 165-166). As Lütge suggests, this can be achieved by perceiving of linguistic-cultural identities in the plural, by overcoming bipolar perspectives, and by relativizing unquestioned norms (ibid., 166). This mirrors my approach of not only acknowledging various degrees of alterity, but also seeing beyond stereotypical representations of ethnic otherness (cf. chapters 5 and 6). Recognizing such changed perspectives could, for example, be realized through texts that present alterity beyond clichés and preconceptions. Yet, and as Lütge correctly qualifies, identity is a concept that cannot be thought without difference: awareness of the individuality of a person is the result of being distinct to otherness (2013a, 164) and changing perspectives is only possible when someone perceives of the other as other. Therefore, reflections on otherness in ELT never aim at assimilating the other, but rather at negotiating meaning with the other and coming to terms with different concepts of being human. A further interesting notion that Lütge adds is that while education has the goal of developing learners' identity, an increased stabilization of identity could also hinder the further development of mutual acceptance and tolerance (2013a, 164).

The references to Norton's "imagined identities" and Welsch's "transcultural identity formation" above reveal that identity formation is strongly future-oriented. It is, therefore, important how learners perceive the community of the foreign language and what kind of images ELT provides. This certainly accounts for the choice of fictional and non-fictional representations in texts, too. When students integrate their opinions and knowledge of other cultures in their identity formation, teachers need to be aware of the implications that are entailed in the resources used in ELT. In this context, the development of the brain offers thought-provoking insights.

Research into psychology and the development of the teen brain suggests that the brain is not fully developed until the early 20s (Giedd et. al, 1999). During the teen years the prefrontal cortex, which inhibits actions that might be culturally or personally inappropriate, and the parts of the brain that are responsible for emotional regulations and responses to external stimuli are still in the process of being formed (cf. Alsup 2006, 3). Subsequently, students' reactions to texts can be linked to their psychological and social developmental stage. This is vital as it "enables a reader to anticipate the future direction of a narrative and fill in the 'gaps' in a text's meaning" (ibid.). Therefore, narratives or storytelling are "central to identity growth and self-perception of identity" (Alsup 2010, 2).

I would like to draw further conclusions: This link can be used to argue in favour of literature as a means to positively influence students' identity formation. Yet, this also underlines how challenging this endeavour could be as students may psychologically not be ready to process and understand certain connections and contents. When literature is read in ELT to increase cultural competences, depictions of fictional otherness are reflected at a time when the brain constructs cultural behavior and appropriateness and perceptions of cultural otherness. Depending on the images that are provided in texts, students can be sustainably influenced in their mindset of perceiving otherness. Thus, students' exposure to certain contexts can be decisive for their identity formation.

Hall points at decisive criticism: "If identity does not proceed, in a straight, unbroken line, from some fixed origin, how are we to understand its formation?" (1990, 226) Holland et al. state that "identities […] are unfinished and in process'" which encourages teachers "to regard students' identities as potential, and to experiment with activities" that offer them choices beyond "'finalized identities'" (in Norton/Toohey 2011, 429). Teachers certainly carry high responsibility for their students' identity formation. They need to be aware of their students' different imagined communities and imagined identities, and take these appropriately into consideration. Teachers need to be careful in selecting or suggesting texts on which inter- and transcultural learning is to be based. In relation to the teaching objectives, national and bi-polar perspectives should be extended by transcultural texts which pay tribute to a more holistic perception of alterity.

Based on these elaborations I believe that a common and generalizing objective of identity formation is quite bold as it is difficult to assume that teaching a specific text and using specific tasks involves diverse students, their diverse imagined identities and develops these. However, language educators need to "recognize that diverse classroom practices offer learners a range of positions from which to speak, listen, read, or write" and that "it is important for educators to explore with students which identity positions offer the greatest opportunity for social engagement and interaction" (Norton/Toohey 2011, 429). While this is certainly valid and an essential foundation for identity work in ELT, Norton's otherwise important scholarship cannot always be applied to all context of transcultural learning.

Norton focuses on second language learners (mostly adult migrants) who are motivated to learn a second language as they plan to immigrate to the target culture or already have done so, and learn the language in the target culture. I think that this offers very different prerequisites compared to young learners who learn a foreign language in schools in which it is a compulsory subject. My perspective puts students' current situations center stage rather than their imagined future identity as in Norton's approach. I would like to raise awareness for the fact that young learners participating in ELT in the middle or also at the end of their school career may not necessarily project the success of their current foreign language education on possibilities of acculturation, assimilation or integration into a target language community. While Norton sees identity as an individual projection of characteristics and motives to the future, I believe that for young learners, identity formation is happening at the moment and is only in parts consciously future directed. New influences and orientations are omnipresent and continuously negotiated, be it consciously or incidentally.

Developmental psychology sees young people, depending on their age, rather oriented at their immediate surroundings (time, space), at their interlocutors (cf. Havighurst 1972, Kohlberg 1975), or concerned with establishing stable group memberships. Although learners need to become aware of their responsibility for global issues, their immediate environment is often effected by their action first. Students' surroundings are often built by a community, which "has traditionally designated a particular form of social organization based on small groups, such as neighborhoods, the small town, or a spatially bounded locality" (Delanty 2003, 2) and which has "produced a worldwide search for roots, identity and aspirations for belonging" (ibid., 1).

Hammer (2012b), who in her work about the effects of globalization on modern foreign language education also elaborates on identity formation and texts in ELT, states that students are caught in processes of establishing identity in the face of 'glocal' connectedness and influences. This becomes apparent when a person tries to make sense of experiences within local rootedness on the one hand and balancing global influences on the other. A hybridization of identity and a plurality of identification have long been characterized as major challenges in processes of identity formation within shifting community constructions in a global sphere (cf. Bhabha 1994). One aspect of this challenge is seen in a "fear of losing identity" (cf. Breidenbach/Zukrigl 1998, 100 in Hammer 2012b, 281) as a locally bound identity formation is increasingly difficult to pursue within a simultaneous opening of locally defined borders.

Arnett regards "hybrid identities," "identity confusion" and "self-selected culture" (2000, 774-783, also in Hammer 2012b, 282, cf. Bhabha 1997a) as possible results of the multitude of local and global influences on identity formation. He estimates that the "central psychological consequence of globalization is that it results in transformations in identity, that is, in how people think about themselves in relation to the social environment" (Arnett 2002, 777). The effects of globalization can take different shapes: First, the decision and ability to live with two or more cultures, seeing part of one's identity rooted in local cultures "while another part stems from an awareness of the relation to the global culture" (ibid.). This results in bi-cultural, global and "hybrid identities." Second, "identity confusion" can occur when "people find themselves at home in neither the local culture nor the global culture" because the local culture is changing rapidly in response to globalization – this often results in an identity crisis. And third, the search for locally-bound identifications of people who "wish to have an identity that is untainted by the global culture and its values" (ibid.) can result in a "self-selected culture" (local-patriotic, nationalistic, fundamentalist) as a form of rejecting a surplus of possibilities of identification (cf. ibid., 774-783). I propose that especially when facing the "insecure conditions of modernity" (Delanty 2003, 1), students' (self-selected) communities play a significant role in their identity formation. Furthermore, it can be derived that education in general needs to guide young people in developing viable and adaptive constructs of identity as well as tools which support this development.[184]

Within these self-selected cultures learners need to be aware of the potentials and challenges involved in being drawn to certain subcultures. On the one hand, self-selected cultures can offer guidance in establishing a sense of self within global cultures that can easily become confusing and overwhelming. On the other hand, those also bear the danger of manipulating learners and leading them against democratic structures and values. An enlightened and critical reflection upon this range of subcultures is increasingly important because choices are getting more diverse. As Arnett observes, "identity becomes based less on prescribed social roles and more on individual choices, on decisions that each person makes about what values to embrace and what paths to pursue" (2002, 781).

Whereas one could assume that modern media in a globalized world offers various orientations and increases young people's exposition to alternative designs and creations of lifestyle, this globalization simultaneously supports a "cultural homogenization" (Jennings 2011, 132-134) and decreases the portrayal of alternative life paths. Additionally, a wide choice for identification does not mean that this choice becomes any easier. Within this conglomeration of pluralization, heterogenization and homogenization of influences on identity, it is important that students are given the chance to focus on the self in order not

---

[184] Additionally, Arnett assumes that "identity explorations in love and work are increasingly stretching beyond the adolescent years [...] into a post-adolescent period of emerging adulthood" (ibid., 777). These psychological consequences of globalization support the call for a new set of competences education needs to develop, yet for my account Arnett focuses too strongly on experiences of migration and cultural/ethnic otherness. However, even within such complex and manifold choices and directions of identity formation and development, students not only need to be able, but also encouraged to develop a sense of self that facilitates active and critical participation in social, political, and economic spheres, if one can assume that these exist separately. Education needs to contribute to the development of tools which are useful to students in order to navigate through different opportunities of self-fulfillment. Interestingly and if the limitation to ethnic identity is permitted for this context, Arnett's differentiation can also be transferred to fictions of migration (cf. Sommer 2001a, 2001b, Freitag-Hild 2010) as many immigration stories reflect how migrants first experience identity confusion and how they, after a certain period of time, either establish hybrid identities or form self-selected cultures, often together with other migrants from the same country or in similar situations. What I consider important in Arnett's differentiation is that it also raises awareness of possible negative consequences. When reading a text in which a member of a certain cultural group has positive or negative experiences in the process of becoming a member of the new society, this should ideally have positive influences on the students' identity formation. They should experience the benefits and challenges of life in globalized and increasingly multicultural societies as broadening their horizons. Yet, it is just as likely that students could be disturbed by what they read when they compare their own experiences to those depicted in the fictional text and may need help in order to deal with the consequences of such disturbance. This underlines that the complexity of processes of identification and identity formation are not to be underestimated. Moreover, this also emphasizes the importance of choosing appropriate texts and tasks for ELT. These need to be designed in a way that students have a chance to come to terms with possible identity confusion.

to feel lost and overcharged in global context. Hence, I would like to use the individuals and their direct surroundings as a starting point for re-considering identity formation.

As a result of increasing influences and dynamic and changing points of references that need to be negotiated, I believe that in order to beneficially integrate identity formation in ELT, identity competence needs to be regarded as a central aspect of transcultural competences and deserves a separate set of descriptions. The concept of identity competence I propose entails the competence to

- question medially conveyed representations of otherness,
- negotiate options of local and global identification in order to establish a sense of belonging,
- negotiate global influences on one's identity and sense of self,
- develop awareness of events, styles, practices and information that are part of global culture (cf. Arnett 2002, 777),
- develop the willingness to take responsibility for oneself, which also includes justifying choices and taking risks,
- balance conformity and flexibility,
- accept the engagement with alterity as a given and on a daily basis, as a matter of course,
- appreciate alterity, maintain a respectful distance and proximity to the other (avoiding assimilation),
- perceive of the other beyond his or her ethnic identity, and
- the competence and willingness to seek direct contact, establish a trustful atmosphere of true conversations and design forms of direct contact with others.

The call for identity competence can be related to Delanty as he characterizes that

> [s]trangeness has become more central to the self today, both in terms of a strangeness within the self and in the relationship between self and other. This experience of strangeness captures the essence of the postmodern sensibility, namely the feeling of insecurity, contingency and uncertainty both in the world and in the identity of the self. (2003, 133)

Based on this insecurity and continuing dynamic shifts and multiple influences on identity, students need to be equipped with skills and competences that allow them to translate these influences according to their needs, make them applicable to themselves or to reject them. They need to develop confidence to discover reliable frames within which they can navigate and take risks, and develop a sense of self. This navigation can be very difficult because "[t]he self can be invented in many ways. The contemporary understanding of the self is that of a social self formed in relations of difference rather than of unity and coherence" (ibid., 135).

Moreover, the concept of identity competence can be supported with Bauman's argumentation for a new set of skills for individuals living in 'liquid modernity.' His analysis of current challenges for educators also includes "the collapse of long-term thinking, planning and acting – and the disappearance or weakening of social structures" (2005, 304). He assumes, and I agree, that young people live in "short-term projects" which no longer merge into consistent life plans that can be described as "'development,' 'maturation,' 'career,' or 'progress'" (ibid.). This fragmentation, he states, demands a new set of skills and competences to be able to accomplish fulfilled lives despite an accumulation of episodes. One feature of such skills is the ability to test, inspect and revise past successes in the face of changing circumstances to see in how far the acquired skills are still beneficial for current situations. Moreover, the future is "now largely out of control and unpredictable" (ibid.) and "responsibility for resolving the quandaries generated by […] changing circumstances is shifted onto the shoulders of individuals" (ibid., 305). While individuals may be free in their choices, they also have to take the risks that are entailed in those choices. The concept of identity competence reflects those aspects and emphasizes that students need to be able to adjust their life concepts and projects to increasingly unreliable and insecure circumstances and developments.

To some, identity competence as suggested above may seem self-evident and obvious, but identity is too important to be left at the margins of reflecting upon transcultural learning. In times in which societies are increasingly diverse and young people have the possibility, and no other choice but to derive identity from manifold models and have to make use of various options, it is essential that they are competent in making decisions, in locating identity in transcultural frames. Identity competence is essential because global changes contribute to "a sense of fragmentation and uncertainty, in which the traditional resources for identity formation are no longer so straightforward or so easily available" (Buckingham 2008, 1). Furthermore, it is important to acknowledge that respectful treatment of alterity, open-mindedness and participation in creating a fulfilled life start with the development of a sense of self that then can be extended toward others (cf. awareness of alterity below).

"Despite teachers' best intentions […] pedagogical decisions can reinforce subordinate student identities, and limit students' access not only to language learning opportunities, but also to their imagination of more desirable identities" (Norton/Toohey 2011, 430). This statement links identity formation to certain decisions that are made in classrooms and, thus, supports my call for implementing texts in ELT that depict balanced multicultural protagonists. Through the choice of texts "pedagogical practices have the potential to be transformative in offering language learners more powerful positions than those they may occupy either inside or outside the classroom" (ibid., 417). This kind of identity formation, however, is only possible when the protagonists with whom the students can identify and grow are not only presented in victim positions but as balanced heroines and heroes as well. Otherwise, narrative constructions of identity, as classified above, only develop along limited lines and do not offer balanced re- and de-constructions of alterity and self.

In order not to lose a sense of self, learners need to gain the competence to come to terms with local identity constructs that change due to global and transcultural influences; they need to be able to cope with constant triggers of self-reflection. This entails a negotiation of meaning in the face of global media, growing and globalized economic sectors and new forms of communication. When acknowledging such changes, learners need to be enabled to select aspects they may incorporate in their hybrid identities and reject others. Being aware of, dealing with and negotiating meaning of hybridizations of identity is the central aspect of identity competence.

9.1.2 Awareness of Alterity

Similar to identity formation, understanding otherness has been described as a central element of cultural learning (cf. chapter 1). Yet, as I reflected throughout this work (cf. chapters 1.1.1, 2.1.1 and 7.1.2), this objective faces criticism on various levels. This regards whether understanding otherness is possible or not, or whether a balance between both positions can be found. What is essential for applying understanding otherness to classrooms is that "processes of understanding usually go unnoticed, since they are automatic and therefore not usually consciously experienced, while a failure to understand is something that people notice as unpleasant and disconcerting" (Reichl 2013, 109). Reichl additionally states that

> [i]f understanding was a straightforward process, a normative one and one with a clear single outcome, there would not be much room for individual or intersubjective learning and construction processes, which are the basis for a realization of the meaning potential as well as the basis for a discussion of the processes involved in understanding. (ibid.)

As I point out in the following, a critical perspective on understanding otherness can be unfolded in different directions.

Just as identity and identity formation are dynamic and flexible constructs and lifelong processes, otherness and understanding otherness need to be seen as non-static, fluid and continuing processes as well. This indicates that the objective of understanding otherness in cultural learning may not only need to be adjusted to various othernesses that students engage with, but may also be revisited after new steps of identity formation have been taken. As self and the other are open to change and further developments, it is challenging to assume that a student has understood a dynamic other – this process continues and demands an ongoing negotiation of self and otherness.

Apart from the problematic constitution of subjectivity and the relation of self and other pointed at above (cf. Fäcke 2006), understanding otherness entails a logical problem, too. When the understanding process results in the perception of too close a familiarity and intimacy, it reduces the other's independent character and negates the other as a meaningful partner in conversations.

> When I think I know, when I think I understand the Other, I am exercising my knowledge over the Other, shrouding the Other in my own totality. The Other becomes an object of *my* comprehension, *my* world, *my* narrative, reducing the Other to me. What is at stake is my ego. (Todd 2011, 73, emphasis in original)

Understanding otherness should not lead to a negation of otherness as it is debatable in how far the other still exists if it is understood. In order to perceive someone as other, differences need to be recognized as these define otherness (cf. Lütge 2013a, cf. above). Too much empathy or a naïve understanding of the other's complexity can reduce the other in its otherness and move it into an even stronger object position than it may already be ascribed. However, in educational discourses students are expected to learn not only about but also from otherness. Therefore, the other needs to remain the other to a certain extent; the other should be permitted space to remain mysterious and secretive, as this offers incentives to further engage with the other. This position sheds light on the value of otherness and that understanding otherness, while possible, should not be the final objective.

Beyond inter- and transcultural perspectives on understanding otherness, the relevance of otherness needs to be acknowledged in intra-cultural encounters as well. A so-called "lighthouse perspective" sees cultural education "as something you do abroad" (Stier 2003, 83). By standing "at the top of the lighthouse and look[ing] towards the foreign, exotic countries on the horizon" students observe cultural identities and otherness in a distance. This may cause them to ignore the cultural diversity "at the foot of the lighthouse – in [their] immediate environment" (ibid.). Yet, societies are becoming increasingly diverse and students need to be enabled to acknowledge and respect such changes and plurality within.

However, as I pointed out in connection to the development of cultural competences, also in dealing with otherness students may actually already be very competent and perform understanding otherness on a high level based on their daily experiences. Cultural learning may problematize otherness in the first place, and classroom scenarios of understanding otherness may indeed focus students' attention on an 'other' they may not have identified as such before.

Therefore, education should be highly sensitive with ascribing otherness and assuming a certain level of cultural competences.

The aforementioned arguments lead to the conclusion that understanding otherness is too advanced and abstract, and also too vague an objective to be reached in ELT. If understanding otherness is seen in its philosophical and ethical complexity, one could even argue for its rejection as an objective of ELT as its strict interpretation could entail negating the other instead of approaching it in its diversity and respectfully acknowledging its dynamic and complex process character. Yet, negotiating cultural identities is one of the central features of cultural learning and needs to be implemented in ELT. Therefore, I would like to suggest 'awareness of alterity' as an alternative and extended objective of cultural learning.

The term "alterity" was coined by Lévinas:

> [I]n the very heart of the relationship with the other that character-
> izes our social life, alterity appears as a nonreciprocal relation-
> ship... The Other as Other is not only an alter ego: the Other is
> what I myself am not. The Other is this, not because of the Other's
> character, or physiognomy, or psychology, but because of the Oth-
> er's very alterity. (1987, 83)

For my concept of awareness of alterity, alterity implies a more holistic view on otherness and a more respectful and modest approach. Rather than assuming an understanding of otherness, awareness leaves students space for certain gaps of understanding and allows them to gradually approximate alterity. A similar, rather careful approach is reflected when Volkmann qualifies intercultural alterity competence developed by Bredella. Bredella's concepts entails an understanding of otherness from within, the interpretation of the other culture not based on values of the self but based on cultural norms and values of the other culture. However, this could only be described in theory and would be doomed to failure. In reality it would only be possible to gradually approximate to the utopia of understanding otherness (cf. Volkmann 2010, 131). Awareness of alterity entails that otherness can exist in its difference and that the self allows itself to use "the time, the space, and the opportunity to appreciate the stranger without and within" (Schutte 1998, 61).

For Antor (2002) the concept of alterity to define alterity competence entails strong notions of understanding the self; intercultural dialog can only exist between two or more cultures. For him, a one-sided effort of understanding otherness without a simultaneous reflection of the self and its own cultural roots would negate one part of the dialog – hence my focus on identity competence in the previous chapter. A constructive and intercultural exchange and the resulting negotiations of meaning are only likely when it is possible to share and convey both cultural points of view. These exchanges are characterized by plurality (cf. Antor 2002, 144). Antor's concept differs from intercultural learning in that it explicitly focuses on understanding the other, understanding the self, awareness of plurality and self-reflection. In his concept of alterity competence he also includes moments of hesitation when he claims that certain expectations of intercultural contacts are too idealistic and too naïve. These expectations may lead to disappointment and, as a consequence, to negative experiences and memories of the cultural encounter (cf. Antor 2007, 116).

What is more, and what offers a point of reference for my suggestion of awareness of alterity, is Antor's inclusion of a hermeneutic competence as a sub-competence to alterity competence. With this he goes beyond a mere understanding of otherness but focuses on a mutual conditionality of identity and alterity, and includes an "enlightened viewpoint" which would be more important than openness and tolerance toward others. An "enlightened viewpoint" implies that the self has established a certain position, but is still open for new experiences, however not in the sense of a total accommodation of and to the other (cf. ibid., 118-119). This idea mirrors Gadamer's "fusion of horizons" (cf. chapter 1.1); the horizons of self and alterity may partly overlap and find similarities, but both do not merge completely. Rather, both horizons are extended and altered. Awareness of alterity as I like to suggest is similar to Antor's alterity competence, yet, I do not assume, or prescribe, an understanding of alterity on the side of the students.

Awareness also takes centre stage in Schulz's suggestion of five fundamental objectives of cultural learning:

1. Students develop and demonstrate an awareness that geographic, historical, economic, social/religious, and political factors can have an impact on cultural perspectives, products, and practices, including language use and styles of communication.
2. Students develop and demonstrate an awareness that situational variables (e.g. context and role expectations, including power differentials, and social variables such as age, gender, social class, religions, ethnicity, and place of residence) shape communicative interaction (verbal, non-verbal, and paralinguistic) and behavior in important ways.
3. Students recognize stereotypes or generalizations about the home and target cultures and evaluate them in terms of the amount of substantiating evidence.
4. Students develop and demonstrate an awareness that each language and culture has culture-conditioned images and culture-specific connotations of some words, phrases, proverbs, idiomatic formulations, gestures, etc.
5. Students develop and demonstrate an awareness of some types of causes (linguistic and non-linguistic) for cultural misunderstanding between members of different cultures. (2007, 17)

Remarkably, Schulz's objectives include references to various degrees of alterity, which provides an understanding of culture in holistic terms, similar to what I suggest. Additionally, instead of using 'understanding' which would indicate rather complex and thorough negotiations of meaning, she remains in the realm of 'awareness,' an objective which, to my mind, is more realistic and appropriate for ELT. Traces of this can also be found in Blell's and Rust's adaptation of Byram's model of ICC, in which they include "critical transcultural awareness." This entails flexibility, awareness of synergy and dissent, and "doing identity" (Blell/Rust 2012, 117).

In close proximity to Antor's and Schulz's ideas and in reaction to the limited options of understanding otherness and its evaluation in ELT, I suggest an extension of cultural competences by awareness of alterity. In this concept, understanding moves to the background, because it can cause neglect and ignorance of alterity. Awareness entails that a certain distance to alterity is acknowledged and that students are conscious about the existence of other lifestyles than their own. It also entails being alert to and recognizing the dynamic and fluid character of self and alterity. However, this suggestion does not entail neglecting or deleting the term 'otherness' from the discourse of cultural learning. Rather, awareness of alterity aims at paying tribute to several forms of othernesses and at extending its perception because otherness has often been limited to ethnic and national otherness. I believe that using alterity offers a more open and holistic concept.

The examples from Canadian young adult fiction show how varied alterity can be. As was argued in chapters 6.3 and 7.2, this alterity could be represented by family relations or egoistic characters. Furthermore, the discussions of the novels in chapter 5 illustrate the different perceptions of otherness and alterity. *Little Voice* depicts a young girl who tries to establish a balanced identity facing two different ethnic influences, First Nation and European Canadian. By tracing Ray's identity challenges which are related to her ethnic identity, readers can engage with ethnic otherness and try to understand mechanisms of exclusion and integration. They can become aware of the severity of such conflicting cultural experiences and see how both influence identity formation.

With *Run* I introduced a young adult novel that presents another form of alterity than ethnic otherness, as Terry develops the will-power and determination to run across Canada despite the amputation of his leg. This novel meets my suggestion of developing awareness of alterity because Terry stands out for his human qualities. It is disputable in how far students are truly able to understand his trials and tribulations or whether such an assumption would reduce the seriousness of his illness. I believe that it is more manageable and likely for younger learners to develop awareness for his "Marathon of Hope" and thus approach his story in a more modest and respectful manner.

The Water of Possibility can also be seen as a novel that supports raising awareness of alterity, but yet again from a different perspective. The main protagonist, Sayuri, is of Japanese Canadian descent, but instead of focusing on her quest for arrival in Canadian society or the troubles this could bring about, the novel tells the adventurous story of her discovering a parallel world in which the powers of the Patriarch threaten the peaceful existence of the other inhabitants and the security and well-being of the land. As Sayuri is not caught in challenging negotiations of ethnic identity but rather in issues of growing up and becoming an adolescent, understanding otherness is not present as in *Little Voice* or other texts that are commonly used for increasing inter- and also transcultural competences (cf. Eberhardt 2008, 2010, 2013, Fäcke 2006, Freitag-Hild 2010, cf. chapter 7). Rather, learners can develop awareness of alterity in interpreting the meaning of Japanese mythological figures or in recognizing Sayuri's behavior when she forgives the Patriarch his terrible deeds (cf. chapter 5.3). This novel and *Run* illustrate how understanding otherness in inter- and multicultural literature changes to awareness of alterity in transcultural literature (cf. chapter 7.2).

My suggestion of awareness of alterity refrains from answering the question whether understanding the other is actually possible and desirable, which I believe veils the central content of this debate. Pursuing awareness of alterity prevents a flat and superficial perception of otherness. As awareness of alterity entails sensitivity, this concept also facilitates an emotional engagement with alterity beyond shallow perceptions. Compared to understanding, awareness is more respectful as the other is not reduced to a simple understanding; it respects the complexity of alterity. The balanced conceptualization of awareness of alterity, which is still based on recognizing boundaries and hermeneutic processes of approaching self and other, reflects the relational characteristics of self and other. This leads to an enriching perception of and respectful attitude to alterity.

What is essential in this approach to awareness of alterity is that it does not entail or demand a separate investigation of various degrees of alterity but rather suggests a holistic competence that enables students to deal with alterity in general, independent of individual realizations of identity. Thus, transcultural learning scenarios could use various sample texts to develop respectful approaches to alterity and guide students in transferring this awareness to further forms of alterity they may encounter.

Discussing and analyzing current issues of inter- and transcultural scholarship in ELT and taking a critical stance toward the literature that is currently used for cultural learning, I suggested certain changes and shifts of cultural learning. The respective results also have consequences for teachers' competences, as indicated in chapter 8.1. These not only regard their methodology and choice of texts, but also their own approach to alterity.

9.2 Teachers' Competences in Transcultural Learning Environments

Crawford and McLaren warn of the dangers if "teachers feel inadequate in their knowledge of the foreign culture" or "may not have been adequately trained in the teaching of culture" (2003, 153). For them, this could lead to pushing cultural negotiations to the margins of lessons. Similarly,

> [i]f teaching about culture in the foreign language classroom is to reflect both the determination to avoid a fetishization of 'other cultures' and the willingness to engage with cultural difference, this first of all requires a corresponding approach from teachers. (Doff/Schulze-Engler 2011, 7)

If teachers are not competent to reflect upon alterity appropriately, this could lead to shallow and one-sided negotiations of meaning. The discussion about new conceptualizations of cultural learning and current changes in this field also needs to refer to teacher education, as successfully developing inter- and transcultural competences and certainly identity competence and awareness of alterity depends on the qualification of teachers.

Doff and Schulze-Engler (2011) distinguish teachers' competences into awareness, skills and knowledge, and emphasize the need that those aspects of cultural learning have to be implemented in teacher trainings as well. Likewise Paige, who takes trainers of intercultural programs into account, differentiates between knowledge, personal, behavioral, technical and situational factors as well as self-awareness, which can be transferred to foreign language teacher education. Personal factors, for example, entail a "high degree of self-awareness, recognition of one's skills limitations, [and] sensibility to the needs of the learners" (Paige/Martin 1983, 57). Furthermore, teachers need to be open to and flexible with new ideas, they need to be able to tolerate ambiguity. When developing awareness of alterity they should be patient, show enthusiasm and commitment, and take students' comments and opinions seriously. Another personal quality entails the "honest respect for the complexities, challenges, and uncertainties of intercultural learning" (Paige 1993, 193). Educators' effectiveness is positively influenced by behavioral skills such as communicative competence, "culturally appropriate role behavior and [the] ability to relate well to others" (ibid., 171). On a personal level, teachers need to respectfully deal with students' identity formation and, if necessary, be able to establish an acknowledging distance to the students and their opinions. This is especially the case if teachers apply methods in which students are allowed to keep parts of their opinions private (cf. chapter 8.2.1). These classroom procedures ask for relationships that are more intensely characterized by trust and respect for one another.

Additionally, Schulz asks in how far teachers can actually be classified as intercultural speakers (cf. Byram 1997, 59). According to the concept of ICC, learners are expected to develop a profound understanding of cultural phenomena of the other culture and to be able to link certain practices to underlying culture-specific concepts. This competence is highly complex and Schulz estimates that

> most teachers lack sufficient background knowledge and experience to determine relationships between those practices [Christmas traditions, greetings, mealtime-related etiquette] and products [Cologne cathedral, special food] and the cultural perspectives that gave (or give) rise to them. [...] To what extent are teachers (and students) equipped to make valid comparisons between the home and target cultures? What is – and who provides – the factual background data necessary to make such comparisons? (2007, 10-11)

The relevance of this background knowledge should not be underestimated: Teachers' skills and competences need to be based on extended knowledge about alterity which includes political, economic, social, cultural, demographic, religious, and historical knowledge of a group. Yet, this also refers to knowledge of mechanisms that bring about the development of subcultures, identity formation in alterity, processes of exclusion, separation, integration and assimilation. This kind of knowledge would facilitate a reflection upon alterity beyond national and ethnic identity and include various shades of forming identity, be it individual or collective.

When teachers themselves have gained these competences, it is important that they are able to transfer these to their own teaching, realized through the contents they approach, the methods they apply, and the tasks they set. Such a reflective approach also has to become visible in the assessment they conduct in their language classrooms. It is paramount for teachers to be able to design learning environments in which students can encounter alterity and diversity, and negotiate meaning. Such environments need to be "sensitive to the history of oppression, discrimination, and intergroup relations of the groups" being discussed (Paige 1993, 187) and based on knowledge of learning processes, didactic concepts and methodological tools. On a cultural level, this also entails the "capacity to provide consciousness-raising education about the nature and impact of racism, sexism, and other forms of prejudice and discrimination" (Paige 1993, 187). Schulz concludes that

> [i]mplementing the culture standards in their present form would necessitate a serious revamping of teacher education to equip teachers with the historical, social, and political insights that would permit them to critically examine attitudes, values, and beliefs and

relate these to concrete examples of products and practices in the target culture as well as their own. (2007, 11)

As teachers are to develop identity competence and awareness of otherness in students, it is necessary that they have those competences themselves; and not only on a performance level, but on a pragmatic competence level as to genuinely teach English in all its complexity and diversity. Their own understanding of transcultural learning will establish the frame for assessing the transcultural competences learners develop in lessons.

However, teachers' development of cultural competences is equally difficult to evaluate as assessment tools at university or other teacher training programs face the same criticism as cultural learning at school. "How can teachers be taught to teach openness?" and "How can it be evaluated whether they are able to do so?" are important questions which are difficult to answer. While a detailed discussion of teacher education in this cultural frame goes beyond the focus of my work, the few comments above nevertheless give insights to an important and complex field which needs more academic attention, in theory and in praxis. The critical discussion of inter- and transcultural learning in the context of Canadian young adult literature leads to further considerations for future research.

9.3 Further Desiderata for Future Research

In chapters 8.4 and 9.1 I suggested certain changes that I believe are necessary in the field of cultural learning and teaching in the 21st century. My work outlines a possible theoretical and conceptual foundation for an altered perspective on transcultural learning. As I hold the view that empirical research in this area faces challenges and that academia needs to establish a solid theoretical basis on which cultural learning can be built, I did not conduct any empirical research. However, my approach to transcultural learning, identity competence and awareness of alterity can only be seen as a first step in this direction and needs to be substantiated by classroom application and teaching experiences. A critical empirical reflection of the concepts suggested here certainly provides an important task for future research.

In order to do so, further tasks, methods and assessment tools need to be designed which allow teachers and researchers to draw conclusions about students' cultural competences. If teachers and researchers expect complex performances of cultural competences, then texts and tasks also need to reflect such complexity; and so do the research tools. TEFL research needs to design valid tools with which cultural competences can be diagnosed and investigated beyond objections such as social desirability. For now I am still doubtful about current procedures as I believe that tasks formats may perhaps raise stereotypic ideas about alterity in the first place, stereotypes that learners may not even have had before ELT focused on the development of ICC. The reflection upon the depiction of alterity in young adult fiction which culminated in a suggestion of transcultural literature and the respective tasks that I introduced could initiate further investigations.

Furthermore, discussing the perception and intersectionality of alterity triggered the question of how alterity is actually defined in multicultural societies. When children grow up with children from other ethnic backgrounds, one could assume that it is likely that they rather see differences in social status, milieu, religion, and in physical challenges, and identify alterity according to markers beyond nationality and ethnicity. In chapter 7, I posed the questions "Who is the other for young learners?" and "When does the other become the Other?" and pointed at a lack of (empirical) investigations of underlying processes from an ELT perspective. How young children and learners of ELT perceive alterity, therefore, is a promising field for empirical but also conceptual research.

In how far can further postmodern and post-structuralist conceptualizations of society and culture be fruitful for developing appropriate concepts of cultural learning in ELT? Koskensalo (2008) reflects upon the potential of transdifference for foreign language teaching and concludes that the concepts' potential for foreign language teaching and learning remains vague. Although Reiche hints at interesting points of references for transcultural learning and transdifference[185] (2011, 84-85), her investigation of African American literature in ELT remains within an intercultural frame. Which further potential is still hidden in concepts like transdifference? Delanoy's recent approaches to transcultural learning go into a similar direction as he explores the potential of the humanities for cultural learning in ELT (2011). However, I am of the opinion that research should uncover the full potential of existing concepts before entering new discussions of more recent concepts that are being developed in neighboring fields which is why I remained within the scope of transcultural learning.

A further aspect that is worth reflecting upon but which goes beyond the focus of this study regards the interplay of (trans)cultural learning and the currently striving field of global education. It could be asked whether global education will, in the long run, replace cultural learning, or whether both will remain intact as differentiated streams that follow different objectives and are based on different assumptions.

Elaborations on transcultural literature could lead to further (re)considerations of formerly canonized literature in ELT. If transcultural learning is taken seriously, 'mainstream' literature should again be focused without hesitation,

---

[185] Transdifference has been developed at Erlangen University. Among other aspects it suggests that identity and difference can be beneficially investigated through exploring how people 'do' identity (cf. Allolio-Näcke/Kalscheuer 2003).

as the transcultural does not attempt to re-establish differences of power between participants of discourse. This aspect is already visible in the inclusion of Walters' *Run* and Sillitoe's *The Loneliness of the Long Distance Runner*. Could it be that regarding critical whiteness theory, transcultural and postcolonial discourses lead toward opposite directions? I see a discrepancy in the inclusion of other others as breaking down traditional hierarchies of 'mainstream' scholarship on the one hand and an exclusion of 'whiteness discourse' on the other. If 'white' literature is omitted from transcultural reflections, such practice does not pay tribute to the fact that 'white' reflects one option for identification and one reality within multiple realities in multicultural societies. In this sense, new conceptual insights could be added to cultural learning, which are worth exploring.

In order to enrich the current selection of transcultural literature as I suggested in chapter 7.2, further children's and young adult fiction needs to be discovered and investigated for its benefits for inter- and transcultural learning. I assume that other cultural and national frames such as the Australia and New Zealand or South Africa offer similar fictions which could be as promising for transcultural learning and developing identity competence and awareness of alterity as the selected Canadian texts I analysed. For example, Niki Daly's *Once upon a Time* (2004), Justine Larbalestier's *Liar* (2009), Toni Morrison's *Peeny Butter Fudge* (2009), Nnedi Okorafor's *Akata Witch* (2011), Manjusha Pawagi's *The Girl who hated Books* (2010), Melanie Prewett's *Two Mates* (2012) or Sean Steward's *Cathy's Book* (2006) depict alterity beyond problem-laden paradigms related to the protagonists' ethnic identity.

Those questions and comments indicate that despite the many recent publications and ongoing research in the field of cultural learning and teaching, the development of inter- and transcultural competences and their empirical investigations, it still holds promises and potential for future research, be it conceptual or empirical. One of the main foci of the last years has been a balancing of standard-orientation and a more holistic perspective on education. In the context of literature and cultural learning, both have recently been brought forward by Eberhardt's (2013) suggestion of a differentiated intercultural competence model and Burwitz-Melzer's (2007) complex, dynamic and open reading-competence model (cf. chapter 8.3). TEFL theory and empirical studies of literary and cultural learning need to further investigate such approaches. As Burwitz-Melzer's model is so far only differentiated for advanced learners, it is for example necessary to extend the model to include all language levels from A1 to C2 (cf. 2007, 156).

Despite such attempts and important contributions to this field, I believe that theoretical developments of the concepts and terminologies which empirical studies work with need to be further explored and adapted to current social, political and cultural changes. Otherwise, research may lose touch with the foundations it actually investigates. TEFL research and ELT need to continue to work on a balanced perception of standard-orientation, operationalization of (cultural) competences and an understanding of holistic education. They need to establish a direction for future research that is able to combine these differing strands. In this view, I consider the extended approach to inter- and transcultural learning and the suggested differentiation of inter- and transcultural literature to be one factor that could contribute to the further investigation and research of cultural and literary learning. The following summary critically reflects upon my research of inter- and transcultural learning in the context of Canadian young adult fiction and draws important conclusions.

Conclusion

"The other has a face, and it is a sacred book in which good is recorded."
(Kapuscinski 2008, 35)

This quote alludes to the important notion that underlies my investigation of transcultural literature, identity competence and awareness of identity, namely the recognition of the other as a person and as a subject in its own right. Only if the other is approached respectfully and modestly is it possible to engage with alterity and establish a relationship from which both self and other can benefit. This connection was analysed and discussed at length in the previous chapters, which brought about remarkable new insights for TEFL theory regarding the implementation of cultural learning.

Inter- and Transcultural Learning in the Context of Canadian Young Adult Fiction was sparked by different observations in the current research of inter- and transcultural learning. Conceptualizations and practical applications of cultural learning have in the past decades taken different forms and focuses. New approaches to cultural competence can be understood as reactions to local and global developments in various spheres such as culture, society, economy and politics which have contributed to increasingly diverse lifestyles. Insights into their significance have led to a stronger reception of inter- and transcultural learning in TEFL theory, as English language education aims at preparing young people for an active and fulfilled life and participation in those spheres.

While intercultural learning is a central foundational concept of ELT, transcultural learning has entered TEFL debates rather recently. The debate whether the one or the other, or a complementary understanding of both is necessary, has not come to a satisfactory end, yet. In the context of this ongoing debate, my study adds important ideas which can help to further differentiate this branch of cultural learning.

The assumption that transcultural learning needs to be based on different – that is, transcultural – literature and texts compared to intercultural learning served as a main thesis of my research. Yet, it is important to note that my approach to cultural learning offers a further development of existing concepts rather than their replacement. The suggestion of transcultural literature does not try to set new normative standards of selecting literature but aims at adding different perspectives on alterity and new options for choosing texts for cultural learning. This new perspective on literature also entails modifications of current principles of using literature in ELT. These reflect a critical view on certain key aspects of teaching literature and culture as well as challenges of methodological procedures and assessment of cultural competences in the EFL classroom. The discussion has proven to be essential in the current debate about standardization and the validity of cultural teaching objectives which seem to evade traditional concepts of evaluation.

The argumentation to support these assumptions was built upon three main pillars represented through the three parts of my work. To lay the theoretical foundation of investigating a different perspective on transcultural learning, Part A centered on the development of conceptualizations of inter- and transcultural learning (chapter 1), and on principles, objectives and challenges that are connected to using literature for increasing cultural competences (chapter 2). Additionally, it offered a Canada-focused analysis of curricula and teaching material, and a reflection upon literatures that are currently used in and suggested for ELT (chapter 3). Part B described the development of Canadian young adult fiction (chapter 4) and provided a critical and detailed discussion of three selected sample texts (chapter 5). The options those entail for transcultural learning were summarized in chapter 6. The conclusions I drew from the interplay of teaching culture and literature in Part A and the reflections on Canadian literature in Part B were merged in Part C: a critical view on the representation of otherness in literature that is used for developing cultural competences led to investigating the potential of Canadian young adult fiction which, in turn, resulted in the suggestion of transcultural literature (chapter 7) as a basis for transcultural learning. The application of certain methods and activities to classroom procedures (chapter 8) paid tribute to an altered view on assessing and evaluating cultural competences which led to extending current concepts of cultural competences to identity competence and awareness of alterity (chapter 9).

One main result of my study is the suggestion of transcultural literature which should be applied to transcultural learning. While I showed that intercultural learning is often based upon literature in which an ethnic protagonist is depicted as struggling for a balanced identity within a malevolent society, I believe that this victim-positioning limits the protagonists to such spheres and reconstructs rather than challenges existing stereotypes. In such literature, also students are limited to perceiving the other within those spheres and need to deconstruct the protagonist's positioning. In comparison, I put forward an understanding of transcultural literature as literature which offers a different perspective and depiction of alterity. In transcultural literature, representations can take different forms, either depicting ethnic and national otherness as active members of society who have power over their own decisions and transcend intrinsic identity struggles, or representing alterity beyond ethnic and national identities altogether. This alterity can then be realized in various shades of identity, like age, class, gender or sexuality.

Using the three Canadian novels *Little Voice*, *Run* and *The Water of Possibility* as a foundation, I justifiably argued in favour of literature in which the protagonist needs to solve 'other-than-ethnicity' quests. In those books, the reader can engage with alterity beyond limited perspectives that entail stereotypes, generalisations and shallowness. In this sense, transcultural literature entails notions of empowerment, enlightenment and emancipation. *Run* and *The Water of Possibility* empower the protagonists from being victimized others based on illness or ethnic identity. Protagonists who were formerly othered are given the opportunity to emancipate from a prevalent dichotomy present in inter- and multicultural literature, while readers are emancipated from reactions of shame and pity for protagonists who are portrayed as suffering from various forms of oppression. Through my work, this alternative perspective on alterity is made part of TEFL research and ELT.

The three novels under investigation reflect a continuum from inter- to transcultural representations of alterity, a perception which allows me to locate my perspective on inter- and transcultural learning in close proximity to Delanoy's line of thought (cf. 2006, 2011, 2012). As outlined in chapters 6.1 and 9.1.2, *Little Voice* reflects the formation of a hybrid identity based on First Nation and Euro-Canadian influences which the protagonist has to balance. This narration was identified as an intercultural text because the focus lies with the protagonist's search for ethnic identity and her development of a hybridized identity as a First Nation Canadian. *Run* extends the perception of alterity to include a prosthesis-wearing and mentally exceptionally strong 'white' protagonist and a teenager who needs to find a place in his social network. In this historic fiction story Terry and Winston Jr. can both be regarded as 'other': Terry, on first sight, because of his amputated leg, but mainly because of his inner strength, will-power and determination, and Winston Jr. based on his family and coming-of-age issues. *The Water of Possibility* lifts the transcultural to yet a different level when the story revolves around a brave Japanese Canadian girl who needs to save her brother and a magical parallel world by growing beyond her wisdom and strength. Instead of suffering from different ethnic influences, Sayuri's lack of self-esteem is grounded in the beginning of puberty and moving to a new home which both cause insecurity and loneliness. While Japanese Canadian culture frames this story, it does not determine the protagonist's quest of self. Her struggle is not based on ethnic identity, but on character. In my argumentation, the diverse representations of alterity and the different developments of the protagonists' identity and self-perception in these three sample texts establish a continuum from inter- to transcultural learning and from inter- to transcultural literature.

My research revealed that the discourse of inter- and transcultural learning in ELT sees challenges in differentiating between thoese two concepts. These challenges center on positions which are in favour of intercultural learning and those that find justifications for a transcultural approach to teaching English:

- The first position maintains that intercultural learning already includes assumptions of transcultural learning and argues that this new model does not necessarily add new insights to cultural learning (e.g. Bredella 2010c).
- The second position bases the development of transcultural competences on Welsch's reflections of transculturality from which conclusions for transcultural learning are derived (e.g. Flechsig 2000).

- A third approach attempts to mediate between both concepts and does not ask whether the one or the other is beneficial for ELT, but rather elaborates on how both concepts can contribute to developing general cultural competences for the 21st century and in how far both can be linked. (cf. Delanoy 2005, 2006, 2008, 2011)

Suggesting a continuum from inter- to a transcultural paradigms, I could offer a solution for the challenge of differentiating between inter- and transcultural learning and competences. Within this discussion, I see myself closer to the transcultural sphere because in my understanding it offers a more differentiated perspective on alterity: transcultural learning transcends a perception of a so-called 'minority' as a struggler for balanced identity and pays tribute to dynamic changes and hybrid identities. This is also visible in my definition of transcultural literature.

Yet, as the diverse opinions of transculturality and transcultural competence have shown, this new approach to teaching culture not only provides a more appropriate perspective on social and political realities in the era of globalization, it also exposes challenges. For example, current societies can be characterized by a "simultaneousness of the inter- and transcultural" (Schulze-Engler 2006, 47). As pointed out, transculturality can offer a beneficial contribution to definitions of self, but at the same time many people have difficulty locating themselves in certain systems. Furthermore, the question of who is affected by transculturality, who are oftentimes people in urban centers and the younger generations, supports this assumption. Not everyone can be included in these specific groups and some may rather find themselves closer to intercultural realities. Thus, the focus on one concept exclusively would not agree to the realities in which learners live; neither interculturality nor transculturality are to be seen as universally applicable to all human experience. Similarly, neither the one nor the other could be seen as the only concept that facilitates successful cultural learning.

Delanoy goes one step further than perceiving of both concepts as complementary and generally asks where the path of cultural learning will lead. He investigates, for example, in how far Anzaldua's *New Mestiza* is applicable to cultural learning and reflects concepts such as Bauman's "liquid modernity" and Lösch's transdifference in more detail. In this conglomerate of concepts, Delanoy ponders whether we really need transculturality as a concept for cultural learning (cf. 2011). I believe that when scholarship takes social changes into consideration, is aware of the different scopes of inter- and transcultural learning, and takes the potential of transcultural literature into account, then differentiating inter- from transcultural learning is indeed beneficial and needed. Nevertheless, this debate has not come to a satisfactory conclusion. Therefore, this work contributes to the discussion by adding new incentives for reconsidering current approaches to transcultural learning and competences. Despite new developments, my scholarship remains within a terminology of inter- and transcultural learning, as I consider it to be more appropriate for the clarity of the research field to fully explore existing concepts before dismissing them when they are still in the process of gaining recognition.

The transcultural reflection of *Run* adds another remarkable notion to transcultural learning as it includes a 'white male' in the cultural frame. In secondary literature about cultural learning, the almost exclusive references to visible ethnic identities seem to indicate that Western cultures are the subjects and starting points of encountering a cultural other. This perspective has its origin in multicultural theory of Western discourses. Yet, as Western cultures are getting increasingly diverse on an intracultural level, and as this concept implies a hierarchy of Western as the norm, this perspective can no longer be justified. Rather, the group which engages in inter- or transcultural encounters itself needs to be perceived as highly diverse including various points of view from which Western cultures could be 'other'. This needs to be taken into account as classrooms become increasingly multicultural as well. Through the inclusion of *Run* in a transcultural paradigm, "being white" is made visible, whereas it used to be the "invisible norm" of cultural engagement (cf. Crawford/McLaren 2003, 145). Winston's issues can be located on a transcultural level, as he has to deal with family issues that are not exclusively identified as white middle-class issues. Furthermore, this hierarchal perspectivity of 'us – white – majority – norm' is challenged as a white middle-class Canadian man with an amputated leg is put into the position of the other, and not because he is an amputee, but because of his courage and determination. In this line of thought, critical theory[186] leaves its marks on concepts of transcultural learning. Multiculturalism is extended to include Western cultures as points of reference, analysis, observation, and interpretation. This view mirrors Kulyk Keefer's argument of applying a more inclusive term of "ethnic" within "multicultural":

> [...] while we can speak of a dominant group within Canadian society, a group comparable, in its traditional hold on power and authority, to the American 'WASP ascendancy,' that group, whether its members are of British or French descent, is as much an 'ethnos,' or distinctive people and culture, as would be a group of Ojibway or Pakistanis. How can we say that Josef Skvorecky and Rohinton Mistry are 'multicultural' while Alice Munro is just Canadian? Isn't a Scottish background as 'ethnic' as a Czech or Parsi one? (1991, 14)

With this statement, Kulyk Keefer includes writers in a literary kaleidoscope who may have been deprived of their ethnicity in order to make space for previously excluded voices. However, as the argument above states, a frame which

---

[186] For an introduction cf. Clark/O'Donnell (1999) and Lopez (2005).

excludes writers like Eric Walters would exclude important contributions to a transcultural mindset.

This assumption leads to re-considering discussions about literary canons in ELT. On the one hand, it needs to be emphasized again that with the selection of Canadian literature for young readers in chapter 5 my research neither establishes new normative requirements for texts in ELT nor does it support arguments for a new canon. Rather, it offers a critical perspective on texts that are currently used in ELT and on the respective teaching aims that result from their implementation. The text selection and the methodological approaches that are elaborated in chapter 8 indicate that a texts' potential for transcultural encounters and learning should in general be unveiled. This would, thus, make it possible to see Sillitoe's *The Loneliness of the Long Distance Runner* from a transcultural perspective as well. Moreover, a reflection upon the transcultural potential of texts also implies that formerly canonized texts in ELT, such as *Brave New World* (Huxley 1932), *Animal Farm* (Orwell 1945) or Shakespeare's works can still be relevant for transcultural learning, as their perception and interpretation could uncover transcultural features.

It is important to note that literature in ELT should not exclusively be functionalized as promoting cultural learning. Especially from a literary-aesthetic perspective, such a reduction is not justifiable. The aesthetic dimension of language learning is only marginally included in curricular guidelines (cf. chapter 2.1 and the criticism of these in chapter 3.1). However, it needs to be anchored more strongly in order to agree with a more holistic approach to teaching language and offer points of reference for a central position of literary literacy.

Certainly, the application of transcultural literature in ELT does not suggest automatisms of developing cultural competences, because apart from texts, the choice of appropriate methods and activities decides upon learning outcomes as well. With regard to methodology and assessment of cultural competences, I suggested a more profound and honest approach. I reflected what kind of answers students offer in cultural learning situations and in how far classroom procedures can have an influence on the students' identity formation. As a result, especially tasks that speak to the affective and pragmatic level find limitations in a potential transfer from classroom performance to inherited competence. It still remains questionable in how far linguistically correct and coherent essays or convincing performances in role-plays can be used as a justification to ascribe cultural competences. As students are aware of expectations of formal and institutionalized education in democratic societies, their in-class answers and opinions may often agree to what is socially desirable. Thus, the conclusions that are drawn from students' in-class performances are decisive.

With this in mind, I suggested new methods and activities which involve the students' right to have private opinions. I argued that learners need to be offered the chance to keep some of their opinions and ideas private, and be treated with respectful distance when reflecting upon personal impressions, experiences and questions of identity. Methods like "Fold Your Answer," "The Other Person" and "Agree and Disagree" differ from other methods for cultural learning as they allow learners to reflect upon cultural issues beyond the teachers' eyes and ears. These methods are applicable for younger learners and take a respectful distance toward affective and pragmatic levels of cultural learning. A further conclusion of critically investigating assessment is a re-evaluation of the cognitive level of cultural learning, as knowledge of certain cultural aspects could prevent cultural conflicts in the first place. Additionally, the cognitive level can be a foundation for assessment when its dynamic and partly subjective character is taken into account.

This new approach to transcultural literature and the methods and activities that have been suggested contributed to reconsidering teaching and learning objectives of cultural learning. In chapters 9.1 and 9.2, I put forward identity competence and awareness of alterity as extensions of cultural competences. Identity competence can be regarded as an overall objective of education in the 21st century because young people need to be enabled to critically view the manifold choices a globalized world offers. Beyond English as a lingua franca, English language education, however, holds a specific position. It is a central part of education and by definition has strong cultural connotations as students learn a foreign language that is closely connected to cultures (supposedly) different to their own. ELT needs to focus on preparing individuals who are members of fluid communities to negotiate meaning with other members of the same or other groups. A changing construction and design of life worlds also needs a changing kaleidoscope of competences which supports individual developments with respect to other individuals, none of whom are static and determined by clearly defined and similar sets of influences. Thus, people are facing a continuous threat of "disembeddment [*sic!*]" as

> few if any 'beds' for 're-embedding' look solid enough to sustain the stability of long occupation. The 'beds' in view look rather like 'musical chairs', of various sizes and styles as well as of changing numbers and mobile positions, forcing men and women to be constantly on the run and promising no rest and no satisfaction of 'arriving', no comfort of reaching the destination where one can disarm, relax and stop worrying. (Bauman 2001, 125)

Students need to be assisted in dealing with such "disembeddment [*sic!*]" which I argued is possible through identity competence and awareness of alterity.

The aforementioned extensions are reactions to a critical discussion of possibilities of understanding otherness. Understanding otherness faces various critical approaches as some positions assume that the other is the absolute other and cannot be fully understood (e.g. Derrida), some assume that the other is a relative other and can be understood (e.g. Gadamer), or some which interpret the will to understand the other as a will to power in the tradition of Foucault and Said. Furthermore, otherness could be seen as a fictional and subjective ascription, not a characteristic of alterity. Understanding the other from one's own perspective exclusively is not beneficial for a reflective understanding of otherness because it runs danger of appropriating the other or neglecting the other's complexity and individuality. I also argued that the other cannot and should not be fully understood because this would neglect and dissolve the existence of the other. The possibility of fully understanding otherness could result in indifference toward otherness and fast and shallow assumptions.

Acknowledging that understanding otherness is a challenging process can lead to conceptualizations which make it less challenging. Therefore, my research reveals that ELT should focus on developing awareness of alterity, which enables learners to respect alterity as such and to refrain from making superficial judgements about others' feelings or wishes. Awareness of alterity presents a more humble form of understanding otherness. It is neither too close to the other to negate it nor too far to assimilate it in a construct of understanding, or too far to be ignored. Being aware of one's own subjectivity and identity evidently leads to perceiving alterity. The assumptions, however, that are derived from this awareness of self and other are essential. When the other is perceived as a worthy being in itself and as a valuable contribution to the perception of self, a reflective, respectful and honest experience of the normalcy of alterity is possible (cf. Hunfeld 1991, 1992). Such processes need to be based on appropriate texts and approaches, as outlined above.

One issue that may still cause ambivalences and appear contradictory at first sight is my reflection upon inter- and transcultural learning based on a nationally defined canon – that is, Canadian literature for young readers. While the Canadian focus should be seen as an example, I argued that it can still be applied despite a 'trans' mindset. As my study shows, a nationally defined canon and transculturalism are not mutually exclusive because, in this case, Canada can serve as a basis for manifold transcultural reflections. Also in reference to ELT practice and theory, Canadian content can be justified as Canada has hardly been considered in ELT and students thus oftentimes lack basic knowledge of Canada. Furthermore, Canadian literature for young readers extends the body of literature in ELT in general. This study makes Canadian literature for young readers available for ELT and puts it into the focus of TEFL research.

This study builds a theoretical foundation for future investigations of transcultural competences and provides an important contribution to the future discourse of transcultural learning. The critical stance on classroom procedures, be it objectives, methods or assessment, unveils the necessity to define theoretical conceptualizations when implementing cultural learning in school. The literature that is used for this research goes beyond a consideration of postmodern and postcolonial approaches, but sees great value in a different depiction of complex and dynamic forms of alterity beyond ethnic or national determinations. The term alterity facilitates the recognition of multifaceted identities and various stages of identity formation.

When taking the different foci of this study together, I can conclude that it offers important insights and enhancements to TEFL research as well as to teaching practices. Teachers can benefit from the discussion of Canadian young adult fiction and inter- and transcultural learning as regards their own classroom practices. The critical perspective on methods and assessment allows them to see their own teaching in a critical light and can contribute to more satisfactory, meaningful and honest discussions of alterity with their students. Expectations of cultural learning based on literature are put into perspective, especially based on the detailed and critical account of empathy, identity formation and toler- ance. The suggestions of Canadian young adult fiction offer a new set of texts which expose students to alterity beyond problem-laden paradigms.

For TEFL research my work offers important insights to concepts of in- ter- and transcultural learning. It refers to a different kind of literature and an extended view on transcultural competences as possible solutions for the con- tinuing debates of contradictory or complementary concepts of inter- and/or transcultural learning. An understanding of transcultural literature could support an approach to transcultural learning in differentiation to intercultural learning, even when both are not mutually exclusive.

For teachers, researchers and politicians involved in laying curricular foundations for cultural learning, my discussion is useful for reviewing such curricula and guidelines of developing cultural competences and for teaching English. Although transcultural topics and global issues are anchored in guide- lines already, current suggestions of literature remain within existing preconcep- tions of otherness and a paradigm that represents the other as an ethnic other searching for balanced ethnic identity. This needs to be altered, because such depictions limit multicultural protagonists to struggler- and victim positions and do not reveal how a constructed distance to this ethnic other is overcome. This, however, would be especially important in multicultural societies.

Using concepts of transculturality, reader-response theory and identity for- mation as a basis, I was able to demonstrate how essential a role the choice of literature for cultural learning processes plays. As a result, this work demands a more critical perspective on central concepts of teaching literature and culture in ELT, and asks for sensitivity toward sociocultural changes which apply more strongly to societies in the 21st century. Based on a perception of transcultural as including various forms of alterity beyond national and ethnic identity and the different perspectives on depicting alterity, this study suggest transcultural liter- ature as a foundation for transcultural learning. The consequential extended view on methodology, the critical remarks on assessing and evaluating cultural learning, and the extension of teaching objectives pay tribute to the challenging but nevertheless central position both identity formation and awareness of alteri- ty play within the concept of cultural competences. When such shifts contribute to reflective negotiations of cultural encounters, these not only mirror the complexities and dynamics of self and other, but may also motivate students to leave the classroom saying "Hey, that was about me!"

Bibliography

I. Primary Literature

Abish, Walter (1980). *How German is it*. New York: W.W. Norton & Company.

Achebe, Chinua (1972). "Akueke", in: Achebe, Chinua. *Girls at War, and Other Stories*. New York: Anchor Books, 1991, 31-36.

Alvarez, Julia (1991). *How the Garcia Girls Lost Their Accent*. New York: Algonquin Books.

Atwood, Margaret (1985). *The Handmaid's Tale*. Toronto: McClelland & Stewart.

Atwood, Margaret (1988). *Cat's Eye*. Toronto: McClelland & Stewart.

Atwood, Margaret (2003). *Oryx and Crake*. Toronto: McClelland & Stewart.

Arato, Rona (2013). *The Last Train: A Holocaust Story*. Toronto: Owlkids Books.

Armstrong, Jeannette (1982). *Enwisteetkwa* (*Walk in Water*). Penticton: Okanagan Indian Curriculum Project/Okanagan Tribal Council.

Armstrong, Jeannette (1984). *Neekna and Chemai*. Penticton: Theytus.

Armstrong, Jeannette (1990). *Slash*. Penticton: Theytus.

Armstrong, Jeannette (2009). *Dancing with the Cranes*. Penticton: Theytus Books.

Armstrong, Kelley (2010). *Waking the Witch*. Toronto: Vintage Canada.

Armstrong, Kelley (2011a). *The Gathering*. Toronto: Vintage Canada.

Armstrong, Kelley (2011b). *Spell Bound*. Toronto: Vintage Canada.

Asher, Jay (2007). *13 Reasons Why*. London: Penguin.

Ballantyne, R. M. (1856). *Snowflakes and Sunbeams; or The Young Fur Traders*. London: Ward, Locke.

Barnes, Julian (1995). "Evermore", in: Korte, Barbara/Einhaus, AnnMarie (Eds.). *The Penguin Book of First World War Stories*. London: Penguin Books, 2007, 345-361.

Bass, Karen (2013). *Graffiti Knight*. Toronto: Pajama Press.

Bastado, Jamie (2006). *On thin Ice*. Markham: Red Deer Press.

Behr, Mark (1995). *The Smell of Apples*. Cape Town: Queillerie.

Bobet, Leah (2012). *Above*. New York: Arthur A. Levine Books

Bonnefons, Amable (1777). *Le Petit livre de vie, qui apprend à bien vivre et bien prier Dieu, à Lùsage de diocese de Quebec./The Little Book of Life*. Montreal Fleury Mesplet & Charles Berger.

Bouchard, David (2008). *The Drum Calls Softly*. Markham: Red Deer Press.

Boyle, T.C. (1994). "Top of the Food Chain" in: Boyle, T.C. *Without a Hero and Other Stories*. New York: Viking Press, 173-178.

Boyle, T.C. (1995). *The Tortilla Curtain*. New York: Viking Press.

Boyne, John (2006). *The Boy in the Striped Pyjamas*. Oxford: David Fickling Books.

Brand, Dionne (1997). *In Another Place, Not Here*. Toronto: Penguin Random House Canada.

Brouwer, Sigmund (2009). *Absolute Pressure*. Victoria: Orca Book.

Browne, Eileen (1994). *Handa's Surprise*. London: Walker.

Buchan, John (1915). *The Thirty-Nine Steps*. Edinburgh: William Blackwood & Sons.

Butler, W.F. (1882). *Red Cloud*. London: Low and Marston.

Campbell, Maria (1973). *Halfbreed*. Toronto: McClelland & Stewart-Bantam.

Cisneros, Sandra (1984). *The House on Mango Street*. Houston: Arte Público Press.

Coetze, J. M. (2000). *Disgrace*. London: Random House.

Collins, Sarah (2011). *What Happened to Serenity?*. Markham: Red Deer Press.

Connor, Ralph (1902). *Glengarry Schooldays*. Toronto: McClelland & Stewart, 1993.

Cook, Lyn (1950). *The Bells on Finland Street*. Markham: Scholastics Canada, 1991.

Cook, Lyn (1951). *The Little Magic Fiddler: The Story of Donna Grescoe*. Winnipeg: Donna Grescoe

Coupland, Douglas (1995). *Microserfs*. New York: HarperCollins.

Cowan, Elizabeth (2008). *Earthgirl*. Toronto: Groundwood Books.

Culleton Mosionier, Beatrice (1983). *In Search of April Raintree*. Winnipeg: Portage & Main Press, 1999.

Culleton Mosionier, Beatrice (2002). *Unusual Friendships*. Penticton: Theytus.

Daly, Niki (2003). *Once upon a Time*. New York: Farrar, Straus and Giroux.

Diersch, Sandra (2011). *Home Court Advantage*. Toronto: Lorimer.

Downie, Mary Alice/Robertson, Barbara/Cleaver, Elizabeth (1968). *The Wind Has Wings*. New Yor: Oxford University Press.

Doyle, Roddy (1987). *The Commitments*. Dublin: King Farouk.

Doyle, Roddy (1990). *The Snapper*. London: Secker & Warburg.

Doyle, Roddy (1991). *The Van*. London: Secker & Warburg.

Doyle, Roddy (1999). *A Star called Henry*. London: Jonathan Cape.

Dueck, Adele (2011). *Racing Home*. Regina: Coteau Books.

Duncan, Frances (1977). *Kap-Sung Ferris*. Toronto: Burns &MacEachern.

Edwardson Dahl, Debby (2003). *Whale Snow*. Watertown: Charlesbridge.

Elliot, Zetta (2008). *A Wish after Midnight*. Las Vegas: AmazonEncore.

Ellis, Deborah (2002). *Parvana's Journey*. Vancouver: Douglas & McIntyre.

Ellis, Deborah (2011). *True Blue*. Toronto: Pajama Press.

Engkent, Garry (1991). "Why My Mother Can't Speak English", in: Bennett, Lee/Wong-Chu, Jim (Eds.). *Many Mouthed Birds: Contemporary Writing by Chinese Canadians*. Seattle: University of Washington Press.

Foon, Dennis (2011). *Double or Nothing*. Vancouver: Annick Press.

Freeman, Minnie Aodla (1980). "Survival in the South", in: Gedalof (Ed.). *Pa-*

per Stays Put: A Collection of Inuit Writing. Edmonton: Hurting, 101-112.

Frost, Robert (1916). "The Road not Taken", in: Frost, Robert. *Mountain Interval.* New York: Henry Holt and Company, 9.

Fullerton, Alma (2010). *Burn.* Toronto: University of Toronto Press.

Gaines, Ernest J. (1993). *A Lesson Before Dying.* New York: Knopf Publishing.

Gay, Marie-Louise (2006). *Caramba.* Toronto: Groundwood Books.

Golding, William (1954). *Lord of the Flies.* London: Faber and Faber.

Gordimer, Nadine (1981). *July's People.* New York: Penguin.

Goto, Hiromi (2001). *The Water of Possibility.* Regina: Coteau Books.

Green, John (2006). *Looking for Alaska.* London: Speak.

Hamilton, Hugo (1996). "Nazi Christmas", in: Hamilton, Hugo. *Dublin Where the Palm Trees Grow.* London: Faber and Faber, 9-15.

Highway, Tomson (1999). *Kiss of the Fur Queen*, Toronto: Doubleday.

Highway, Tomson (2011). *Fox on the Ice/Maageesees Maskwameek Kaapit.* Markham: Fifth House.

Holbrook, Frances (1898). *The Hiawatha Primer.* Toronto: s.n.

Hornby, Nick (1992). *Fever Pitch.* London: Gollancz.

Hughes, Monica (1983). *My Name is Paula Popowich!.* Toronto: Lorimer.

Huxley, Aldous (1932). *Brave New World.* London: Chatto & Windus..

Ipellie, Alootook (1983). *Arctic Dreams and Nightmares.* Penticton: Theytus.

Johnson, E. Pauline (1911). *Legends of Vancouver.* Vancouver: Thompson.

Johnson, E. Pauline (1912). *The Shagganappi.* Toronto: Briggs.

Johnson, E. Pauline (1913). *The Mocassin-Maker.* Toronto: Briggs.

Katz, Welwyn Wilton (1987). *False Face.* Toronto: Groundwood Book, 2001.

Keneally, Thomas (1992). *Schindler's Ark.* London: Hodder & Stoughton.

Kincaid, Jamaica (2000). *A Small Place.* New York: Farrar, Straus, and Giroux.

King, Thomas (1993a). *Green Gras, Running Water.* Boston: Houghton Mifflin.

King, Thomas (1993b). "How Corporal Colin Sterling Saved Blossom, Alberta, and Most of the Rest of the World as Well", in: King, Thomas. *One Good Story, That One: Stories.* Toronto: HarperCollins, 49–65.

King, Thomas (1993c). "Borders", in: King, Thomas. *One Good Story, That One: Stories*, Toronto: HarperCollins, 131–147.

Kogawa, Joy (1981). *Obasan.* Toronto: Penguin.

Kogawa, Joy (1986). *Naomi's Road.* Markham: Fitzhenry & Whiteside, 2005.

Kureishi, Hanif (1990). *Buddha of Suburbia.* London: Faber and Faber.

Kureishi, Hanif (1994). "My Son the Fanatic", in: Kureishi, Hanif (1997). *Love in a Blue Time.* New York: Simon & Schuster, 119-131.

Kusak, Marcus (2005). *The Book Thief.* London: Black Swan.

Larbalestier, Justine (2009). *Liar.* Crows Nest: Allen & Unwin.

Laurence, Margaret (1964). *The Stone Angel.* Toronto: McClelland & Stewart.

Laurence, Margaret (1974). *The Diviners.* Toronto: McClelland & Stewart.

Laurence, Margaret (1979). *Six Darn Cows.* Toronto: Lorimer.

Laurence, Margaret (1982). *The Olden Days Coat*. Toronto: McClelland & Stewart.

Little, Jean (1972). *From Anna*. New York: HarperTrophy.

Little, Jean (1977). *Listen for the Singing*. New York: HarperCollins, 1991.

Lee, Harper (1960). *To Kill a Mockingbird*. New York: HarperCollins.

Lee, Sky (1990). *Disappearing Moon Café*. Toronto: Douglas & McIntyre.

Lodge, David (1970). *Out of the Shelter*. London: Macmillan.

Longfellow, Henry Wadsworth (1858). *The Song of Hiawatha*. New York: Hurst and Company.

Lunn, Janet (1981). *The Root Cellar*. Toronto: Lester and Orpen Dennys.

Lunn, Janet (1997). *The Hollow Tree*. Toronto: Lester and Orpen Dennys.

MacLennan, Hugh (1945). *Two Solitudes*. Toronto: McClelland & Stewart.

Marineau, Michelle (1992). *Road to Chlifa*. Markham: Red Deer Press, 2003.

Martin Bossley, Michele (2006). *Jumper*. Victoria: Orca Book.

Martin Bossley, Michele (2007). *Kicker*. Victoria: Orca Book.

Maupin, Armistead (1978). *Tales of the City*. New York: Harper & Row.

Mayhew, James (2003). *Katie in London*. London: Hodder & Stoughton, 2014.

McClung, Nellie (1908). *Sowing Seeds in Danny*. New York: Grosset & Dunlap Publishers.

McEwan, Ian (1987). *The Child in Time*. London: Jonathan Cape.

McKee, David (2007). *Elmar*. New York: HarperCollins.

Meknyk, Bohdan (1978). *Fox Mykyta*. Newmarket: Tundra Books.

Miller, Arthur (1992). *The Last Yankee*. London: Bloomsbury, 2011.

Mistry, Rohinton (1987). *Tales from Firozsha Baag*. Toronto: Penguin

Mo, Timothy (1982). *Sour Sweet*. Brighton & Hove: Paddleless Press, 1999.

Moloney, James (1998). *Angela*. Brisbane: University of Queensland Press.

Montgomery, Lucy Maude (1908). *Anne of Green Gables*. Boston: L.C. Page & Co.

Montgomery, Mercedes (2008). *www.walkwithapolarbear.com*. Regina: Your Nickel's Worth.

Moorhouse, Frank (1972). "Five Incidents Concerning the Flesh and Blood", in: Moorhouse, Frank. *The Americans, Baby: A Discontinuous Narrative of Stories and Fragments*. Sydney: Angus and Robertson, 79-100.

Moorhouse, Frank (1972). "A Person of Accomplishment", in: Moorhouse, Frank. *The Americans, Baby: A Discontinuous Narrative of Stories and Fragments*. Sydney: Angus and Robertson, 133-147.

Morrison, Toni (2009). *Peeny Butter Fudge*. New York: Simon & Schuster.

Okorafor, Nnedi (2011). *Akata Witch*. New York: Viking Juvenile.

Ondaatje, Michael (1987). *In the Skin of a Lion*. Toronto: McClelland & Stewart.

Orwell, George (1945). *Animal Farm*. London: Secker & Warburg.

Parr Traill, Catherine (1852). *Canadian Crusoes: A Tale of the Rice Lake Plains*. London: Hall, Virtue.

Parr Traill, Catherine (1856). *Lady Mary and her Nurse; or, A Peep into Canadian Forest.* London: Hall,

Pawagi, Manjusha (2010). *The Girl who hated Books.* Toronto: Second Story Press.

Pinter, Harold (1993). *Moonlight.* London: Faber and Faber.

Prewett, Melanie (2012). *Two Mates.* Broome: Magabala Books.

Prinz, Yvonne (2009). *The Vinyl Princess.* Toronto: HarperColins.

Reid, Raziel (2014). When Everything Feels like the Movies: Vancouver: Arsenal Pulp Press.

Renaud, Anne (2008). *Missuk's Snow Geese.* Vancouver: simply read books.

Richler, Mordecai (1989). *Solomon Gurskey was Here.* Toronto: Viking Canada.

Roberts, Charles G. D. (1902). *The Kindred of the Wild.* Boston: L. C. Page & Company, 1953.

Robinson, Eden (2000). *Monkey Beach.* Toronto: Vintage Canada.

Ross, Jeff (2011). *Powerslide.* Victoria: Orca Book.

Roy, Arundhati (1997). *The God of Small Things.* New Delhi: IndiaInk.

Saigeon, Lori (2009). *Fight for Justice.* Regina: Coteau Books.

San Souci, Robert (1989). *The Talking Eggs.* New York: Dial Books for Young Readers.

Saro-Wiwa, Ken (1995). *A Month and a Day: A Detention Diary.* New York: Penguin.

Saunders, Marshall (1894). *Beautiful Joe: The Autobiography of a Dog.* Philadelphia: American Baptist Society.

Sendak, Maurice (1963). *Where the Wild Things Are.* New York: HarperCollins, 1984.

Seton, Earnest T. (1898). *Wild Animals I have Known.* New York: Scribner.

Shahraz, Qaisra (1988). "A Pair of Jeans", in: *Caught Between two Cultures.* Stuttgart: Klett English Editions, 166-186.

Shakespeare, William (1597). *Romeo and Juliet.* Leipzig: Reclam, 1994.

Shepard, Sam (1981). *True West.* New York: Samuel French Inc.

Sillitoe, Alan (1968). *The Loneliness of the Long Distance Runner.* Copenhagen: Grafisk Forlag.

Slipperjack, Ruby (2002). *Little Voice.* Regina: Coteau Books.

Smucker, Barbara (1978). *Underground to Canada.* London: Puffin, 2008.

Snicket, Lemony (2013). *The Dark.* New York: Little, Brown Books for Young Readers.

Steptoe, John (1987). *Mufaro's Beautiful Daughters: An African Tale.* New York: Lothorp, Lee, & Shepard.

Steward, Sean (2007). *Cathy's Book.* Philadelphia: Running Press Kids.

Stinson, Kathy (1992). *Fish House Secrets.* Saskatoon: Thistledown Press.

Swamp, Chief Jake (1995). *Giving Thanks – A Native American Good Morning Message.* New York: Lee and Low Books.

Syal, Meera (1999). *Life isn't all Ha Ha He He.* New York: Doubleday.

Sydor, Colleen (2008). *My Mother is a French Fry and other Proof of my Fuzzed up Life*. Toronto: Kids Can Press.

Symchych, Victoria/Vesey, Olga (1975). *The Flying Ship*. Boston: Holt Rinehart & Winston.

Taylor, Drew Hayden (1998). *Funny You Don't Look Like One*. Penticton: Thytus.

Taylor, Drew Hayden (2000). *alterNatives*. Vancouver: Talonbooks.

Taylor, Drew Hayden (2007). *The Night Wanderer*. Vancouver: Annick Press.

Teller, Janne (2010). *Nothing*. New York: Atheneum.

Thomas, Erin (2010). *Boarder Patrol*. Victoria: Orca Book.

Ulrich, Maureen (2007). *Power Plays*. Regina: Coteau Books.

Ulrich, Maureen (2010). *Face Off*. Regina: Coteau Books.

Vassanji, M. G. (1997). *No New Land*. Toronto: McClelland & Stewart.

Waboose, Bourdeau (1997). *Morning on the Lake*. Toronto: Kids Can Press.

Walshe, Elizabeth (1863). *Cedar Creek: From the Shanty to the Settlement*. London: Religious Tract Society.

Walters, Eric (2003). *Run*. Toronto: Penguin.

Walters, Eric (2007a). *Sketches*. Toronto: Viking Juvenile.

Walters, Eric (2007b). *Save as Houses*. Toronto: Doubleday Canada.

Weale, David (2012). *Doors in the Air*. Victoria: Orca Book Publisher.

Wolfe, Tom (2004). *I am Charlotte Simmons*. New York: Farrar, Straus and Giroux.

Yee, Paul (1994). *Breakaway*. Toronto: Groundwood Books.

Film

Kunuk, Zacharias (dir., 2001). *Atanarjuat: The Fast Runner*. Sony Pictures.

II. Secondary Literature

Abendroth-Timmer, Dagmar (1998). *Der Blick auf das andere Land. Ein Vergleich der Perspektiven in Deutsch-, Französisch- und Russischlehrwerken.* Tübingen: Gunter Narr.

AFS Orientation Handbook (1984). Vol. 4. New York.

Aho, Tanja N. (2013). "The Body and Embodiment in Disability Studies", unpublished manuscript, University at Buffalo.

Ahrens, Rüdiger (2010). "The Enigmatic Asian Face: Is there a Future for English I South-East Asia?" in: Eisenmann, Maria/Grimm, Nancy/Volkmann, Laurenz (Eds.) (2010). *Teaching the New English Literatures & Cultures.* Heidelberg: Winter, 91-106.

Aigner, Georg (2002). "Interkulturelles Lernen an beruflichen Schulen", in: Volkmann, Laurenz/Stierstorfer, Klaus/Gehring, Wolfgang (Eds.). *Interkulturelle Kompetenz.* Tübingen: Narr, 99-119.

Allolio-Näcke, Lars/Kalscheuer, Britta (2003). "Doing Idenity - Von Transdifferenz und dem alltäglichen Skepitzismus", in Fitzek, Herbert/Ley, Michael (Eds.). *Alltag im Aufbruch: Ein psychologisches Profil der Gegenwartskultur.* Gießen: Psychosozial-Verlag, 152-162.

Alsup, Janet (2006). *Teacher Identity Discourses: Negotiating Personal and Professional Spaces.* Mahwah, NJ: Erlbaum/NCTE.

Alsup, Janet (2010). *Young Adult Literature and Adolescence Identity across Cultures and Classrooms – Contexts for the Literary Lives of Teens.* New York/London: Routledge.

Alter, Grit (2010). "Searching for a Place of One's Own – The Sense of Belonging in First Nations Children's Books by Jeannette Armstrong and Ruby Slipperjack", in: Rana, Marion (Ed.). *Interjuli – Internationale Kinder- und Jugendliteraturforschung* 2, 15-26.

Alter, Grit (2011a). "From Finding a Voice to Being Heard: Overcoming Current Challenges of Canadian Children's Literature", in: *ZAA – Zeitschrift für Anglistik und Amerikanistik, a Quarterly of Language, Literature and Culture,* 59/2, 149-161.

Alter, Grit (2011b). "Living Between Two Worlds: Künstlerische Darstellungen zum Leben der Inuit analysieren und verstehen", in: *Englisch 5-10,* 6/2011, 30-33.

Alter, Grit (2011c). "Run! – Leseerlebnis über einen Mann, der durch Kanada rannte – mit einem Bein", in: *Praxis Englisch,* 6/2011, 14-18.

Alter, Grit (2012a). "Reflections on Multiculturalism in Canadian Fiction for Young People since 1950: A Contribution to National Identity Formation", in: *jeunesse,* 4/1. University of Winnipeg, 178-189.

Alter, Grit (2012b). "Balancing Cultures – Multicultural Canadian Children's Literature", in: Bruti-Liberati, Luigi (Ed.). *Interpreting Canada: New Perspectives From Europe.* The European Network for Canadian Studies, 7-23.

Alter, Grit (2013). "Developing Intercultural Competence through First Nations' Children's Books", in: Bland, Janice/Lütge, Christiane (Eds.). *Children's Literature in Language Education. From Picture Books to Young Adult Fiction*. London: Continuum, 151-158.

Alter, Grit (2014). "The World is not your Garbage Can - Transmediale Elemente eines Jugendromans untersuchen", in: *Der Fremdsprachliche Unterricht Englisch*, 38-42.

Altmayer, Claus (2001). "Bredella, Lothar, Meissner, Franz-Joseph, Nünning, Ansgar & Rößler, Dietmar. (Hrsg.). (2000). *Wie ist Fremdverstehen lehr- und lernbar? Vorträge aus dem Graduiertenkolleg 'Didaktik des Fremdverstehens'* Tübingen: Narr (= Giessener Beiträge zur Fremdsprachendidaktik). ISBN 3-8233-5304-7. LII, 290 Seiten, DM 64" Rezension in: *ZIF* 6(2), online: http://zif.spz.tu-darmstadt.de/jg-06-2/beitrag/fremdverstehen.htm, June 17, 2014.

Altmayer, Claus (2002). "Kulturelle Deutungsmuster von Texten. Prinzipien und Verfahren einer kulturwissenschaftlichen Textanalyse im Fach Deutsch als Fremdsprache", in: *Zeitschrift für Interkulturellen Fremdsprachenunterricht*. Online: http://zif.spz.tu-darmstadt.de/jg-06-3/beitrag/deutungs muster.htm, Aug 16, 2013.

Anderson, Benedikt (1991). *Imagined Communities: Reflections on the Origin and Spread of Nationalism*. New York: Verso.

Anderson, Beatrice (2012). *Nlakapmux Grandmothers' Stories: How Generations of Indigenous Grandmothers of British Columbia Carried out their Responsibilities to Transmit Knowledge*. Saarbrücken: LAP Lambert Academic Publishing.

"Angry Young Man" (2013). In: *Encyclopedia Britannica*. Online: http://www.britannica.com/EBchecked/topic/25251/Angry-Young-Men, Aug 23, 2013.

Antor, Heinz (2000). "Postcolonial Pedagogy, or Why and How to Teach the New English Literatures", in: Reitz, Bernhardt/Rieuwerts, Sigrid (Eds.). *Anglistentag. Proceedings of the Conference of the German Association of University Teachers of English: 1999 Mainz*. Trier: WVT, 245-262.

Antor, Heinz (2002). "Die Vermittlung interkultureller Kompetenz an der Universität: Das Beispiel Kanada", in: Volkmann, Laurenz/Stierstorfer, Klaus/Gehring, Wolfgang (Eds.). *Interkulturelle Kompetenz*. Tübingen: Narr, 143-163.

Antor, Heinz (2006). *Inter- und Transkulturelle Studien: Theoretische Grundlagen und interdisziplinäre Praxis*. Heidelberg: Winter.

Antor, Heinz (2007). "Inter-, multi- und transkulturelle Kompetenz: Bildungsfaktor im Zeitalter der Globalisierung", in: Antor, Heinz (Ed.). *Fremde Kulturen Verstehen – fremde Kulturen Lehren, Theorie und Praxis der Vermittlung interkultureller Kompetenz*. Heidelberg: Winter, 111-126.

Antor, Heinz (2010). "From Postcolonialism and Interculturalism to the Ethics of Transculturalism in the Age of Globalization", in: Antor, Heinz/

Merkl, Matthias/Stierstorfer, Klaus/Volkmann, Laurenz (Eds.). *From Interculturalism to Transculturalism: Mediating Encounters in Cosmopolitan Contexts.* Heidelberg: Winter, 1-13.

Anzaldua, Gloria (1999). *Borderlands/La Frontera. The New Mestiza.* San Francisco: Aunt Lute Books.

Appiah, Kwame (1996). "Race, Culture, Identity: Misunderstood Connections", in: Appiah, Kwame Anthony/Gutmann, Amy (Eds.). *Color Consciousness. The Political Morality of Race.* Princeton: Princeton University Press, 30-105.

Arnett, Jeffrey Jensen (2002). "The Psychology of Globalization", in: *American Psychologist,* 57/2000, 774-783.

Ashcroft, Bill (2011). "Reading the Other: Constitutive Transculturality in a Hong Kong Classroom", in: Doff, Sabine/Schulze-Engler (Eds.). *Beyond 'Other Cultures' – Transcultural Perspectives on Teaching the New Literatures in English.* Trier: WVT, 17-30.

Ashcroft, Bill/Griffiths Gareth/Tiffin, Helen (Eds.) (1995). *The Post-Colonial Reader.* London: Routledge.

Ashcroft, Bill/Griffiths, Gareth/Tiffin, Helen (2003). *Post-Colonial Studies: The Key Concepts.* London: Routledge.

Atkinson, Dwight (1999). "TESOL and culture", in: *TESOL Quarterly*, 33(4), 625-654.

Atwood, Margaret (1972). *Survival. A Thematic Guide to Canadian Literature.* Toronto: Anansi.

Atwood, Margaret (1999). "Margaret Atwood", in: Dickson, Margaret/Longpré, Kerry (Eds.). *22 Provocative Canadians: In the Spirit of Bob Edwards.* Calgary: Bayeux Arts, Inc., 10-18. [Similar in Atwood, Margaret (2003). "Survival Then and Now", in: Gaffield, Chad/Gould, Karen L. (Eds.). *The Canadian Distinctiveness into the XXIst century.* Ottawa: University of Ottawa Press, 47-55.]

Audale, Debra van/Feagin, Joe R. (2001). *The First R: How Children Learn Race and Racism.* Lanham: Rowman & Littlefield.

Bachmann-Medick, Doris (2004). "Multikultur oder kulturelle Differenzen? Neue Konzepte von Weltliteratur und Übersetzung in postkolonialer Perspektive", in: Bachmann-Medick, Doris. *Kultur als Text. Die anthropologische Wende in der Literaturwissenschaft.* Tübingen: Francke, 262-296.

Bainbridge, Joyce/Carbonaro, Mike/Green, Nicole (2005). "Canadian Children's Literature: An Alberta Survey", in: *The Alberta Journal of Educational Research*, 51/4, 311-327.

Bamford, Julian/Day, Richard D. (Eds.) (2008). *Extensive Reading Activities for Teaching Language.* Cambridge: CUP.

Bandura, Albert (1986). *Social Foundations of Thought and Action.* Englewood Cliffs, NJ: Prentice-Hall.

Banerjee, Mita (2011). "Fremdverstehen Meets Indo Chic", in: Doff, Sabine/Schulze-Engler (Eds.). *Beyond 'Other Cultures' – Transcultural Perspectives on Teaching the New Literatures in English.* Trier: WVT, 31-46.

Banks, James/McGee Banks, Cherry. (1989). *Multicultural Education: Issues and Perspectives.* Boston: Allyn & Bacon.

Bär, Marcus (2013). "Standardisierung vs. Individualisierung: Zur Rolle von (komplexen) Lernaufgaben in einem kompetenzorientierten Fremdsprachenunterricht", in: Gründewald, Andreas/Plikat, Jochen/Wieland, Katharina (Eds.). *Bildung – Kompetenz – Literalität. Fremdsprachenunterricht zwischen Standardisierung und Bildungsanspruch.* Seelze: Klett/Kallmeyer, 98-109.

Barker, Joanne (2015). "Gender", in: Warrior, Robert (Ed.). *The World of Indigenous North America.* New York: Routledge.

Bartz, Walter/Vermette, Rosalie (1996). "Testing Cultural Competence", in: Nostrand, Howard/Grundstrom, Allan/Singerman, Alan (Eds.). *Acquiring Cross-cultural Competence. Four Stages for Students of French.* Lincolnwood: National Textbook Company, 75-83.

Bartosch, Roman/Grimm, Sieglinde (2014). *Teaching Environments. Ecocritical Encounters.* Frankfurt: Peter Lang.

Basseler, Michael (2014). "Environmental Learning. Ökodidaktische Konzepte für den Englischunterricht", in: *Der Fremdsprachliche Unterricht Englisch*, 129, 2-8.

Bauman, Zygmunt (1992). *Intimations of Postmodernity.* London: Routledge.

Bauman, Zygmunt (2000). *Liquid Modernity.* Cambridge: Blackwell Publishers.

Bauman, Zygmunt (2001). "Identity in the Globalising World", in: *Social Anthropology* 9/2, 121-129.

Bauman, Zygmunt (2005). "Education in Liquid Modernity", in: *The Review of Education, Pedagogy & Cultural Studies*, 27/4, 303-317.

Baumgratz-Gangl, Gisela (1990). *Persönlichkeitsentwicklung und Fremdsprachenerwerb. Transnationale und transkulturelle Kommunikationsfähigkeit im Französischunterricht.* Paderborn: Schöningh.

Bausch, Karl-Richard/Christ, Herbert/Krumm, Hans-Jürgen (Eds.). *Interkulturelles Lernen im Fremdsprachenunterricht. Arbeitspapiere der 14. Frühjahrskonferenz zur Erforschung des Fremdsprachenunterrichts.* Tübingen: Narr.

Bennett, Donna (2002). "Nation and Its Discontents: Atwood's *Survival* and After", in: Oliva, Julio Ingacio (et al.) (Ed.). *Canadística Canaria, 1991-2000: Ensayos Literarios Anglocanadienses.* La Laguna: Servicio de Publicaciones, Universidad de La Laguna, 13-29.

Benwell, Tara (2004). "Canadian English – a linguistic pot-pourri", in: *Klett Magazin close-up*, 4/11, 3-5.

Beres, Laura (1999). "Beauty and the Beast: The Romanticization of Abuse in Popular Culture", in: *European Journal of Cultural Studies*, 2, 191-207.

Bernhardt, Elizabeth B./Berman, Russell A. (1999). "From German I to German Studies 001: A Chronicle of Curricular Reform", in: *Die Unterrichtspraxis/Teaching German*, 32/1, 22-31.

Bezirksregierung NRW (2008) (Ed.). "Didaktisch methodische Fortbildung Englisch in der Grundschule; Modul 7: (Kinder-) Literatur im Englischunterricht der Grundschule". Materialien für die Lehrerfortbildung in Nordrhein-Westfalen.

Bhabha, Homi (1994). *The Location of Culture.* New York: Routledge.

Bhabha, Homi (1997a). "Die Frage der Identität", in: Bronfen, Elisabeth/Marius, Benjamin/Steffen, Therese (Eds.). *Hybride Kulturen. Beiträge zur anglo-amerikanischen Multikulturalismusdebatte.* Tübingen: Stauffenberg, 97-122.

Bhabha, Homi (1997b). "Verortungen der Kultur", in: Bronfen, Elisabeth/Marius, Benjamin/Steffen, Therese (Eds.). *Hybride Kulturen. Beiträge zur anglo-amerikanischen Multikulturalismusdebatte.* Tübingen: Stauffenberg, 123-148.

Bhabha, Homi (1997c). "DissemiNation: Zeit, Narrative und die Ränder der modernen Nation", in Bronfen, Elisabeth/Marius, Benjamin/Steffen, Therese (Eds.). *Hybride Kulturen. Beiträge zur anglo-amerikanischen Multikulturalismusdebatte.* Tübingen: Stauffenberg, 149-194.

Biebricher, Christine (2008). *Lesen in der Fremdsprache: Eine Studie zu Effekten extensives Lesens.* Tübingen: Narr.

Bishop, Rudine Sims (Ed.) (1994). *Kaleidoscope: A Multicultural Booklist for Grades K-8.* Urbana: NCTE.

Bishop, Rudine Sims (1997). "Selecting Literature for a Multicultural Curriculum", in: Harris, Violet J. (Ed.). *Using Multiethnic Literature in the K-8 Classroom.* Norwood, MA: Christopher-Gordon, 1-19.

Bissoondath, Neil (1994). *Selling Illusions: The Cult of Multiculturalism in Canada.* Toronto: Penguin.

Bland, Janice/Lütge, Christiane (Eds.) (2013). *Children's Literature in Second Language Education.* London: Bloomsbury Academic.

Blell, Gabriele/Rust, Ina (2012). "E-Begegnungen und transkulturelles Lernen in der literaturdidaktischen Ausbildung von Lehramtsstudierenden", in: Blell, Gabriele/Lütge, Christiane (Eds.). *Fremdsprachendidaktik und Lehrerbildung – Konzepte, Impulse, Perspektiven.* Münster: Lit-Verlag, 113-132.

Blell, Gabriele (2013). "Sprach(en)lernen und Identität im Kontext eines literatur- und kulturdidaktischen Fremdsprachenunterrichts", in: Burwitz-Melzer, Eva/Königs, Frank G./Riemer, Claudia (Eds.). *Identität und Fremdsprachenlernen – Anmerkungen zu einer komplexen Beziehung.* Tübingen: Narr, 29-38.

Block, David (2007). *Second Language Identities.* London: Continuum.

Borrelli, Michele (1991). "Intercultural Pedagogy: Foundation and Principles", in: Buttjes, Dieter/Byram, Michael (Eds.). *Mediating Language and*

Culture: Towards an Intercultural Theory of Foreign Language Education. Multilingual Matters: Clevedon, 275-286.

Botelho, Maria José/Rudman, Masha K. (2009). *Critical Multicultural Analysis of Children's Literature: Mirrors, Windows, and Doors*. New York: Routledge.

Bourdieu, Pierre (1977). "The Economics of Linguistic Exchanges", in: *Social Science Information,* 16, 645-668.

Bradford, Clare (2011). "Multiculturalism and Post-Colonialism", in: Grenby, Matthew O./Reynolds, Kimberly (Eds.). *Children's Literature Studies – A Research Handbook*. New York: Palgrave Macmillan, 162-170.

Brandl, Florian/Kretschmer, Simone (2011). "Kidnapped in Vancouver: Im Kontext einer Kriminalgeschichte landeskundliches Wissen erwerben", in: *Englisch 5-10*, 6, 14-17.

Bräuer, Gerd/Keller, Martin/Winter, Felix (2012). *Portfolio macht Schule: Unterrichts- und Schulentwicklung mit Portfolio*. Stuttgart: Klett/ Kallmeyer.

Bredella, Lothar (1988). "How is Intercultural Understanding Possible?", in: Bredella, Lothar/Haack, Dietmar (Eds.). *Perceptions and Misperceptions: The United States and Germany*. Tübingen, Narr, 1-25.

Bredella, Lothar (1993). "Ist das Verstehen fremder Kulturen wünschenswert?", in: Bredella, Lothar/Christ, Herbert (Eds.). *Zugänge zum Fremden*. Gießen: Verlag der Ferber'schen Universitätsbuchhandlung, 11-36.

Bredella, Lothar (Ed.) (1995). *Verstehen und Verständigung durch Sprachenlernen? Dokumentation des 15. Kongresses für Fremdsprachendidaktik, veranstaltet von der Deutschen Gesellschaft für Fremdsprachenforschung (DGFF), Gießen 4.-6. Oktober 1993*. Bochum: Brockmeyer.

Bredella, Lothar (2002a). *Literarisches und interkulturelles Verstehen*. Tübingen: Narr.

Bredella, Lothar (2002b). "Fremdverstehen mit literarischen Texten", in: Bredella, Lothar. *Literarisches und interkulturelles Verstehen*. Tübingen: Narr, 306-330.

Bredella, Lothar (2007). "Die welterzeugende und die welterschließende Kraft literarischer Texte: Gegen einen verengten Begriff von Literarischer Kompetenz und Bildung", in: Bredella, Lothar/Hallet, Wolfgang (Eds.). *Literaturunterricht, Kompetenzen und Bildung*. Trier: WVT, 65-85.

Bredella, Lothar (2008). "Dramatische Texte im interkulturellen Fremdsprachenunterricht: alterNatives von Drew Hayden Taylor", in: Ahrens, Rüdiger/Eisenmann, Maria/Merkl, Matthias (Eds.). *Moderne Dramendidaktik für den Englischunterricht*. Heidelberg: Universitätsverlag Winter, 177-210.

Bredella, Lothar (2010a). "How to Conceive of Intercultural Understanding. Considering the Tensions Between the Liberal and the Communal Concept of the Self?", in: Antor, Heinz/Merkl, Matthias/Stierstorfer, Klaus/Volkmann, Laurenz (Eds.). *From Interculturalism to Transcul-*

turalism: Mediating Encounters in Cosmopolitan Contexts. Heidelberg: Winter, 15-38.

Bredella, Lothar (2010b). "Fremdverstehen und interkulturelles Lernen", in: Hallet, Wolfgang/Königs, Frank (Eds.). *Handbuch Fremdsprachenunterricht.* Seelze-Velber: Klett, 120-125.

Bredella, Lothar (2010c). *Das Verstehen des Anderen. Kulturwissenschaftliche und Literaturdidaktische Studien.* Tübingen: Narr.

Bredella, Lothar (2010d). "Trans- oder Interkulturalität als Bildungsziel des Fremdsprachenlehrens und -lernens?", in: *ForumSprache*, 4, 21-41.

Bredella, Lothar (2012). *Narratives und interkulturelles Verstehen.* Tübingen: Narr.

Bredella, Lothar/Burwitz-Melzer, Eva (2004). *Rezeptionsästhetische Literaturdidaktik mit Beispielen aus dem Fremdsprachenunterricht.* Tübingen: Narr.

Bredella, Lothar/Christ, Herbert (Eds.) (1993). *Zugänge zum Fremden.* Gießen: Verlag der Ferber'schen Universitätsbuchhandlung.

Bredella, Lothar/Christ, Herbert (Eds.) (1995). *Didaktik des Fremdverstehens.* Tübingen: Narr.

Bredella, Lothar/Christ, Herbert (Eds.) (2007). *Fremdverstehen und interkulturelle Kompetenz.* Tübingen: Narr.

Bredella, Lothar/Christ, Herbert/Legutke, Michael (Eds.) (1997). *Thema Fremdverstehen. Arbeiten aus dem Graduiertenkolleg „Didaktik des Fremdverstehens".* Tübingen: Narr, 11-33.

Bredella, Lothar/Christ, Herbert/Legutke, Michael (1997b) "Einleitung", in: Bredella, Lothar/Christ, Herbert/Legutke, Michael (Eds.). *Thema Fremdverstehen. Arbeiten aus dem Graduiertenkolleg „Didaktik des Fremdverstehens".* Tübingen: Narr, 11-33.

Bredella, Lothar/Delanoy, Werner (Eds.) (1999). *Interkultureller Fremdsprachenunterricht.* Tübingen: Narr.

Bredella, Lothar/Delanoy, Werner (Eds.) (1999). *Interkultureller Fremdsprachenunterricht: Das Verhältnis von Fremdem und Eigenem.* Tübingen: Narr.

Bredella, Lothar/Hallet, Wolfgang (Eds.) (2007). *Literaturunterricht, Kompetenzen und Bildung.* Trier: WVT.

Bredella, Lothar/Christ, Herbert/Legutke, Michael K. (Eds.) (2000). *Fremdverstehen zwischen Theorie und Praxis. Arbeiten aus dem Graduiertenkolleg „Didaktik des Fremdverstehens".* Tübingen: Narr.

Bredella, Lothar/Meißner, Franz-Josef/Nünning, Ansgar/Rösler, Dietmar (Ed.) (2000). *Wie ist Fremdverstehen lehr- und lernbar?* Tübingen. Narr.

Breen, Michael (1985). "Authenticity in the Language Classroom", in: *Applied Linguistics* 6/1, 60-70.

Bremicker, Monika (2004). "Blame Canada", in: *Englisch betrifft uns – Canada,* 1, 28-32.

Bretzmann, Sina (2011). "It's getting wild: Kanadas Tierwelt kennen- und schätzen lernen", in: *Englisch 5-10*, 6, 4-9.

Brown, Jean E./Stephens, Elaine C. (Eds.) (1998). *United in Diversity – Using Multicultural Young Adult Literature in the Classroom*. Urbana: National Council for teachers of English.

Buckingham, David (2008). "Introducing Identity", in: Buckingham, David (Ed.). *Youth, Identity, and Digital Media*. Cambridge, MA: The MIT Press, 1-24.

Burford, Roger Mason (1992). *Colourful Canada*. Berlin: Cornelsen English Library.

Burwitz-Melzer, Eva (2003). *Allmähliche Annäherungen: Fiktionale Texte im interkulturellen Fremdsprachenunterricht der Sekundarstufe I*. Beiträge zur Gießener Fremdsprachendidaktik. Tübingen: Narr.

Burwitz-Melzer, Eva (2007). "Ein Lesekompetenzmodell für den fremdsprachlichen Literaturunterricht", in: Bredella, Lothar/Hallet, Wolfgang (Eds.). *Literaturunterricht, Kompetenzen und Bildung*. Trier: WVT, 127-157.

Burwitz-Melzer, Eva (2013a). "Approaching Literary and Language Competence: Picturebooks and Graphic Novels in the EFL Classroom", in: Lütge, Christiane/Bland, Janice (Eds.). *Children's Literature in Language Education*. London: Bloomsbury, 55-70.

Burwitz-Melzer, Eva (2013b). "Sprache und Identität im Fremdsprachenunterricht", in: Burwitz-Melzer, Eva/Königs, Frank G./Riemer, Claudia (Eds.). *Identität und Fremdsprachenlernen – Anmerkungen zu einer komplexen Beziehung*. Tübingen: Narr, 39-49.

Burwitz-Melzer, Eva/Königs, Frank G./Riemer, Claudia (Eds.) (2013). *Identität und Fremdsprachenlernen – Anmerkungen zu einer komplexen Beziehung*. Tübingen: Narr.

Bushman, John H./Parks Haas, Kay (2006). *Using Young Adult Literature in the English Classroom*. Upper Saddle River: Person/Merrill Prentice Hall.

Butler, Judith (1993). *Bodies that Matter. On the Discursive Limits of Sex*. London/New York: Routledge.

Buttjes, Dieter (1990). "Culture in German Foreign Language Teaching: Making Use of an Ambiguous Past", in: Buttjes, Dieter/Byram, Michael (Eds.). *Mediating Language and Culture: Towards an Intercultural Theory of Foreign Language Education*. Multilingual Matters: Clevedon, 47.-62.

Butzkamm, Wolfgang (1973). *Aufgeklärte Einsprachigkeit: Zur Entdogmatisierung der Methode im Fremdsprachenunterricht*. Heidelberg: Quelle & Meyer.

Butzkamm, Wolfgang (2003). "We Only Learn Language Once: The Role of the Mother Tongue in FL Classrooms – Death of a Dogma", in: *Language Learning Journal*, 28, 29-39.

Butzkamm, Wolfgang (2011). "Why Make Them Crawl if They Can Walk. Teaching with Mother Tongue Support", in: *RELC Journal*, 42,3, 379-391.

Butzkamm, Wolfgang/Schmid-Schönbein, Gisela (2008). "Funktionale Fremdsprachigkeit", in: *Grundschulmagazin Englisch/The Primary English Magazine*, 5, 6-8.

Butzkamm, Wolfgang/Caldwell, John A. W. (2009). *The Bilingual Reform: A Paradigm Shift in Foreign Language Teaching*. Tübingen: Narr.

Byram, Michael (1997a). *Teaching and Assessing Intercultural Communicative Competence*. Clevedon: Multilingual Matters.

Byram, Michael (1997b). "The Intercultural Dimension in 'Language Learning for European Citizenship'", in: Byram, Michael (Ed.). *The Sociocultural and Intercultural Dimension of Language Learning and Teaching*. Straßbourg: Council of Europe, 17-20.

Byram, Michael (1999). "Developing the Intercultural Speaker for International Communication", in: Chambers, Angela/Baoill, D.P.Ó. (Eds.) (1999). *Irish Association for Applied Linguistics: Intercultural Communication and Language Learning*. Dublin: Irish Association for Applied Linguistics, 17-35.

Byram, Michael (2000). "Learning English Without a Culture? The Case of English as a Lingua Franca", in: Bredella, Lothar/Meißner, Franz-Joseph/Nünning, Ansgar/Rösler, Dietmar (Eds.). *Wie ist Fremdverstehen lehr- und lernbar? Vorträge aus dem Graduierten Kolleg „Didaktik des Fremdverstehen"*. Tübingen: Narr, 1-17.

Byram, Michael (2009). "Evaluation and/or Assessment of Intercultural Competence", in: Hu, Adelheid/Byram, Michael (Eds.). *Interkulturelle Kompetenz und fremdsprachliches Lernen – Modelle, Empirie, Evaluation/Intercultural Competence and Foreign Language Learning – Models, Empiricism, Assessment*. Tübingen: Narr, 215-252.

Byram, Michael/Fleming, Michael (Eds.) (1998). *Language Learning in Intercultural Perspective*. Cambridge: CUP.

Byram, Michael/Fleming, Michael (Eds.) (1998). *Language Learning in Intercultural Perspective. Approaches through Drama and Ethnography*. Cambridge: CUP.

Byram, Michael/Gribkova, Bella/Starkey, Hugh (2002). *Developing the Intercultural Dimension in Language Teaching: a Practical Introduction for Teachers*. Strasbourg: Council of Europe.

Byram, Michael/Nichols, Adam/Stevens, David (2001) (Eds.). *Developing Intercultural Competence in Practice*. Clevedon: Multilingual Matters.

Byram, Michael/Zarate, Geneviéve (1994). *Definitions, Objectives and Assessment of Sociocultural Competence*. Council of Europe: Strasbourg.

Byram, Michael/Zarate, Geneviève (1996). "Defining and Assessing Intercultural Competence: Some Principles and Proposals for the Europeans

Context", in: *language teaching – The international abstracting journal for language teachers and applied linguists*, 29/4, 239-243.

Byram, Michael/Zarate, Geneviéve (1997). "Definitions, Objectives and Assessment of Sociocultural Competence", in: Byram, Michael/Zarate, Geneviéve/Neuner, Gerhardt (Eds.). *Sociocultural Competence in Language Learning and Teaching*. Strasbourg: Council of Europe, 9-43.

Cadden, Mike (2011). "Genre as Nexus", in: Wolf, Shelby, A./Coats, Karen/Enciso, Patricia/Jenkins, Chinstine A (Eds.). *Handbook of Research on Children's and Young Adult Literature*. New York: Routledge, 302-313.

The Canada Council for the Arts/The Writer's Trust of Canada (2002). "English-Language Canadian Literature in High Schools." Online: http://www.canadacouncil.ca/publications_e/research/aud_access/di127 234254927656250.htm, Oct 1, 2010.

Candlin, Christopher N. (1987). "Towards Task-Based Language Learning", in: Candlin, Christopher/Murphy, Dermot (Eds.). *Language learning tasks*. Englewood Cliffs, NJ: Prentice-Hall International, 5-22.

Carducci, Bernardo J. (2009). *The Psychology of Personality: Viewpoints, Research, and Applications*. Oxford: Wiley-Blackwell.

Carolli, Piera (2008). *Literature in Second Language Education: Enhancing the Role of Texts in Learning*. London: Continuum.

Carrell, Patricia/Carson Joan (1997). "Extensive and Intensive Reading in an EAP setting", in: *English for Specific Purposes*, 16/1, 47-60.

Carter, Robert/Cheuvront, Samuel/Harrison, C./Proctor, Larry/Myburgh, Kathryn/Brown, Michael/Malina, Robert (2010). "Success, Race and Athletic Performance", in: *Journal for the Study of Sports and Athletes in Education* 4(3), 207-229.

Casper-Hehne, Hiltraut (2008). "Überlegungen zur Bewertung der Qualität von interkulturellem DaF- und DaZ-Unterricht", in: Schulz, Renate/Tschirner, Erwin (Eds.). *Communication across Borders. Developing Intercultural Competence in German as a Foreign Language*. München: Iudicium, 310-327.

Castanheira, Maria L./Green, Judith/Dixon, Carol/Yeagerb, Beth (2007). "(Re) Formulating Identities in the Face of Fluid Modernity: An Interactional Ethnographic Approach", in: *International Jounral of Educational Research* 46, 172-189.

Clark, Christine/O'Donnell, James (Eds.) (1999). *Becoming and Unbecoming White: Owning and Disowning A Racial Identity*. Westport: J.F. Bergin & Garvey.

Clifford, James (1988). *The Predicament of Culture*. Cambridge, MA: Harvard University Press.

Coats, Karen (2011). "Young Adult Literature: Gorwing up, In Theory", in: Wolf, Shelby, A./Coats, Karen/Enciso, Patricia/Jenkins, Chinstine A

(Eds.). *Handbook of Research on Children's and Young Adult Literature*. New York: Routledge, 315-329.

Collie, Joanne/Slater, Stephen (2007). *Literature in the Language Classroom. A Resource Book of Ideas and Activities*. Cambridge: CUP.

Collins, Patricia H. (2000). "Gender, Black Feminism, and Black Political Economy", in: *Annals of the American Academy of Political and Social Science*, 568, *The Study of African American Problems: W.E.B. DuBois's Agenda, Then and Now*, 41–53.

Council of Europe (Ed.) (2001). *Common European Framework of Reference for Languages: Learning, Teaching, Assessment*. Council of Europe: Straßbourg.

Council of Europe (Ed.) (n.y.). "European Language Portfolio". Online: http://www.coe.int/t/dg4/education/elp/ELP-REG/Default_EN.asp, July 2, 2013.

Craven, Allison (2002). "Beauty and the Belles: Discourses of Feminism and Femininity in Disneyland", in: *The European Journal of Women's Studies*, 9/2, 123-142.

Crawford, Linda M./McLaren, Peter (2003). "A Critical Perspective on Culture in the Second Language Classroom", in: Lange, Dale L./Paige, Michael R. (Eds.). *Culture as Core: Perspectives on Culture in Second Language Learning*. Charlotte: Information Age Publishing, 127-157.

Crenshaw, Kimberlé (1989). "Demarginalizing the Intersection of Race and Sex: A Black Feminist Critique of Antidiscrimination Doctrine", in: *The University of Chicago Legal Forum*, 139-167.

Crenshaw, Kimberlé (1991). "Mapping the Margins: Intersectionality, Identity Politics, and Violence against Women of Color", in: *Stanford Law Review*, 43/6, 1241-1299.

Cunningham, Aliel (2010). "Engaging and Enchanting the Heart: Developing Moral Identity through Young Adult Fantasy Literature", in: Alsup, Janet (Ed.). *Young Adult Liteature and Adolescent Identity across Cultures and Classrooms – Contexts for the Literary Lives of Teens*. New York/London: Routledge, 111-132.

Dantas-Whitney, Maria/Rilling, Sarah (Eds.) (2010). *Authenticity in the Language Classroom and Beyond: Children and Adolescent Learners*. TESOL Press.

De Luca, Anna Pia (2009). "Migrant Women: Transnational/Transcultural Identities across Borders in Canadian Female Writing", in: Löschnigg, Maria/Löschnigg, Martin (Eds.). *Migration and Fiction. Narratives of Migration in Contemporary Canadian Literature*. Heidelberg: Winter, 59-72.

Decke-Cornill, Helene/Volkmann, Laurenz (2007). *Gender Studies and Foreign Language Teaching*. Tübingen: Narr.

Delanoy, Werner (1995). "Fremdsprachenunterricht und interkulturelle Verständigung", in: Bredella, Lothar (Ed.). *Verstehen und Verständigung durch Sprachenlernen? Dokumentation des 15. Kongresses für Fremd-sprachendidaktik, veranstaltet von der Deutschen Gesellschaft für Fremdsprachenforschung (DGFF), Gießen 4.-6. Oktober 1993.* Bochum: Brockmeyer, 284-291.

Delanoy, Werner (1999). "Fremdsprachenunterricht als 'dritter Ort' bei inter-kultureller Begegnung", in: Bredella, Lothar/Delanoy, Werner (Eds.) (1999). *Interkultureller Fremdsprachenunterricht.* Tübingen: Narr, 121-159.

Delanoy, Werner (2000). "Prozessorientierungund interkultureller Fremdspra-chenunterricht", in: Bredella, Lothar/Meißner, Franz-Joseph/Nünning, Ansgar/Rösler, Dietmar (Eds.). *Wie ist Fremdverstehen lehr- und lern-bar? Vorträge aus dem Graduierten Kolleg „Didaktik des Fremdver-stehens".* Tübingen: Narr, 191-230.

Delanoy, Werner (2005). "A Dialogic Model for Literature Teaching", in: *ABAC Journal,* 25/1, 53-66.

Delanoy, Werner (2006). "Transculturality and (Inter-)Cultural Learning in the EFL Classroom", in: Werner Delanoy/Laurenz Volkmann (Ed.). *Cultu-ral Studies in EFL Classroom.* Heidelberg: Winter, 233-248.

Delanoy, Werner (2008). "Transkulturalität und Literatur im Englischunter-richt", in: Gnutzmann, Claus/Königs, Frank G./Zöfgen, Ekkehard (Eds.). *Fremdsprachen Lehren und Lernen (FLuL),* 37/2008, 95-123.

Delanoy, Werner (2008b). "Dialogic Communicative Competence and Langu-age Learning", in: Delanoy, Werner/Volkmann, Laurenz (Eds.). *Future Perspectives for English Language Teaching.* Heidelberg: Winter, 173-188.

Delanoy, Werner (2011). "Do We Really Need Transculturality as a Concept for Cultural Learning", in: Vasta, Nicoletta/Riem, Antonella, Bortuluz-zi, Maia/Saidero, Deborah (Eds.). *Identities in Transition in the Eng-lish-Speaking World.* Udine: Forum, 277-290.

Delanoy, Werner (2012). "From 'Inter' to 'Trans'? Or: Quo Vadis Cultural Learning?", in: Eisenmann, Maria/Summer, Theresa (Eds.). *Basic Is-sues in EFL Teaching and Learning.* Heidelberg: Winter, 157-169.

Delanoy, Werner/Volkmann, Laurenz (Eds.) (2006). *Cultural Studies in the EFL Classroom.* Heidelberg: Winter.

Delanty, Gerard (2003). *Community.* London: Routledge.

Dervin, Frank (2010). "Assessing Intercultural Competence in Language Learn-ing and Teaching: A Critical Review of Current Efforts", in: Dervin, Frank/Suomela-Salmi, Eija (Eds.). *New Approaches to Assessment in Higher Education.* Bern: Lang, 157-173.

DESI-Konsortium (Ed.) (2008). *Unterricht und Kompetenzerwerb in Deutsch und Englisch: Ergebnisse der DESI-Studie.* Weinheim: Beltz.

Devine, Dympna/Kelly, Mary (2006). "'I Just Don't Want to Get Picked on by Anybody': Dynamics of Inclusion and Exclusion in a Newly Multi-Ethnic Irish Primary School", in: *Children and Society*, 20/2, 128-139.

Devine, Dympna/Kenny, Mairin/Macneela, Eileen (2008). "Naming the 'Other': Children's Construction and Experience of Racism in Irish Primary Schools", in: *Race Ethnicity and Education*, 11/4, 369-385.

Dewaele, Jean-Marc/Nakano, Seiji (2013). "Multilinguals' Perceptions of Feeling Different when Switching Languages", in: *Journal of Multilingual and Multicultural Development*, 34/2, 107-120.

Diakiw, Jerry (1997). "Children's Literature and Canadian National Identity: A Revisionist Perspective", in: *Canadian Children's Literature* 87, 36-49.

Djikic, Maja/Oatley, Keith/Zoeterman, Sara/Peterson, Jordan B. (2009). "On Being Moved by Art: How Reading Fiction Transforms the Self", in: *Creativity Research Journal,* 21, 24-29.

Doff, Sabine (2005). *O Canada! History, Country and Cultures from Sea to Sea.* Viewfinder Topics Resource Book. Munich: Langenscheidt ELT.

Doff, Sabine (2006). "Die Frühphase der Englischdidaktik in der BRD: Eine konzeptuelle Analyse", in: Doff, Sabine/Wegner Anke (Eds.) (2006). *Fremdsprachendidaktik im 20. Jahrhundert* (MAFF). Munich: Langenscheidt, 193-207.

Doff, Sabine (2008). *Englischdidaktik in der BRD 1949-1989* (MAFF). Munich: Langenscheidt.

Doff, Sabine (2010). "Beyond Beavers and Bilingualism: Reasons and Suggestions for Teaching Modern Canada in the EFL Classroom", in: Eisenmann, Maria/Nancy Grimm/Laurenz Volkmann (Eds.). *Teaching the New English Cultures & Literatures.* Heidelberg: Winter, 3-17.

Doff, Sabine/Wegner Anke (Eds.) (2006). *Fremdsprachendidaktik im 20. Jahrhundert* (MAFF). München: Langenscheidt.

Doff, Sabine/Schulze-Engler (2011). "Beyond 'Other Cultures': An Introduction", in: Doff, Sabine/Schulze-Engler (Eds.). *Beyond 'Other Cultures' – Transcultural Perspectives on Teaching the New Literatures in English.* Trier: WVT, 1-14.

Douglas, Matthew (2011). "Canadian School Life", in: *Praxis Englisch*, 6, 9-13.

Dreßler, Constanze/Schmidt, Torben (2011). "Multiculturalism in Canada", in: *Praxis Englisch*, 6, 40-43.

Dreyer, Dagmar (2010). "Canada in Darkness: 'Happy Multicultural Land'?", in: Ernst, Jutta/Glaser, Brigitte (2010). *The Canadian Mosaic in the Age of Transnationalism.* Heidelberg: Winter, 75-90.

Dundes, Lauren (2001). "Disney's Modern Heroine Pocahontas: Revealing Age-old Gender Stereotypes and Role Discontinuity under a Façade of Liberation", in: *Social Science Journal*, 38, 353-365.

Düwel, Dieter-Hermann/Grün, Jennifer von der (Eds.) (2004). *Englisch betrifft uns – Canada.* Aachen: Bergmoser + Höller Verlag, 1.

Düwel, Dieter-Hermann/Grün, Jennifer von der (2004). "Vancouver – an Ideal Venue for the Winter Olympics 2010?", in: *Englisch betrifft uns – Canada*, 1, 33-36.

Dyck, Karen van (2010). "'Beginning with O, the O-mega': Translingual Literature and its Lessons for Translation". Online: Institut für Byzantinistik und Neogräzistik, Vienna. http://www.byzneo.univie.ac.at/oester reichische-gesellschaft-fuer-neugriechische-studien/gehaltene-vortraege /?key=1-13, Aug 26, 2013.

Dyck, Karen van (2012). "Trankulturelle Literatur und Übersetzungen", in: Cremer-Renz, Christa/Jansen-Schulz, Bettina (Eds.). *Von der Internationalisierung der Hochschule zur Transkulterllen Wissenschaft* (Proceedings of the Internationalisation of Higher Education to Transcultural Science Conference, 2010 at Leuphana University, Luneberg, Germany). Baden-Baden: Nomos, 267-282.

Eberhardt, Jan-Oliver (2008). "Interkulturelle Kompetenz bei Französischlernern. Eine explorative Studie mit Schülern der Jahrgangsstufe 10", in: *Zeitschrift für Fremdsprachenforschung*, 19/2, 273-296.

Eberhardt, Oliver (2009). "'Flaggen, Baguettes, auch wenn's komisch klingt, das Aussehen der Leute erinnert an Frankreich'. Von den Herausforderungen, interkulturelle Kompetenz im Kontext von Fremdsprachenunterricht zu evaluieren", in: Hu, Adelheid/Byram, Michael (Eds.). *Interkulturelle Kompetenz und fremdsprachliches Lernen – Modelle, Empirie, Evaluation/Intercultural Competence and Foreign Language Learning – Models, Empiricism, Assessment*. Tübingen: Narr, 253-272.

Eberhardt, Jan-Oliver (2010). "Interkulturelle Kompetenz als Bildungsstandard von Fremdsprachenunterricht: zwischen Anspruch und Wirklichkeit", in: *Grenzen überschreiten: sprachlich, fachlich, kulturell: Dokumentation zum 23. Kongress für Fremdsprachendidaktik der DGFF, Leipzig, 30.9.-1.10.2009*. Hohengehren: Schneider, 205-218.

Eberhardt, Jan-Oliver (2013). *Interkulturelle Kompetenzen im Fremdsprachenunterricht. Auf dem Weg zu einem Kompetenzmodell für die Bildungsstandards*. Trier: WVT.

Eckert, Johannes/Wendt, Michael (Eds.) (2003). *Interkulturelles und transkulturelles Lernen im Fremdsprachenunterricht*. Frankfurt a.M.: Peter Lang.

Eggers, Maureen (2008). "Rassifizierung und kindliches Machtempfinden: Wie schwarze und weiße Kinder rassifizierte Machtdifferenz verhandeln auf der Ebene von Identität", Kiel: Universitätsbibliothek Kiel. Online publication, June 18, 2013. http://macau.uni-kiel.de/receive/disserta tion_diss_00002627.

Einhoff, Jürgen (2003). "MULTI-CULTI. Didaktische Ansätze, Zielvorstellungen und Themen im Englischunterricht des 21. Jahrhunderts", in: Sonderheft *PRAXIS/fsu - MULTI-CULTI im Fremdsprachenunterricht*, 6-10.

Eisenmann, Maria (2004). *Das Amerikabild im Werk Edward Albees: Eine imagologisch-didaktische Analyse*. Heidelberg: Winter.

Eisenmann, Maria/Grimm, Nancy/Volkmann, Laurenz (Eds.) (2010). *Teaching the New English Literatures & Cultures*. Heidelberg: Winter.

Eisenmann, Maria (2010). "Jane Harrison's Stolen: Physical, Psychological and Sexual Abuse of Aboriginal Children in Australia", in: Eisenmann, Maria/Grimm, Nancy/Volkmann, Laurenz (Eds.) (2010). *Teaching the New English Literatures & Cultures*. Heidelberg: Winter, 125-137.

Egoff, Sheila (1967). *The Republic of Childhood: A Critical Guide to Children's Literature in English*. Oxford: OUP.

Ellis, Deborah (2010). *We Want You to Know*. Regina: Coteau Books.

Erdmenger, Manfred/Istel, Hans-Wolf (1973). *Didaktik der Landeskunde*. Tübingen: Hueber.

Ernst, Jutta/Glaser, Brigitte (Eds.). *The Canadian Mosaic in the Age of Transnationalism*. Heidelberg: Winter.

Ertelt, Barbara (2007). "The Story of the Totem Pole", in: *Grundschulmagazin Englisch "Cowboys and Indians"*. Munich: Oldenbourg Schulbuch GmbH Verlag, 13-16.

Ewers, Hans-Heino (2000). "Was ist Kinder- und Jugendliteratur? Ein Beitrag zu ihrer Definition und zur Terminologie ihrer wissenschaftlichen Beschreibung", in: Günter Lange (Ed.). *Taschenbuch der Kinder- und Jugendliteratur. Band 1 Grundlagen-Gattungen*. Baltmannsweiler: Schneider-Verlag Hohengehren, 2-16.

Fäcke, Christiane (2005). "Französischunterricht heute: Theoretische Positionen, didaktische Leitlinien, konkrete Umsetzungen. Eine Bestandsaufnahme – insbesondere im Hinblick auf interkulturelles Lernen", in: *Neusprachliche Mitteilungen aus Wissenschaft und Praxis* 58/4, 5-16.

Fäcke, Christiane (2006). *Transkulturalität und fremdsprachliche Literatur. Eine empirische Studie zu mentalen Prozessen von primär mono- oder bikulturell sozialisierten Jugendlichen*. Frankfurt a.M.: Peter Lang.

Feurle, Gisela (2010). "Teaching South African Literatures: A Diversity of Writings and Experiences", in: Eisenmann, Maria/Grimm, Nancy/Volkmann, Laurenz (Eds.) (2010). *Teaching the New English Literatures & Cultures*. Heidelberg: Winter, 43-57.

Flächer, Tina (2009). *Portfolioarbeit im gymnasialen Fremdsprachenunterricht: Themenorientierter Unterricht mit dem Europäischen Portfolio der Sprachen*. Frankfurt a.M.: Peter Lang.

Flechsig, Karl-Heinz (2000). "Transkulturelles Lernen". Interne Arbeitspapiere des Instituts für interkulturelle Didaktik, Göttingen, 2/2000. Online: http://wwwuser.gwdg.de/~kflechs/iikdiaps.htm, April 4, 2012.

Fox, Dana L./Short, Kathy G. (2003) (Eds.). *Stories Matter: The Complexity of Cultural Authenticity in Children's Literature*. Urbana: National Council of Teachers of English.

Franzbecker, Rolf (1988). "Der Flugdrachen als Lebenssymbol in der kanadischen Literatur", in: *Der Fremdsprachliche Unterricht: Kanada*, 89, 8-12.

Freitag-Hild, Britta (2010). *Theorie, Aufgabentypologie und Unterrichtspraxis inter- und transkultureller Literaturdidaktik: British Fictions of Migration im Fremdsprachenunterricht.* Trier: WVT.

Freitag-Hild, Britta (2011). "Searching for New Identities: Inter- and Transcultural Approaches to Black and Asian British Literature and Film", in: Doff, Sabine/Schulze-Engler (Eds.). *Beyond 'Other Cultures' – Transcultural Perspectives on Teaching the New Literatures in English.* Trier: WVT, 65-78.

Fröhlich, Veronika (2007). "Native Americans", in *Grundschulmagazin Englisch "Cowboys and Indians"*, 1, 39.

Frye, Northrop (1965). "Conclusion", in: Klinck, Carl F. (Ed.). *Literary History of Canada.* Toronto: University of Toronto Press. [Frye, Northrop (1995). "Conclusion to a Literary History of Canada", in: Frye, Northrop. *The Bush Garden: Essays on the Canadian Imagination.* Toronto: Anansi, 215-254.]

Gadamer, Hans-Georg (1972/1990). *Wahrheit und Methode.* Tübingen: Narr.

Gadamer, Hans-Georg (1997). *Truth and Method.* New York: Continuum.

Gally, Johanna/Herold, Hanne (2007). "Town and Country Life", in::*in Englisch – Come along to Canada*, 6, 30-35.

Galway, Elizabeth (2008). *From Nursery Rhymes to Nationhood – Children's Literature and the Construction of Canadian Identity.* New York: Routledge.

Gamble, Nikki/Yates, Sally (2008). *Exploring Children's Literature.* London: SAGE. Gandhi, Leela (1998). *Postcolonial Theory: A Critical Introduction.* New York: Columbia University Press.

Garland-Thomson, Rosemarie (1997). *Extraordinary Bodies: Figuring Physical Disability in American Culture and Literature.* Columbia University Press.

Gerring, Richard J. (1990). "The Construction of Literary Character: A View from Cognitive Psychology", in: *Style* 24, 380-391.

Gerson, Carole/Strong-Boag, Veronic (2000). *Paddling her Own Canoe: The Times and Texts of E. Pauline Johnson (Tekahionwake).* Toronto: University of Toronto Press.

Giedd, Jay/Blumenthal, Jonathan/Jeffries, Neal/Castellanos, F. Xavier/Liu, Hong/Zijdenbos, Alex/Paus, Tomáŝ/Evans, Alan/Rapoport, Judith (1999). "Brain Development during Childhood and Adolescence: A Longitudinal MRI Study", in: *Nature Neuroscience*, 2/10, 861-863.

Gilmore, Alex (2007). "Authentic Materials and Authenticity in Foreign Language Teaching", in: *Language Teaching*, 40, 97-118.

Glaap, Albert-R. (1988). "'That True North, whereof we lately heard': Kanada", in: *Der Fremdsprachliche Unterricht: Kanada*, 89, 4-7.

Glaap, Albert-R. (2010). "Plays from Aotearoa in the English Language Classroom", in: Eisenmann, Maria/Grimm, Nancy/Volkmann, Laurenz (Eds.) (2010). *Teaching the New English Literatures & Cultures.* Heidelberg: Winter, 139-150.

Glaap, Albert-R./Rau, Albert (1993). "Canada: a 'toronto' for Students of English. Themen und Texte", in: *Zeitschrift für Kanadastudien,* 13/2/24, 107-125.

Göbel, Kerstin (2003). "Critical Incidents – aus schwierigen Situationen lernen", presentation at "Fachtagung Lernnetzwerk Bürgerkompetenz", 17./18. December 2003, Bad Honnef. http://www.dipf.de/de/projekte/pdf/critical-incidents-2013-aus-schwierigen-situationen-lernen, Aug 8, 2013.

Göbel, Kerstin (2007). *Qualität im interkulturellen Englischunterricht. Eine Videostudie.* Münster: Waxmann.

Göbel, Kerstin/Hesse, Herman-Günter (2004). "Vermittlung interkultureller Komnpetenz im Englischunterricht – eine curriculare Perspektive", in: *Zeitschrift für Pädagogik* 50/6, 818-834.

Göbel, Kerstin/Hesse, Herman-Günter (2007). "Interkulturelle Kompetenz", in: Klieme, Eckhard/Beck, Bärbel (Eds.). *Sprachliche Kompetenzen: Konzepte und Messung. DESI-Studie (Deutsch Englisch Schülerleistungen International).* Weinheim: Beltz, 256-272.

Göbel, Kerstin/Hesse, Herman-Günter (2008). "Vermittlung interkultureller Kompetenz im Englischunterricht", in: DESI-Konsortium (Ed.). *Unterricht und Kompetenzerwerb in Deutsch und Englisch. Ergebnisse der DESI-Studie.* Weinheim: Belz, 398-410.

Göbel, Kerstin/Hesse, Herman-Günter/Jude, Nina (2008). "Interkulturelle Kompetenz", in: DESI-Konsortium (Ed.). *Unterricht und Kompetenzerwerb in Deutsch und Englisch. Ergebnisse der DESI-Studie.* Weinheim: Belz, 180-190.

Goffman, Erving (1959). *The Presentation of Self in Everyday Life.* New York: Anchor Books.

Gooding-Williams, Robert (1995). "Disney in Africa and the Inner City: On Race and Space in The Lion King", in: *Social Identities*, 1, 373-379.

Goodley, Dan (2011). *Disability Studies: An Interdisciplinary Introduction.* London: SAGE.

Goshn, Irma K. (2002). "Four Good Reasons to use Literature in Primary School ELT", in: *ELT Journal* 56/2, 172-179.

Goto, Hiromi (n.y.). "The Water of Possibility". Online: http://www.hiromigoto.com/books/the-water-of-possibility, March 10, 2010.

Grenz, Dagmar (1999). "Fremdverstehen – interkulturelle Literaturdidaktik – Kinderliteratur", in: Decke-Cornill, Helene/Reichart-Wallrabenstein, Maike (Eds.). *Sprache und Fremdverstehen.* Frankfurt a.M.: Peter Lang, 193-210.

Grigoryan, Anna/King, John Mark (2008). "Adbusting: Critical Media Literacy in a Multi-Skills Academic Writing Lesson", in: *English Teaching Forum*, 4, 2-9.

Grimm, Nancy (2009). *Beyond the "Imaginary Indian": Zur Aushandlung von Stereotypen, kultureller Identität & Perspektiven in/mit indigener Gegenwartsliteratur.* Heidelberg: Winter.

Grimm, Nancy (2010). "Australia & New Zealand: Beyond the "Toursist Kit" Approach in the EFL Classroom", in: Eisenmann, Maria/Grimm, Nancy/Volkmann, Laurenz (Eds.) (2010). *Teaching the New English Literatures & Cultures.* Heidelberg: Winter, 19-41.

Grimm, Nancy (2012). "Digital Media: Promise for or Threat to Education?", in Eisenmann, Maria/Summer, Theresa (Eds.). *Basic Issues in EFL Teaching and Learning.* Heidelberg: Winter, 229-239.

Groß, Konrad (1990). "Kanada in Lehrplänen und Lehrwerken für das Fach Englisch", in: *Internationale Schulbuchforschung, Zeitschrift des Georg Eckert-Instituts*, 12, 173-190.

Groß, Konrad (2004). "First Nations Literature from Canada in the EFL Classroom: A Modest Proposal", in: Heinze, Michael/Müller-Schneck, Elke (Eds.). *Canadian, Literary and Didactic Mosaic. Essays in Honour of Albert-Reiner Glaap on the Occasion of his 75th Birthday.* Trier: WVT, 121-136.

Grünewald, Andreas (2010). "Medienkompetenz", in: Surkamp, Carola (Ed.). *Metzler Lexikon Fremdsprachendidaktik.* Stuttgart: Metzler, 213-214.

Grünewald, Andreas/Küster, Lutz (2009). *Fachdidaktik Spanisch: Tradition, Innovation, Praxis.* Seelze: Klett/Kallmeyer.

Gulden, Brigitte (1986). "'Aca nada' oder 'Kanata': Kanadische Literatur im Englischunterricht der gymnasialen Oberstufe", in: Klooß, Wolfgang/Lutz, Hartmut (Eds.). *Kanada: Geschichte Politik Kultur, Gulliver, Deutsch-Englische Jahrbücher*, 19. Berlin: Argument Verlag, 13-30.

Hall, Edward T. (1976). *Beyond Culture.* New York: Anchor Books.

Hall, Edward T. (1989). *The Dance of Life: The Other Dimension of Time.* New York: Doubleday/Anchor Books.

Hall, Geoff (2005). *Literature in Language Education.* New York: Palgrave.

Hall, Stuart (1990). "Cultural Identity and Diaspora", in: Rutherford, Jonathan (Ed.). *Identity: Community, Culture, Difference.* London: Lawrence and Wishart, 222-237.

Hall, Stuart (1991). "Old and New Identities. Old and New Ethnicities", in: King, Anthony D. (Ed.). *Culture, Globalization and the World-System. Contemporary Conditions for the Representation of Identity.* London: Mcmillan, 41-68.

Hall, Stuart (1992a). "Race, Culture, and Communications: Looking Backward and Forward at Cultural Studies", in: *Rethinking Marxism*, 5/1, 10-18.

Hall, Stuart (1992b). "The Question of Cultural Identity", in: Hall, Stuart/Held, David/McGrew, Tony (Eds.). *Modernity and its Futures*. Cambridge: Polity Press, 273-325.

Hall, Stuart (2000). "Who needs 'Identity'?", in: du Gay, Paul/Evans, Jessica/Redman, Peter (Eds.). *Identity: A Reader*. London: SAGE, 15-30.

Hallet, Wolfgang (2001). "Interplay der Kulturen: Fremdsprachenunterricht als ,hybrider Raum'. Überlegungen zu einer kulturwissenschaftlich orientierten Textdidaktik", in: *Zeitschrift für Fremdsprachenforschung* 12/1, 103-130.

Hallet, Wolfgang (2002). *Fremdsprachenunterricht als Spiel der Texte und Kulturen. Intertextualität als Paradigma einer kulturwissenschaftlichen Didaktik*. Trier: WVT.

Hallet, Wolfgang (2005). "La rue Bleue n'est pas bleue. L'Arabe n'est pas arabe'. Das Spiel der Texte und Kulturen in Monsieur Ibrahim et les fleurs du Coran und im Fremdsprachenunterricht", in: Schuhmann, Adelheid (Ed.). *Kulturwissenschaften und Fremdsprachendidaktik im Dialog. Perspektiven eines interkulturellen Fremdsprachenunterrichts*. Frankfurt a.M.: Peter Lang, 99-112.

Hallet, Wolfgang (2007a). "Literatur und Kultur im Unterricht. Ein kulturwissenschaftlicher didaktischer Ansatz", in: Hallet, Wolfgang/Nünning, Ansgar (Eds.). *Neue Ansätze und Konzepte der Literatur- und Kulturdidaktik*. Trier: WVT, 31-47.

Hallet, Wolfgang (2007b). "*Scientific Literacy* und Bilingualer Sachfachunterricht", in: Gnutzmann, Claus/Henrici, Gert/Zöfgen, Ekkehard (Eds.). *Fremdsprache als Arbeitssprache in Schule und Studium. Fremdsprachen Lehren und Lernen* 36, 95-110.

Hallet, Wolfgang (2008). "Die Visualisierung des Fremdsprachenlernens. Funktionen von Bildern und visual literacy im Fremdsprachenunterricht", in: Lieber, Gabriele (Ed.). *Lehren und Lernen mit Bildern. Ein Handbuch zur Bilddidaktik*. Hohengehren: Schneider, 212-222.

Hallet, Wolfgang (2009a). "Available Design. Kulturelles Handeln, Diskursfähigkeit und generisches Lernen im Englischunterricht", in: Abendroth-Timmer, Dagmar/Lütge, Christiane/Elsner, Daniela/Viebrock, Britta (Eds.). *Handlungsorientierung im Fokus: Impulse und Perspektiven für den Fremdsprachenunterricht im 21. Jahrhundert*. Frankfurt a.M.: Peter Lang, 117-142.

Hallet, Wolfgang (2009b). "This Is What My Day Is Like. Generische Schreibaufgaben, Diskursfähigkeit und generisches Lernen", in: *Der fremdsprachliche Unterricht Englisch* 43/97, 20-25.

Hallet, Wolfgang (2009c). "Semiotic Translation, Literacy Learning and Teacher Development". Online: http://clil.uni.lu/images/stories/hallet_expert-statement.pdf, June 3, 2013.

Hallet, Wolfgang (2010a). "Kulturdidaktik", in: Surkamp, Carola (Ed.). *Metzler Lexikon Fremdsprachendidaktik: Ansätze, Methoden, Grundbegriffe.* Stuttgart: Metzler, 152-156.

Hallet, Wolfgang (2010b). "Fremdsprachliche *literacies*", in: Hallet, Wolfgang/Königs, Frank G. (Eds.). *Handbuch Fremdsprachendidaktik,* Seelze-Velber: Klett/Kallmeyer, 66-70.

Hallet, Wolfgang (2011). "Transcultural Fictions and Identities in the EFL Classroom: Zadie Smith, White Teeth", in: Doff, Sabine/Schulze-Engler (Eds.). *Beyond 'Other Cultures' – Transcultural Perspectives on Teaching the New Literatures in English.* Trier: WVT, 47-64.

Hallet, Wolfgang (2012a). "Die komplexe Kompetenzaufgabe. Fremdsprachliche Diskursfähigkeit als kulturelle Teilhabe und Unterrichtspraxis", in: Hallet, Wolfgang/Krämer, Ulrich (Eds.). *Kompetenzaufgaben im Englischunterricht. Grundlagen und Unterrichtsbeispiele.* Seelze: Klett/ Kallmeyer, 8-19.

Hallet Wolfgang (2012b). "Die Entwicklung von Unterrichtseinheiten, Kompetenzaufgaben und Evaluationsaufgaben für den Englischunterricht", in: Hallet, Wolfgang/Krämer, Ulrich (Eds.). *Kompetenzaufgaben im Englischunterricht. Grundlagen und Unterrichtsbeispiele.* Seelze: Klett/ Kallmeyer, 92-97.

Hallet, Wolfgang (2013). "Generisches Lernen im Fachunterricht", in: Becker-Mrotzek, Michael/Schramm, Karen/Thürmann, Eike/Vollmer, Helmut Johannes (Eds.). *Sprache im Fache – Sprachlichkeit und fachliches Lernen.* Münster: Waxmann, 59-76.

Hallet, Wolfgang/Königs, Frank G. (2010). "Lehrpläne und Curricula", in: Hallet, Wolfgang/Königs, Frank G. (Eds.). *Handbuch Fremdsprachendidaktik.* Seelze-Velber: Klett/Kallmeyer, 54-58.

Hallet, Wolfgang (2013). "Multimodale Jugendromane und autobiographisches Erzählen im Fremdsprachenunterricht", in: Grünewald, Andreas/Plikat, Jochen/Wieland, Katharina (Eds.). *Bildung – Kompetenz – Literalität. Fremdsprachenunterricht zwischen Standardisierung und Bildungsanspruch.* Seelze: Klett Kallmeyer, 138-149.

Halliwell, Stephen (2002). *The Aesthetics of Mimesis: Ancient Texts and Modern Problems.* Princeton: Princeton University Press.

Hammer, Julia (2012a). "Friedenserziehung durch Literatur: Deborah Ellis' *Parvana's Journey*", in: Hammer, Julia/Eisenmann, Maria/Ahrens, Rüdiger (Eds.). *Anglophone Literaturdidaktik. Zukunftsperspektiven für den Englischunterricht.* Heidelberg: Winter, 441-456.

Hammer, Julia (2012b). *Die Auswirkungen der Globalisierung auf denmodernen Fremdsprachenunterricht.* Heidelberg: Winter.

Hammer, Mitchell R./Bennett, Milton J./Wiseman, Richard (2003). "Measuring Intercultural Sensitivity: The Intercultural Development Inventory", in: *International Journal of Intercultural Relations,* 27/4, 421–443.

Hansen, Joyce (1998). "Multicultural Literature: A Story of Our own", in: Brown, Jean E./Stephens, Elaine C. (Ed.). *United in Diversity – Using Multicultural Young Adult Literature in the Classroom*. Urbana: National Council of Teachers, 13-19.

Hansen, Klaus P. (2003). *Kultur und Kulturwissenschaft. Eine Einführung*. Tübingen/Basel: Francke.

Harmon, James L. (2002). *Take my Advice. Letters to the Next Generation from People who Know a Thing or Two*. New York: Simon & Schuster.

Havighurst, Robert J. (1972). *Developmental Tasks and Education*. New York: McKay.

Haun, Beverly (2003). "The Rise of the Aboriginal Voice in Canadian Adolescent Fiction 1970-1990", in: Hudson, Aida/Cooper, Susan-Ann (Eds.). *Windows and Words - A Look at Canadian Children's Literature in English*. Ottawa: University of Ottawa Press, 35-48.

Harker, John W. (1987). "Canadian Literature in Canadian Schools: From the Old to the New Internationalism", in: *Canadian Journal of Education/Revue canadienne de l'éducation* 12.3, 417-427.

Harvighurst, Robert (1972). *Developmental Tasks and Education*. New York: David McKay.

Hermes, Liesel (2007). "To Read or not to Read. A Plea for Graded Readers", in: Kindermann, Wolf (Ed.). *Transcending Boundaries. Festschrift in Honor of Gisela Hermann-Brennecke*. Münster: LIT-Verlag, 105-126.

Heidrich, Nicole (2011). "White Fang and Buck – two Dogs in the Northwest of Canada", in: Kuty, Margitta (Ed.). *English 5-10, – Canada,* 6, 18-23.

Henke, Jürgen (1980). *Aspekte des heimlichen Lehrplans in Schulbüchern: eine deskriptive Gruppenanalyse von Sachbüchern der Grundschule unter dem Gesichtspunkt soziosexuellen Lernens*. Frankfurt/Main: Haag-Herchen.

Hermes, Liesel (2007). "To Read or not to Read. A Plea for Graded Readers", in: Kindermann, Wolf (Ed.). *Transcending Boundaries. Festschrift in Honor of Gisela Hermann-Brennecke*. Münster: LIT-Verlag, 105-126.

Hesse, Mechthild (2009). *Teenage Fiction the Active English Classroom*. Stuttgart: Klett.

Hestermann, Sandra (2006). "Teaching the Harry Potter 'Phenomenon' in the EFL Classroom: Harry Potter and the Prisoner of Azkaban", in: Delanoy, Werner/Volkmann, Laurenz (Eds.). *Cultural Studies in the EFL Classroom*. Heidelberg: Winter, 313-322.

Hillman, Judith (2003). *Discovering Children's Literature*. Upper Saddle River: Merrill Prentice Hall.

Hoffman, Diane M. (1996). "Culture and Self in Multicultural Education: Reflections on Discourse, Text, and Practice", in: *American Educational Research Journal*, Vol. 33/3, 545-569.

Hofstede, Geert (1991). *Cultures and Organizations – Software of the Mind*. New York: McGraw-Hill.

Holland, Norman (1968). *The Dynamics of Literary Response*. London: Oxford University Press.

Hollindale, Peter (1988). "Ideology and the Children's Book", in: *Signal: Approaches to Children's Books 55*, 1988, 3-22.

Honegger, Jana/Honegger Thomas (2006). "Tolkin's The Lord of the Rings – Beyond the Printed Text", in: Delanoy, Werner/Volkmann, Laurenz (Eds.). *Cultural Studies in the EFL Classroom*. Heidelberg: Winter, 323-336.

Horner, Marion/Probst, Ingmar (2012). *Canada Themeheft – Abi Workshop English*. Stuttgart: Klett.

Hoyte, Carol-Ann (2007). "Book Week Past and Present", in: *Canadian Children's Book News*, 30/3, 20-21.

Hu, Adelheid (1996). *"Lernen" als "Kulturelles Symbol". Eine empirisch qualitative Studie zu subjektiven Lernkonzepten im Fremdsprachenunterricht bei Oberstufenschülerinnen und -schülern aus Taiwan und der Bundesrepublik Deutschland*. Bochum: Brockmeyer.

Hu, Adelheid (1997). "Warum Fremdverstehen? Anmerkungen zu einem leitenden Konzept innerhalb eines ‚interkulturell' verstandenen Sprachunterrichts", in: Bredella, Lothar/Christ, Herbert/Legutke, Michael (Eds.). *Thema Fremdverstehen. Arbeiten aus dem Graduiertenkolleg „Didaktik des Fremdverstehens"*. Tübingen: Narr, 34-54.

Hu, Adelheid (2008). "Interkulturelle Kompetenz. Ein Leitziel sprachlichen Lehrens und Lernens im Spannungsfeld von kulturwissenschaftlicher Didaktik, pädagogischer Psychologie und Testtheorie", in: Schulz, Renate/Tschirner, Erwin (Eds.). *Communication across Borders. Developing Intercultural Competence in German as a Foreign Language*. München: Iudicium, 284-309.

Humboldt. Wilhelm von (1973). *Schriften zur Sprache*. Stuttgart: Reclam.

Hunfeld, Hans (1990). *Literatur als Sprachlehre, Ansätze eines hermeneutisch orientierten Fremdsprachenunterrichts*. Berlin/Munich: Langenscheidt.

Hunfeld, Hans (1991). "Zur Normalität des Fremden", in: *Der fremdsprachliche Unterricht Englisch*, 25/3, 50-52.

Hunfeld, Hans (1992). "Noch einmal: Zur Normalität des Fremden", in: *Der fremdsprachliche Unterricht: Englisch*, 26/1, 42-44.

Hunfeld, Hans (1994). "Fern vom versöhnten Zustand", in: Bausch, Karl-Richard/Christ, Herbert/Krumm, Hans-Jürgen (Eds.). *Interkulturelles Lernen im Fremdsprachenunterricht. Arbeitspapiere der 14. Frühjahrskonferenz zur Erforschung des Fremdsprachenunterrichts*. Tübingen: Narr, 94-100.

Hunfeld, Hans (1997). "Zur Normalität des Fremden: Voraussetzungen eines Lehrplanes für interkulturelles Lernen", in: BMW AG (Ed.). *LIFE, Ideen und Materialien für interkulturelles Lernen (Grundwerk)*. München: mimeo, 1-10.

Hunfeld, Hans (2004). *Fremdheit als Lernimpuls: skeptische Hermeneutik - Normalität - des Fremden - Fremdsprache Literatur*. Meran: Alpha beta.

Hunt, Jonathan (2007). "Borderland. Redefining the Young Adult Novel", in: *The Horn Book Magazine*, March/April. Online: http://archive.hbook. com/magazine/articles/2007/mar07_hunt.asp, Sept 20, 2011.

Hurley, Dorothy L. (2005). "Seeing White. Children of Color and the Disney Fairy Tale Princess", in: *The Journal of Negro Education,* 74/3, 221-232.

Hutcheon, Linda (1990). *Other Solitudes. Canadian Multicultural Fictions*. Toronto: Univeristy of Toronto Press.

Iljassova-Morger, Olga (2009). "Transkulturalität als Herausforderung für die Literaturwissenschaft und Literaturdidaktik", in: Hegemann, Jens (Ed.). *Das Wort. Germanistisches Jahrbuch Russland, Translation und Translationswissenschaften. Über-Setzen als Kulturtransfer" Beiträge der XXV. Germanistikkonferenz des DAAD vom 14. bis 17. Mai 2008 in Sankt-Peterburg*, 37-57.

Ing, Tiffanie (n.y.). "Publishing for Children: McClelland & Stewart's Long Legacy", in: *Historical Perspectives of Canadian Publishing*. Online: http://hpcanpub.mcmaster.ca/case-study/publishing-children-mcclelland - amp-stewart039s-long-legacy, July 26, 2013.

Iser, Wolfgang (1972). *Der Akt des Lesens*. München: Wilhelm Fink Verlag.

Iser, Wolfgang (1974). *The Implied Reader: Patterns of Communication in Prose Fiction from Bunyon to Beckett*. Baltimore: Johns Hopkins UP.

Iser, Wolfgang (1980). "The Reading Process: A Phenomenological Approach", in: Tompkins, Jane P. (Ed.). *Reader-Response Criticism: From Formalism to Post-Structuralism.* Baltimore: John Hopkins University Press, 50-69.

Jarvie, Grant (1991). *Sport, Racism and Ethnicity*. London: Falmer Press.

Jenkins, Richard (1996). *Social Identity*. New York: Routledge.

Jenkins, Henry (2007). "Transmedia Storytelling 101." Online: Official Weblog of Henry Jenkins: http://henryjenkins.org/2007/03/transmedia_story telling_101.html, July 15, 2014.

Jennings, Justin (2011). *Globalization and the Ancient World*. Cambridge University Press.

Johnston, Gordan (1983). "Obiquadj: Instruction and Delight for Children in White Versions of Indian Stories", in: *CCL: Canadian Children's Literature/Littérature canadienne pour la jeunesse* 31/32, 80-92.

Johnston, Ingrid (2000). "Literature and Social Studies: Exploring the Hyphenated Spaces of Canadian Identity", in: *Canadian Social Studies*, 35/1, Fall. Online: http://www2.education.ualberta.ca/css/CSS_35_1/ literature_and_social_studies.htm, Sept 13, 2011.

Johnston, Ingrid/Bainbridge, Joyce/Mangat, Jyoti/Skogen, Rochelle (2006). "National Identity and the Ideology of Canadian Multicultural Picture

Books: Pre-Service Teachers Encountering Representations of Difference", in: *jeunesse* 32.2, 76-96.

Jones, Raymond E./Stott , Jon C. (2000). *Canadian Children's Books: A Critical Guide to Authors and Illustrators*. Don Mills: OUP.

Jordan, Sarah (1997). "Student Responses to Culturally Diverse Texts", in: Cruz, Gladys/Jordan, Sarah/Meléndez, José/Ostrowski, Steven/Purves, Alan C. (Eds.). *Beyond the Culture Tours, Studies in Teaching and Learning with Culturally Diverse Texts*. Mahwah: Lawrence Erlbaum Associates, 9-34.

Joshua, Marilyn (2002). "Inside Picture Books: Where are the Children of Color?", in: *Educational Horizons*, 80, 125-131.

Kaikkonen, Pauli (1995). "Entwicklung des Kulturbildes der Fremdsprachenlernenden", in: Bredella, Lothar et al. (Ed.). *Verstehen und Verständigung durch Sprachenlernen? Dokumentation des 15. Kongresses für Fremdsprachendidaktik, veranstaltet von der Deutschen Gesellschaft für Fremdsprachenforschung (DGFF), Gießen 4.-6. Oktober 1993*. Bochum: Brockmeyer, 159-168.

Kamboureli, Smaro (2007). *Making a Difference: Canadian Multicultural Literature*. Toronto: OUP.

Kapuscinski, Ryszard (2008). *The Other*. London: Verso.

Kazaki, Vasiliki (2011). "Hollywood North. Warum die kanadische Filmindustrie zum ernstzunehmenden Rivalen Hollywoods wurde", in: *Praxis Englisch*, 6, 34-38.

Keen, Suzanne (2006). "Theory of Narrative Empathy", in: *Narrative,* 14/3, 207-236.

Keen, Suzanne (2007). *Empathy and the Novel*. New York: OUP.

Kelley, Colleen/Mayers, Judith (1993). *Cross-cultural Adaptability Inventory Manual*. Minneapolis: National Computer Systems.

Kellner, Douglas/Share, Jeff (2005). "Toward Critical Media Literacy: Core Concepts, Debates, Organizations, Policy", in: *Discourse: Studies in the Cultural Politics of Education* 26.3, 369-386.

Kiesling, Scott F./Paulston, Christina Bratt (Eds.) (2005). *Intercultural Discourse and Communication – The Essential Readings*. Oxford: Blackwell Publishing.

King, Thomas (1990). *All my Relations: An Anthology of Contemporary Canadian Native Fiction*. Toronto: McClelland & Stewart.

Kinzel, Till (2010). "Transcending Multiculturalism? Neil Bissoondath and the Question of Canadian Identity", in: Ernst, Jutta/Glaser, Brigitte (2010). *The Canadian Mosaic in the Age of Transnationalism*. Heidelberg: Winter, 61-74.

Kisch, Conrad (Ed.) (2005). *Destination: Canada: Textheft*. Berlin: Cornelsen.

Klein, Kerstin (2007). "I'm a happy cowboy", in: *Grundschulmagazin Englisch "Cowboys and Indians"*, 1, 29-30.

Klewitz, Bernd (Ed.) (2011). *Canada – Dreams and Realities. Schwerpunktthema Abitur Englisch*. Berlin: Cornelsen.

Klieme, Eckhardt/Beck, Bärbel (Eds.) (2007). *Sprachliche Kompetenzen - Konzepte und Messung*. DESI-Studie (Deutsch Englisch Schülerleistungen International). Weinheim: Beltz.

Klippel, Friederike (1994). *Englischlernen im 18. und 19. Jahrhundert Die Geschichte der Lehrbücher und Unterrichtsmethoden*. Münster: Nodus Publikation.

Klippel, Friederike (2000) . "Zum Verhältnis von altsprachlicher und neusprachlicher Methodik im 19. Jahrhundert", in: *Zeitschrift für Fremdsprachenforschung*, 11, 41-61.

Klippel, Friederike (2001). "Grammatik als Sprachlehre im 18. und 19. Jahrhundert", in: Börner, Wolfgang/Vogel, Klaus (Eds.). *Grammatik lehren und lernen*. Bochum: AKS Verlag, 61-81.

Klippel, Friederike (2005a). "Fremdsprachenunterricht im Spannungsfeld von Tradition und Innovation – Rückblick und Ausblick", in: Gebert, Doris (Ed.). *Innovation aus Tradition*. Dokumentation der 23. Arbeitstagung 2004. Bochum: AKS-Verlag, 17-32.

Klippel, Friederike (2005b). "Englische Literatur im Englischunterricht des 19. Jahrhunderts", in: Klippel, Friederike/Hüllen Werner (Eds.). *Sprachen der Bildung - Bildung durch Sprachen im Deutschland des 18. und 19. Jahrhunderts*. Wiesbaden: Harrassowitz, 185-209.

Klippel, Friederike (2006). "Perspektiven der Fremdsprachendidaktik am Ende des 20. Jahrhunderts", in: Doff, Sabine/Wegner Anke (Eds.) (2006). *Fremdsprachendidaktik im 20. Jahrhundert* (MAFF). Munich: Langenscheidt, 273-287.

Klippel, Friederike/Schmid-Schönbein, Gisela (2001). "Forschung in der Fremdsprachendidaktik", in: Bayrhuber, Horst/Finkbeiner, Claudia/Spinner, Kaspar H./Zwergel, Herbert A. (Eds.). *Lehr- und Lernforschung in den Fachdidaktiken*. Innsbruck: Studienverlag, 111-119.

Klippel, Friederike/Kolb, Elisabeth/Sharp, Felicitas (2013). "Einführung: Sprachenpolitische und fremdsprachendidaktische Diskurse im 19. und 20. Jahrhundert", in: Klippel, Friederike/Kolb, Elisabeth/Sharp, Felicitas (Eds.). *Schulsprachenpolitik und fremdsprachliche Unterrichtspraxis*. Münster: Waxmann, 7-11.

Klippel-Mostert, Dagmar (Ed.) (2003). *Bausteine Englisch - English Around the World* 1/4, 1-50.

Knapp, Karlfried/Knapp-Potthoff, Annelie (1990). "Interkulturelle Kommunikation", in: *Zeitschrift für Fremdsprachenforschung,* 1, 62-93.

Kohlberg, Lawrence (1975). "Moral Education for a Society in Moral Transition", in: *Educational Leadership* 33/1, 46-54.

Kordes, Hagen (1990). "Intercultural Learning at School: Limits and Possibilities", in: Buttjes, Dieter/Byram, Michael (Eds.). *Mediating Languages and Cultures. Towards an Intercultural Theory of Foreign Language Education.* Clevedon: Multicultural Matters, 287-305.

Korte, Barbara (1990). "Vorschläge zur Behandlung anglo-kanadischer Romane im Englischunterricht der gymnasialen Oberstufe", in: *Neusprachliche Mitteilungen*, 1, 33-38.

Koskensalo, Annikki (2008). "Transdifferenz und Transkulturalität: Neue Konzepte für die Fremdsprachendidaktik?", in: Tella, Seppo (Ed.). *From Brawn to Brain: Strong Signals in Language Education.* Proceedings of the ViKiPeda-2007 Conference in Helsinki, May 21–22, 2007. Helsinki: Department of Applied Sciences of Education, 85-98.

Krajewska-Kułak, Elżbieta et al. (2012). "Perception of Disabled Persons held by Children and Adolescents based on their Artwork", in: *Prog Health Sci*, 2/2, 116-124.

Kramsch, Claire (1993). *Context and Culture in Language Teaching.* Oxford: OUP.

Kramsch, Claire (1995). "Andere Worte – andere Werte: Zum Verhältnis von Sprache und Kultur", in: Bredella, Lothar et al. (Ed.). *Verstehen und Verständigung durch Sprachenlernen? Dokumentation des 15. Kongresses für Fremdsprachendidaktik, veranstaltet von der Deutschen Gesellschaft für Fremdsprachenforschung (DGFF), Gießen 4.-6. Oktober 1993.* Bochum: Brockmeyer, 51-66.

Kramsch, Claire (1998). "The Privilege of the Intercultural Speaker", in: Byram, Michael/Fleming, Michael (Eds.) (1998). *Language Learning in Inter-cultural Perspective.* Cambridge: CUP, 16-31.

Kramsch, Claire (2006). "From Communicative Competence to Symbolic Competence", in: *The Modern Language Journal*, 90, 249-252.

Kramsch, Claire (2009a). "Third Culture and Language Education", in: Cook, Vivian/Wei, Li (Eds.). *Contemporary Applied Linguistics. Language Teaching and Learning.* London: Continuum, 233-254.

Kramsch, Claire (2009b). *The Multilingual Subject.* Oxford: OUP.

Kramsch, Claire (2011). "The Symbolic Dimension of the Intercultural", in: *language teaching, surveys and studies*, 44/03, 354-367.

Kramsch, Claire/Whiteside, Anne (2008). "Language Ecology in Multilingual Settings: Towards a Theory of Symbolic Competence", in *Applied Linguistics* 29, 645-671.

Krebes, Sebastian (2002). "Zum Bild des nordamerikanischen Indianers im Deutschland des 21. Jahrhunderts: Versuch einer empirischen Analyse vorherrschender Stereotypen und Untersuchungen ihres realhistorischen Ursprungs", State examination thesis, unpublished. Rostock: University of Rostock.

Kulyk Keefer, Janice (1991). "From Mosaic to Kaleidoscope: Out of the Multicultural Past Comes a Vision of a Transcultural Future", in: *Books in Canada* 20/6, 13-16.

Kuty, Margitta (Ed.) (2011). *Englisch 5-10 – Canada,* 6. Seelze: Friedrich.

Küster, Lutz (2003). "Der Gegensatz ,Transkulturalität und ,Interkulturalität' aus Sicht der deutschen Erziehungswissenschaft – Anschlussmöglichkeiten für die Fremdsprachendidaktik?", in: Eckert, Johannes/Wendt, Michael (Eds.). *Interkulturelles und transkulturelles Lernen im Fremdsprachenunterricht.* Frankfurt a.M.: Peter Lang, 41-52.

Küster, Lutz (2005). "Kulturverständnisse in Kulturwissenschaft und Fremdsprachendidaktik", in: Schuhmann, Adelheid (Ed.). *Kulturwissenschaften und Fremdsprachendidaktik im Dialog. Perspektiven eines interkulturellen Fremdsprachenunterrichts.* Frankfurt a.M.: Peter Lang, 59-70.

Küster, Martin/Keller, Wolfram R. (2002). "Beyond *Fleur de Lis* and *Maple Leaf*: Ethnicity in Contemporary Canadian Literature", in: Küster, Martin/Keller, Wolfram R. (Eds.). *Writing Canadians: The Literary Construction of Ethnic Identities.* Marburg: Universitätsbibliothek, 9-27.

Lado, Robert (1957). *Linguistics across Cultures: Applied Linguistics for Language Teachers. A Guide for Building the Modern Curriculum.* Ann Arbor: University of Michigan Press.

Larkey, Edward (2008). "Intercultural Assessment Instruments in Foregin Language Teaching", in: Schulz, Renate/Tschirner, Erwin (Eds.). *Communication across Borders. Developing Intercultural Competence in German as a Foreign Language.* München: Iudicium, 259-283.

Larsson, Thomas (2001). *The Race to the Top: The Real Story of Globalization.* Washington, D.C.: Cato Institute.

Latrobe, Kathy/Drury, Judy (2009). *Critical Approaches to Young Adult Literature.* New York: Neal-Schuman.

Lazar, Gillian (2009). *Literature and Language Teaching.* Cambridge: CUP.

Lindner, Oliver (2010). "India: The Jewel in the Classroom", in: Eisenmann, Maria/Grimm, Nancy/Volkmann, Laurenz (Eds.) (2010). *Teaching the New English Literatures & Cultures.* Heidelberg: Winter, 59-72.

Litmann, Deanne Aline (2011). "Canada is not Another American State, it is a Country", in: Kuty, Margitta (Ed.). *English 5-10 – Cana da,* 6, 44-45.

Lemieux, Louise (1972). *Pleins feux sur la littérature de jeunesse au Canada français.* Montréal: Lemeac Editeur.

Lessard-Clouston, Michael (1992). "Assessing Culture Learning: Issues and Suggestions", in: *The Canadian Modern Language Review,* 49/2, 326-341.

Lévinas, Emmanuel (1987). *Time and the Other and Additional Essays.* Pittsburgh: Duquesne University Press

Lévinas, Emmanuel (1991). *Totality and Infinity.* Dordrecht: Kluwer Academic Publishers.

Levine, Deena R./Adelman, Mara B. (1993). *Beyond Language. Cross-Cultural Communication.* Upper Saddle River: Prentice Hall Regents.

Lohmann, Christa/Schmidt, Torben (Eds.) (2011). *Praxis Englisch* 6. Braunschweig: Bildungshaus Schulverlage.

Lösch, Klaus (2005). "Begriff und Phänomen der Transdifferenz: Zur Infrage-stellung binärer Differenzkonstrukte", in: Allolio-Näcke, Lars/Kal-scheuer, Britta/Manzesche, Arne (Eds.). *Differenz anders Denken. Bau-steine zu einer Kulturtheorie der Transdifferenz.* Frankfurt a.M.: Cam-pus, 26-49.

Löschmann, Martin (1998). "Stereotype, Stereotype und kein Ende", in: Löschmann, Martin/Stroinska, Magda (Eds.). *Stereotype im Fremdspra-chenunterrich*t. Frankfurt a.M.: Peter Lang, 7-33.

Löschmann, Martin/Stroinska, Magda (Eds.) (1998). *Stereotype im Fremdspra-chenunterrich*t. Frankfurt a.M.: Peter Lang.

Löschnigg, Maria/Löschnigg, Martin (Eds.) (2009). *Migration and Fiction. Narratives of Migration in Contemporary Canadian Literature.* Heidel-berg: Winter.

Luke, Carmen (1997). "Media Literacy and Cultural Studies", in: Muspratt, Sandy/Luke, Alan/Freebody, Peter (Eds.). *Constructing Critical Litera-cies: Teaching and Learning Textual Practice.* Creskill, NJ: Hampton Press, 19-49.

Lütge, Christiane (Ed.) (2012a). *Praxis Fremdsprachenunterricht: Global Edu-cation*, 5. München: Oldenburg Schulbuchverlag.

Lütge, Christiane (2012b). "Developing "Literary Literacy"? Towards a Pro-gression of Literary Learning", in: Eisenmann, Maria/Summer, Theresa (Eds.). *Basic Issues in EFL Teaching and Learning.* Heidelberg: Win-ter, 191-202.

Lütge, Christiane (2013a). "Sprachenlernen und Identität(en) im Fremdspra-chenunterricht", in: Burwitz-Melzer, Eva/Königs, Frank G./Riemer, Claudia (Eds.) (2013). *Identität und Fremdsprachenlernen – Anmer-kungen zu einer komplexen Beziehung.* Tübingen: Narr, 163-170.

Lütge, Christiane (2013b). "Otherness in Children's Literature: Perspectives for the EFL Classroom", in: Lütge, Christiane/Bland, Janice (Eds.). *Chil-dren's Literature in Language Education.* London: Bloomsbury, 97-105.

Lütge, Christiane (2013c) "Conclusion", in: Bland, Janice/Lütge, Christiane (Eds.). *Children's Literature in Second Language Education.* London: Bloomsbury Academic, 219-224.

Lutz, Hartmut (2002). "Images of Indians in German Children's Books", in Lutz, Hartmut (Ed.). *Approaches: Essays in Native North American Studies and Literatures.* Augsburg: Wißner Verlag, 13-47.

Lynch-Brown, Carol/Tomlinson, Carl M./Short, Kathy G. (2011). *Essentials of Children's Literature.* Boston: Pearson.

Madore, Edith (1994). *La littérature pour la jeunesse au Québec.* Montréal: Éditions du Boréal.

Maijala, Minna (2006). "Klischees im Spiegel landeskundlicher Inhalte von Sprachlehrwerken. Über stereotype Darstellungen fremder Kultur(en)", in: *Jahrbuch Deutsch als Fremdsprache 32*, 126-139.

Maillet, Gregory (2003). "A Parliament of Stories: Multiculturalism and the Contemporary Children's Literature of Saskatchewan", in: Hudson, Aida/Cooper, Susan-Ann (Eds.). *Windows and Words: A Look at Canadian Children's Literature in English*. Ottawa: University of Ottawa Press, 49-60.

Mandel, Eli/Taras, David (Eds.) (1987). *A Passion for Identity: An Introduction to Canadian Studies*. Toronto/New York: Methuen.

Mar, Raymond A./Djikic, Maja/Oatley, Keith (2008). "Effects of Reading on Knowledge, Social Abilities, and Selfhood", in: Zyngier, Sonia/ Bortolussi, Marisa/Chesnokova, Anna/Auracher, Jan (Eds.). *Directions in Empirical Studies in Literature: In Honor of Willie van Peer*. Amsterdam: Benjamins, 127-137.

Martin-Rodriguez, Manuel M. (2000). "Hyenas in the Pride Lands: Latinos/as and Immigration in Disney's The Lion King", in: *Aztlan*, 25/1, 47-66.

Mathews, Gordon (2000). *Global Culture/Individual Identity: Searching for a Home in the Cultural Supermarket*. London: Routledge.

May, Jill (1995). *Children's Literature and Critical Theory: Reading and Writing for Understanding*. New York: OUP.

McCallum, Robyn/Stephens, John (2011). "Ideology and Children's Books", in: Wolf, Shelby, A./Coats, Karen/Enciso, Patricia/Jenkins, Christine A. (Eds.). *Handbook of Research on Children's and Young Adult Literature*. New York: Routledge, 359-371.

McGrath, Robin (1983). "Genuine Eskimo Literature; Accept No Substitutes", in: *CCL: Canadian Children's Literature/Littérature canadienne pour la jeunesse,* 31/32, 23-29.

McKenzie, Andrea (2003). "The Changing Faces of Canadian Children: Pictures, Power and Pedagogy", in: Hudson, Aida/Cooper, Susan-Ann (Eds.). *Windows and Words: A Look at Canadian Children's Literature in English*. Ottawa: University of Ottawa Press, 201-218.

McLaughlin, Eithne (2007). "Cultural Memory and Regional Identities in Northern Ireland and Southern Carinthia: A Cross-Cultural Comparison", in: Delanoy, Werner/Helbig, Jörg/James, Allan (Eds.). *Towards a Dialogic Anglistics*. Wien/Münster: LIT, 29-46.

Melde, Wilma (1987). *Zur Integration von Landeskunde und Kommunikation im Fremdsprachenunterricht*. Tübingen: Narr.

Mercer, Sarah (2011). *Towards an Understanding of Language Learner Self-Concept*. Heidelberg: Springer.

Merkl, Matthias (2005a). "Images of Canada: from a Eurocentric Perspective to Multiperspectivity", in: Merkl, Matthias (Ed.). *Revue LISA/LISA e-jounral - Views of Canadian Cultures*, Vol. 3/2, 1-10. Online: http://lisa. revues.org/1169, Dec 18, 2011.

Merkl, Matthias (2005b). "Teaching Canadian Identity and Multiculturalism in Germany", in: Merkl, Matthias (2011) (Ed.). *Revue LISA/LISA e-*

jounral - Views of Canadian Cultures, 3/2, 246-273. Online: http://lisa.
revues.org/1169, Dec 18, 2011.

Merkl, Matthias (2005c). "What makes a Canadian? Strategies of Presenting
Canadianness in Teaching Materials", in: Antor, Heinz/Bölling, Gor-
don/Kern-Stähler, Annette/Stierstorfer, Klaus (Eds*.). Refractions of Canada in European Literature and Culture*. Berlin/New York: de Gruy-
ter, 281–295.

Merkl, Matthias (2013). *Identität und Fremdverstehen. Eine kulturwissenschaftliche und fachdidaktische Untersuchung der kanadischen Minoritätenli-
teratur der Gegenwart*. Oldenburg: BIS-Verlag.

Miall, David S. (1988). "Affect and Narrative. A Model of Response to Stories", in: *Poetics 17*, 259-272.

Miller, Partick B. (1998). "The Anatomy of Scientific Racism: Racialist Responses to Black Athletic Achievement", in: *Journal of Sport History*
25/1, 119-151.

Mitchell, David T./Snyder, Sharon L. (Eds.) (2000). *Narrative Prosthesis: Disability and the Dependency of Discourse*. Ann Arbor: University of
Michigan Press.

Mitchell, Michael (2010). "'Nobody or a Nation': Intercultural Adventures in
the Caribbean", in: Eisenmann, Maria/Grimm, Nancy/Volkmann, Laurenz (Eds.) (2010). *Teaching the New English Literatures & Cultures*.
Heidelberg: Winter, 73-89.

Mukherjee, Arun P. (1998). *Postcolonialism: My Living*. Toronto: TSAR.

Mukherjee, Bharati (1981). "An Invisible Woman", in: *Saturday Night*, March,
36-40.

Mukherjee, Bharati (1997). "American Dreamer", *MotherJones*. Online:
http://www.motherjones.com/politics/1997/01/american-dreamer, July
14, 2013.

Müller, Gertrud (2007). *Bausteine Englisch - Native Americans/Indiane*r.
Aachen: Bergmoser + Höller Verlag, 3/2007.

Müller, Klaus Peter (Ed.) (1990/2003). *Contemporary Canadian Short Stories*.
Ditzingen: Reclam.

Müller-Hartmann, Andreas (1999). "Auf der Suche nach dem 'dritten Ort': Das
Eigene und das Fremde im virtuellen Austausch über literarische Tex-
te", in: Bredella, Lothar/Delanoy, Werner (Eds.). *Interkultureller
Fremdsprachenunterricht*. Tübingen: Narr, 160-182.

Müller-Hartmann, Andreas (2001). "Literatur im virtuellen Lerndreieck – ein
interkulturelles Begegnungsprojekt", in: *Der fremdsprachliche Unterricht Englisch,* 49, 35-40.

Müller-Hartmann, Andreas/Richter, Annette (2002). "Von Holden Caulfield zu
Ahn Jo. Multikulturelle Jugendliteratur", in: Kieweg, Werner et al.
(Ed.). *Der Fremdsprachliche Unterricht Englisch*, 5. Seelze: Friedrich-
Verlag, 4-9.

Nadolny, Arnd (2004). "Two of the Toughest Sled Dog Races in the World: the Iditarod Sled Dog Race and the Yukon Quest", in: *Englisch betrifft uns – Canada*, 1, 7-11.

Nell, Victor (1988). *Lost in a Book – The Psychology of Reading for Pleasure*. New Haven: Yale University Press.

Neuhoff, Antje (2008). "E-Learning am LSK – Fallstudie Language On-Line Portfolio Project (LOLIPOP): Ein neues webbasiertes Europäisches Sprachenportfolio", MDC-Reihe: Perspektiven im E-Learning, TU Dresden, Lehrzentrum Sprachen und Kulturen. Online: http://tu-dresden.de/die_tu_dresden/zentrale_einrichtungen/mz/veranstaltungen/kolloquia/vortragsreihe/archiv/vortragsreihe/2008/neuhoff-2008-06-20.pdf, June 1, 2013.

Nevid, Jeffey S. (2009/2013). *Psychology: Concepts and Applications*. Belmont: Wadsworth.

New, William H. (Ed.) (2002). *Encyclopedia of Literature in Canada*. Toronto: University of Toronto Press.

Newby, David/Fenner, Anne-Brit/Jones, Barry (Eds.) (2011). *Using the European Portfolio for Student Teachers of Languages.* Graz: European Center for Modern Languages/Council of Europe.

Ngugi wa Thiong'o (1986). *Decolonising the Mind*. Harare: Zimbabwe Publishing House.

Nicholas, Lionel (Ed.) (2008). *Introduction to Psychology*. Cape Town: UCT Press.

Nieweler, Andreas (1995). "Fremdsprachlicher Literaturunterricht als Hermeneutik des Fremden", in: Bredella, Lothar (Ed.). *Verstehen und Verständigung durch Sprachlernen? Dokumentation des 15. Kongresses für Fremdsprachendidaktik, veranstaltet von der Deutschen Gesellschaft für Fremdsprachenforschung (DGFF), Gießen 4.-6. Oktober 1993*. Bochum: Brockmeyer, 292-298.

Niergarden, Göran (2010). "'Carving out me identity': Caribbean Poetry as a Travel Guide to Postcolonial Awareness and Intercultural Competence", in: Eisenmann, Maria/Grimm, Nancy/Volkmann, Laurenz (Eds.). *Teaching the New English Literatures & Cultures*. Heidelberg: Winter, 197-215.

Nilsen, Alleen Pace/Donelson, Kenneth L. (2009). *Literature for Today's Young Adults*. Boston: Person.

Nischik, Reingard (2000). "Multiculturalism in Canadian Culture: A Didactic Approach", in: *Zeitschrift für Kanadastudien*, 20/1/37, 27-40.

Nodelman, Perry (1983). "Non-Native Primitive Art: Elizabeth Cleaver's Indian Legends", in: *CCL: Canadian Children's Literature/Littérature canadienne pour la jeunesse* 31/32, 69-79.

Nodelman, Perry (1992). "The Other: Orientalism, Colonialism, and Children's Literature", in: *Children's Literature Association Quarterly*, 17, 29–35.

Nodelman, Perry (1997). "What is Canadian about Canadian Children's Literature?", in: *CCL: Canadian Children's Literature/Littérature canadienne pour la jeunesse,* 87, 23/3, University of Winnipeg, 15-35.

Nodelman, Perry (2008). "At Home on Native Land: A Non-Aboriginal Canadian Scholar Discusses Aboriginality and Property in Canadian Double-Focalited Novels for Young Adults", in: Reimer, Mavis (Ed.). *Home Words – Discourses of Children's Literature in Canada.* Waterloo: Wilfrid Laurier Press, 107-128.

Nodelman, Perry/Reimer, Reimer (2003). *The Pleasures of Children's Literature.* New York: Allyn & Bacon.

Norales, Francisca (Ed.) (2006). *Cross-cultural Communication. Concepts, Cases and Challenges.* New York: Cambria Press.

Norton, Bonny (1997). "Language, Identity, and the Ownership of English", in: *TESOL Quarterly* 31/3, 409-429.

Norton, Bonny (2000). *Identity and Language Learning: Gender, Ethnicity, and Educational Change.* Harlow, England: Longman/Pearson.

Norton, Bonny (2001). "Non-Participation, Imagined Communities, and the Language Classroom", in: Breen, Michael (Ed.). *Learner Contributions to Language Learning: New Directions in Research.* London: Pearson Education Limited, 159-171.

Norton, Bonny/Pavlenko, Aneta (2007). "Imagined Communities, Identity, and English Language Learning", in: Cummins, Jim/Davison, Chris (Eds.). *International Handbook of English Language Teaching, Part II*, New York: Springer, 669-680.

Norton, Bonny/Toohey, Kelleen (2011). "Identity, Language Learning, and Social Change", in: *Language Teaching* 44/4, 412-446.

Norton, Donna E. (1995). *Through the Eyes of a Child: An Introduction to Children's Literature.* Englewood Cliffs: Merrill-Prentice.

Norton, Donna E. (2009). *Multicultural Children's Literature: Through the Eyes of Many Children.* Boston: Pearson.

Norton, Donna E. (2011). *Through the Eyes of a Child: An Introduction to Children's Literature.* Boston: Pearson.

Nunan, David/Choi, Julie (Eds.) (2010). *Language and Culture. Reflective Narratives and the Emergence of Idenity.* New York: Routeldge.

Nünning, Ansgar (1994). "Das Image der (häßlichen) Deutschen. Möglichkeiten der Umsetzung der komparatistischen Imagologie in einer landeskundlichen Unterrichtsreihe für den Englischunterricht", in: *Die Neueren Sprachen* 93/2, 160-184.

Nünning, Ansgar (2000). "'Intermisunderstanding' Prolegomena zu einer literaturdidaktischen Theorie des Fremdverstehens: Erzählerische Vermittlung, Perspektivwechsel und Perspektivübernahme", in: Bredella, Lothar/Meißner, Franz-Joseph/Nünning, Ansgar/Rösler, Dietmar (Eds.). *Wie ist Fremdverstehen lehr- und lernbar?* Tübingen: Narr, 84-132.

Nussbaum, Martha (2008). "Beyond Toleration to Equal Respect", in: *Seminar New Delhi*, 581, Malyika Singh, 100-104.

Oatley, Keith (2011). "Why Fiction is Good for You", in: *LRC*, July/August. Online: http://reviewcanada.ca/essays/2011/07/01/why-fiction-is-good-for-you/, July 5, 2013.

O'Reilly, Carolyn (2011). "Optimism, Commitment & Growth – 35 Years of the Canadian Children's Book Centre", in: *booknews* 34/2, 17-19.

O'Sullivan, Emer/Rösler, Dietmar (1999). "Stereotype im Rückwärtsgang. Zum didaktischen Umgang mit Heterostereotypen in kinderliterarischen Texten", in: Bredella, Lothar/Delanoy, Werner (Eds.) (1999). *Interkultureller Fremdsprachenunterricht: Das Verhältnis von Fremdem und Eigenem*. Tübingen: Narr, 312-321.

O'Sullivan, Emer/Rösler, Dietmar (2002). "Fremdsprachenlernen und Kinder- und Jugendliteratur: Eine kritische Bestandsaufnahme", in: *Zeitschrift für Fremdsprachenforschung* 13/1, 63-111.

Pache, Walter (1974). "Forschungsbericht. Moderne kanadische Literatur: Ein Überblick über wichtige Hilfsmittel", in: *Literatur in Wissenschaft und Unterricht*, 7/2, 122-133.

Paige, Michael R. (1993). "Trainer Competencies for International and Intercultural Programs", in: Paige, Michael R. (Ed.). *Education for the Intercultural Experience*. Yarmouth: Intercultural Press, 169-199.

Paige, Michael R./Martin, Jusith N. (1983). "Ethical Issues and Ethics in Cross-Cultural Training", in: Landis, Dan/Brislin, Richard W. (Eds.). *Handbook of Intercultural Training, Vol. 1, Issues in Theory and Design*. New York: Pergamin Press, 36-60.

Paige, Michael R./Jacobs-Cassuto, Melody/Yershova, Yelena A./DeJaeghere, Joan (1999). "Assessing Intercultural Sensitivity: A Validation Study of the Hammer and Bennett (1998) Intercultural Development Inventory", paper presented at the International Academy of Intercultural Research Conference. Kent: Kent State University.

Paige, Michael R./Jorstad, Helen L./Siaya, Laura/Klein, Francine/Colby, Jeanette (2003). "Culture Learning in Language Education: A Review of the Literature", in: Lange, D.L./Paige, R. Michael. (Eds.). *Culture as Core: Perspectives on Culture in Second Language Learning*. Greenwich, CT: Information Age Publishing, 173-236.

Pantaleo, Sylvia (2002). "Children's Literature across the Curriculum: An Ontario Survey", in: *Canadian Journal of Education/Revue canadienne de l'éducation*, 27/2/3, 211-30.

Pearson, Joseph (2011). "I will never be a German – How a Canadian experiences life in Berlin", in: *Praxis Englisch*, 6, 39.

Petzold, Dieter (2000). "Multiculturalism in Canadian Children's Books: The Embarrassments of History", in: McGillis, Roderick (Ed.). *Voices of the Other. Children's Literature and the Postcolonial Context*. New York: Routledge, 177-192.

Phinney, Jean S./Rotherman, Mary J. (Eds.). *Ethnic Socialization of Children: Pluralism and Development*. Beverly Hills: Sage Publications.

Piornak, Heike (2007). "A Canadian E-mail Friend", in:*:in Englisch – Come along to Canada*, 6, 2-8.

Plitsch, Axel (2007). "A Canadian Kaleidoscope", in:*:in Englisch – Come along to Canada*, 6, 9-20.

Pratt, Linda/Beaty, Janice J. (1999). *Transcultural Children's Literature*. Englewood Cliffs, NJ: Prentice-Hall.

Raith, Thomas/Möhrle, Solveig (2006). "Global Englisch hören und erforschen. Aufgabenorientierte Arbeit mit Radioaufnahmen", in: *Der Fremdsprachliche Unterricht Englisch*, 84, 17-25.

Ramsey, Patricia G./Myers, Leslie C. (1990). "Salience of Race in Young Children's Cognitive, Affective, and Behavioral Responses to Social Environments", in: *Journal of Applied Developmental Psychology*, 11, 49-67.

Rasmussen, Ricky/Esgate, Anthony/Turner, David (2005). "On Your Marks, Get Stereotyped, Go! Novice Coaches and Black Stereotypes in Sprinting", in: *Journal of Sport and Social Issues* 29(4), 426-436.

Rau, Albert (1988). "Canada in the German Classroom - Necessarily an 'Alien Continent'?", in: *Der Fremdsprachliche Unterricht: Kanada,* 89, 21-24.

Rau, Albert (Ed.) (2005/2011). *Short Stories from Canada*. Berlin: Cornelsen.

Rau, Albert (2010). "Margaret Atwood's *The Handmaid's Tale*: A Dystopian Novel in the EFL Classroom", in: Eisenmann, Maria/Grimm, Nancy/Volkmann, Laurenz (Eds.) (2010). *Teaching the New English Literatures & Cultures.* Heidelberg: Winter, 109-124.

Rau, Albert (2012). "Margaret Atwoods Kurzgeschichte "Dancing Girls" – ein multikultureller Traum", in: Hammer, Julia/Eisenmann, Maria/Ahrens, Rüdiger (Eds.). *Anglophone Literaturdidaktik. Zukunftsperspektiven für den Englischunterricht*. Heidelberg: Winter, 127-140.

Reiche, Sofie (2011). "The Transcultural Approach in the Foreign Language Classroom: Teaching Octavia Butler's *Kindred*", in: Doff, Sabine/Schulze-Engler (Eds.). *Beyond 'Other Cultures' – Transcultural Perspectives on Teaching the New Literatures in English*. Trier: WVT, 79-96.

Reichl, Susanne (2013). "Doing Identity, Doing Culture: Transcultural Learning through Young Adult Fiction", in: Bland, Janice/Lütge, Christiane (Eds.). *Children's Literature in Second Language Education*. London: Bloomsbury Academic, 107-117.

Rembis, Michael A. (2013). "Athlete First: A Note on Passing, Disability and Sport", in: Brune, Jeffrey A./Wilson, Danial J. (Eds.) (2013). *Disability and Passing. Blurring the Lines of Identity*. Philadelphia: Temple University Press, 111-142.

Richter, Annette (2000). "Fremdverstehen mit multikulturellen Jugendbüchern: Laurence Yeps *Dragonwings*", in: Bredella, Lothar/Christ, Herbert/Legutke, Michael (Eds.). *Fremdverstehen zwischen Theorie und Praxis – Arbeiten aus dem Graduiertenkolleg „Didakitik des Fremdverstehens".* Tübingen: Narr, 87-110.

Richter, Miriam (2011). *Creating the National Mosaic: Multiculturalism in Canadian Children's Literature from 1950 to 1994.* Amsterdam: Rodopi.

Risager, Karen (1998). "Language Teaching and the Process of European Integration", in: Byram, Michael/Fleming, Michael (Eds.). *Language Learning in Intercultural Perspective. Approaches through Drama and Ethnography.* Cambridge: CUP, 242-254.

Risager, Karen (2012). "Introduction: Intercultural Learning: Raising Cultural Awareness", in: Eisenmann, Maria/Summer, Theresa (Eds.). *Basic Issues in EFL Teaching and Learning.* Heidelberg: Winter, 143-155.

Robert-Bosch-Stiftung/Payer, Peter (Eds.) (1982). *Fremdsprachenunterricht und internationale Beziehungen – Stuttgarter Thesen zur Rolle der Landeskunde im Französischunterricht.* Gerlingen: Robert-Bosch-Stiftung, Ludwigsburg Deutsch-Französisches Institut.

Roche, Jörg (2001). *Interkulturelle Sprachdidaktik. Eine Einführung.* Tübingen: Narr Studienbücher.

Rosaldo, Renato (1989). *Culture and Truth: The Remaking of Social Analysis.* Boston: Beacon Press.

Rosenblatt, Louise M. (1970). *Literature as Exploration.* London: Heinemann.

Rutherford, Jonathan (1990). "The Third Space. Interview with Homi Bhabha", in: Rutherford, Jonathan (Ed.). *Identity: Community, Culture, Difference.* London: Lawrence and Wishart, 207-221.

Ryan, Marie-Laure (2010). "Narration in Various Media", in: Hühn, Peter/Pier, John/Schmid, Wolf/Schöner, Jörg (Eds.). *The Living Handbook of Narratology.* Hamburg: Hamburg University Press. Online: http://www.lhn.uni-hamburg.de/article/narration-various-media, July 11, 2014.

Ryan, Marie-Laure (2013): "Transmedial Storytelling and Transfictionality", *Poetics Today* 34/3, Durham: Duke University Press, 361-388.

Ryan, Marie-Laure/Thon, Jan-Noël (Eds.) (2014). *Storyworlds across Media. Towards a Media-Conscious Narratology.* Nebraska: University of Nebraska Press.

Said, Edward (1978). *Orientalism.* New York: Vintage Books.

Said, Edward (1994). *Culture and Imperialism.* London: Vintage.

Saldanha, Louise (2000). "Bedtime Stories: Canadian Multiculturalism and Children's Literature", in: McGillis, Roderick (Ed.). *Voices of the Other. Children's Literature and the Postcolonial Context.* New York: Routledge, 165-176.

Saltman, Judith (1987). *Modern Canadian Children's Books.* Toronto: OUP.

Saltman, Judith (2003). "Children's Literature at the Millenium", in: Hudson, Aïda/Cooper, Susan-Ann (Eds.). *Windows and Words: A Look at Canadian Children's Literature in English.* Ottawa: University of Ottawa Press, 23-34.

Samson, Natalie. "Toronto Scientists Determine that Fiction Can Change Personalities", in *Quill & Quire*, August 11, 2011. Online: http://www.quill andquire.com/google/article.cfm?article_id=11929, Nov 3, 2012.

Saussure, Ferdinand de (1983). *Course in General Linguistics*. La Salle: Open Court.

Schardin, Andrea (2011). "Famous Canadians: Who is Amanda Marschall?: Eine Pro- und Kontra-Diskussion über Ein-/Auswanderung führen", in: *Englisch 5-10*, 6, 24-29.

Scheller, Ingo (1998). *Szenisches Spiel*. Berlin: Cornelsen.

Schlee, Fridtjof (2007). "Canada's National Parks", in: *:in Englisch – Come along to Canada*, 6, 21-29.

Schmid-Schönbein, Gisela (Ed.) (2007). *Grundschulmagazin Englisch "Cowboys and Indians"*, 1. Munich: Oldenbourg Schulbuch GmbH Verlag.

Schuhmann, Adelheid (2008). "Transkulturalität in der Romanistischen Literaturdidaktik. Kulturwissenschaftliche Grundlagen und didaktische Konzepte am Beispiel der *littérature beur*", in: *Fremdsprachen Lehren und Lernen (FLuL)*, 37, 81-94.

Schulz, Renate (2007). "The Challenge of Assessing Cultural Understanding in the Context of Foreign Language Instruction", in: *Foreign Language Annals*, 40/1, 9-26.

Schulze-Engler, Frank (2006). "Von 'Inter' zu 'Trans': Gesellschaftliche, kulturelle und literarische Übergänge", in: Antor, Heinz (Ed.). *Inter- und Transkulturelle Studien. Theoretische Grundlagen und interdisziplinäre Praxis*. Heidelberg: Winter, 41-53.

Schulze-Engler, Frank (2007). "Theoretical Perspectives: From Postcolonialism to Transcultural World Literature", in: Eckstein, Lars (Ed.). *English Literatures around the Globe. A Companion*. München/Stuttgart: Fink/ UTB, 20-32.

Schulze-Engler, Frank (2009). "Introduction", in: Schulze-Engler, Frank/Helff, Sissy (Eds.). *Transcultural English Studies. Theories, Fictions, Realities*. Amsterdam: Rodopi, ix-xvi.

Schutte, Ofelia (1998). "Cultural Alerity: Cross-Cultural Communication and Feminist Theory in North-South Contexts", in: *Hypatia*, 13/2, 53-72.

Schwartz, Helmut (2011). *Topics in Context: Canada – Changes and Challenges*. Berlin: Cornelsen.

Seelye, Ned (1974). *Teaching Culture: Strategies for Foreign Language Educators*. Skokie, Ill.: National Textbook Co.

Seelye, Ned (1988). *Teaching Culture*. Lincolnwood. Ntc Group.

Sercu, Lies (2004). "Assessing Intercultural Competence: a Framework for Systematic Test Development in Foreign Language Education and Beyond", in: *Intercultural Education*, 15/1, 73-89.

Sercu, Lies (2010). "Assessing Intercultural Competence: More Questions than Answers", in: Paran, Amos/Sercu, Lies (Eds.). *Testing the Untestable in Language Education*. Buffalo: Multilingual Matters, 17-34.

Shavit, Zohar (1986). *Poetics of Children's Literature*. Athens: University of Georgia Press.

Shirts, Garry (1973). *BAFA/BAFA: A Cross-Cultural Simulation*. Delmar: Smile II.

Siebold, Jörg (2006). "Zur kommunikativen Sicht in der Methodik des Englischunterrichts in der DDR", in: Doff, Sabine/Wegner Anke (Eds.) (2006). *Fremdsprachendidaktik im 20. Jahrhundert* (MAFF). Munich: Langenscheidt, 177-192.

Siepmann, Dirk (2012). "Spracherwerb in komplexen Kompetenzaufgaben. Einige Leitlinien und Beispiele für deren Umsetzung", in: Hallet, Wolfgang/Krämer, Ulrich (Eds.). *Kompetenzaufgaben im Englischunterricht. Grundlagen und Unterrichtsbeispiele*. Seelze: Klett/Kallmeyer, 30-44.

Sims, Rudine (1982). *Shadow and Substance: Afro-American Experience in Contemporary Children's Fiction*. Urbana, IL: National Council of Teachers of English.

Smith-D'Arezzo, Wendy M./Moore-Thomas, Cheryl (2010). "Children's Perceptions of Peers with Disabilities", in: *Teaching Exceptional Children Plus*, 6/3, 2-16. Online: http://journals.cec.sped.org/tecplus/vol6/iss3/art2, Sept 3, 2013.

Sommer, Doris (1999). *Proceed with Caution, when Engaged by Minority Writing in the Americas*. Cambridge, MA: Harvard University Press.

Sommer, Roy (2000). "Fremdverstehen durch Literaturunterricht: Prämissen und Perspektiven einer narratologisch orientierten interkulturellen Literaturdidaktik", in: Bredella, Lothar/Christ, Herbert/Legutke, Michael (Eds.). *Fremdverstehen zwischen Theorie und Praxis.* Tübingen: Narr, 19-42.

Sommer, Roy (2001a). *Fictions of Migration. Ein Beitrag zur Theorie und Gattungstypologie des zeitgenössischen interkulturellen Romans in Großbritannien.* Trier: WVT.

Sommer, Roy (2001b). "Fictions of Migration. Fremdverstehen durch multikulturelle Romane", in: *Der Fremdsprachliche Unterricht Englisch* 35/53, 36-39.

Spivak, Gayatri C. (1990). "Questions of Multi-Culturalism", in: Harasym, Sarah (Ed.). *The Post-Colonial Critic: Interviews, Strategies, Dialogues.* New York: Routledge, 59-66.

Stier, Jonas (2003). "Internationalisation, Ethnic Diversity and the Acquisition of Intercultural Competencies", in: *Intercultural Education*, 14/1, 78-91.

Stott, Jon C. (1983a). "The Circle and the Square", in: *CCL: Canadian Children's Literature/Littérature canadienne pour la jeunesse* 31/32, 2-4.

Stott, Jon C. (1983b). "A Conversation with Maria Cambell", in: *CCL: Canadian Children's Literature/Littérature canadienne pour la jeunesse* 31/32, 15-22.

Strauss, Marina (2001). "U.S. Demands Trample Canadian Kid's Lit", in: *The Globe and Mail*. June 1, M1.

Striegler, Marion (2007). "A Way of Life Collapses for Canada's Inuit", in: *Englisch betrifft uns – Canada*, 1, 37-40.

Surkamp, Carola (2012). "Literarische Texte im kompetenzorientierten Fremdsprachenunterricht", in: Hallet, Wolfgang/Krämer, Ulrich (Eds.). *Kompetenzaufgaben im Englischunterricht. Grundlagen und Unterrichtsbeispiele*. Seelze: Klett/Kallmeyer, 77-90.

Surkamp, Carola/Nünning, Ansgar (2008). *Englisch Literatur unterrichten 1: Grundlagen und Methoden*. Seelze: Klett/Kallmeyer.

Surkamp, Carola/Nünning, Ansgar (2009). *Englische Literatur unterrichten 2: Unterrichtsmodelle und Materialien*. Seelze: Klett/Kallmeyer.

Susemihl, Geneviève (2008). "The Imaginary Indian in German Children's Non-Fiction Literature", in: Knopf, Kerstin (Ed.). *Aboriginal Canada Revisted*. Ottawa: University of Ottawa Press, 122-157.

Susemihl, Geneviève (2011a). "From Umiak and Qamutik to Snowmobiles and Quads: Das Leben der Inuit früher und heute vergleichen", in: *Englisch 5-10*, 6, 10-13.

Susemihl, Geneviève (2011b). "'Most Canadians live in the woods, in huts and igloos…': Stereotype über Kanada ermitteln und diskustieren", in: *Englisch 5-10*, 6, 34-39.

Sutherland, Zena (1997). *Children and Books*. New York: Longman.

Tasillo, Mary (2006). "Heroism: What Does It Mean to be a Hero?", in: Trupe, Alice (Ed.). *Thematic Guide to Young Adult Literature*. Westport: Greenwood, 107-114.

Taylor, Charles (1993). *Multikulturalismus und die Politik der Anerkennung. Mit Kommentaren von Amy Gutmann (Ed.), Steven C. Rockefeller, Michael Walzer, Susan Wolf und einem Beitrag von Jürgen Habermas*. Frankfurt a.M.: Fischer.

Tesch, Bernd (2013). "De nouveaux ingredients pour une approche ancienne: Kompetenzorientierte Lernaufgaben im neuen Licht", in: Gründewald, Andreas/Plikat, Jochen/Wieland, Katharina (Eds.). *Bildung – Kompetenz – Literalität. Fremdsprachenunterricht zwischen Standardisierung und Bildungsanspruch*. Seelze: Klett/Kallmeyer, 86-97.

Thaler, Engelbert (2008). *Teaching English Literature*. Paderborn: Schöningh UTB.

Titchener, Edward B. (1915). *A Beginner's Psychology*. London: Macmillan.

Titchkosky, Tanya/Michalko, Rod (Eds.) (2009). *Rethinking Normalcy*. Toronto: Canadian Scholar's Press.

Thonhauser, Josef (1995). "Das Schulbuch im Spannungsfeld zwischen Wissenschaft und Ideologie", in: Olechowski, Richard (Ed.). *Schulbuchforschung*. Frankfurt a.M.: Peter Lang, 175-194.

Teepe, Harald (2004). "Saving Canada's Great Bear Rainforest. Focus on Environmental Issues", in: *Englisch betrifft uns,* Canada, 1, 12-17.

Todd, Sharon (2001). "On Not Knowing the Other, or Learning from Lévinas", in: *Philosophy of Education 2001*, 67-73. Online: http://ojs.ed.uiuc. edu/index.php/pes/article/view/1871/582, Feb 20, 2012.

Tomalin, Barry/Stempleski, Susan (1993). *Cultural Awareness*. Oxford: Oxford University Press.

Toohey, Kelleen (2000). *Learning English at School: Identity, Social Relations and Classroom Practices*. Clevedon: Multilingual Matters.

Towbin, Mia Adessa/Haddock, Shelley A./Schindler Zimmerman, Toni/Lund, Lori K./Tanner, Litsa Renée (2003). "Images of Gender, Race, Age, and Sexual Orientation in Disney Feature-Length Animated Films", in: *Journal of Feminist Family Therapy*, 15/4, 19-44.

Trompenaars, Frans/Hampden-Turner, Charles (Eds.) (1997). *Riding the Waves of Culture: Understanding Global Diversity in Global Business*. New York: McGraw-Hill.

Truchan-Tataryn, Maria (2011). *(In)visible Images: Seeing Disability in Canadian Literature, 1823-1974*. Lambert Academic Publishing.

Tunkel, Nora (2012). *Transcultural Imaginaries. History and Globalization in Contemporary Canadian Literature.* Heidelberg: Winter.

Vanderbeke, Dirk (2006). "Comics and Graphic Novels in the Classroom", in: Delanoy, Werner/Volkmann, Laurenz (Eds.). *Cultural Studies in the EFL Classroom*. Heidelberg: Winter, 365-380.

Viebrock, Britta (2012). "Zwischen Medieneuphorie und vermeintlicher "Demokratisierung des Lernens": Einige kritische Überlegungen zur Nutzung des Web 2.0 im Englischunterricht", in Reinfried, Marcus/Volkmann, Laurenz (Eds.). *Medien im neokommunikativen Fremdsorachenunterricht: Einsatzformen, Inhalt, Lernerkompetenzen.* Frankfurt a.M.: Peter Lang, 183-198.

Vogt, Susanne (2007). "The Boys in the Cave", in: *Grundschulmagazin Englisch "Cowboys and Indians"*, 1, 17-20.

Volkmann, Laurenz (2002). "Aspekte und Dimension interkultureller Kompetenz", in: Volkmann, Laurenz/Stierstorfer, Klaus/Gehring, Wolfgang (Eds.) (2002). *Interkulturelle Kompetenz. Theorie und Praxis des fremdsprachlichen Unterrichts.* Tübingen: Narr, 11-47.

Volkmann, Laurenz (2005). "'Demokratisierung des Lernens' oder ‚Medienverwahrlosung'? Überlegungen zum didaktischen Umgang mit dem Internet", in: Blell, Gabriele & Kupetz, Rita (Eds.). *Fremdsprachenlernen zwischen ‚Medienverwahrlosung und Medienkompetenz. Beiträge zu einer kritisch-reflektierten Mediendidaktik.* Frankfurt a.M.: Lang, 43-66.

Volkmann, Laurenz (2005). "Die Vermittlung kulturwissenschaftlicher Inhalte und Methoden", in: Volkmann, Laurenz/Stierstorfer, Klaus (Eds.). *Kulturwissenschaft Interdisziplinär.* Tübingen: Narr, 271-301.

Volkmann, Laurenz (2007). "*The Global Village*: Von der interkulturellen zur multikulturellen Kompetenz", in: Antor, Heinz (Ed.). *Fremde Kulturen verstehen, fremde Kulturen lehren: Theorie und Praxis der Vermittlung interkultureller Kompetenz.* Heidelberg: Winter, 127-157.

Volkmann, Laurenz (2008). "Arundhati Roy: The God of Small Things", in: Peters, Susanne/Stierstorfer, Klaus/Volkmann, Laurenz (Eds.). *Teaching Contemporary Literature and Culture: Novels II.* Trier: WVT, 463-480.

Volkmann, Laurenz (2009). "Trotz Bildungsstandards und Output-Orientierung: Literatur auch und gerade in der Sekundarstufe I!", in: Hollm, Jan (Ed.). *Literaturdidaktik und Literaturvermittlung im Englischunterricht der Sekundarstufe I.* Trier: WVT, 23-40.

Volkmann, Laurenz (2010). *Fachdidaktik Englisch: Kultur und Sprache.* Tübingen: Narr.

Volkmann, Laurenz (2011). "The 'Transcultural Moment' in English as a Foreign Language", in: Doff, Sabine/Schulze-Engler (Eds.). *Beyond 'Other Cultures' – Transcultural Perspectives on Teaching the New Literatures in English.* Trier: WVT, 113-128.

Volkmann, Laurenz (2012). "Intercultural Learning and Postcolonial Studies: "Never the Twain Shall Meet"?", in: Eisenmann, Maria/Summer, Theresa (Eds.). *Basic Issues in EFL Teaching and Learning.* Heidelberg: Winter, 169-180.

Volkmann, Laurenz/Stierstorfer, Klaus/Gehring, Wolfgang (Eds.) (2002). *Interkulturelle Kompetenz. Theorie und Praxis des fremdsprachlichen Unterrichts.* Tübingen: Narr.

Vollmer, Helmut Johannes (2010). "Kompetenzstandards und Aufgabenentwicklung", in: Hallet, Wolfgang/Königs, Frank G. (Eds.). *Handbuch Fremdsprachendidaktik,* Seelze-Velber: Klett/Kallmeyer, 372-376.

Wagner, Sebastian (2011). "My Name is Seepeetza: Shirley Sterlin's novel My Name is Seepeetza – an Indian Residential School Experience", in: *Praxis Englisch*, 6, 29-33.

Waszak, Marion (2007). "Time to Dress Up!", in: *Grundschulmagazin Englisch "Cowboys and Indians"*, 1, 27-28.

Waterston, Elizabeth (1992). *Children's Literature in Canada,* New York: Twayne Publishers.

Watson, Victor (2001). *The Cambridge Guide to Children's Books in English.* Cambridge: CUP.

Wauer, Sylvia/Zocholl, Peter (2004). "The Button Factory – The Rise and Fall of a Canadian Family. An Ecerpt from Margarte Atwood's novel 'The Blind Assassin'", in: *Englisch betrifft uns*, 1, 18-27.

Weaver, Gary R. (1993). "Understanding and Coping with Cross-Cultural Adjustment Stress", in: Paige, Michael (Ed.). *Education for the Intercultural Experience.* Yarmouth: Intercultural Press, 137-167.

Weeks, Jeffrey (1990). "The Value of Difference", in: Rutherford, Jonathan (Ed.). *Identity, Community, Culture, Difference.* London: Lawrence & Wishart, 88-100.

Weinbrenner, Peter (1995). "Grundlagen und Methodenprobleme sozialwissen-schaftlicher Schulbuchforschung", in: Olechowski, Richard (Ed.). *Schulbuchforschung*. Frankfurt a.M.: Peter Lang, 21-45.

Weissharr, Harald (Eds.) (2007). *:in Englisch – Come along to Canada*. Aachen: Bergmoser + Höller Verlag, 6/2007.

Welsch, Wolfgang (1999). "Transculturality – the Puzzling Form of Cultures Today", in: Featherstone, Mike/Lash, Scott (Eds.). *Spaces of Culture: City, Nation, World*. London: Sage, 194-213.

Welsch, Wolfgang (2000). "Transkulturalität. Zwischen Globalisierung und Partikularisierung", in: *Jahrbuch Deutsch als Fremdsprache*, 26, 327-351.

Wenger, Etienne (1998). *Communities of Practice: Learning, Meaning, and Identity*. Cambridge: CUP.

West, Alan/Harris, Lee (2003). "Secrecy and Space: Glenn Gould and Tim Wynne-Jone's *The Maestro*", in: Hudson, Aida/Cooper, Susan-Ann (Eds.). *Windows and Words – A Look at Canadian Children's Literature in English*. University of Ottawa Press, 77-86.

Whalen-Levitt, Peggy (1983). "Pursuing the Reader in the Book", in: May, Jill (Ed.). *Children and their Literature: A Readings Books*. West Fafayette: ChLA, 154-159.

Whitaker, Muriel (1983). "The Raven Cycle: Mythology in Process", in *CCL: Canadian Children's Literature/Littérature canadienne pour la jeunesse* 31/32, 46-52.

Wigod, Rebecca (2008). "New Rules Coming to get Canadian Literature in School", in: *Vancouver Sun*, July 26, 2008, n.p.

Wilson, Rosemary (2013). "Another Language is Another Soul", in: *Language and Intercultural Communication*, 13/3, 298-309.

Witte, Arnd (2006a). "Cultural Progression in Teaching and Learning Foreign Languages", in: Harden, Theo/Witte, Arnd/Köhler, Dirk (Eds.). *The Concept of Progression in the Teaching and Learning of Foreign Languages*. Bern: Lang, 205-232.

Witte, Arnd (2006b). "Überlegungen zu einer (inter)kulturellen Progression im Fremdsprachenunterricht", in: *Fremdsprachen Lehren und Lernen (FLuL)*, 35, 28-43.

Witte, Arnd (2007). "Das Verstehen des fremdkulturellen Kontextes – eine ver-nachlässigte Komponente im Fremdsprachenunterricht", in: *eDUSA* 2, 7-17.

Xie, Shaobo (2000). "Rethinking the Identity of Cultural Otherness: The Discourse of Difference as an Unfinished Project", in: McGillis, Roderick (Ed.). *Voices of the Other. Children's Literature and the Postcolonial Context*. New York: Routledge, 1-16.

Yeoman, Elizabeth (1999). "How does it get into my Imagination? Elementary School Children's Intertextual Knowledge and Gendered Storylines", in: *Gender and Education*, 11/4, 427-440.

Zaharka, Sharon E. (2002). *Interkulturelles Lernen mit multi-ethnischen Texten aus den USA*. Tübingen: Narr.

Zarate, Geneviève (2003). "Identities and Plurilingualism: Preconditions for the Recognition of Intercultural Competences", in: Byram, Michael (Ed). *Intercultural Competence*. Strasbourg: Council of Europe Publishing, 85-118.

Ziaja-Buchholtz, Miroslawa (2002). "Singing Snakes and Artistic Hens: Ethnic Diversity in Canadian Children's Books of the 1980s and 90s", in: Küster, Martin/Keller, Wolfram R. (Eds.). *Writing Canadians: The Literary Construction of Ethnic Identities*. Marburg: Universitätsbibliothek, 67-81.

Zydatiß, Wolfgang (1992). "Integrierte Text-Sprach-Arbeit: Plädoyer für einen systematischen Sprachunterricht in der Oberstufe", in: *Der fremdsprachliche Unterricht: Englisch*, 6/3, 34-39.

Zydatiß, Wolfgang (2005a). "Bildungsstandards für den Fremdsprachenunterricht in Deutschland: Eine hervorragende Idee wird katastrophal implementiert – oder: Von der Endkontrolle der Schüler zu strukturverbessernden Maßnahmen", in: Bausch, Karl-Richard/Burwitz-Melzer, Eva/Königs, Frank G./Krumm, Hans-Jürgen (Eds.). *Bildungsstandards auf dem Prüfstand. Arbeitspapiere der 26. Frühjahrskonferenz zur Erforschung des Fremdsprachenunterrichts*. Tübingen: Narr, 272-280.

Zydatiß, Wolfgang (2005b). *Bildungsstandards und Kompetenzniveaus im Englischunterricht. Konzepte, Empirie, Kritik und Konsequenzen*. Frankfurt a.M.: Peter Lang.

Zydatiß, Wolfgang (2006). "Stehen wir vor einem *meltdown* der Persönlichkeitsbildung im schulischen Fremdsprachenunterricht? – vermutlich ja, aber gerade deshalb sollten empirisch erprobte, integrierte Lern- und Überprüfungsaufgaben für diese Bereiche entwickelt werden", in: Bausche, Karl-Richard et a. (Eds.). *Aufgabenorientierung als Aufgabe*. Tübingen: Narr, 256-264.

III. Textbooks

Edelbrock, Iris (Ed.) (2010). *The New Pathway to Summit. Einführungsband Sekundarstufe II*. Braunschweig: Schöningh.

Edelbrock, Iris (Ed.) (2011). *The New Pathway Advanced*. Braunschweig: Schöningh.

Edelhoff, Christoph (Ed.) (2006a). *Camden Town 1*. Braunschweig: Diesterweg.

Edelhoff, Christoph (Ed.) (2006b). *Camden Town 2*. Braunschweig: Diesterweg.

Edelhoff, Christoph (Ed.) (2007a). *Camden Town 3*. Braunschweig: Diesterweg.

Edelhoff, Christoph (Ed.) (2007b). *Camden Town 4*. Braunschweig: Diesterweg.

Edelhoff, Christoph (Ed.) (2009a). *Camden Town 5*. Braunschweig: Diesterweg.

Edelhoff, Christoph (Ed.) (2010a). *Camden Town 6*. Braunschweig: Diesterweg.

Edelhoff, Christoph (Ed.) (2007c). *Notting Hill Gate 1*. Braunschweig: Diesterweg.

Edelhoff, Christoph (Ed.) (2008a). *Notting Hill Gate 2*. Braunschweig: Diesterweg.

Edelhoff, Christoph (Ed.) (2009b). *Notting Hill Gate 3a*. Braunschweig: Diesterweg.

Edelhoff, Christoph (Ed.) (2009c). *Notting Hill Gate 3b*. Braunschweig: Diesterweg.

Edelhoff, Christoph (Ed.) (2010b). *Notting Hill Gate 4a*. Braunschweig: Diesterweg.

Edelhoff, Christoph (Ed.) (2010c). *Notting Hill Gate 4b*. Braunschweig: Diesterweg.

Edelhoff, Christoph (Ed.) (2005). *Portobello Road 1*. Braunschweig: Diesterweg.

Edelhoff, Christoph (Ed.) (2006c). *Portobello Road 2*. Braunschweig: Diesterweg.

Edelhoff, Christoph (Ed.) (2007d). *Portobello Road 3*. Braunschweig: Diesterweg.

Edelhoff, Christoph (Ed.) (2008b). *Portobello Road 4*. Braunschweig: Diesterweg.

Edelhoff, Christoph (Ed.) (2009d). *Portobello Road 5*. Braunschweig: Diesterweg.

Edelhoff, Christoph (Ed.) (2011). *Portobello Road 6*. Braunschweig: Diesterweg.

Hanus, Pamela et.al. (Eds.) (2005a). *Camden Town 1*, Braunschweig: Diesterweg.

Hanus, Pamela et.al. (Eds.) (2005b). *Camden Town 2*. Braunschweig: Diesterweg.

Hanus, Pamela et.al. (Eds.) (2007). *Camden Town 3*. Braunschweig: Diesterweg.

Hanus, Pamela et.al. (Eds.) (2008). *Camden Town 4*. Braunschweig: Diesterweg.

Hanus, Pamela et.al. (Eds.) (2004). *Camden Town 5*. Braunschweig: Diesterweg.

Hanus, Pamela et.al. (Eds.) (2005c). *Camden Town 6*. Braunschweig: Diesterweg.

Hass, Frank (Ed.) (2005a). *Orange Line 1*, Stuttgart: Klett.

Hass, Frank (Ed.) (2007a). *Organe Line 2*. Stuttgart: Klett.

Hass, Frank (Ed.) (2007b). *Organe Line 3 Grundkurs*. Stuttgart: Klett.

Hass, Frank (Ed.) (2007c). *Organe Line 3 Erweiterungskurs*. Stuttgart: Klett.

Hass, Frank (Ed.) (2008a). *Organe Line 4 Grundkurs*. Stuttgart: Klett.

Hass, Frank (Ed.) (2008b). *Organe Line 4 Erweiterungskurs*. Stuttgart: Klett.

Hass, Frank (Ed.) (2009a). *Organe Line 5 Grundkurs*. Stuttgart: Klett.

Hass, Frank (Ed.) (2009b). *Organe Line 5 Erweiterungskurs*. Stuttgart: Klett.

Hass, Frank (Ed.) (2010a). *Organe Line 6 Grundkurs*. Stuttgart: Klett.

Hass, Frank (Ed.) (2010b). *Organe Line 6 Erweiterungskurs*. Stuttgart: Klett.

Hass, Frank (Ed.) (2005b). *Red Line 1*, Stuttgart: Klett.

Hass, Frank (Ed.) (2007d). *Red Line 2*. Stuttgart: Klett.

Hass, Frank (Ed.) (2008c). *Red Line 3*. Stuttgart: Klett.

Hass, Frank (Ed.) (2009c). *Red Line 4*. Stuttgart: Klett.

Hass, Frank (Ed.) (2010c). *Red Line 5*. Stuttgart: Klett.

Hass, Frank (Ed.) (2010d). *Red Line 6*. Stuttgart: Klett.

Hellyer-Jones, Rosemary/Horner, Marion/Parr, Robert/Parsons, Carolyn (Eds.) (2004). *Red Line new Bayern*. Stuttgart: Klett.

Schwarz, Helmut (Ed.) (2006a). *English G21 – A1*. Berlin: Cornelsen.

Schwarz, Helmut (Ed.) (2007a). *English G21 – A2*. Berlin: Cornelsen.

Schwarz, Helmut (Ed.) (2008a). *English G21 – A3*. Berlin: Cornelsen.

Schwarz, Helmut (Ed.) (2009a). *English G21 – A4*. Berlin: Cornelsen.

Schwarz, Helmut (Ed.) (2006b). *English G21 – D1 Grundausgabe*. Berlin: Cornelsen.

Schwarz, Helmut (Ed.) (2007b). *English G21 – D2 Grundausgabe*. Berlin: Cornelsen.

Schwarz, Helmut (Ed.) (2008b). *English G21 – D3 Grundausgabe*. Berlin: Cornelsen.

Schwarz, Helmut (Ed.) (2008c). *English G21 – D3 Erweiterte Ausgabe*. Berlin: Cornelsen.

Schwarz, Helmut (Ed.) (2009b). *English G21 – D4 Grundausgabe*. Berlin: Cornelsen.

Schwarz, Helmut (Ed.) (2009c). *English G21 – D4 Erweiterte Ausgabe*. Berlin: Cornelsen.

Schwarz, Helmut/Rademacher, Jörg (Eds.) (2010). *English G21 – A5*. Berlin: Cornelsen.

Schwarz, Helmut/Rademacher, Jörg (Eds.) (2011). *English G21 – A6*. Berlin: Cornelsen.

Schwarz, Helmut/Rademacher, Jörg (Eds.) (2010a). *English G21 – D5 Grundausgabe*. Berlin: Cornelsen.

Schwarz, Helmut/Rademacher, Jörg (Eds.) (2010b). *English G21 – D5 Erweiterte Ausgabe*. Berlin: Cornelsen.

Schwarz, Helmut/Rademacher, Jörg (Eds.) (2010c). *English G21 – D6 Grundausgabe*. Berlin: Cornelsen.

Schwarz, Helmut/Rademacher, Jörg (Eds.) (2010d). *English G21 – D6 Erweiterte Ausgabe*. Berlin: Cornelsen.

Schwarz, Helmut/Whittaker, Marvyn (Eds.) (2010). *Context 21*. Berlin: Cornelsen.

Thaler, Engelbert (2007) (Ed.). *The New Summit – Texts and Methods*. Braunschweig: Schöningh.

Thaler, Engelbert (2010) (Ed.). *Summit G8 – Texts and Methods*. Braunschweig: Schöningh.

Weisshaar, Harald (Ed.) (2006a). *Green Line 1*, Stuttgart: Klett.

Weisshaar, Harald (Ed.) (2006b). *Green Line 2*. Stuttgart: Klett.

Weisshaar, Harald (Ed.) (2007). *Green Line 3*. Stuttgart: Klett.

Weisshaar, Harald (Ed.) (2008). *Green Line 4*. Stuttgart: Klett.

Weisshaar, Harald (Ed.) (2009a). *Green Line 5*. Stuttgart: Klett.

Weisshaar, Harald (Ed.) (2010). *Green Line 6*. Stuttgart: Klett.

Weisshaar, Harald (Ed.) (2009b). *Green Line Oberstufe*. Stuttgart: Klett.

IV. Curricula

Government of Alberta/Education (2003). *High School English Language Arts Program of Study* (Senior High). Online: https://education.alberta. ca/media/645805/srhelapofs.pdf [Nov 13, 2014]

Hessisches Kultusministerium (2012). "Hinweise zur Vorbereitung auf die schriftlichen Abiturprüfungen im Landesabitur 2014". Online http:// berufliche.bildung.hessen.de/bg/archiv/LA14-Hinweise_zur_Vorbereitung _auf_die_schriftlichen_Abiturpruefungen. pdf, Oct 12, 2011.

KMK (2003). *Bildungsstandards für die erste Fremdsprache (Englisch/Französisch) für den Mittleren Schulabschluss.* München: Luchterhand.

KMK (2004). *Bildungsstandards für die erste Fremdsprache (Englisch/Französisch) für den Hauptschulabschluss.* München: Luchterhand.

KMK (2012). *Bildungsstandards für die fortgeführte Fremdsprache (Englisch/Französisch) für die Allgemeine Hochschulreife (Beschluss der Kultusministerkonferenz vom 18.10.2012.* München: Carl Link Verlag.

Manitoba Education and Training (2000). *Senior 4 English Language Arts.*

Ministerium für Schule und Weiterbildung des Landes Nordrhein-Westfalen (2005). *Schulgesetz für das Land Nordrhein-Westfalen.* Frechen: Ritterbach-Verlag.

Ministerium für Bildung, Wissenschaft und Kultur (2010). *Schulgesetz für das Land Mecklenburg-Vorpommern.* Online: http://www.landesrecht-mv.de/jportal/portal/page/bsmvprod.psml?showdoccase=1&doc.id=jl SchulGMV2010rahmen&doc.part=X&doc.origin=bs&st=lr, Oct 12, 2011.

Ministry of Education, Province of British Columbia (2007). *English Language Arts 8-12.*

Ministry of Education, Saskatchewan curriculum (2011). *English Language Arts 10.*

Ministry of Education (2007). *The Ontario Curriculum 11 and 12, English.*

Ministère de l'Education, du Loisir et du Sport (n.y.). *Secondary Language Arts.*

MSJK/Ministerium für Schule, Jugend und Kinder (Ed.) (2004). *Kernlehrplan für die Gesamtschule Sekundarstufe I in Nordrhein-Westfalen Englisch,* Düsseldorf.

MSJK/Ministerium für Schule, Jugend und Kinder des Landes Nordrhein-Westfalen (Ed.) (2011). *Kernplan für die Hauptschule in Nordrhein-Westfalen: Englisch.*

MSW/Ministerium für Schule und Weiterbildung des Landes Nordrhein-Westfalen (2007). *Kernlehrplan für den verkürzten Bildungsgang des Gymnasiums – Sekundarstufe I (G8) in Nordrhein-Westfalen – Englisch.* Frechen: Ritterbach-Verlag.

MSW/Ministerium für Schule und Weiterbildung des Landes Nordrhein-Westfalen (2008). *Lehrplan Englisch für die Grundschulen des Landes Nordrhein-Westfalen.* Frechen: Ritterbach-Verlag.

MSW/Ministerium für Schule und Weiterbildung des Landes Nordrhein-Westfalen (2011). *Kernlehrplan für die Hauptschule in Nordrhein-Westfalen.* Frechen: Ritterbach-Verlag.

MSWWF/Ministerium für Schule, Weiterbildung, Wissenschaft und Forschung des Landes Nordrhein-Westfalen (Ed.) (1999). *Richtlinien und Lehrpläne für die Sekundarstufe II, Gymnasium/Gesamtschule in Nordrhein-Westfalen: Englisch.*

Niedersächsisches Kultusministerium (2010). *Hinweise zur schriftlichen Abiturprüfung 2012 im Fach Englisch.* Online http://www.nibis.de/nli1/gohrgs/zentralabitur/zentralabitur_2012/02EnglischHinweise2012.pdf, Oct 12, 2011.

V. Online References

Publishers

Annick Press. http://www.annickpress.com/, Aug 15, 2011.
Coteau Books. http://coteaubooks.com/, Aug 15, 2011.
    http://coteaubooks.com/index.php?p=Education%20Resources, July 27, 2013.
Groundwood Books. http://www.groundwoodbooks.com/, Aug 15, 2011.
Red Deer Press. http://www.reddeerpress.com/, Aug 15, 2011.
Theytus. http://www.theytus.com/, Aug 15, 2011.
Orca Books. http://www.orcabook.com/, Aug 15, 2011.

Further Online References

Accessibility for Ontarians with Disabilities Act (2005).
    http://www.e-laws.gov.on.ca/html/statutes/english/elaws_statutes_05a1
    1_e.htm, Aug 6, 2013.
Canada.com.
    http://www.canada.com/vancouversun/news/arts/story.html?id=e8b7b8
    26-9837-4d9b-9972-73997b23b045, Aug 6, 2013.
Canada Council Homepage/Governor General Literary Award.
    http://www.canadacouncil.ca/prizes/ggla/ww128020470294038311.htm
    http://ggbooks.canadacouncil.ca/, Dec 8, 2011.
The Canadian Children's Book Centre.
    http://www.bookcentre.ca/resources/publishers_booksellers_wholesaler
    s, July 25, 2013.
    http://www.bookcentre.ca/resources/publishers_booksellers_wholesaler
    s#Related+Publications, July 26, 2013.
    http://www.bookcentre.ca/award, Aug 24, 2012.
    http://www.bookcentre.ca/news/ccbc_announces_new_monica_hughes_
    award_science_fiction_and_fantasy, July 26, 2013.
Canadian Children's Literature/Littérature canadienne pour la jeunesse.
    http://ccl-lcj.ca/index.php/ccl-lcj/index, Aug 9, 2011.
Canadian Journal of Disability Studies.
    http://cjds.uwaterloo.ca/index.php/cjds/index, July 25, 2013.
Canadian Society of Children's Authors, Illustrators and Performers.
    http://www.canscaip.org/content/join-canscaip, Aug 10, 2011.
Centre for the Research in Young People's Texts and Cultures.
    http://crytc.uwinnipeg.ca/about.php, Aug 9, 2011.
Chapters/Indigo Bookstore. http://www.chapters.indigo.ca/our-company/time-
    line/, Aug 9, 2011.
Chapters/Indigo. "Canadian Books for Teens".

http://www.chapters.indigo.ca/en-ca/teens/canadian-books-canadian-teens/, Jan 20, 2015.

Children's Writers and Illustrators of British Columbia Society. http://www.cwill.bc.ca/, Aug 15, 2011.

Deutsche Gesellschaft für Fremdsprachenforschung/German Association of Research into Language Learning and Teaching. http://kongress.dgff.de/en/panels.html, Sept 5, 2013.

Historical Perspectives on Canadian Publishing. http://hpcanpub.mcmaster.ca/case-study/publishing-children-mcclelland-amp-stewart039s-long-legacy, Dec 8, 2011.

Jeunesse: Young People, Texts, Cultures. http://www.jeunessejournal.ca/index.php/yptc, Aug 9, 2011.

LOLIPOP-Portfolio. http://lolipop-portfolio.eu/teams.html, Dec 9, 2011.

McNally Robinson Bookstore. http://www.mcnallyrobinson.com/teens/browse/category/891/, Dec 9, 2011.

Ontarians with Disabilities Act (2001). http://www.canlii.ca/en/on/laws/stat/so-2001-c-32/latest/so-2001-c-32.html, Aug 10, 2011.

Society of Children's Book Writers and Illustrators, Canada East Chapter. http://www.scbwicanada.org/east/aboutscbwi.htm, Aug 10, 2011.

Terry Fox Foundation. http://www.terryfox.org/cgi/page.cgi/InternationalRun/Run_site_listings.html, Dec. 8, 2014.

The Vinyl Princess. http://www.thevinylprincess.com/about-me, Sept 13, 2011.

Young Alberta Book Society. http://www.yabs.ab.ca/About-Yabs.asp, Aug 10, 2011.